Critical Thinking Unleashed

Critical Thinking Unleashed

Elliot D. Cohen

ROWMAN & LITTLEFIELD PUBLISHERS, INC.
Lanham • Boulder • New York • Toronto • Plymouth, UK

ROWMAN & LITTLEFIELD PUBLISHERS, INC.

Published in the United States of America
by Rowman & Littlefield Publishers, Inc.
A wholly owned subsidiary of The Rowman & Littlefield Publishing Group, Inc.
4501 Forbes Boulevard, Suite 200, Lanham, Maryland 20706
www.rowmanlittlefield.com

Estover Road
Plymouth PL6 7PY
United Kingdom

British Library Cataloguing in Publication Information Available

Library of Congress Cataloging-in-Publication Data

Cohen, Elliot D.
  Critical thinking unleashed / Elliot D. Cohen.
    p. cm.
  Includes bibliographical references and index.
  ISBN 978-0-7425-6431-2 (cloth : alk. paper) — ISBN 978-0-7425-6432-9 (pbk. : alk. paper)
— ISBN 978-1-4422-0005-0 (electronic)
  1. Critical thinking—Textbooks. I. Title.
B809.2.C65 2009
160—dc22   2009009411

Printed in the United States of America

∞™ The paper used in this publication meets the minimum requirements of American
National Standard for Information Sciences—Permanence of Paper
for Printed Library Materials, ANSI/NISO Z39.48-1992.

Contents

x Contents

Preface to the Student

This book is about using your powers of critical thinking to think freely about life issues. Being such a freethinker requires a persistent habit of accepting conclusions only after careful examination of the reasoning put forth to support them. This is an awesome challenge, given the personal, social, and political obstacles each of us confronts in the course of everyday living.

By reading this book and working through its exercises, I hope you will begin to hone the rational skills necessary to meet this challenge. This is a lifelong project that does not terminate with the end of a course of study such as the one you are about to undertake.

So, will it be worth the effort?

If you think about it, most of the problems we face in the world today (and have faced in the past) are largely due to irrational thinking. Be they personal emotional challenges, familial conflicts, unjust domestic policies, or global policies that threaten the environment, balance of power, or the prospects for world peace, if you look carefully at the reasoning behind such problems, you are likely to find irrational thinking of the sort examined in this book.

True, this is a complex world with many problems and few simple solutions. But unless we begin to tackle these problems with a sense of what is rational and what is not, we are not likely to make any real progress toward their resolution. As you will see, it is a fallacy to demand perfection since the world is not a perfect place. But, assuredly, the world could be a *better* place.

This is where you come in. As a citizen in a democratic society, you can strengthen the tides of freedom—but not by jumping on a bandwagon of blind worshippers of authority. The popular slogans that have moved many to such blind following (e.g., "You are either with us or with the terrorists") have succeeded in slowing the progress toward improving the condition of the world. Freethinkers are the ones who can see through these manipulative facades. The nation and the world need more freethinkers. As a freethinker, you can carry the torch of freedom.

It is not freedom to worship blind authority and to follow the leader into a sink-hole of war, economic meltdown, and even annihilation of the planet. Freedom is the product of reason harnessed to solve problems in the world without surrendering to fears arising from magical, superstitious, and antiscientific thinking. When out of fear we shut down our civil rights and wage war on our enemy in the name of freedom, we have already lost the war.

The United States will never be the same since the September 11, 2001, attacks. They have taught the new generation the devastating effects of hatred and fear. But we cannot benefit from these lessons by responding with hatred and fear. This places us in a self-perpetuating, vicious cycle in which we all become terrorists terrorizing each other. The lesson to be learned is that we must harness the powers of reason to work toward peace—not to become ourselves invaders, merchants of war, torturers, and world dictators.

This will not eliminate the occasional need for self-defense in the form of physical force when there is evidence and proof (and not just appeals to ignorance and fear) that it is needed. We cannot afford to run our personal lives or our lives as citizens of a nation or of the world by the argument of the club. I hope that this book will provide you some of the tools needed to make the world a better place—your own personal sphere of it as well as that shared with others.

Elliot D. Cohen, PhD
Indian River State College

Introduction

Freethinking

In his classic book *The Open Society and Its Enemies*, philosopher Karl Popper distinguishes between two types of societies—one "open," the other "closed." An open society, he says, "sets free the critical powers of man," while a closed society stresses "submission to magical forces."[1] The "critical powers" unleashed in an open society engage the rational capacity of human beings to reach conclusions on the basis of evidence and to revise these conclusions as the evidence changes. This openness to evidence distinguishes it from closed societies, which submit to ritualistic, superstitious, and blind thinking impervious to evidence.

In an open society, political leaders are not to be idolized and worshipped as gods among humans. Like anyone else, their views can be called into question if they fail to fit the facts as rationally determined. Such a society is antiauthoritarian, realistic, and democratic in its emphasis on enlightened self-governance. In contrast, a closed society is authoritarian, and its leaders lead by demanding blind obedience. Here there is typically an appeal to the supernatural instead of reason and a tendency to make the facts fit the political policy rather than vice versa.

WHAT FREETHINKING IS

In Popper's words, freethinking is the kind of thinking that "sets free the critical powers of man." It is such "critical thinking" that would be welcome in an open society and shunned in a closed one. It is the lifeline of a free nation: that is, a nation whose citizens shape their own destinies through rational self-determination instead of dronelike obedience.

This book is a primer for freeing such critical powers of reason. It aims at helping to expose the irrational, self-defeating, and destructive ideas that foreclose

---

1. Karl R. Popper, *The Open Society and Its Enemies*, vol. 1, *The Spell of Plato* (London: Routledge & Kegan Paul, 1993).

the human potential for productivity and happiness. It aims at overcoming these irrational ideas and replacing them with rational ones. It provides the logical tools and skill-building exercises that can help you see through the sophistry and twisted logic that underlies a closed society—one that fails to apply rational methods to come to grips with human problems.

Freethinking is *self-reflective* thinking: that is, thinking that takes thinking itself as the primary subject. Like the popular bumper sticker that asks, "How's my driving?" freethinkers ask the same of their own thinking. Asking this question is the first step toward constructive change since it is not likely that one will give up irrational ideas without subjecting them to careful scrutiny. It is therefore *analytical* thinking that methodically dissects reasoning, divining its parts and inspecting them. But it is also *reparative* and *ameliorative* thinking. This means that it engages in logical inspection in order to make repairs and, thereby, to make things better.

Freethinking therefore emphasizes the practical side of thinking. Its theoretical principles and methods aim at enhancing human life. Here, there is reciprocity. To paraphrase philosopher Immanuel Kant, theory without practice is pointless, but practice without theory is blind.

Freethinkers aspire to worship no sacred cows. While no human being can be perfectly unbiased, to be a freethinker means that one is prepared to think critically on any subject. Freethinkers are not ordinarily constrained from questioning the reasoning behind any political, social, religious, or cultural agenda. This means that they are likely to clash with those who dogmatically cling to their beliefs and take criticism of them personally. Socrates, who was executed for allegedly corrupting the youth of Athens, is a good example of such clashing. Socrates was not afraid to question the religious and cultural views of his fellow Athenian citizens, and for doing so, he was brought to court and sentenced to death. Freethinkers, as the example of Socrates suggests, are not easily intimidated by personal attacks, appeals to force, or other forms of manipulation.

THE CONTEXT OF FREETHINKING

Freethinking is thus critical thinking unleashed from social, political, cultural, and religious bondage. Freethinkers follow the path of reason and evidence rather than the path most traveled.

Still, we human beings live in a technologically savvy world in which "information" is hurled at us from many quarters. The theory and practice of freethinking therefore recognizes that making rational choices amid this "blooming, buzzing universe" can be an onerous task. Thus, it stresses the usefulness of understanding the context in which practical reasoning occurs—that is, the sociopolitical influences and human vulnerabilities that can undermine it.

Mass Media Manipulation

One major influence on our thinking is the mass media. TV and radio provide us with "news" often intertwined with editorializing and propagandizing. Media organizations, owned and operated by gigantic media companies, from News Corporation's Fox News to General Electric's NBC, are driven by corporate bottom-line interests that largely determine what filters down to us and in what form. For example, in 1999, General Electric, the world's second largest nuclear reactor manufacturer, removed all references to "radioactive waste transport" from its NBC made-for-TV movie *Atomic Train*. The plot originally involved a train carrying commercial high-level atomic waste, which was detonated by a nuclear weapon smuggled onboard, destroying the city of Denver. In order to avoid giving any negative press to nuclear energy, the plot was changed such that the train carried unidentified "hazardous" waste.[2]

By controlling the conduits of information—the airwaves, cables, and phone lines—media and telecom companies have been able to manipulate and control the content of what is transmitted. The end result is that consumers of information are left with information tailored to fit the narrow, self-interested perspective of corporate shareholders.

Government agencies are also intertwined within the corporate media web, and the content of television and radio programming and motion pictures may be censored and altered under corporate and political pressures. The major media corporations have powerful lobbies in Congress and at the Federal Communications Commission (FCC) that seek to influence government policy regarding media ownership and cross-ownership caps, tax breaks, and other corporate incentives. As the result of such lobbying activities, in 1996, the Clinton administration passed sweeping legislation known as the 1996 Telecommunications Act, which substantially increased the ability of the giant media corporations to monopolize and control the national media market. Large media and telecom companies also have interests in lucrative government contracts such as military defense contracts. For example, General Electric makes jet engines for aircraft used in military defense. Media self-censorship to the beat of the prevailing administration's interests is accordingly part of the cost of doing business for these companies, and it affects what consumers of information see and hear.

For example, as early as the first Clinton administration and escalating during the administration of George W. Bush, the major news networks, including Fox News and CNN, allowed government agencies to inject "fake news"—self-serving propaganda—into the programming of local network affiliate stations. These prepackaged videos were produced by pubic relations firms, and the reporters were actually public relations officers masquerading as real journalists. To viewers, these news feeds looked like real news items. For example, one segment included a jubilant Iraqi American thanking President Bush for invading Baghdad. Another touted the Bush administration's "success" in strengthening airport security, calling it "one of the most remarkable campaigns in aviation history."[3] Such propagandizing by

---

2. Michael Mariotte, "Atomic Train: The Truth Is Out There," Nuclear Information and Resource Service, May 12, 1999. Retrieved online on April 6, 2009, from www.nirs.org/factsheets/atomic trainfacts.htm.

3. David Barstow and Robin Stein, "Under Bush, a New Age of Prepackaged TV News," *New York Times*, March 13, 2005. Retrieved online on January 10, 2009, from www.nytimes.com/2005/03/13/politics/13covert.html.

government in cooperation with corporate media underscores the danger of believing everything aired on the nightly news.

In contrast to mainstream media, the Internet is an incredibly rich resource for *independent* media—that is, news agencies not connected to giant corporations with vested financial interests in what they report. The Internet's vast sea of information, however, also contains its sludge. One challenge to surfing the net is thus deciphering credible from bogus claims. Further, giant media and telecommunications corporations have already achieved a strong Internet presence. If this trend continues, the Internet may itself become an extension of the corporate media.

Within this corporate media–governmental web, corporate sponsors also exert pressures of their own to promote their products. It is not uncommon to see references within movies and television shows to specific businesses—from the Pottery Barn and Bed, Bath, and Beyond to Wal-Mart—as well as to specific products—from Coca-Cola to Nikes. The commercial landscape frequently contains images of successful, happy people whose prosperity, we are led to believe, is somehow bound up with the product being promoted.

Government agencies such as the Food and Drug Administration (FDA) and the Environmental Protection Agency (EPA) have also been complicit with giant corporations in exposing human beings to dangers under their seal of approval. For example, under the George W. Bush administration, the EPA permitted pesticide companies to test suspected carcinogens and neurotoxicants on human beings without informed consent. According to one congressional study,

> The experiments deliberately exposed human subjects to dangerous pesticides, such as organophosphates, which were developed in the 1930s for use in nerve gas, and methyl isothiocyanate, which is closely related to the chemical that killed thousands in Bhopal, India. In one experiment, human subjects were placed in a chamber with vapors of chloropicrin, an active ingredient in tear gas, at levels substantially greater than the federal exposure limit, causing some subjects to experience "severe" adverse effects. An older experiment administered the pesticide carbofuran to human subjects for the explicit objective of determining "the minimum dose necessary to induce toxic effects (e.g. headache, nausea, and vomiting)." In many of the experiments, the subjects were instructed to swallow capsules of toxic pesticides with orange juice or water at breakfast.[4]

Genetically engineered foods have sprouted up in the supermarkets albeit without adequate FDA oversight. Testing for toxic effects and health risks has not been systematically undertaken, and the environmental consequences are far from clear; yet these products are available for human consumption.

Cultural Bias

Enculturation, or the socialization of children to cultural norms, is another factor in creating barriers to rational thinking. Prejudice and bias are "taught," and

---

4. Sen. Barbara Boxer and Rep. Harry A. Waxman, "Human Pesticide Experiments," Committee on Government Reform, U.S. House of Representatives (Minority Staff) and Office of Sen. Barbara Boxer, U.S. Senate (Environmental Staff), June 2005. Retrieved online on April 6, 2009, from boxer.senate.gov/news/pesticidereport.pdf.

conformity to slanted norms routinely replaces self-reflective thinking. Here the mass media also play a significant role in propagating stereotypes. For example, a popular media image of a gay male is one who is "flaming." For example, the eight-year run of the popular NBC TV sitcom *Will & Grace* dignified this stereotype in the flamboyant comic character of Jack. While viewers were encouraged to laugh at his "gay antics," they were also being encouraged not to take gay people seriously as human beings.

It was not so funny when in October 1998 Matthew Shepard, a twenty-one-year-old student at Colorado State University, was brutally murdered because he was gay. He was tied to a fence, beaten, and tortured by two men who lured him from a campus bar by telling him they were gay. Matthew was left for dead in a remote area of Wyoming. A cyclist who found him some hours later tied to the fence in near freezing temperatures had at first mistaken him for a scarecrow.

While Matthew lay dying in a hospital from massive brain stem injuries sustained at the hands of his assailants, a group of Colorado State University students rode atop a homecoming float displaying a scarecrow intentionally made to look like Matthew's tortured body. The figure bore a sign saying "I'm gay" with an obscene message painted on the back of the scarecrow's shirt. To these students, Matthew Shepard was not to be taken seriously, not even after he was so brutally assaulted.

Desensitization to the Pain and Suffering of Others

Such desensitization to the pain and suffering of other human beings is also a manifestation of a related problem endemic to society. Graphic violence, as commonly depicted in movies such as the *Texas Chain Saw Massacre*, video games like Doom or Mortal Combat, and sexually violent and dehumanizing pornography, has made wanton cruelty, sexual sadism, and destruction of human life a marketable commodity in contemporary Western society. Such desensitization through graphic depictions of sex and violence has made it easier to tolerate exposure in real life, and there is some evidence to suggest that it encourages at least some very susceptible human beings to imitate what they have seen.

Inherent Insecurity of Human Beings

The more we watch horror films and other violent depictions, the more desensitized we become and the more graphic the depiction must be in order to hold our interest. Yet what attracts us to such brutality in the first place and keeps us watching may be our own sense of personal vulnerability. Were humans not aware of their own mortality, the sight of a brutal massacre would not be "horrifying" in the first place.

The entertainment industry and advertisers alike play upon human insecurity in order to turn a profit. We watch slashers because we fear for our own lives. We purchase when advertisers appeal to our fear of being without their products (can you afford to be without a deodorant that really works?) Be it from fear of losing favor with others or missing out on "the chance of a lifetime," human insecurity drives a lucrative market of manipulation.

Our insecurity also leads us to jump on bandwagons, demand perfection in an imperfect world, catastrophize, suffer anxiety about the future, and dutifully torment ourselves with worry. It is human insecurity that keeps us stuck, afraid to advance, and it is human insecurity that leads us to leap blindly for fear of never having another opportunity to succeed. It is such fear that leads the poor and gullible to give up their hard-earned cash to the electronic evangelist and other snake oil salespersons.

As existential philosophers such as Jean-Paul Sartre and Martin Heidegger emphasized, human beings have only a finite time on the meter of life, and this is the object of considerable angst. How we spend our hours, days, months, and years requires judgment, and this judgment is fallible. Reaching out for standards to guide us in this pursuit becomes a formidable task for human beings.

Here, then, are some of the sociopolitical and human pitfalls with which all of us must inevitably reckon in our practical lives. We are subject to an intricate web of manipulation and deception spun off by big media, industry, advertisers, and government. We are socialized into a climate of cultural bias that can work insidiously to undermine our own happiness and that of others. Our vulnerability to fear is exploited until we require greater and greater increments of horror to satisfy our craving, while all the while we have become increasingly numb to the pain and suffering of others. Our inherent human insecurity makes us vulnerable to those who use it to turn a profit, and we, ourselves, can be our own worst enemies when we squander much of our own mortal existences by making irrational demands, needlessly obsessing over things, and leaping blindly into the fire.

Freethinking as Critical Thinking Unleashed

In one clear, sociological sense, critical thinking is a course taught at most institutions of higher learning and in some high schools. The discipline taught in these courses consists of a beginning introduction to logic. This discipline includes a set of technical terms such as *argument, premise, conclusion, induction,* and *deduction,* which it uses to introduce students to rules and techniques for checking reasoning for its validity and soundness. Quite often these courses seek to illustrate mistakes in reasoning (called *fallacies*) in the contexts of ordinary life.

However, these courses usually do not apply, in any careful and comprehensive way, the logical tools they develop to the irrational lines of thinking woven into the fabric of a nation that threaten its status as, or prospects for becoming, an open society. In contrast, this text aims at putting critical thinking to work to help us to overcome dangerous impediments to an open society. From the Bush administration's justification for going to war in Iraq to the mainstream media's coverage of criminal investigations such as the Duke rape case, from the attempt by giant corporations to curb Internet neutrality to the problem of distinguishing reliable from unreliable content on the Web, from the methodological errors researchers sometimes make in attempting to find the causes of life-threatening diseases such as AIDS to the processes of reasoning behind debilitating emotional problems such as depression and anxiety, this text tackles current affairs, scientific research, the difficulties of a digital age, psychological problems, and many other twenty-first-century challenges. *These issues are treated not merely as benign illustrations of logical rules or techniques but as important subjects in their own right.*

In its emphasis on freethinking, this text does not expect students to accept every argument or claim made but offers abundant exercises in which they are encouraged to provide their own reflective responses that cut through the sludge of dogmatic, ritualistic, superstitious, antiscientific, and dronelike acceptance of the status quo. If this text becomes a gadfly that shakes up preconceptions and hits nerves in an effort to teach the difference between sound reasoning and its counterfeit, then it has done its job. It is to this task that we now shall turn.

I

KINDS OF REASONING

1

The Nuts and Bolts
of Reasoning

ARGUMENTS

Reasoning is the activity of making *inferences*. This is when you attempt to justify or prove one statement by appealing to another statement or statements. To prove or justify a statement means *to give a good reason for believing it*.[1] The statement that you are trying to justify is called the *conclusion*, whereas the justifying statements are called *premises*. All reasoning has a conclusion (implied or explicit) and at least one (and typically more than one) premise. Logicians also refer to inferences as *(logical) arguments*.

For example, in 1923, in *The Philosophy of Civilization*, Albert Schweitzer concluded that "we have entered a new medieval period": that is, a period of "spiritual" and "moral" decline, because "the majority renounce the privilege of thinking as free personalities, and let themselves be guided in everything by those who belong to the various groups and cliques."[2] Thus, Schweitzer's *argument* was that civilization was in decline because the majority of people (the masses) had become blind conformists instead of freethinkers.

When Schweitzer looked about him, he perceived industrialization usurping the skilled artisan and replacing his "creative and artistic powers" with a menial job on an assembly line, a postwar environment in which "the control of thought was made complete" and "propaganda definitely took the place of truth," the dumbing down of education, the seeking of entertainment that made the "least demand" upon a person's intellect, lack of intellectual curiosity, superficial interpersonal relationships, and talk about war and conquest as though these involved "operations on a chessboard" rather than the sacrifice of flesh-and-blood human beings. In short, Schweitzer perceived a national climate in which free and independent

---

1. Alternatively, to prove or justify a statement might be defined in terms of providing *adequate evidence* for believing it.
2. Albert Schweitzer, *The Philosophy of Civilization* (Amherst, N.Y.: Prometheus Books, 1987), 18.

thinking had disappeared en masse. This, he argued, was good reason to believe that we had entered "a new medieval period."[3]

Can a similar *argument* be made about post-9/11 America?

STATEMENTS THAT DO NOT FORM ARGUMENTS

Arguments need to be distinguished from statements. While arguments contain statements, not every statement, or set of statements, constitutes an argument. Again, in order to have an argument, one must be attempting to prove or justify one statement (the conclusion) by using other statements (the premises).

Mere Opinions

Consider the following statements asserted by actor-comedian Charlie Chaplin:

> I remain just one thing, and one thing only, and that is a clown. It places me on a far higher plane than any politician.

Here Chaplin is not attempting to prove or justify anything. Rather, he is stating his low *opinion* of politicians without attempting to justify it. Without any attempt to justify his opinion by adding premises, there is no argument—just opinion. While it is commonly said that one opinion is just as good as the next, this is not strictly speaking true. Opinions that are justified are better than ones that are not justified.

Expressions of Desire

Like mere opinions, statements expressing one's desires or wishes do not constitute arguments. For example, consider black activist Rosa Parks's wish for herself:

> I would like to be remembered as a person who wanted to be free and wanted other people to be also free.

While Parks's refusal in 1955 to obey a bus driver's order to give up her seat for a white passenger marked an important beginning in the struggle of black people for civil rights in America, Parks is not here trying to prove that she *should* be remembered *because of* her contribution to the civil rights movement. This would have constituted an argument. Rather, her statement is simply the expression of a wish to be remembered as a person who, as a matter of fact, wanted to be free and wanted the same for others.

Reports

Reports also do not, as such, qualify as arguments. For example, consider what the ancient Greek historian Thucydides says about the Greeks:

---

3. Schweitzer, *The Philosophy of Civilization*, ch. 2.

> We are lovers of the beautiful, yet simple in our tastes, and we cultivate the mind without loss of manliness.

Here, Thucydides does not provide any argument to prove the veracity of his account. Nor does he have to insofar as he knew this culture firsthand. Notice, however, that in the twenty-first century we can only *infer* from the testimony of Thucydides and other ancient sources that things were as described. So, our acceptance of Thucydides' account as historically accurate must be based on argument. In this manner, all historical accounts, insofar as they are not purely speculative, must be justified or proven by way of argument.

With the exception of editorials, newspaper articles seldom present arguments. This is especially true of the lead sentences at the beginning of a newspaper article. For example, look at these lead sentences from the *New York Times*, April 29, 2004:

> American soldiers at a prison outside Baghdad have been accused of forcing Iraqi prisoners into acts of sexual humiliation and other abuses in order to make them talk, according to officials and others familiar with the charges. The charges, first announced by the military in March, were documented by photographs taken by guards inside the prison, but were not described in detail until some of the pictures were made public.

Notice that these sentences make factual claims but do not draw any conclusions from them. Notice, too, that the article cautiously qualifies its claims. For example, instead of saying that American soldiers forced Iraqi prisoners into acts of sexual humiliation, it says that they were accused of doing so, according to officials and others familiar with the charges. Clearly, newspapers are reluctant to draw conclusions that may later be proven false. This opens them up to civil suits as well as embarrassing retractions, which can adversely affect these companies' bottom lines. Such caution, however, has a negative feature. As discussed in chapter 14, by simply reporting what government officials tell them rather than drawing inferences from their own careful investigations, the mainstream media run the risk of misleading the public. In short, by not advancing their own arguments, newspapers play it safe—but not necessarily to the advantage of the public whom they serve.

Literary Metaphors

Literary metaphors are also often used to make statements that do not form arguments. A literary metaphor is an explanation of an object or idea by way of relating it to something else that is seemingly disparate and unrelated. For example, consider Albert Einstein's characterization of nationalism, which he called "an infantile disease," "the measles of mankind." Here Einstein is using "measles" and "infantile disease" to drive home the idea that nationalistic thinking, which involves zealous devotion to one's own nation over and above any other, is immature and maladaptive. And while Einstein's metaphor works to get his point across in a vivid manner, the metaphor is not itself an argument.

Nor does such use of metaphor support the drawing of (literal) conclusions. For example, from the comparison of nationalism with measles, one would not be justified in drawing the conclusion that nationalistic thinkers have red spots. Similarly, one could present a vivid picture of a woman with beautiful, large eyes by saying, "Her eyes were like two pools of water," but that wouldn't mean that we could realistically go swimming in them. Literary metaphors can be useful in enlivening our viewpoint, but they are not useful for purposes of forming arguments.

Explanations of Facts

In other cases, a statement or set of statements can be used to *explain why* another statement is true without trying to prove or justify it. In such cases, the statements do not form an argument. For example, consider what guitarist Eric Clapton had to say about the influence Buddy Holly had on him:

> One summer I remember, I got exposed to Chuck Berry and Buddy Holly and Buddy Holly . . . made a very big impression on me. Because of a lot of things, you know, the way he looked and his charisma.

Notice Clapton is not trying to prove or justify the assertion that Buddy Holly made a big impression on him. That is, he is not trying to give a good reason to believe that Holly made such an impression on him. Instead, he is explaining what aspects of Holly had this effect.

However, explaining why something is (or is not) the case is not the same thing as trying to justify or prove that a given explanation is the correct one. For example, in stating, "I was late because I got caught in traffic," I would not ordinarily be trying to give a good reason *for believing* that I was late.[4] Indeed, this fact claim would not be in question. Rather, I would simply be explaining *why* I was late. On the other hand, if you were to say of another person, "He must be caught in traffic because he is late," you may well be trying to provide a good reason for believing that he is caught in traffic. Here, the statement that he is caught in traffic would be in question. Accordingly, in this latter case, you would be advancing an argument: you would be trying to give a good reason for believing this statement. As a rule, an argument does not *merely* explain why something is the case but also attempts to give a good reason to believe it.

PRESENTING AN ARGUMENT VERSUS
PRESENTING A GOOD ARGUMENT

But *attempting* to give a good reason to believe something is not necessarily the same thing as successfully giving one. Consider, for example, these statements made by seventeenth-century philosopher John Locke:

---

4. Note that there is also a difference between my giving an acceptable or excusable reason for my being late and my giving a good reason for believing that I was late. In this sense, getting caught in traffic might be excusable, whereas sleeping in might not be. However, trying to provide an acceptable explanation for my being late is logically distinct from my trying to give a good reason for *believing* that I was late.

The end of law is not to abolish or restrain, but to preserve and enlarge freedom. For in all the states of created beings capable of law, where there is no law, there is no freedom.

These statements form an argument because Locke is using one statement to try to prove or justify another statement. That is, he is trying to give us a good reason to believe that the end (purpose) of law is to enlarge our freedom. So this is the conclusion of his argument. And he is trying to justify this conclusion with the statement that "where there is no law, there is no freedom," which is therefore his premise. So Locke's argument is that the end of law must be to enlarge our freedom because where there is no law there is no freedom.

But, although Locke is making an argument, this does not mean he is making a *good* argument. In fact, Locke's argument is not a good one. That is, he does not succeed in giving us a good reason to believe that the end (purpose) of law is to enlarge our freedom. For, even if it is true that where there is *no* law there is *no* freedom, this doesn't mean that where there *is* law, there must be freedom (let alone the "enlargement" of it). As you will see (chapter 3), this is a fallacy. It's like arguing that where there is no fruit, there are no apples. Therefore, where there *is* fruit, there must be apples. What about pears, peaches, bananas, and grapes? Similarly, what about tyrannical governments that have laws, albeit very oppressive ones, which aim at stifling freedom?

It should therefore be clear that something can be an argument without necessarily being a good argument. But before you can determine if an argument is a good one, you must be able to distinguish an argument from a nonargument in the first place.

Exercise Set 1.1

Determine whether each of the following is or is not an argument. That is, determine whether or not the author is trying to give a good reason to believe one statement by appealing to another statement or statements.

1.1.1
"Bodybuilding is much like any other sport. To be successful, you must dedicate yourself 100 percent to your training, diet, and mental approach." —Arnold Schwarzenegger

1.1.2
"Generally speaking, the errors in religion are dangerous; those in philosophy only ridiculous." —David Hume

1.1.3
"I love kids. I was a kid myself once." —Tom Cruise

1.1.4
"I had this beer brewed just for me. I think it's the best I ever tasted. And I've tasted a lot. I think you'll like it too." —Billy Carter (brother to President Jimmy Carter)

1.1.5
"Do something every day for no other reason than you would rather not do it, so that when the hour of dire need draws nigh, it may find you not unnerved and untrained to stand the test." —William James

(continued)

1.1.6
"He that is taken and put into prison or chains is not conquered, though overcome; for he is still an enemy." —Thomas Hobbes

1.1.7
"Logic is the last scientific ingredient of philosophy; its extraction leaves behind only a confusion of non-scientific, pseudo problems." —Rudolph Carnap

1.1.8
"It's always felt natural, because I'm generally very comfortable with people." —Bruce Springsteen

1.1.9
"In so far as a scientific statement speaks about reality, it must be falsifiable; and in so far as it is not falsifiable, it does not speak about reality." —Karl Popper

1.1.10
"The meaning of life is not to be discovered only after death in some hidden, mysterious realm; on the contrary, it can be found by eating the succulent fruit of the Tree of Life and by living in the here and now as fully and creatively as we can." —Paul Kurtz

1.1.11
"Cheney is a terrorist. He terrorizes our enemies abroad and innocent citizens here at home indiscriminately." —Alec Baldwin

1.1.12
"Our society is run by insane people for insane objectives. I think we're being run by maniacs for maniacal ends, and I think I'm liable to be put away as insane for expressing that. That's what's insane about it." —John Lennon

1.1.13
"I think it's really terrifying that a country based on the foundations and ideals of God is now systematically removing God from everything. Everything!" —Stephen Baldwin

1.1.14
"U.S. and coalition forces launched missiles and bombs at targets in Iraq as Thursday morning dawned in Baghdad, including a 'decapitation attack' aimed at Iraqi president Saddam Hussein and other top members of the country's leadership." —CNN, Thursday, March 20, 2003

1.1.15
"I'm not the type of guy who enjoys one-night stands. It leaves me feeling very empty and cynical. It's not even fun sexually. I need to feel something for the woman and entertain the vain hope that it may lead to a relationship." —Ben Affleck

1.1.16
"Life is like an onion: you peel it off one layer at a time, and sometimes you weep." —Carl Sandburg

1.1.17
"Every night, I have to read a book, so that my mind will stop thinking about things that I stress about." —Britney Spears

1.1.18
"To be a good actor you have to be something like a criminal, to be willing to break the rules to strive for something new." —Nicolas Cage

1.1.19
"I want a world without war, a world without insanity. I want to see people do well. I don't even think it's as much as what I want for myself. It's more what I want for the people around me. That's what I want." —Tom Cruise

1.1.20
"Patriotism is a kind of religion; it is the egg from which wars are hatched." —Guy de Maupassant

INDUCTIVE AND DEDUCTIVE ARGUMENTS

Both of the inferences in table 1.1 present arguments. In inference 1, the premises together make the conclusion *probable*. Given the truth of both premises, the conclusion seems reasonable—at least in the absence of any further disconfirming facts. Notice that it is still possible for the conclusion to be false even if both premises are true. For example, there could be a clogged fuel line and a broken gas gauge. On the other hand, in inference 2, the conclusion follows *necessarily* from the premises. That is, as long as both premises are true, the conclusion will also have to be true come hell or high water! Inferences like inference 1 (where the premises can only make the conclusion probable) are called *inductive* inferences, while inferences like inference 2 (where the premises necessitate the conclusion) are called *deductive* inferences.

Table 1.1

	INFERENCE 1	*INFERENCE 2*
Premises	1. The car won't start	1. If the car is out of gas, it won't start unless we put more gas in the tank.
	2. The gas gauge is pointing to empty	2. The car is out of gas
Conclusion	The car is out of gas	The car won't start unless we put more gas in the tank

Inductive reasoning typically provides the content of the premises from which you deduce things. For example, notice that in table 1.1 the conclusion of the inductive inference (inference 1) provides the content of premise 2 of the deductive inference (inference 2).

Exercise Set 1.2

Indicate whether each of the following arguments is inductive or deductive. If you think it is inductive, provide a case in which its conclusion would be false while all its premises would be true. To determine the status of each argument as inductive or deductive, you should assume that all premises are true.

(continued)

1.2.1

The earth is getting warmer.

Over the past fifty years, this rise in temperature has been correlated with human activities that emit greenhouse gases, such as the burning of fossil fuel.

Therefore, if these activities continue, the earth will continue to get warmer.

1.2.2

The way the parts of a watch work together displays purpose and design.

The universe displays similar purpose and design.

But a watch has a designer (a watchmaker).

Therefore, the universe also has a designer (God).[1]

1.2.3

In response to an editorial written by newspaper editor Horace Greeley, Abraham Lincoln stated, "My paramount object in this struggle is to save the Union, and is not either to save or to destroy slavery. If I could save the Union without freeing any slave I would do it, and if I could save it by freeing all the slaves I would do it; and if I could save it by freeing some and leaving others alone I would also do that. What I do about slavery, and the colored race, I do because I believe it helps to save the Union."

Therefore, Lincoln's motive for freeing the slaves was to save the union and not to help the slaves.

1.2.4

If a factual claim is true and it is censored, we are deprived of the opportunity of exchanging error for truth.

If it is false, and it is censored, we are deprived of the clearer perception of truth produced by its collision with error.

Factual claims are either true or false.

Therefore, if a factual claim is censored, we are either deprived of the opportunity of exchanging error for truth or of the clearer perception of truth produced by its collision with error.[2]

1.2.5

If a category 5 hurricane strikes New Orleans and the levees don't hold, the city will be under water once again.

The maximum category the levees can withstand is a category 3 hurricane.

Therefore, if a category 5 hurricane strikes New Orleans, the city will be under water once again.

1.2.6

"It is . . . evident to our senses, that in the world some things are in motion. Whatever is in motion must be put in motion by another. If that by which it is put in motion be itself put in motion, then this also must needs be put in motion by another, and that by another again. But this cannot go on to infinity, because then there would be no first mover, and, consequently, no other mover; seeing that subsequent movers move only inasmuch as they are put in motion by the first mover. . . . Therefore it is necessary to arrive at a first mover, put in motion by no other; and this everyone understands to be God."[3]

---

1. This is a formulation of an argument advanced by William Paley in *Natural Theology* (1802).

2. This is a formulation of a famous argument presented by John Stuart Mill in *On Liberty*.

3. This is Saint Thomas Aquinas's first of "Five Ways" for proving God's existence. See St. Thomas Aquinas, *Summa Theologica*, Part 1, Question 2, Article 3. Italics added. Retrieved online on October 12, 2008, from www.newadvent.org/summa/1002.htm.

IDENTIFYING PREMISES AND CONCLUSIONS IN ARGUMENTS

In ordinary language, arguments are generally not "set up" like those in table 1.1, with the premises and conclusion clearly distinguished. Instead, you may have to determine what the conclusion and premises are. This can sometimes be accomplished by looking for certain key words that signal premises and others that signal conclusions. For example, consider the following argument made by American philosopher Sydney Hook:

> Those who say that life is worth living at any cost have already written an epitaph of infamy, for there is no cause and no person that they will not betray to stay alive.

Notice the word "for." This term is serving as a premise indicator. That is, it indicates an oncoming premise in support of the conclusion that those who say that life is worth living at any cost have already written an epitaph of infamy. Accordingly, here is how the argument looks in terms of its premise and conclusion:

> *Premise:* There is no cause and no person that those who say that life is worth living at any cost will not betray to stay alive.
> *Conclusion:* Those who say that life is worth living at any cost have already written an epitaph of infamy.

Here Hook is drawing out the self-defeating implication of holding out an unconditional commitment to staying alive. He is drawing the conclusion that the life such a person seeks at all cost to preserve will, in the end, be diminished by ending in disgrace. Hook's argument is important because it helps us to see that absolutistic thinking, even about the value of life itself, can have unwelcome consequences.

Speaking of absolutistic thinking, philosopher Peter Singer advances this argument:

> I'm a Utilitarian, so I don't see the rule against lying as absolute; it's always subject to some overriding utility which may prevent its exercise.

Notice Singer's use of the word "so" to indicate an oncoming conclusion, namely, that he doesn't see the rule against lying as absolute. Notice also that Singer is giving additional information that really isn't germane to the central argument. True, Singer's being a "utilitarian" explains why he doesn't see the rule against lying as absolute, but what he is really trying to prove is that the rule against lying is not absolute. That's why he goes on to say that this rule is always subject to some overriding utility that may prevent its exercise. This latter statement is in fact the premise Singer is using to defend his position on lying. Accordingly, Singer's central argument, with the information about himself removed, is as follows:

> *Premise:* The rule against lying is always subject to some overriding utility which may prevent its exercise.
> *Conclusion:* The rule against lying is not absolute.

The ethical theory of utilitarianism to which Singer aligns himself assesses the morality of actions according to their ability to promote "utility": that is, according to the goodness of their consequences. Thus, Singer's premise says that lying can at least sometimes be acceptable, such as when it serves some overriding good purpose—for example, saving the lives of innocent persons. So, he concludes, this rule cannot be absolute (that is, it is not unconditional).

As you can see from the above examples, the use of premise and/or conclusion indicators can help us to grasp the meaning and intent of an argument. Such use makes it less likely that one might misconstrue the intent of the argument. Consider, for example, the following argument made by Aristotle:

> Both oligarch and tyrant mistrust the people. . . . [They] deprive them of their arms.

As the argument is presented above, it is not clear whether Aristotle is concluding that oligarchs and tyrants mistrust the people because they deprive them of their arms or that they deprive the people of their arms because they mistrust them. However, this ambiguity disappears when the original text of the argument is restored:

> Both oligarch and tyrant mistrust the people, and *therefore* deprive them of their arms.

The insertion of the word "therefore" immediately clears up this ambiguity. Aristotle is clearly arguing that oligarchs and tyrants deprive the people of their arms because they mistrust the people. He is not trying to prove that they mistrust the people by appealing to the purported fact that they deprive the people of their arms. This would be a different argument.

It is therefore a good idea to include appropriate premise/conclusion indicators when you are formulating your own arguments. Remember, just because you are clear about what you are arguing does not mean that those to whom you are addressing your argument also know what you are arguing.

Table 1.2 is a partial list of some premise and conclusion indicators. *A useful general rule is that any word that means the same as "therefore" is a conclusion indicator, while any word that means the same as "because" is a premise indicator.* However, although such words can often provide useful cues as to an oncoming premise or conclusion, they do not always function this way.

For example, as you should have already surmised from the previous section, the word "because" can be used in an explanatory sense that does not give an argument. Consider, for instance, the statement "The patient died because he suffered a massive heart attack." The latter use of the word "because" does not attempt to give a good reason for believing that the patient died. The patient's death is already presented as fact and therefore is not argued. Instead, the word "because" is used to indicate the cause of the patient's death.

Further, arguments in ordinary language do not always contain premise or conclusion indicators. In such cases, you will need to rely on context to glean the direction of the argument. For example, look at this argument from philosophy professor Angela Davis:

Table 1.2

Some Premise Indicators	*Some Conclusion Indicators*
because	therefore
since	so
inasmuch as	thus
for	hence
as	consequently
for the reason that	it follows that
may be deduced/inferred/derived from	accordingly
this is why	in conclusion
as a result/consequence of	conclude that
follows from	which implies/entails/means/shows that
establishes that	may deduce/infer that
proves/justifies that	means that
provides evidence for	for these reasons

Well, of course, there's been a great deal of progress over the last forty years. We don't have laws that segregate black people within the society any longer.

In this argument, Davis does not provide any structural indicators such as "because" and "therefore," but we can still glean her argument from its context:

Premise: We don't have laws that segregate black people within the society any longer.
Conclusion: There has been a great deal of progress over the last forty years.

Apparently, the conclusion Davis is trying to prove is that there has been a great deal of progress (in the United States) over the last forty years regarding the civil rights of black people. This, she argues, is because we no longer have segregation laws (premise). Notice, she is not arguing that we no longer have racial discrimination, only that there has been substantial progress. We should be careful not to read into an argument any more than is being argued. Indeed, the fact that we no longer subscribe to the old racial segregation laws does not mean that there aren't any other ways in which the civil rights of blacks (and other minority groups) are still being abridged.

Speaking about civil rights is not merely academic. Whether such rights are recognized can have serious consequences for the way people live. In the Old South, black people were not permitted to drink from the same water fountains, use the same bathrooms, and attend the same schools as white people.

The thinking that led to such oppressive actions was based on a dangerous argument that black people were inferior to white people and *therefore* should not be treated as peers.[5] It took many years before even the courts began to recognize that the premise of this argument was groundless. But the progress of which

---

5. As announced in the landmark Supreme Court decision *Brown v. Board of Topeka*, "separate" was not truly "equal."

Davis speaks was only possible because we were willing to take another, more careful look at our premises and to abandon them in favor of more rational ones. This process of reexamination is always a work in progress. As soon as we refuse to hold open our premises to the possibility of future challenges, we foreclose the possibility of making further progress.

Exercise Set 1.3

Each of the following is an argument. Pick out the premise and conclusion indicators, if any, and state the conclusion and the premises. Then discuss briefly whether you agree with the premises.

1.3.1
"The time I burned my guitar it was like a sacrifice. You sacrifice the things you love. I love my guitar." —Jimi Hendrix

1.3.2
"One of the first signs of being depressed is that you lose interest in things. That's why I think it is important to stay passionate." —Nicolas Cage

1.3.3
"Courage is the greatest of all virtues because if you haven't courage, you may not have an opportunity to use any of the others." —Samuel Johnson

1.3.4
"First of all, the Jewish religion has a great deal in common with the Christian religion because, as Rabbi Gillman points out in the show, Christianity is based on Judaism. Christ was Jewish." —Barbara Walters

1.3.5
"We will always remember. We will always be proud. We will always be prepared, so we will always be free." —Ronald Reagan

1.3.6
"I don't get worked up or excited about situations I can't control because it's not in my power, so I might appear crazy to some people." —50 Cent

1.3.7
"It is possible to be a master in false philosophy, easier, in fact, than to be a master in the truth, because a false philosophy can be made as simple and consistent as one pleases." —George Santayana

1.3.8
"Every therapeutic cure, and still more, any awkward attempt to show the patient the truth, tears him from the cradle of his freedom from responsibility and must therefore reckon with the most vehement resistance." —Alfred Adler

1.3.9
"It's hard to do it because you gotta look people in the eye and tell 'em they're irresponsible and lazy. And who's gonna wanna do that? Because that's what poverty is, ladies and gentlemen. In this country, you can succeed if you get educated and work hard. Period. Period." —Bill O'Reilly

1.3.10
"Most people do not really want freedom because freedom involves responsibility, and most people are frightened of responsibility." —Sigmund Freud

1.3.11

"All thought must, directly or indirectly, by way of certain characters, relate ultimately to intuitions, and therefore, with us, to sensibility, because in no other way can an object be given to us." —Immanuel Kant

1.3.12

"The liberally educated person is one who is able to resist the easy and preferred answers, not because he is obstinate but because he knows others worthy of consideration." —Allan Bloom

2

+

Deductive Reasoning

In chapter 1 we distinguished between deductive and inductive reasoning. As you have seen, in the former the conclusion follows necessarily from the premises, whereas in the latter the conclusion follows from the premises with a degree of probability. In this chapter we examine some basic concepts of deductive logic.

BASICS OF DEDUCTIVE REASONING

Logical Form

All deductive arguments have argument forms. An *argument form* is a symbolic representation of an argument with all references to the world stripped away and replaced with variables (placeholders). For example, look carefully at the following three arguments and their respective argument forms presented in table 2.1. The letters *p* and *q* in the forms of arguments 1 and 2 are called *statement variables*. That is, they are placeholders for statements that replace them in their respective arguments.

All three arguments are called *syllogisms*. A syllogism is a deductive argument with two premises. Each, however, is a different type of syllogism. Argument 1 is called a *hypothetical* (or *conditional*) *syllogism* because its first premise (referred to as the "major premise") is a conditional ("if-then") statement. A hypothetical syllogism is a syllogism with at least one conditional statement. Logicians refer to the *if* part of the major premise ("Global warming continues to increase at the current rate") as the *antecedent* and the *then* part ("The earth is in imminent danger") as the *consequent*. In these terms, the minor premise (second premise) of argument 1 can be said to *affirm the antecedent*, while its conclusion *affirms the consequent*.

Argument 2 is called a *disjunctive syllogism* because its major premise (first premise) is a disjunctive ("or") statement. Logicians refer to each alternate in the

Table 2.1

Argument	Argument Form
1. If global warming continues to increase at the current rate, then the earth is in imminent danger.	If p then q
Global warming is continuing to increase at the current rate.	p
Therefore, the earth is in imminent danger.	Therefore q
2. The Iraq war was based on shoddy intelligence or the Bush administration deliberately deceived the American people.	p or q
The Iraq war was not based on shoddy intelligence.	Not p
Therefore, the Bush administration deliberately deceived the American people.	Therefore q
3. All deliberate killing of innocent persons is wrong.	All M is P
All mercy killing is the deliberate killing of innocent persons.	All S is M
Therefore, all mercy killing is wrong.	Therefore, All S is P

major premise as a *disjunct*. In these terms, the minor premise can be said to be denying one disjunct, while the conclusion is affirming the other.

Finally, argument 3 is called a *categorical syllogism* because it consists of statements that relate classes, or "categories" (the deliberate killing of innocent people, mercy killings, and wrong acts), and uses quantifiers ("all" and "no") to relate these classes. Thus, the capital letters S, P, and M in the form of argument 3 are placeholders for three distinct classes.

We will look more carefully at each of these three types of syllogisms in the chapters that follow this one.

Formal Validity

All three arguments are *formally valid*. A deductive argument is *formally valid* if and only if it has a valid form. A valid form is one such that any consistent substitution instances of the variables that make all of the premises true will also make the conclusion true. For example, consider the following substitutions for the statement variables in argument 1:

p = July 4 is a federal holiday.
q = the U.S. Post Office is closed on July 4

When the above statements are consistently substituted for their respective statement variables in the argument form of argument 1, we get the following argument:

If July 4 is a federal holiday, then the U.S. Post Office is closed on July 4.
July 4 is a federal holiday.
Therefore, the U.S. Post Office is closed on July 4.

Notice that these substitutions make the premises of the resulting argument true. But also notice that this automatically makes the conclusion true. The form of this argument automatically makes its conclusion true just as long as its statement variables are consistently replaced with statements that yield true premises. The same thing can be said about all formally valid arguments. You are free to try to find substitution instances of the variables of any of the three above argument forms that make the premises true and the conclusion false. Try as you may, you will not be able to do this!

On the other hand, some argument forms are *invalid*. Such argument forms have some substitution instances in which the premises are true and the conclusion false. For example, consider this argument form:

> If p, then q.
> Therefore, if not p, then not q.

It is not difficult to find substitution instances of p and q for this argument form that would make the premise true and the conclusion false.[1] For example, let p be the statement "John is a Baptist," and let q be "John is a Christian." These substitution instances yield this argument:

> If John is a Baptist, then John is a Christian.
> Therefore, if John is not a Baptist, then John is not a Christian.

Clearly the conclusion is false. John could belong to another Christian denomination; for example, he could be a Catholic or a Protestant. Accordingly, since you can find substitution instances of the variables in the above form that make its premise true and its conclusion false, this argument form must be invalid; therefore, any argument of this form is also formally invalid.

Exercise Set 2.1

Some of the below argument forms are valid while others are not. Determine which of them are invalid by finding substitution instances of their statement variables that make their premises true and their conclusions false.

2.1.1
p/therefore q

2.1.2
p or q/therefore q

2.1.3
p/therefore p or q

2.1.4
If p then q/therefore, if q then p

2.1.5
p and q/therefore q

(continued)

---

1. Note that this form is not a syllogistic form since it only has one premise, whereas a syllogism always has two premises.

2.1.6
q/therefore p and q

2.1.7
If p then q
If r then q/therefore, if p then r

2.1.8
If p then q
q/therefore p

2.1.9
p/therefore p

2.1.10
p/therefore not p

Soundness

The conclusions of formally valid syllogisms are not necessarily true. For example, consider this hypothetical syllogism:

Major premise: If the United States has an accurate system of counting ballots, then election outcomes will not deviate widely from the results of the exit polls.
Minor premise: The United States has a fair and accurate system of counting ballots.
Conclusion: Election outcomes will not deviate widely from the results of the exit polls.

Here is what the argument form of this syllogism looks like:

If p, then q.
p.
Therefore, q.

As you have already seen, the above argument form is *valid*. Again, this means that if you substitute statements for each of the statement variables, p and q, which make the premises true, the conclusion will also automatically turn out to be true. However, just because this argument has a valid form doesn't mean you can count on its conclusion to be true. In fact, in the 2004 presidential election, the results of exit polling did not bear out this argument's conclusion but instead deviated widely from the official election results. This means that in the case of the 2004 presidential election, at least one of the premises of this argument had to be false. This is because, given the validity of the argument's form, if both premises were indeed true, the conclusion would also have had to be true, but the conclusion was not in fact true in the case of the 2004 presidential election.

Some skeptics about the fairness of the 2004 presidential election have pointed to the falsehood of the minor premise, claiming that the wide divergence of exit polling from the actual results was statistically almost impossible in a fair and accurate election. If this is correct, then the above argument, insofar as the 2004 presidential election was concerned, rested on a false minor premise.

This shows that a formally valid argument can have a false conclusion if it rests on a false premise. There are accordingly two equally important questions to ask in assessing a deductive argument:

1. Is its argument form valid?
2. Are all its premises true?

If the answer to *both* of these questions is yes, then the argument can be said to be a *sound* argument. Thus, *a sound deductive argument must satisfy two conditions: (1) it is formally valid—that is, it has a valid form—and (2) all of its premises are true.* Insofar as you have good reason for thinking that a deductive argument satisfies both of these conditions, you have good reason for thinking that the argument is sound—and therefore good reason for believing its conclusion.

In our study of deductive arguments, each of these two conditions will be treated with equal importance. As critical and free thinkers, we should not believe things unless we have good reason for believing them. Since arguments that are formally valid can have false conclusions if their premises are false, the formal validity of an argument should not be enough to satisfy us. And, since deductive arguments that have only true premises can still have false conclusions if their forms are invalid, we must be careful not to assume that the conclusions of such arguments must also be true. In other words, both the form and content of deductive reasoning merit our attention.

Exercise Set 2.2

For each of the following arguments, apply the two standards of soundness to decide whether it is a deductively sound argument. That is, decide whether (1) each of the premises of the argument is true and (2) the form of the argument is valid. To determine the truth of the premises, you may need to do some Internet research (for example, Google the relevant terms, such as "Geneva Conventions" and "2006 Military Commissions Act" in the first problem).

2.2.1
If an act gives the president the authority for the United States to interpret the meaning and application of the Geneva Conventions, then the president has the authority to decide whether the treatment of a detainee is or is not torture.
The 2006 Military Commissions Act gives the president the authority for the United States to interpret the meaning and application of the Geneva Conventions.
Therefore, the president has the authority to decide whether the treatment of a detainee is or is not torture.

2.2.2
The First Amendment of the United States protects the right of the people to be secure in their persons, houses, papers, and effects against unreasonable searches and seizures.
Therefore, either the First Amendment of the United States protects against unreasonable searches and seizures or it gives the people the right to peacefully assemble.

(continued)

2.2.3
Either the 1960s folk-rock song "Turn! Turn! Turn!" was written by Pete Seeger and was based on a passage from the Bible (Ecclesiastes), or it was recorded by a rock group called The Byrds.
The 1960s folk-rock song "Turn! Turn! Turn!" was not recorded by a rock group called The Byrds.
Therefore, the folk-rock song, "Turn! Turn! Turn!" was written by Pete Seeger and was based on a passage from the Bible (Ecclesiastes).

2.2.4
J. K. Rowling is a British author.
Therefore, J. K. Rowling is a British author and the author of the Harry Potter series.

2.2.5
The national intelligence estimate of November 2007 judged with high confidence that in fall 2003 Tehran (Iran) halted its nuclear weapons.
Therefore, Tehran poses no immediate homeland-security threat to the United States.

2.2.6
In July 2008, Britney Spears ended her child custody battle with her ex-husband Kevin Federline in exchange for visitation rights.
Therefore, in July 2008, Britney Spears gave up custody of her two sons, Sean Preston and Jayden James, to K-Fed in exchange for visitation rights, which may increase over time.

2.2.7
In the state of Texas, if a person is convicted of a capital felony (such as murder of a police officer) and the state seeks the death penalty, then he or she can be sentenced to death.
Therefore, in the state of Texas, if a person can be sentenced to death, then he or she is convicted of a capital felony (such as murder of a police officer), and the state seeks the death penalty.

2.2.8
According to the Fifth Amendment of the U.S. Constitution, no person shall be held to answer for a capital or otherwise infamous crime unless on a presentment or indictment of a grand jury, except in cases arising in the land or naval forces, or in the militia, when in actual service in time of war or public danger; nor shall any person be subject for the same offense to be twice put in jeopardy of life or limb; nor shall be compelled in any criminal case to be a witness against himself, nor be deprived of life, liberty, or property, without due process of law; nor shall private property be taken for public use, without just compensation.
Therefore, according to the Fifth Amendment of the U.S. Constitution, no person shall be compelled in any criminal case to be a witness against himself or deprived of life, liberty, or property without due process of law.

Formal Logic

Within this more inclusive context of concern for soundness, we will now look more carefully at how to determine whether the first of the above two conditions is satisfied—that is, how to distinguish valid from invalid forms. This study of how to distinguish valid from invalid forms is called *formal logic*.

In formal logic, if the argument form of a deductive argument is invalid, it is said to commit a *formal fallacy*. A fallacy is a mistake in reasoning. A formal fallacy is thus *a mistake in reasoning resulting from the use of an invalid form*.

Being able to recognize fallacies is important because, as we will see, they can lead us to respond (cognitively, behaviorally, and emotionally) in ways that are regrettable. Indeed, the point of flagging a mistake in reasoning and calling it a fallacy is to help us avoid being misled through its commission.

In the next chapter, we will examine the hypothetical syllogism with an eye toward identifying the different types of formal fallacies it can contain.

3

✦

Hypothetical Syllogisms

As stated in chapter 2, a hypothetical syllogism is a syllogism with at least one conditional premise—that is, at least one "if-then" premise. The "if-then" relationship may be expressed in ordinary language by using a number of different terms. In checking hypothetical syllogisms expressed in ordinary language for their validity, it is therefore useful to be able to translate such conditional vocabulary into *standard conditional form*.

THE VOCABULARY OF CONDITIONAL STATEMENTS

A conditional statement can be said to be in standard conditional form when it is stated with the antecedent stated first and the consequent stated second, and when the antecedent is preceded by the word "if" and the consequent by the word "then." For example, the following statement is in standard conditional form:

If it rains, then the roof will leak.

In contrast, the following statement is *not* in standard conditional form:

The roof will leak if it rains.

Table 3.1 provides some common conditional vocabulary and illustrates how to translate it into standard conditional form. Notice that "only if" does not mean the same thing as "if." In asserting that "p only if q," I am asserting that you cannot have p without q, which translates into standard conditional form as "If p then q." Consider our example: "It rains only if there are clouds." This means that it cannot rain unless there are clouds, which translates into standard conditional form as "If it rains, then there are clouds."[1]

---

1. Notice also that if q is a necessary condition of p, then p is also a sufficient condition of q. That is, if you can't have p without q, then *if* you have p, you will also have q.

Table 3.1

Conditional Vocabulary	Example	Standard Conditional Form
only if	It rains only if there are clouds. Only if there are clouds does it rain.	If it rains, then there are clouds.
if and only if	You are eligible to vote if and only if you have a valid voter registration card.	If you have a valid voter registration card, then you are eligible to vote. & If you are eligible to vote, then you have a valid voter registration card.
on condition that	I will go on condition that you pay me.	If I you pay me, then I will go.
entails, implies	Bachelorhood entails being unmarried. Bachelorhood implies being unmarried.	If one is a bachelor, then one is unmarried.
in the event that	In the event that there's a fire, take the stairs.	If there is a fire, then take the stairs.
when	When he lies, his left eye twitches.	If he lies, then his left eye twitches.
where	Where there's smoke, there's fire.	If there's smoke, then there's fire.
assuming that, given that	Assuming that weather permits, the graduation will be outdoors. Given that the weather permits, the graduation will be outdoors.	If the weather permits, then graduation will be outdoors.
provided that	The bill will become law provided that the president signs it. Provided that the president signs it, the bill will become law.	If the president signs the bill, then the bill will become law.

In translating "only if" statements into standard conditional form, a useful rule is that *whatever immediately follows the "only if" becomes the consequent*. So, in the statement "Only if there are clouds does it rain," the consequent is "there are clouds," since this is what immediately follows the "only if."

Notice that the term "if and only if" yields *two* conditional statements, each of which reverses the order of the other's antecedent and consequent. This is because this term says two things: it says "if" and it says "only if." Thus, "p if and only if q" means "p if q" *and* "p only if q." And since p only if q is translated as "If p then q," the result is two conditionals in reverse order: "If p then q" and "If q then p." For example, "You are eligible to vote if and only if you have a valid voter registration card" says two things: "You are eligible to vote if you have a valid voter registration card" and "You are eligible to vote only if you have a valid voter registration card." Translating this into standard conditional form accordingly yields two conditions: "If you have a valid voter registration card, then you are eligible to vote" and "If you are eligible to vote, then you have a valid voter registration card."

NECESSARY VERSUS SUFFICIENT CONDITIONS

Since "p only if q" means that you can't have p unless you also have q, q can also be said to be a *necessary condition* of p. On the other hand, since this translates into standard form as "If p then q," it also means that p is a *sufficient condition* of q—that is, if p is the case, then so too is q. Therefore, if q is a necessary condition of p, then p is also a sufficient condition of q. For example, in saying that clouds are a necessary condition of rain, we mean, "If it rains, then there are clouds"—that is, you can't have rain unless you also have clouds. On the other hand, this conditional also asserts that rain is a sufficient condition of clouds since it says that if you have rain, then you also have clouds.

If p is true *if, and only if* q is true, then p can also be said to be *both a necessary and sufficient condition* of q. Since "p is a necessary condition of q" translates into standard conditional form as "If q then p," and since "p is a sufficient condition of q" translates as "If p then q," this means that "p is both a necessary and sufficient condition of q" translates into two conditionals: if p then q, *and* if q then p. So, for example, if having a valid voter registration card is both a necessary and sufficient condition of being eligible to vote, then the following two conditionals are true: "If you are eligible to vote, then you have a valid voter registration card" *and* "If you have a valid voter registration card, then you are eligible to vote."

Table 3.2 illustrates the standard conditional form of statements expressing necessary and/or sufficient conditions. It is important to keep the difference between necessary and sufficient conditions straight. If p is a *sufficient* condition of q (that is, if p then q), and if you know that p is true, you can validly deduce that q is true.

Table 3.2

Conditional Vocabulary	Example	Standard Conditional Form
necessary condition	Clouds are a necessary condition of rain.	If it rains, then there are clouds.
sufficient condition	Rain is a sufficient condition of clouds.	If it rains, then there are clouds.
necessary and sufficient condition	Having a valid voter registration card is a necessary and sufficient condition of being eligible to vote.	If you are eligible to vote, then you have a valid voter registration card. & If you have a valid voter registration card, then you are eligible to vote.

In contrast, as you will see in the next section of this chapter, if you know that q is a *necessary* condition of p (if p then q), and if you know that q is true, you *cannot* validly deduce that p is true.

For example, in contract law, a *necessary* condition of a legally binding contract is that the contract be executed between mutually consenting parties. However, this is not a *sufficient* condition of a legally binding contract. Other conditions must also be true, such as that the consent was informed and not coerced, the contract was between competent parties, and it was entered into for a legal purpose. Thus, you cannot deduce that a contract is legally binding from the fact that it fulfills any one of these necessary conditions of a legally binding contract. For example, the fact that you may have signed on the dotted lines does not by itself mean that you are bound by the contract because signing a contract is not a sufficient condition of its being legally binding. The signed contract would not be legally binding if, for instance, consent was forced or cajoled.

Exercise Set 3.1

Translate each of the below statements into standard conditional form.

3.1.1
"Only if people live free of illness to the very end and then die suddenly will medical progress really result in cheaper medicine." —Leon R. Kass and Eric Cohen

3.1.2
HIV is necessary (but not sufficient) for AIDS.

3.1.3
Destruction of the eardrum is a sufficient condition of deafness.

3.1.4
"The desire to avoid negative outcomes accompanied by a negative expectation of being able to do so has been found a necessary and sufficient condition for the experience of anxiety" —Howard R. Pollio, Tracy B. Henley, and Craig J. Thompson, *The Phenomenology of Everyday Life*

3.1.5
The defendant was given a suspended sentence on condition that he undergo therapy.

3.1.6
"'The present king of France is bald,' entails that 'The present king of France exists.'"
—Bertrand Russell

3.1.7
"[The President] shall have Power, by and with the Advice and Consent of the Senate, to make Treaties, provided two thirds of the Senators present concur." —Article 2, Sec. 2, U.S. Constitution

3.1.8
"After 12 weeks, abortion is allowed only if the foetus has a genetic deficiency or to preserve the physical and mental health of the mother." —Conditions of permissible abortion in Italy

3.1.9
"Given that any representation of Mohammed, whether satirical or otherwise, is going to offend a strict follower of Islam, any move to legislate against hurting someone's feelings is I agree a dangerous slippery slope." —Blog comment

3.1.10
"Given that Google is so central to the web, whatever attitude it takes toward privacy has massive implications for the rest of the web in general, and for other search engines in particular." —Googlewatch.org

3.1.11
"I will burn an American flag if and ONLY if a constitutional amendment against flag burning is ratified but only if 100 other citizens of the United States of America will do the same." —Domingo Galdos, American citizen (Pledgebank.com)

3.1.12
"Supposing that there were a machine so constructed as to think, feel, and have perception, we could conceive of it as enlarged and yet preserving the same proportions, so that we might enter into it as into a mill. And this granted, we should only find on visiting it, pieces which push one against another but never anything by which to explain perception." —Nicholas Humphrey, *A History of the Mind: Evolution and the Birth of Consciousness*

3.1.13
"Only if the president knew his subordinates were engaged in criminal acts (rather than, more loosely, 'dirty tricks') and only if the president knew of the criminal acts either before they took place or soon thereafter during the period when he repeatedly told the American people that White House personnel were not engaged in burglary or other nefarious activities, could impeachment be entertained." —Michael Schudson, *Watergate in American Memory*

3.1.14
"Life has meaning only if one barters it day by day for something other than itself." —Antoine de Saint Exupéry

FORMS OF HYPOTHETICAL SYLLOGISM

You have just seen how to translate conditional statements in ordinary language into standard conditional form. With this ability to "set up" hypothetical syllogisms in ordinary language, you can in turn distinguish those that have valid forms from those that have invalid forms.

Table 3.3 should help you distinguish the formally valid hypothetical syllogisms from those that are invalid and therefore commit fallacies.

The Fallacy of Denying the Antecedent

As you can see from table 3.3, the first two forms are valid, while the last three commit formal fallacies.[2] To illustrate the second of these fallacies, the *fallacy of*

2. Note that these fallacies are identified by describing what their minor premises are doing.

Table 3.3

Form	Minor Premise	Conclusion	Status
If p then q p Therefore q	Affirms antecedent	Affirms consequent	Valid
If p then q Not q Therefore not p	Denies consequent	Denies antecedent	Valid
If p then q q Therefore p	Affirms consequent	Affirms antecedent	Invalid: Fallacy of Affirming the Consequent
If p then q Not p Therefore not q	Denies antecedent	Denies consequent	Invalid: Fallacy of Denying the Antecedent
If p then q r Therefore q	Relation between premises is uncertain	Affirms consequent	Invalid: Fallacy of Uncertain Relations between Premises
If p then q P Therefore r	Affirms antecedent	Conclusion does not follow	Invalid: Non-Sequitur

denying the antecedent, suppose that while driving, you approach a traffic light, which you observe to have just changed from red to green. So you reason, "The light is not red. It just turned green, so I don't have to stop." Suppose that as a result of drawing this conclusion, you proceed through the intersection, overlooking a police officer standing in the road directing you to stop. Accordingly, when you run down the officer, you have only bad logic to blame! This is because from the fact that the light is not red, it does not necessarily follow that you don't have to stop. The relevant traffic rule says, "If the light is red, you have to stop," which doesn't mean there can't be any other lawful reasons that constitute sufficient conditions for stopping.

This syllogism, with both of its premises articulated, looks like this:

Major premise/traffic rule: If the light is red, then I have to stop.
Minor premise: The light is not red.
Conclusion: I do not have to stop.

Notice that the form of this argument is as follows:

If p, then q.
Not p.
So, not q.

As you can see, this is the *fallacy of denying the antecedent* since the minor premise denies the antecedent, while the conclusion denies the consequent (see table 3.3). The form of the argument is invalid; therefore, so too is the *argument* itself. You can prove that this form is invalid just by substituting statements for the letters that make the premises true and the conclusion false.[3] This is easy to do. For example, try substituting "This is an apple" for p and "This is a fruit" for q. Given that "this" is a peach, you can see how the premises could be true while the conclusion is false.

It is important not to confuse the fallacy of denying the antecedent with the valid form of denying the consequent. On a cursory inspection, this latter form may appear to be the same as the fallacious form, but notice that the conclusion and the minor premise are in the reverse order of the fallacy of denying the antecedent:

If p, then q.
Not q.
So, not p.

It is easy to see that this form is valid. It is, in essence, saying that since p implies something q that is false, then p is itself false. That is, a statement that implies a false statement is itself false. For example, since "This is an apple," implies "This is a fruit," and since it's false that this is a fruit, it follows that this is not an apple. In this form, there are no substitution instances that would make the premises true and the conclusion false. This is impossible.

The Fallacy of Affirming the Consequent

While denying the consequent is valid, *affirming* it is a fallacy. And, like other irrational inferences, it can have serious consequences. Here is an illustration.

During the years immediately following the September 11, 2001, attacks, many Americans believed that the leader of Iraq, Saddam Hussein, supported al-Qaeda largely because he engaged in terrorism against his own people. As you will see (chapter 14), in the absence of concrete evidence linking Hussein to al-Qaeda (and therefore to the 9/11 attacks), the Bush administration's case for such a linkage was made to rest largely on the fact that Hussein was undeniably a terrorist. For example, the following is quoted from President George W. Bush's 2002 State of the Union address:

> Iraq continues to flaunt its hostility toward America and to support terror. The Iraqi regime has plotted to develop anthrax, and nerve gas, and nuclear weapons for over a decade. This is a regime that has already used poison gas to murder thousands of its own citizens—leaving the bodies of mothers huddled over their dead children. . . . States like these, and their terrorist allies, constitute an axis of evil, arming to threaten the peace of the world.

The "terrorist allies" referred to here are not explicitly mentioned by Bush, but he was quite explicit in other speeches, and it is clear that he was referring to the

---

3. Since you cannot substitute statements for the variables of a valid form that make the premises true and the conclusion false, constructing such an example constitutes a proof that the argument form is indeed invalid.

terrorist organization known as al-Qaeda. Moreover, Vice President Dick Cheney didn't mince words when, during an interview with journalist Tim Russert in 2003 on the news show *Meet the Press*, he said of Hussein, "We know that he has a long-standing relationship with various terrorist groups, including the al-Qaeda organization."[4] In fact, this alleged link between al-Qaeda and Hussein was later refuted in 2004,[5] and in the end, the alleged link between Hussein and al-Qaeda rested largely on this flimsy argument:

> *Major premise:* If a group supports al-Qaeda, it supports terrorism.
> *Minor premise:* The Iraqi regime (Hussein and company) supports/has supported terrorism.
> *Conclusion:* The Iraqi regime supports al-Qaeda.

Both premises are clearly true. However, the conclusion does not follow from the premises. This is because someone can support terrorism without being an al-Qaeda supporter. In other words, while supporting terrorism may be a *necessary* condition of being an al-Qaeda supporter, it is not a sufficient condition. In fact, while Hussein did indeed support terrorism, his largely secular regime did not support the radical Muslim sectarian group.

The form of this argument is

> If p, then q.
> q.
> Therefore, p.

As you can plainly see, this is the fallacy of affirming the consequent. This fallacy confuses a necessary condition with a sufficient condition. The major premise says that q is a necessary condition of supporting al-Qaeda, not a sufficient one. It is regrettable that the evidence the Bush administration had to support invading a sovereign nation rested largely on false claims and invalid inferences.

The Fallacy of Uncertain Relationship between Premises in Hypothetical Syllogisms

You have already seen that the case of affirming the antecedent is valid. However, care should be taken not to confuse a statement that affirms the antecedent with one that really does not. Consider the following case.

In March 2006, Crystal Mangum, a black woman, accused three white male Duke University students who played for the Duke lacrosse team of gang-raping her at an off-campus party on March 13. As the case unfolded, it became evident that there was no evidence linking the three men to the rape and that the district attorney, Michael Nifong, was pursuing the case to garner favor with the black community in order to be reelected.

---

4. Interview with Vice President Dick Cheney, NBC, "Meet the Press," transcript for March 16, 2003. Available at www.mtholyoke.edu/acad/intrel/bush/cheneymeetthepress.htm.

5. Walter Pincus and Dana Milbank, "Al-Qaeda-Hussein Link Is Dismissed," *Washington Post*, June 17, 2004. Retrieved on February 1, 2008, from www.washingtonpost.com/wp-dyn/articles/A47812 -2004Jun16.html.

The atmosphere in Durham, North Carolina, home to Duke University, was one of fear and racial tension while this case came to a head over the course of several months. Amid community protests, eighty-eight Duke University professors signed a campus newspaper ad condemning "what happened to this young woman" and proclaiming it to be a "social disaster."

Mangum, a student at North Carolina Central University, a black cross-town college, was also a single mother who worked part-time as a stripper and escort. The national media framed Mangum as an underprivileged, struggling single mom victimized by three rich white kids from a prestigious university. The case thus became a symbol of racial, sexual, and economic oppression. Unfortunately, the disingenuous nature of the charges did not help the true victims of these social circumstances.

Among the journalists who ran with this story of oppression was CNN host Nancy Grace. Here are excerpts from her show, which aired on March 31, 2006:[6]

> Grace: . . . first tonight: At Duke University, they consider themselves the cream of the crop—top grades, top scores, rich endowment, top athletics. Duke University squares off with Lady Justice. Tonight, legal smackdown, Duke's entire lacrosse team under the microscope on the alleged multiple rape of another student. . . .

> Grace: Straight out to a reporter with WPTF radio, Kevin Miller. Kevin, what is going on at Duke University?

> Kevin Miller, WPTF Radio: Well, Duke University, Nancy, has been slow to respond to these terrible allegations of what has happened with the lacrosse team and other members. They've been playing catch-up. They actually played two games before the community found out what actually happened. We've had protests there. . . .

> Grace: You know what, Kevin? I'm so glad they didn't miss a lacrosse game over a little thing like gang rape! Go ahead.

> Miller: Well, Nancy, you know, it's good you bring that up. They played a game against Cornell and UNC, and they would have played another game against George-town, if the community had not heard about what happened and got together and really started these protests. There were protests at the lacrosse game. . . .

> Grace: Let's go to prosecutor Holly Hughes. She's a veteran sex crimes prosecutor.

> . . .

> Holly Hughes: . . . this woman was beaten. She was bruised. She was battered. And you can call her a stripper. You can call her a hooker. You can use all kinds of derogatory terms about the victim. But no matter how rough someone claims the victim liked it, no one wants to be beaten. And based on the bruising and the beating and the broken nails, Nancy, this is rape. If, in fact, there's DNA, they can say consent all they want, but the other evidence speaks volumes, and it's going to negate that.

> Grace: But, of course, you know, Holly, you've heard the words "not guilty" in a case where you have bruising, where you have DNA results. You've got these probably rich kids, lacrosse players, claiming consent or I didn't do it. This is going to be a courtroom showdown like no other.

---

6. transcripts.cnn.com/TRANSCRIPTS/0603/31/ng.01.html.

As is evident from the tenor of the above exchanges, the presumption of innocence has been replaced with the presumption of guilt. Grace's sarcasm ("a little thing like gang rape") already assumes that the Duke players are guilty of gang-raping Mangum. Kevin Miller's remark that the three men would have played another game had the community "not heard about what happened" assumes that *something* (namely, a gang rape) did in fact *happen*. Notice, too, how Holly Hughes, Grace's expert on sex crime, has already decided that the three defendants are guilty.

Also notice, however, that Grace and Miller move between assuming that the gang rape actually happened and speaking of the "*alleged* multiple rape of another student" and the "terrible *allegations* of what has happened." But, clearly, an *allegation* is not the same thing as a guilty verdict.

Predictably, in response to Hughes, Grace emphasizes the privileged status of the three defendants and questions whether even DNA evidence would convict them.[7] Here, in essence, is one of Grace's key arguments, which kept viewers tuning in for further updates:

> *Major premise:* If rich (white) kids who play lacrosse for a prestigious university like Duke gang-rape a (black) stripper, then they may still, in the end, get away with it.
> *Minor premise:* There are allegations that the three white Duke lacrosse players gang-raped Mangum, a black stripper.
> *Conclusion:* The three Duke students may still, in the end, get away with having gang-raped Mangum.

This inflammatory argument may have had the power to keep viewers' ongoing attention and thus to help CNN turn a profit, but notice that its minor premise does not affirm the antecedent. This is because there is a difference between an *alleged* gang rape and a proven one. Only by fudging on this distinction can Grace and company draw the above conclusion.[8] This reasoning, however, is invalid. Its form is as follows:

> If p, then q.
> r.
> Therefore, q.

This is the fallacy of uncertain relations between premises (see table 3.3).

In the end, the three men were acquitted, and Nifong was disbarred. However, the stigma of being accused of rape in the public eye on prime-time national TV does not easily fade away. "Lady Justice," as Grace called it, would have been better served by sound argument!

---

7. Also, at other junctures Grace assumed that Mangum's work as a stripper would be used against her: "But let's get real, Holly. How badly is it going to hurt her credibility if she is a stripper? She's also a student at a nearby college, but if she's a stripper, the prosecution's got to deal with that."

8. Notice that without the presumption of innocence removed, Grace's conclusion would have been that *if* the defendants are guilty, they might still get away with it. But, even if this provisional conclusion could have been rationally defended, it would not have been nearly as provocative and engaging as the one Grace tried to get her audience to accept—namely that there was a good chance that these rich white kids from Duke, *who were guilty as charged*, would get away with gang rape.

Non Sequitur

The Latin term *non sequitur* literally means "It does not follow." *This fallacy arises when one attempts to deduce a conclusion that does not follow from the premises.* A non sequitur differs from the fallacy of uncertain relations between premises. In the latter fallacy, the minor premise does not affirm the antecedent, whereas in a non sequitur, the conclusion does not affirm the consequent.

Consider, for example, the following argument:

> If I have mitral valve prolapse, then I have a heart condition. The doctor said that I have mitral valve prolapse. It was confirmed by an ultrasound. So, I am going to die of a heart attack.

Mitral valve prolapse is a common condition of the heart in which one of the heart values, the mitral valve, closes irregularly. It is a relatively benign condition that does not cause heart attacks. The above argument illustrates a non sequitur in which one sets oneself up for intense fear by jumping to a dreaded conclusion not supported by the evidence.

In standard hypothetical form, this argument is as follows:

> *Major premise:* If I have mitral valve prolapse, then I have a heart condition.
> *Minor premise:* I have mitral valve prolapse.
> *Conclusion:* I am going to die of a heart attack.

The form of this argument is

> If p, then q.
> p.
> Therefore, r.

As you can see, the form of this argument is invalid. The minor premise (p) affirms the antecedent, but the conclusion (r) does not affirm the consequent (q).

In this instance, the valid conclusion to be drawn is the consequent, "I have a heart condition." But one cannot infer that one will have a heart attack from the fact that one has a heart condition. In fact, this so-called heart condition does not increase the risk of having a heart attack. The logical gap here is bridged by fear rather than by evidence.

Consider this other argument:

> The Earth is about 4.5 billion years old; life has been present for at least the last 3 billion of those years, and possibly got started even earlier. Complex, multicelled plants and animals go back about 600 million years, so for half the Earth's history or more, bacteria had the place to themselves.[9]

Let E = the earth is about 4.5 billion years old, *and* life has been present for at least the last 3 billion of those years, *and* complex, multicelled plants and animals go back about 600 million years.

---

9. Dan Ibekwe, Comment, "Is There Life on Other Planets?" About.com, May 9, 2008. Retrieved online on April 8, 2009, from space.about.com/b/2008/05/09/friday-question-is-there-life-on-other-planets.htm.

Let C = for at least half the earth's history, organisms that were not complex, multicelled plants and animals had the earth to themselves.

Let B = for at least half the earth's history, bacteria had the earth to themselves.

The argument in question can now be represented as follows:

If E, then C.
E.
Therefore, B.

Notice that this argument is a non sequitur. The conclusion that for at least half the earth's history, bacteria had the earth to themselves (B) does not follow. Rather, all that follows is that for at least half the earth's history, organisms that were not complex, multicelled plants and animals had the earth to themselves (C). Since there are other types of non-multicellular life besides bacteria, for example protozoa and algae, the premises do not support a conclusion about bacteria.

While some hypotheses about the origins of life on earth do claim that primitive bacteria were probably the first life forms[10] and, accordingly, probably did inhabit the earth for at least half of the earth's history, this conclusion simply does not follow from the evidence provided. To establish this conclusion, further premises that attempt to establish the primacy of bacteria over other organisms would have to be added. For example, viruses could be ruled out because they are parasitic, which means they need hosts, which in turn suggests that they would have had to have developed later on in the food chain.

The Pure Hypothetical Syllogism

We have so far looked at hypothetical syllogisms that have just one conditional premise. However, some of them have not just one but two such premises. This form of hypothetical syllogism is called a *pure hypothetical syllogism*. Consider, for example, the following argument:

Major premise: If the president approved the torture of prisoners of war, then the president violated the Geneva Conventions.
Minor premise: If the president violated the Geneva Conventions, then the president has committed a war crime.
Conclusion: If the president approved the torture of prisoners of war, then the president has committed a war crime.

The form of this argument is:

If p, then q.
If q, then r.
Therefore, if p, then r.

---

10. "Origins of Life on Earth," Biology Online. Retrieved online on April 8, 2009, from www.biology-online.org/10/1_first_life.htm.

This form is valid; that is, any consistent substitution instances for its statement variables, p, q, and r, that make the premises true, will also make the conclusion true. For example, let p = this is an apple, q = this is a fruit, and r = this has seeds. Notice that given these substitution instances, the premises turn out to be true, but so too does the conclusion: "If this is an apple, then this has seeds."

Arguably, the argument is also *sound*. Its major premise appears to be true. According to Article 17 of the 1949 Geneva Conventions,[11]

> No physical or mental torture, nor any other form of coercion, may be inflicted on prisoners of war to secure from them information of any kind whatever. Prisoners of war who refuse to answer may not be threatened, insulted, or exposed to any unpleasant or disadvantageous treatment of any kind.

The argument's minor premise also appears to be true. This is because the Geneva Conventions require all signatory nations to pass national laws that make serious violation of its provisions a punishable criminal offense. The United States is such a signatory, and in fact, under the 1996 U.S. War Crimes Act, it is a punishable criminal offense for U.S. military personnel and government officials to commit war crimes as defined by the Geneva Conventions.

Therefore, given that the form of this argument is valid and both premises are true, it follows that the conclusion must also be true. But notice that the conclusion of a pure hypothetical syllogism is itself a conditional statement. In particular, the conclusion of the argument in question does not state (unconditionally) that the president has committed a war crime. Rather, it states that *if* the president approved the torture of prisoners of war, *then* he has committed a war crime. Therefore, in order to establish that President Bush has committed a war crime, the following argument has to be defended:

Major premise: If the president approved the torture of prisoners of war, then he has committed a war crime.
Minor premise: The president approved the torture of prisoners of war.
Conclusion: The president has committed a war crime.

Notice that this hypothetical syllogism is valid (a case of affirming the antecedent). However, its minor premise was a source of intense debate between the Bush administration and its critics.

Much of the controversy surrounded whether a form of "enhanced interrogation" known as "waterboarding" constitutes torture. Waterboarding, which dates back to the Spanish Inquisition, consists of strapping down a person, placing a cloth over his or her face, and pouring water onto the cloth, thereby creating the condition and painful sensation of drowning.[12] During 2002 and 2003, President Bush authorized the use of this technique on at least three detainees—accused al-Qaeda members

---

11. The Geneva Conventions set the standards of international law governing noncombatants and prisoners of war.

12. This is not simulated drowning but, rather, actual drowning because water does in fact enter the lungs. Unless this technique is discontinued before the lungs fill with water, stopping respiration, there is the real possibility that the person will actually drown.

Khalid Sheikh Mohammed, Abu Zubaydah, and Abd al-Rahim al-Nashiri—allegedly to gain information to avoid further attacks by al-Qaeda.

Waterboarding has been condemned by nations around the world, the *Army Field Manual* explicitly forbids it, and U.S. courts have previously obtained convictions for its use. Further, this method of interrogation appears to fit the ordinary language definition of torture. For example, according to the Oxford English Dictionary, torture is "the infliction of severe bodily pain, as punishment or a means of persuasion."

We have just seen how a valid pure hypothetical syllogism could be used in establishing or defending a claim (in this case that the president was guilty of a war crime). However, not all pure hypothetical syllogisms are valid. Here is an example of an invalid argument:

> If waterboarding is against the Geneva Conventions, then it is illegal.
> If waterboarding is torture, then it is illegal.
> If waterboarding is torture, then it is against the Geneva Conventions.

Don't be fooled by the fact that both premises and the conclusion are true. The validity of an argument is a function of its form, and the form of this argument is invalid. Here is its form:

> If p, then q.
> If r, then q.
> Therefore, if r, then p.

Notice that you can easily find substitution instances of the variables of the above form that make the premises true and the conclusion false. For example, let p = this is an apple, q = this is a fruit, and r = this is an orange. The conclusion then turns out to be "If this is an orange, then this is an apple." Therefore, this form is invalid, and any argument that has this form is formally invalid.

Exercise Set 3.2

For each of the following hypothetical syllogisms, (1) determine whether it is valid or invalid, (2) state its form, and (3) if the argument is invalid, indicate the fallacy that it commits.

3.2.1
If the Internet is taken over by the giant telecom corporations, such as Comcast and ATT, which are obedient to the federal government, then Net neutrality will be destroyed, and the Internet will no longer be a free and open democratic forum.
These giant telecom corporations have already taken some steps toward taking over the Internet.
Therefore, Net neutrality will be destroyed, and the Internet will no longer be a free and open democratic forum.

3.2.2
If the FBI permits racial profiling for purposes of searches and seizures, then it violates the equal protection clause of the Fourteenth Amendment of the U.S. Constitution.

On October 1, 2008, the FBI adopted new rules that permit racial profiling for purposes of searches and seizures.
Therefore, the FBI violates the equal protection clause of the Fourteenth Amendment of the U.S. Constitution.

3.2.3
If Britney Spears gets back together with K-Fed, then she will be reunited with her children, who are presently in the custody of K-Fed.
Britney Spears is not going to get back together with K-Fed.
Therefore, Britney Spears will not be reunited with her children, who are presently in the custody of K-Fed.

3.2.4
If Vice President Dick Cheney disclosed the identity of covert CIA operative Valerie Plame, then he placed her life as well as those of her associates at risk.
Vice President Cheney did indeed disclose the identity of covert CIA operative Valerie Plame.
Therefore, Vice President Cheney should be tried for treason.

3.2.5
If there is a depression, then the housing market will get even worse.
Economists are predicting that the housing market will indeed get even worse.
Therefore, there will be a depression.

3.2.6
If millions of liters of radioactive waste from European nuclear plants are pumped into the ocean, then this will present a serious health hazard for millions of Europeans and a threat to the environment.
Every year millions of liters of radioactive waste are routinely pumped into the ocean from European nuclear plants.
Therefore, the nuclear waste that is routinely pumped into the ocean will present a serious health hazard for millions of Europeans and a threat to the environment.

3.2.7
If bacteria were the first life forms on earth, then human beings must have evolved from bacteria.
Human beings evolved from bacteria.
Therefore bacteria were the first life forms on earth.

3.2.8
If the big bang theory is true, then the universe must have come into being ex nihilo ("out of nothing").
But something cannot come from nothing.
Therefore, the big bang theory is false.

3.2.9
If God created the earth five thousand years ago, then the big bang theory is false.
According to some Christian theologians, God did create the earth five thousand years ago.
Therefore, the big bang theory is heretical and should not be taught.

3.2.10
If you don't believe in God's existence, then if there is a God, you will burn in hell.
But you do believe in God's existence.
Therefore, it's not the case that if there's a God, you will burn in hell.

(*continued*)

> 3.2.11
> If the United States deploys an antiballistic missile system in Europe, then it will put the Russians and the Chinese on the defensive.
> If that happens, then it will encourage both the Russians and the Chinese to escalate buildup of their nuclear arsenals.
> Therefore, if the United States deploys an antiballistic missile system in Europe, then it will encourage both the Russians and the Chinese to escalate buildup of their nuclear arsenals.

NONSYLLOGISTIC CONDITIONAL ARGUMENTS

Next, let's consider some conditional arguments that are not syllogisms. Consider the argument forms in table 3.4. Notice that the valid form does two things: (1) *switches* the order of and (2) *negates* each of the variables. And notice that the two invalid forms fail to do either (1) or (2). More exactly, the inversion fallacy *forgets to switch*, while the conversion fallacy *forgets to negate*. So you need to remember to switch and negate when you draw conclusions from one conditional premise, such as in the forms given in table 3.4.

Table 3.4

Form	Conclusion	Status
1. If p then q Therefore, if not q then not p	Switches order of variables and negates them	Valid
2. If p then q Therefore, if not p then not q	Negates each variable	Invalid: Inversion Fallacy (Forgetting to Switch)
3. If p then q Therefore, if q then p	Switches order of variables	Invalid: Conversion Fallacy (Forgetting to Negate)

> **Exercise Set 3.3**
>
> For each of the following nonsyllogistic conditional arguments, construct its form using the statement variables p and q and indicate whether it is valid or invalid. If it is invalid, state which fallacy the argument commits—namely the inversion fallacy (forgetting to switch) or the conversion fallacy (forgetting to negate).
>
> 3.3.1
> If there is evil, then God does not exist.
> Therefore, if God exists, then there is no evil.
>
> 3.3.2
> If abortion is the killing of an innocent person, then it is wrong.
> Therefore, if abortion is not the killing of an innocent person, then it is not wrong.
>
> 3.3.3
> If capital punishment deters crime, then it is a good idea.
> Therefore, if capital punishment does not deter crime, then it is not a good idea.

3.3.4

If same-sex marriage is not legalized, then the family and the institution of marriage will not be destroyed.

Therefore, if same-sex marriage is legalized, then the family and the institution of marriage will be destroyed.

3.3.5

If "safe" sex is to be taught in the schools, then our young people must buy the lie that condoms prevent unwanted pregnancies and STDs.

Therefore, if our young people do not buy the lie that condoms prevent unwanted pregnancies and STDs, then "safe" sex cannot be taught in the schools.

3.3.6

If Christians sit idly by and allow black-robed radical judges to tear away at our moral foundation through their judicial activism, then they will shape our culture as they see fit.

Therefore, if black-robed radical judges shape our culture as they see fit, then Christians will sit idly by and allow them to tear away at our moral foundations through their judicial activism.

3.3.7

If people have a fundamental right to reproduce, then human cloning should be a legal reproductive option.

If it is false that human cloning should be a legal reproductive option, then it is false that people have a fundamental right to reproduce.

SETTING ORDINARY LANGUAGE ARGUMENTS UP AS HYPOTHETICAL SYLLOGISMS

Enthymemes

When people express their reasoning, they often *assume* certain parts of their arguments instead of explicitly stating them. We must rely on the context of the argument to determine what the argument is missing. Such arguments are called enthymemes or enthymematic arguments. That is, an enthymeme is an argument that has a missing premise or conclusion. In the case of syllogisms, enthymemes may be missing a major premise, minor premise, or conclusion. In fact, arguments that are expressed in everyday life tend to be enthymematic in one of these ways.

An Enthymeme with a Missing Minor Premise: The Case for Religious Worship without the Church

Consider the following argument advanced by William Ames, the highly influential seventeenth-century theologian and religious reformer:

> Therefore, the church is not absolutely necessary as an object of faith . . . for then Abraham and the other prophets would not have given assent to those things which were revealed to them from God without any intervening help of the church.

The first step in analyzing an argument in ordinary language is to locate the conclusion. In the above, notice that the word "therefore" indicates the conclusion:

> The church is not absolutely necessary as an object of faith.

Notice also the premise indicator "for" that follows the conclusion, which indicates the premise:

> Then Abraham and the other prophets would not have given assent to those things which were revealed to them from God without any intervening help of the church.

Notice that this premise begins with "then," which signifies an oncoming consequent of a conditional statement. While the antecedent of this premise is not explicitly stated, it is clear from the context that the premise is referring to what would be true *if* the church were absolutely necessary as an object of faith. Thus, fully articulated this premise states,

> *If* the church were absolutely necessary as an object of faith, *then* Abraham and the other prophets would not have given assent to those things which were revealed to them from God without any intervening help of the church.

Since the above premise is the only conditional premise, it is clearly the major premise of the argument. Thus, the argument so far looks like this:

> *Major premise: If* the church were absolutely necessary as an object of faith, *then* Abraham and the other prophets would not have given assent to those things which were revealed to them from God without any intervening help of the church.
> *Conclusion:* The church is not absolutely necessary as an object of faith.

Therefore, what is missing from the argument is its minor premise. However, it is easy enough to figure out what this premise is from the context. Clearly, Ames is assuming that Abraham and the other prophets did indeed give their assent to things revealed to them from God without any intervening help from the church. So the argument, when fully formulated, looks like this:

> *Major premise: If* the church were absolutely necessary as an object of faith, *then* Abraham and the other prophets would not have given assent to those things which were revealed to them from God without any intervening help of the church.
> *Minor premise:* Abraham and the other prophets *did* give assent to those things which were revealed to them from God without any intervening help of the church.
> *Conclusion:* The church is not absolutely necessary as an object of faith.

Notice that the minor premise as presented above denies the consequent of the major premise,[13] while the conclusion denies the antecedent of the major premise. It is therefore formally valid.[14]

---

13. To say that Abraham and the other prophets *did give assent* is to deny that they would *not have given assent*.

14. The argument therefore has this valid form:

If p, then q.
Not q.
Therefore, not p.

Once we have explicated the argument, carefully spelling out its premises and conclusion, and checked its validity, we are then in a position to assess the argument for its *soundness*.

Indeed, Ames's argument, if sound, has very important implications for religiosity. This is because many theists (believers in God) believe that they cannot worship God unless they are involved in church life. However, if Ames's reasoning is correct, then one can worship God directly without the help of the church. And, clearly, this has significant implications for the role of the church in the life of theists.

Obviously, for those who are nontheists, the minor premise would not hold water because it assumes the existence of God in the first place. Hence, unless one is prepared to provide a further argument that proves the minor premise, the argument rests largely on faith. Nevertheless, the argument provides a serious challenge to the belief system of those who share this faith, yet believe that they can worship God only with the help of the church. You are accordingly left to decide for yourself whether this argument is sound.

An Enthymeme with a Missing Major Premise:
The Case for Living in Your House

Consider the following argument advanced by sixteenth-century philosopher and statesman Sir Francis Bacon:

> Houses are built to live in, and not to look on: therefore let use be preferred before uniformity.

Notice the word "therefore," which signals the conclusion "Let use be preferred before uniformity," which Bacon attempts to prove with the premise "Houses are built to live in and not to look on." Accordingly, here is what is given of the argument:

> Houses are built to live in and not to look on.
> Therefore, let use be preferred before uniformity.

Clearly, we can see that Bacon is assuming the *major premise*: "If houses are built to live in and not to look on, then let use be preferred before uniformity." Thus, fully articulated, his argument looks like this:

> *Major premise:* If houses are built to live in and not to look on, then let use be preferred before uniformity.
> *Minor premise:* Houses are built to live in and not to look on.
> *Conclusion:* Let use be preferred before uniformity.

Since the minor premise affirms the antecedent of the major premise, and the conclusion affirms the consequent of the major premise, this argument is formally valid.[15]

---

15. Accordingly, the valid form of this argument is

If p, then q.
p.
Therefore, q.

Those who think of their houses as both functional objects and works of art may take issue with Bacon's minor premise. Perhaps this objection could be accommodated by changing the minor premise to read, "Houses are *primarily* built to live in and not to look on." Then, this change would also have to be made to the antecedent of the major premise.

Notice that Bacon's argument is telling us *what we should do*—namely arrange our homes in a manner conducive to living and not merely for show.[16] For those who *obsessively* seek "uniformity" (orderliness) in their homes, Bacon's syllogism might present a challenge!

An Enthymeme That Is Missing a Conclusion: The Case of a Nation without a Soul

You have just seen examples of enthymemes with missing premises. However, sometimes arguments are missing their conclusions. For example, consider the following argument advanced by Winston Churchill:

> A nation without a conscience is a nation without a soul. A nation without a soul is a nation that cannot live.

Here there are two premises that can be expressed as conditional statements:

> If a nation is without a conscience, then it is without a soul.
> If it is without a soul, then it cannot live.

Clearly, Churchill wants us to conclude that "If a nation is without a conscience, then it cannot live." This conclusion would follow validly as the conclusion of a pure hypothetical syllogism. That is, fully formulated, its form would be

> If p, then q.
> If q, then r.
> Therefore, if p, then r.

Unfortunately, we may question the veracity of Churchill's minor premise. That is, can a nation survive without a soul, and for how long? Presumably, this means without a system of internalized moral principles. This is a complex question since it raises the question of how to distinguish between moral principles that are binding and those that are not. Indeed, virtually all nations would at least claim to have "a soul," even Nazi Germany. However, even if we can get past this hurdle, we may still wonder how some nations that do not appear to qualify as ones with souls have lasted as long as they have. For example, apartheid lasted in South Africa for more than thirty years! True, this oppressive system did finally come to an end, but then again, this might also be said of just nations. Perhaps all nations, with or without a soul, eventually die out or undergo radical changes in their moral structure.

---

16. This type of syllogism is called a practical syllogism and will be examined in chapter 14.

Arguments That Include Additional Information
Not Essential to the Main Argument

In ordinary language arguments, authors quite commonly embellish their arguments with statements that are not essential to the main argument. Thus, it is up to you to locate and formulate the major premise, minor premise, and conclusion of the main argument and to distinguish these from other statements that are not essential to this argument.

Consider the following argument advanced by one of the founding fathers of the United States, James Madison:

> Let us weigh the objections which have been stated against the number of members proposed for the House of Representatives. . . . The number of which this branch of the legislature is to consist, at the outset of the government, will be sixty-five. . . . The true question to be decided then is whether the smallness of the number, as a temporary regulation, be dangerous to the public liberty? . . . I am unable to conceive that the people of America, in their present temper, or under any circumstances which can speedily happen, will choose, and every second year repeat the choice of, sixty-five or a hundred men who would be disposed to form and pursue a scheme of tyranny or treachery.[17]

The passage excerpted above contains no conclusion indicators.[18] Nevertheless, it is clear from the context what Madison is trying to prove—namely that a temporary (and gradually increasing) number of sixty-five members of the House of Representatives would be large enough to guard against the abuse of power by these members. And it is also clear from the context that his primary reason for this conclusion is his confidence in the capacity of the American people to choose their representatives wisely.

This confidence in the power of human beings to self-govern, including their ability to choose their representatives, is itself a judgment that requires defending, and Madison attempts to do exactly that in the following passage:

> As there is a degree of depravity in mankind which requires a certain degree of circumspection and distrust, so there are other qualities in human nature which justify a certain portion of esteem and confidence. Republican government presupposes the existence of these qualities in a higher degree than any other form. Were the pictures which have been drawn by the political jealousy of some among us faithful likenesses of the human character, the inference would be that there is not sufficient virtue among men for self-government; and that nothing less than the chains of despotism can restrain them from destroying and devouring one another.[19]

Here, it is again clear from the context what conclusion he is drawing—namely that human beings possess certain qualities "worthy of esteem or confidence." So, how does he defend *this*?

---

17. James Madison, Federalist 55. Retrieved online on March 25, 2009, from jim.com/federalist/fed55.htm.
18. Note that the word "so" in the first sentence really means "also" and not "therefore."
19. James Madison, Federalist 55. Retrieved online on March 25, 2009, from jim.com/federalist/fed55.htm.

Well, he says, "republican government"[20] presupposes these qualities more so than any other form of government. That is, if we didn't have these qualities, we couldn't have self-government (government that derives its power from the people) but would instead have despotism (dictatorship) in order to prevent us from destroying each other. So here's Madison's argument:

> *Major premise:* If there were not qualities in human nature that justify a certain portion of esteem and confidence, then we would have despotism to keep us from destroying each other and not self-government.
>
> *Minor premise:* We do not have despotism to keep us from destroying ourselves; we have self-government.
>
> *Conclusion:* Therefore, there are qualities in human nature that justify a certain portion of esteem and confidence.

Clearly, the above argument is formally valid because the minor premise denies the consequent of the major premise.[21]

Notice that not all of what Madison has stated is included in this formulation. For example, notice that Madison admits that there are human vices: "a degree of depravity . . . which requires a certain degree of circumspection and distrust." And notice that he also speaks of "the pictures which have been drawn by the political jealousy of some among us." However, while this information provides useful background for the argument, it is not essential to the *formulation* of the main argument and is therefore not included in it. As with any "editing" process, some measure of discretion goes into deciding what exactly to include in the argument and how exactly to word it. As for the choice of words, one useful rule of thumb is to include language that approximates the author's language. Sticking as closely as possible to the original language can help the editor guard against introducing his or her own ideas or values into the formulation of the argument.

Notice also that Madison never states but instead assumes the minor premise. However, writing in 1787 prior to the ratification of the U.S. Constitution by all states, the American experiment in democracy was in its infancy, and the question of whether it would truly work was still an open question. Thus, Madison is defending the conclusion of his argument by appealing to a minor premise that itself assumes the truth of this very conclusion. As you will see,[22] this is called a

---

20. Here is how Madison elsewhere defines "republican government": "We may define a republic to be, or at least may bestow that name on, a government which derives all its powers directly or indirectly from the great body of the people; and is administered by persons holding their offices during pleasure, for a limited period, or during good behaviour. It is *essential* to such a government, that it be derived from the great body of the society, not from an inconsiderable proportion, or a favored class of it; otherwise a handful of tyrannical nobles, exercising their oppressions by a delegation of their powers, might aspire to the rank of republicans, and claim for their government the honorable title of republic" (Federalist 39, retrieved online on March 25, 2009, from press-pubs.uchicago.edu/founders/documents/v1ch4s24.html).

21. The valid form of this argument is therefore

If p, then q.
Not q.
Therefore, not p.

22. See chapter 21.

circular argument (assuming the very statement you are trying to prove), and circular arguments are, indeed, not useful arguments.

Further, this same minor premise has long been a bone of contention of some political thinkers. Chief among these critics has been the ancient Greek philosopher Plato, who thought that "self-government," or "democracy," was the final stage in the movement toward despotism (dictatorship). For Plato, the average person was very gullible and lacked the intellectual capacity to manage government. Eventually, he said, the citizens of a democratic state would be enticed by a demagogue who would seize control of state power and erect a despotic form of government.

In the sixteenth century, British philosopher Thomas Hobbes also denied that human beings have the virtues necessary to hold the reins of government. In contrast to Madison, Hobbes emphasized the competitive, distrustful, and self-aggrandizing nature of human beings and held that unless a strong, dictatorial, central government constrained this nature, we would be propelled into a treacherous state of anarchy in which we would all live without security. Thus, while Hobbes looked askance at the minor premise of the above argument, he was quite willing to accept its major premise. Indeed, Hobbes was willing to draw out the implications of Madison's major premise, which Madison himself flatly denied. Effectively, Hobbes turned Madison's argument on its head and (validly) argued like this:

> *Major premise:* If there were not qualities in human nature that justify a certain portion of esteem and confidence, then we *should* have despotism to keep us from destroying each other and not self-government.
> *Minor premise:* We do not possess the qualities in human nature that justify a certain portion of esteem and confidence.
> *Conclusion:* We *should* have despotism to keep us from destroying each other and not self-government.

True, Plato and Hobbes wrote prior to the American experiment in democracy, and we may be able to boast of some success in the more than two centuries since the founding of this nation in 1776. Nevertheless, still with us today is the specter of doubt raised by these critics of democracy about the capacity of human beings to self-govern and to elect representatives who truly represent the collective wisdom and will of the people.

Consider, for example, U.S. history over the last decade or so. Do you think that the will of the people has been adequately represented by its elected officials? Indeed, given the fact that the Supreme Court—and not, strictly speaking, the American people—decided the outcome of the 2000 presidential election, one might even meaningfully ask whether our government officials have really been "elected" by the people.

As you can see, boiling ordinary language arguments down to their basic premises, checking for validity, and then carefully examining these premises for soundness can help to focus our attention on what is important and therefore help us to ask relevant questions. This is what it means to be a free and critical thinker. Arguably, the survival of democracy in a free ("open") society may depend on how well we, the people, harness and apply these thinking skills! Such was the challenge that America's founding fathers faced, and we face the same challenge today in contemporary America.

Exercise Set 3.4

For each of the following arguments, (1) set it up in standard hypothetical form, (2) supply any missing parts if necessary, (3) state the form of the argument, (4) indicate whether the argument is valid or invalid, and (5) if the argument is invalid, state the fallacy it commits, and (6) briefly discuss its soundness.

3.4.1
"If each man had a definite set of rules of conduct by which he regulated his life he would be no better than a machine. But there are no such rules, so men cannot be machines." —A. M. Turing, "Computing Machinery and Intelligence," *Mind* 59 (1950)

3.4.2
"I very clearly see that the certitude and truth of all science depends on the knowledge alone of the true God, insomuch that, before I knew him, I could have no perfect knowledge of any other thing. And now that I know him, I possess the means of acquiring a perfect knowledge respecting innumerable matters." —Rene Descartes, *Meditations V*, ch. 16

3.4.3
"I don't believe I'll ever get credit for anything I do in foreign affairs, no matter how successful it is, because I didn't go to Harvard." —Lyndon B. Johnson

3.4.4
"Politics gives guys so much power that they tend to behave badly around women." —Bill Clinton, to a woman friend while he was a Rhodes scholar at Oxford

3.4.5
"A house divided against itself cannot stand. I believe this government cannot endure permanently half-slave and half-free. I do not expect the Union to be dissolved—I do not expect the house to fall—but I do expect it will cease to be divided." —Lincoln's "House-Divided" speech in Springfield, Illinois, June 16, 1858

3.4.6
God does not exist because there is evil; and if God existed then there would be no evil.

3.4.7
"I truly believe that people like myself, who are in a position of entertainers in the limelight, should keep their mouth shut on politics. . . . Because at the end of the day I'm good at writing songs and singing. What I'm not educated in is the field of political science. And so for me to be sharing my views and influencing people of who I think they should be voting for . . . I think would be very irresponsible on my part." —Kid Rock

3.4.8
"The terrorists are fighting freedom with all their cunning and cruelty because freedom is their greatest fear—and they should be afraid, because freedom is on the march." —George W. Bush

3.4.9
"The solution to Iraq—an Iraq that can govern itself, sustain itself, and defend itself—is more than a military mission. Precisely the reason why I sent more troops into Baghdad." —George W. Bush

3.4.10
"Joe Biden . . . stated that paying higher taxes was 'the patriotic thing to do.' . . . If one takes Joe Biden at his word, paying more taxes is a way to show your patriotism. Therefore, any American who does not want to pay more taxes is unpatriotic." —Rational_Thinker (a blogger)

3.4.11

"I agree with Senator McCain that it is time for a radical change in our health care system, and I agree that health insurance should be divorced from employment. But radical reform is useful only if it addresses the problems in our current health care system, and McCain's plan does not do that." —Susanne King, MD

3.4.12

"The sad truth is that the U.S. is experiencing a staggering increase in violent crime among inner-city teens. The murder rate for black males, ages 15–24, has increased by a factor of three in the last six years. Since there has not been a significant increase in firearms during this period, the cause of this increase in violence must be sought elsewhere." —Gerry Roston

3.4.13

"What has bothered me the most about those who support gay marriage is that they refuse to support pedosexuals and help protect their rights. I will only support gay marriage if and only if EVERYONE gets the same rights and privilages. . . . The problem I have with gay marriage is not gay people. It's that people that support gay marriage aren't open-minded enough [to allow] others who are struggling to have 'equal rights.' And until that is done, I will continue to oppose gay marriage." —Blogger

3.4.14

If gay marriage is legalized, it will destroy the institution of marriage; and if it destroys the institution of marriage, then it will destroy society.

3.4.15

"Identical twins have identical genes. If homosexuality was a biological condition produced inescapably by the genes (e.g. eye color), then if one identical twin was homosexual, in 100% of the cases his brother would be too. But we know that only about 38% of the time is the identical twin brother homosexual. Genes are responsible for an indirect influence, but on average, they do not force people into homosexuality." —N. E. Whitehead, PhD

4

✢

Disjunctive Syllogisms

As described in chapter 2, a disjunctive syllogism has a disjunctive ("or") state-ment as its major premise. As also stated, each of the alternatives given in the major premise of a disjunctive syllogism is called a *disjunct*.

THE CORE MEANING OF "OR"

The core meaning of any disjunctive statement p or q is that *at least one of the two disjuncts is true*. However, this is also quite consistent with both being true—since when both are true, *at least one* is true.

Nevertheless, in some contexts, when we state that p or q is true, what we may intend to convey is that *only one* of the two disjuncts is true. However, in this case, we must glean this intention of the speaker from the context in which the statement is made and not from the core meaning of "or" itself, which simply is that at least one disjunct is true. For example, if you go to a restaurant and the waiter tells you that you can have a choice of soup or salad with any entrée, you are supposed to assume that this "or" is exclusive and you can therefore have one of the two alternatives *but not both*. However, this addition of "but not both" is what we glean from the ordinary conventions of ordering soup or salad with an entrée in a restaurant. Thus, the uninitiated patron who responded, with respect to an offering of soup or salad, "Both of those would be fine," would likely be told that he could have only one of these alternatives unless he wanted to pay extra for both.

It is also a mistake to suppose that the word "either" in "either p or q" necessar-ily makes the "or" exclusive. For example, the statement "She is either ill or tired" might still be true even if the person in question turned out to be both ill and tired. In fact, in some contexts, it could be risky to assume that a disjunctive statement is intended to convey an exclusive disjunction. For example, if a penal statute stated that the punishment for a given offense was *a specific fine or term of incarceration*, you would not be justified in assuming that you would not be subject to receiving *both* the fine and term of incarceration if you were found guilty of the crime in question. In interpreting a contract, it can also be risky to assume a disjunction is exclusive, and you may need to ask for clarification. Such ambiguities can sometimes be cleared up by making inclusiveness or exclusiveness explicit by using "and/or" for inclusiveness and "but not both" for exclusiveness.

However, where such explication is not possible or feasible, and where there is no information to the contrary, it is rational to interpret "or" inclusively. This general rule is justified because it assumes no more than what the core meaning of "or" provides. In short, this rule avoids making assumptions for which there is no evidence.

FORMS OF DISJUNCTIVE SYLLOGISMS

Table 4.1 can help you to distinguish formally valid from formally invalid disjunctive syllogisms.[1] As you can see from the first two cases (forms 1 and 2 in table 4.1), it doesn't matter whether the minor premise of a disjunctive syllogism denies the first or the second disjunct of the major premise. In either case, the syllogism will be valid just as long as the conclusion affirms the other disjunct. This is because the disjunctive statement p or q says that *at least one of the two disjuncts is true*. Therefore, if any one of these two disjuncts is false, the other will necessarily be true.

One commonplace use of this eliminative logic is in forensic evaluation. For example, consider the death of Heath Ledger, a twenty-year-old movie star who gained fame for his role in the blockbuster movie *Brokeback Mountain.*

Ledger, who was found dead in his Manhattan apartment, had had anxiety problems and insomnia, for which he was taking a number of prescribed medications and sleeping pills. Prior to the toxicology report, there was speculation about whether his death was an accident or suicide. In the end, the medical examiner ruled that Ledger's death was accidental due to acute intoxication by the combined effects of five different medications: three antianxiety medications (Xanax, Valium, and Ativan), a sleeping medication (Lunesta), and a sedative (Restoril). The disjunctive syllogism that led to this conclusion was basically this:

> Ledger's death was accidental or a suicide.
> His death was not a suicide.
> Therefore, it was accidental.

The toxicology report did not reveal a large dosage (overdose) of any one medication, which would have probably been the case had Ledger's death been a suicide. The medical examiner used this evidence to rule out suicide and therefore to conclude that the death was accidental—due to an accidental abuse of medications. Notice that the toxicology report only indirectly showed that Ledger's death was

---

1. Cases 3 and 4 apply the stated rule of inclusive "or." That is, these cases assume that the "or" means simply that at least one disjunct is true.

Table 4.1

Form	Minor Premise	Conclusion	Status
1 p or q not p Therefore q	Denies first disjunct	Affirms second disjunct	Valid: Denies a disjunct
2 p or q not q Therefore p	Denies second disjunct	Affirms first disjunct	Valid: Denies a disjunct
3 p or q p Therefore not q	Affirms first disjunct	Denies second disjunct	Invalid: Fallacy of Affirming a Disjunct
4 p or q q Therefore not p	Affirms second disjunct	Denies first disjunct	Invalid: Fallacy of Affirming a Disjunct
5 p or q, but not both p & q p Therefore not q	Affirms first exclusive disjunct	Denies second exclusive disjunct	Valid: Affirms an exclusive disjunct
6 p or q, but not both p & q q Therefore not p	Affirms second exclusive disjunct	Denies first exclusive disjunct	Valid: Affirms an exclusive disjunct
7 p or q r Therefore q	Neither affirms nor denies a disjunct	Affirms second disjunct	Invalid: Fallacy of Uncertain Relations between Premises
8 p or q r Therefore p	Neither affirms nor denies a disjunct	Affirms first disjunct	Invalid: Fallacy of Uncertain Relations between Premises

accidental by ruling out (more exactly, making it improbable) that Ledger had committed suicide.[2]

Valid disjunctive syllogisms need not, however, be restricted to just two alternatives. For example, the following would also be valid:

p or (q or r).
Not p.
Therefore, q or r

For instance, in the Ledger case there was also at first some speculation that he might have been murdered, but this was dismissed after investigation:

Ledger's death was a murder, accident, or suicide.
His death was not a murder.
Therefore, it was an accident or suicide.

---

2. This "ruling-out" process is part of the method of hypothesis, which will be examined in chapter 12.

Notice that the conclusion here is itself a disjunction, which in turn can serve as a major premise of a further disjunctive syllogism. In this manner, any number of disjuncts can be eliminated.

Affirming an Exclusive Disjunct

Notice that forms 5 and 6 in table 4.1 explicitly use an exclusive "or" in the disjunctive statement "p or q." Each of these argument forms is valid because each says that *not both p and q are true*, and since one of the exclusive disjuncts is true, it necessarily follows that the other is false. But notice that these forms are not valid because of the core meaning of "or" but rather because of the meaning of "but not both."

Let us call syllogisms having such a form *valid excusive "or" syllogisms*. For example, the following is such a syllogism:

> The president's proposed tax plan will benefit the middle class or the rich but not both.
> The president's proposed tax plan will benefit the rich.
> Therefore, the president's proposed tax plan will not benefit the middle class.

This syllogism is valid because of the "but not both" and would be invalid if this added information was not given, in which case it would then commit the fallacy of affirming a disjunct.

The Fallacy of Affirming a Disjunct

Notice that in cases 3 and 4 in table 4.1, no information is provided that allows us to add that not both of the disjuncts are true. In such cases, where this additional information is absent, we cannot deduce anything about the truth status of one disjunct, given the truth of the other. This is because the core meaning of "or" says that at least one disjunct is true, which is consistent with *both* being true. Thus, given the truth of one disjunct, the other might also be true since both *can* be true, or it might be false since we know only that at least one disjunct is true. Therefore, such an inference would be invalid.

This fallacy can sometimes be subtle and go unnoticed. Yet it can have serious consequences. This appears to be the case with regard to a little-publicized Supreme Court decision that could have serious negative impacts on the future of the Internet as a free, neutral, universal bastion of democratic thought.

On June 27, 2005, in a 6–3 decision in the case of *National Cable & Telecommunications Association v. Brand X Internet Services*, the Supreme Court ruled that giant Internet cable companies like Comcast and Verizon are not required to share their cables with other Internet service providers (ISPs). Prior to the decision, these cable companies were governed by the rule of "common carriage," which required that the broadband Internet cables be treated like the phone lines. Just as anyone could use the phone lines to send and receive information, so too could anyone use the Internet cables to send and receive information. However, the Brand X decision ended this by giving these giant corporations the right to exclude independent ISPs from operating on the cables. The Brand X decision also left open the option for giant phone companies like AT&T to exclude other independent ISPs from operating on the phone lines, and three weeks after this decision, the Federal Communications Commission (FCC) granted this legal right to these giant telephone companies.

The decision was based on an argument that attempted to prove that ISPs do not offer telecommunication services. This argument was important because the 1996 Telecommunications Act requires companies offering telecommunications services to be subject to common carriage as a means of maintaining fair competition.

The classic example of a telecommunications service is a phone company that provides its customers the facilities to make and receive phone calls. The Court maintained that ISPs provided information services and not telecommunications services. A classic example of information services is a cable TV network that provides television programming to its customers.

The Court argued that cable companies do not "offer" the telecommunications aspects of its services to consumers because it "offers end users information-service capabilities inextricably intertwined with data transport."

Here is the basic argument put forth by the Court:

> Cable companies either offer telecommunications services or information services.
> Cable companies offer information services.
> Therefore, cable companies do not offer telecommunications services.

The fallacy here is clearly that of affirming a disjunct. To build a valid argument, the additional information of "but not both" would need to be added to the major premise. Thus,

> Cable companies either offer telecommunications services or information services, *but not both*.
> Cable companies offer information services.
> Therefore, cable companies do not offer telecommunications services.

However, while valid, this argument is not sound. It is far from clear why cable companies cannot offer *both* telecommunications and information services. As the Court itself acknowledged, a cable company "offers end users information-service capabilities *inextricably intertwined with data transport.*"

In criticizing the majority opinion, Justice Antonin Scalia, writing the minority opinion for the Court, argued that you might as well say that a pizza service doesn't deliver pizzas because it also bakes them. Responding to Scalia, the majority view argued, you might as well say that a car dealership "offers" engines to consumers because it offers them cars. According to the majority view, since the car is the final product, not the engine, it makes more sense to say that they offer consumers cars rather than engines. Analogously, it contended, the cable companies offer their consumers such capabilities as surfing the Internet and not simply transmitting data over a wire.

However, this reasoning is oversimplified. First, the analogy with cars is not convincing because consumers of cars are interested in the type of engine a car has (whether it is a V8, V6, 2.0L, 3.8L, etc.). From this viewpoint, the car dealership is indeed "offering" engines (as well as bucket seats, antilock breaks, dual airbags, and many other automotive components that concern drivers). Analogously, consumers of Internet services are not merely interested in surfing the Internet; they are also interested in sending and receiving e-mail messages, which sounds more like telecommunications services than the information services a cable TV network provides. Further, consumers are also concerned about speed and connectivity, which again are services that consumers are seeking when they purchase services "offered" by cable companies.

Consequently, the main argument of the Court rested on either the fallacy of affirming a disjunct or on a valid disjunctive syllogism with a false or highly questionable major premise. Nevertheless, this is the logic the Court used to give giant cable corporations (and three weeks later, giant phone companies) a monopoly on the provision of Internet services.

With this legal victory in hand, these companies have removed a chief obstacle in controlling Internet content. If these companies can decide who sends information down their pipes, then they can also determine what information can be sent down them. This means that in the not so distant future, the landscape of the Internet may look much like that of the cable TV networks. It will have primarily a corporate presence, and the days of the small website operator may be numbered.

Indeed, these behemoth corporations are now heading in this direction. They now have powerful lobbies in Congress and the FCC that are attempting to institute a "pay-for-play" system in which fast lanes and slow lanes will be set up for Internet website operators. In order to get into the fast lane (that is, to receive bandwidth that permits fast and secure connectivity), one will have to have deep pockets. This means the giant corporations.

The rest of us will then have to settle for operating in the slow lane, where our messages will not likely get the same attention as those of the large corporations. In consequence, "Net neutrality"—where everyone has an equal right to speak in the grandest democratic forum ever devised by humankind—may well become a thing of the past.

Fallacy of Uncertain Relations in Disjunctive Syllogisms

Cases 7 and 8 in table 4.1 display the forms of disjunctive syllogism in which the minor premise neither affirms nor denies a disjunct of the major premise. One example of this form of disjunctive syllogism occurs in some cases of so-called crisis of faith in which one perceives God's existence as a condition of the meaningfulness of life but has doubts about whether God truly exists. Philosopher Thomas Carlyle classically expressed this position in his attempt to cope with his own loss of faith:

> For man's well-being, Faith is properly the one thing needful; . . . with it, Martyrs, otherwise weak, can cheerfully endure the shame and the cross; and without it, Worldlings puke-up their sick existence, by suicide, in the midst of luxury. . . . For a

pure moral nature, the loss of his religious Belief was the loss of everything. Unhappy young man![3]

Such loss of faith proceeds from a major premise that can be put in terms of an "either-or": "Either God exists, or life is meaningless." But the problem is not that many in Carlyle's position have found peace in disbelief but rather that they are caught in a state of gnawing doubt.

Here, then, is how the premises of this syllogism proceed:

Either God exists, or life is meaningless.
I don't know if God exists.

The minor premise of the above premises does not deny God's existence. That would yield the valid conclusion that life is meaningless. Rather, it expresses agnosticism: that is, doubt about whether God exists. This premise neither affirms nor denies the first disjunct: that God exists. Therefore, there is an uncertain relation between premises, and the conclusion that life is meaningless cannot be validly deduced from them.

Instead, the premises in question leave one in a state of uncertainty about whether there is a point to one's life. Philosophers have approached such "existential anxiety" in different ways. For example, for theistic thinkers like Søren Kierkegaard, the solution is to make a "leap of faith" amid the uncertainty of not having a rational basis for belief and to find hope in having faith. For atheistic thinkers like Jean-Paul Sartre and Friedrich Nietzsche the solution is to accept the premise that God is "dead" (that is, does not exist) and to rely upon one's own free choices as the source of values and meanings in life. According to these philosophers, by abandoning the belief in God, one is free to pursue one's own values and meanings rather than having to live in conformity with what others decree.

Accordingly, these atheistic philosophers avoid existential anxiety by rejecting the major premise that "either God exists, or life is meaningless." In their view, *both* of these disjuncts can be false.

Exercise Set 4.1

Each of the following arguments can be set up as a disjunctive syllogism. For each argument, (1) identify the major premise, minor premise, and conclusion (note that you may need to edit the arguments to exclude nonessential information), (2) state the form of the argument, (3) determine whether it is valid or invalid, and (4) if the argument is invalid, state the fallacy committed. In assessing whether the disjunction is inclusive or exclusive, consider the ordinary meanings of the disjuncts. For example, in "Either the door is open, or it is shut," we know that the disjunction is exclusive because a door can't be both open and shut at the same time. As a rule, if both disjuncts can possibly be true in the given context, assume that the disjunction is inclusive.

(continued)

---

3. Thomas Carlyle, "Sartor Resartus: The Life and Opinions of Herr Teufelsdrockh," ch. 7. Retrieved online on April 17, 2009, from melbecon.unimelb.edu.au/het/carlyle/sartor.html#bk2Ch7.

4.1.1
Either God does not exist, or there is no evil in the world. Since, as anyone can see, there is evil in the world, it follows that God does not exist.

4.1.2
The only conclusion to be drawn from history is that the Iranians are not going to recognize the existence of Israel because we know that either they must recognize the existence of Israel, or there will never be peace in the Middle East; after all this time, it is obvious that there will never be peace in the Middle East.

4.1.3
In these hard economic times, either Congress will have to cut all or most of the pork from the budget, or it will have to cut corners on major priorities such as health care and education. Fortunately, in his State of the Union address, the president said he does not intend to cut corners on major priorities such as health care and education. So we can rest assured that Congress will cut all or most of the pork from its budget.

4.1.4
Either there should be a required course on ethics in medical school, or there should be a concerted attempt to incorporate the teaching of ethics into other courses in the medical school curriculum. However, there should not be a required course on ethics in medical school because there are simply too many other courses vital to the medical school curriculum that need to be covered. This is why there should be a concerted attempt to incorporate the teaching of ethics into other courses in the medical school curriculum.

4.1.5
Disconnecting the feeding tube of a terminally ill patient is either active euthanasia or passive euthanasia. It is not active euthanasia because active euthanasia involves killing a patient, and in disconnecting a feeding tube, one doesn't kill the patient. Rather the patient dies of his or her disease. So, it must be passive euthanasia.

4.1.6
Either one is a theist, an atheist, or an agnostic. Obviously, since Christians are theists, they are neither atheists nor agnostics.

4.1.7
Either personhood begins at conception, or it begins at a later point in embryological development. According to *Row v. Wade*, "The 'compelling' point is at viability. This is so because the fetus then presumably has the capability of meaningful life outside the mother's womb." Therefore personhood does not begin at conception.

4.1.8
"Deep Throat," the secret informant who helped *Washington Post* reporters Robert Woodward and Carl Bernstein break the Watergate story, was either Mark Felt or an FBI agent. After thirty years, the identity of this secret informant was finally revealed. Alas, it was Mark Felt. Therefore, the secret informant was not an FBI agent.

4.1.9
Either Senator John Kerry or President George W. Bush or President Bill Clinton belonged to Skull and Bones, a powerful secret society of Yale University. However, although Clinton went to Yale, he was not a member of the Skull and Bones. This can only mean that either George W. Bush or John Kerry belonged to Skull and Bones.

4.1.10
Human nature can be either good or evil. But human nature is evil, as anyone can see from a cursory look at the history of humankind. Therefore, we can in the very least conclude that human nature is not good.

BLACK OR WHITE MAJOR PREMISES
IN DISJUNCTIVE SYLLOGISMS

When each of the disjuncts of a disjunctive statement is false, the statement itself is false. One commonplace type of false disjunctive statement is a "black-or-white" statement. This is a disjunctive statement that divides things into opposites ("black or white") without recognizing that there can be any alternatives ("shades of gray") in between. In so doing, the statement leaves no room for cases in which both opposites are false and therefore the disjunctive statement is also false.

Consider, for example, the following statement that President George W. Bush made in an address to a joint session of Congress and to the American people on September 20, 2001, only nine days after the September 11, 2001, attacks on American soil:

> We will pursue nations that provide aid or safe haven to terrorism. Every nation, in every region, now has a decision to make. Either you are with us, or you are with the terrorists. [Applause.] From this day forward, any nation that continues to harbor or support terrorism will be regarded by the United States as a hostile regime.[4]

When Americans' emotions were up to concert pitch, it was easy for many of us to applaud fighting words; however, it is harder to justify such applause on rational grounds. Take a look at Bush's disjunctive premise, which he proposes to use as a basis for determining who among the world community is to be regarded as "hostile" to America:

> Either you are with us, or you are with the terrorists.

Is it really true that all of us must fall into one or the other of these classes?

In 2003, prior to the U.S. invasion of Iraq, when France, Germany, and Belgium refused to join the United States and the British in a "coalition of the willing," they were branded "the axis of weasels," a derogatory term intended as a pun on Bush's prior use of "axis of evil" to apply to Iraq, Iran, and North Korea, and which implied that these dissenting nations were duplicitous cowards. In fact, the *New York Post*, a media holding of Rupert Murdoch's News Corporation, included on the front page of its January 24, 2003, issue, a picture of a United Nations meeting convened to consider the case for war with Iraq depicting the presidents of France and Germany as having giant weasel heads.

The disjunctive syllogism at work here clearly traded upon a "black-or-white" major premise that divided the world into those who were with us and those who were against us. According to this premise, since the Germans and French were not "with us," they were necessarily "against us."

Here there was no room for serious disagreement on a serious issue of war that ultimately cost the lives of hundreds of thousands of Americans and Iraqis alike. Nor was there room for respect for others' right to dissent.

---

4. George W. Bush, Address to Joint Session of Congress following 9/11 Attacks, September 20, 2001. Retrieved online on April 8, 2009, from www.americanrhetoric.com/speeches/gwbush 911jointsessionspeech.htm.

Contrary versus Contradictory Terms

A disjunctive syllogism that contains such a major premise that divides the world into black or white, with no possible shades of gray between, is unsound. Unfortunately, such black-or-white thinking is prevalent in everyday reasoning.

In fact, the popular religious idea that people either go to heaven or hell is itself a testament to the human tendency to divide the world neatly into two tidy camps with nothing in between.[5] Philosopher David Hume notes,

> Heaven and hell suppose two distinct species of men, the good and the bad. But the greatest part of mankind float betwixt vice and virtue.

As Hume makes clear, there is nothing self-contradictory about saying that most people do not fit into either class of good and bad. Consider the "square of opposition" in figure 4.1, which plots the logical relationships between the terms "good" and "bad." "Good" and "bad" are *contrary terms*: neither of them has to be true, but both of them cannot at once be true. Thus, as Hume notes, a person may be neither good nor bad. But a person cannot at once be both good and bad.[6]

However, notice that the terms "good" and "not good" (like the terms "bad" and "not bad") are not contrary but *contradictory terms*: one or the other, but not both, must be true of a thing. Thus, a person cannot at once be both good and not good (at least in the same respect); however, a person will be either good or not good.

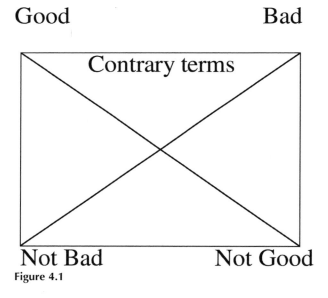

Figure 4.1

___

5. Perhaps the idea of purgatory is one way in which some religious groups, notably Roman Catholics, have attempted to accommodate the fact that not everyone is either good or bad. Nonetheless, purgatory is supposed to be temporary. Therefore, even this notion assumes that everyone will sooner or later be determinably good or bad.

6. At least not in the same respect. Thus, someone can't at once be both morally good and morally bad when the same standards of morality are consistently used to assess the morality of persons.

Black-or-white thinking accordingly confuses contraries with contradictories. For example, Bush's terms "with us" and "against us" are contraries and not contradictories. Like "good" and "bad," neither of these terms need apply to individuals or nations. In dividing the world into black or white, we purchase tidiness at the expense of oversimplifying reality.

Exercise Set 4.2

Which of the following disjunctive statements contains a black-or-white fallacy?

4.2.1
"I wish the American media would take a great look at the views of the people in Congress and find out, are they pro-America or anti-America?" —Rep. Michele Bachmann (R-MN)

4.2.2
Medicines no longer protected under patent can be gotten in brand name or generic.

4.2.3
"Smile-Measuring Device Knows How Happy or Sad You Are . . . It's a 'smile detector'— essentially a piece of software capable of objectively measuring the smiles of humans (and eventually humanoids, we presume) and attributing to them a percentage rating." —Internet posting

4.2.4
"Is Best Buy's Geek Squad Competent or Incompetent?" —Title of an Internet post

4.2.5
"Is Your Lifestyle Fat or Skinny? Take our quiz and find out if you're living fit." —Internet posting

4.2.6
"I will assume that positions persons adopt (or the justifications they use) are either reasonable or unreasonable." —Chandran Kukathas

4.2.7
"Let us . . . say, 'God is, or he is not.' . . . What will you wager? . . . Let us weigh the gain and the loss in wagering that God is. Let us estimate these two chances. If you gain, you gain all; if you lose, you lose nothing. Wager, then, without hesitation that He is." —Blaise Pascal

4.2.8
"To be, or not to be: that is the question: Whether 'tis nobler in the mind to suffer the slings and arrows of outrageous fortune, or to take arms against a sea of troubles, and by opposing end them? To die: to sleep."—William Shakespeare

4.2.9
"Marriage isn't about happiness. . . . It is a business relationship. Someone has to be the boss." —Internet posting

4.2.10
"Are You a Man or a Mouse?
A husband was advised by his psychiatrist to assert himself. 'Don't let your wife henpeck you. Go home and show her you're the boss.' On fire with enthusiasm, the man rushed home, slammed the door, and growled at his wife. 'From now on, you're taking orders from me. . . .'" —*Saturday Evening Post* article

4.2.11
"You either get tired fighting for peace, or you die." —John Lennon

FALSE DILEMMAS

One form of disjunctive syllogism that sometimes contains a black-or-white major premise is called a *dilemma argument*. In a dilemma one has only two alternatives, both of which have undesirable consequences, so that no matter which alternative is chosen, there is an undesirable consequence. Such popular expressions as "catch 22" and "caught between a rock and hard place" are often used to capture the logic of such an argument. When a dilemma argument contains one or more false premises, it is called a *false dilemma*.

Consider, for example, the following dilemma argument, which author A. V. Campbell uses to begin his book titled *Moral Dilemmas in Medicine*:

> A patient in the ward in which I worked was visited by the surgeon in the evening after his operation. The surgeon asked how the patient was, and being told that he appeared to be suffering severe pain prescribed five milligrams of diamorphine injected intramuscularly. The patient was give the injection, but had a restless sleep and clearly was still in pain. When the surgeon returned to the ward in the morning and was told of the patient's condition he ordered an increase of dosage to fifty milligrams. Knowing that an increase of this magnitude was almost certainly lethal, I questioned the surgeon's instruction. He appeared rather taken back by my questioning, but explained that while operating the previous day he had found that the patient's abdomen was riddled with carcinoma. . . . I went to the ward clinic to draw up the injection knowing full well that it would kill the patient. I hesitated to think what I was doing. To end the patient's life was against all my upbringing, my nursing experience, and my religious conviction. But could I refuse? I had been in the hospital only a week after qualifying as a registered mental nurse and this was one of my first difficult situations. If I refused to give the injection that might be the end of my career in general nursing. What was I to do?

In this case, the nurse recognized only two alternatives: either give the injection or refuse to give it. Moreover, she perceived a negative result no matter which option she took. If she gave the injection, she would go against her upbringing, nursing experience, and religious convictions. On the other hand, if she refused, then she would risk ending her career in general nursing. Accordingly, her conclusion was that she would have to endure one or the other of these two unsavory consequences. Formally expressed, here is the dilemma this nurse painted for herself:

> *Major premise:* Either I give the (almost certainly) lethal injection, or I refuse to give it.
> *Minor premise:* If I give it, then I go against my upbringing, nursing experience, and religious convictions; if I refuse to give it, then I risk ending my career in general nursing.
> *Conclusion:* I either go against my upbringing, nursing experience, and religious convictions, or I risk ending my career in general nursing.

Here is the form of this argument:

> Either p or q.
> (If p, then r) and (if q, then s).
> Therefore, either r or s.

Let us say that any argument expressed in this form is in *standard dilemma form*, which is a valid form. Therefore, the argument in question is valid. Since it is valid, at least one of the unpalatable alternatives of its conclusion will have to be true, provided that all its premises are also true. Thus, the only way for our nurse to escape this conclusion is to show that at least one of the premises of the argument is false.

The nurse could "escape between the horns" of her dilemma by attempting to come up with alternatives besides the two given in her major premise. Indeed, since giving the lethal injection and refusing to give it are contrary terms, she could decide not to do either of these things. For example, she could instead give a lesser dosage, or she could simply decide to lie about having given the injection.[7]

She could also attempt to "break a horn" of her dilemma by determining that one of the conditionals expressed in her minor premise is false. For example, according to the professional ethics of nurses, a nurse is justified in refusing to participate in practices she considers to be unethical.[8] Thus, she would have strong professional grounds for refusing to give the injection and therefore a reasonable expectation of not ending her career in general nursing.

Exercise Set 4.3

Express each of the below dilemmas in standard dilemma form, and discuss whether it is sound. In discussing the soundness of each argument, consider whether it is possible to "break a horn" or "escape between the horns." Finally, consider what you would do if you were in each of the given situations.

4.3.1
You are a lawyer representing a client to help him obtain custody of his six-year-old son, presently in the custody of the child's mother. You have reasonable belief from discussions with him that your client is sexually attracted to children. Your client admits to enjoying child pornography depicting little boys and downloads it frequently from the Internet, but he stops short of saying that he has sexually molested his own son. As a result of such reasonable belief, you now also have reasonable belief that allegations of sexual abuse of the child, which had previously been investigated by the Department of Children and Families and deemed to be unfounded, were probably true and that the timely complaint of the child that "Daddy touches my private parts" was also probably true and not really the result of the mother's having coached the child—as your client consistently maintained. You now also have reasonable belief that evidence allegedly establishing that the mother has been coaching the child to accuse the father of child abuse (namely, the client's prospective testimony that his wife threatened to destroy him by fabricating sexual abuse) is probably false.

According to the American Bar Association's code of ethics, "A lawyer shall not knowingly offer evidence that the lawyer knows to be false." On the other hand, "A lawyer may refuse [but is not required to refuse] to offer evidence . . . that the lawyer reasonably believes

(continued)

---

7. No claim is here being made that either of these options is necessarily ethical, only that they are logical possibilities.
8. See, for example, the American Nurses Association Code of Ethics at nursingworld.org/Main MenuCategories/ThePracticeofProfessionalNursing/EthicsStandards/CodeofEthics.aspx.

is false."[1] Insofar as you only have reasonable belief but not knowledge that the evidence in question is false, should you attempt to use it to establish that the mother has been coaching the child?

On the one hand, you are your client's advocate and have learned the incriminating information only because your client has confided in you. On the other hand, you are an officer of the court and the welfare of a child may hang in the balance.[2]

4.3.2

I am writing for advice on a personal dilemma of the most personal nature. I am male, mid-40s, married 20 years.

After all these years, I still long to make love to my wife two or three times per week, while she seems to prefer two or three times per year, if ever. Best I can tell, she no longer enjoys making love whatsoever and hasn't for the last 10 years.

While all this seems dismal, the problem I am seeking advice on is more a moral issue. First, let me make sure you know that I have been faithful to my wife since the day I met her. I would never consider sex outside my marriage vows. That goes against every moral fiber of my being. Additionally, pornographic materials and gentlemen's clubs go against my beliefs and would only make matters worse. I will say after all these years I do understand why some men succumb to weakness and fall prey to sex outside their marriage.

Please do not tell me to have a meaningful conversation with my wife. I tried that and failed miserably. In February 2000, after years of trying to get through to her, I felt I couldn't take it anymore. I told her I long for the intimacy only a married couple can share. She offered no reason, except she is always tired and has too much on her plate. While I acknowledge that she shoulders plenty of responsibility with work and home, she can find the time to walk the dogs or work herself to the bone on something that can wait until tomorrow. I pleaded with her to get whatever physical, medical, emotional, or psychological help she might need to get our marriage back on track. I offered to attend any sessions she felt comfortable with me participating in. I offered to do anything in our lovemaking that would make it more enjoyable for her. I told her I would not pressure her into making love, but would wait for her to let me know when she was ready.

For four weeks things improved as we made love three times. However, she never sought outside help and began to fall into her old comfortable habits. Over the next 17 months we made love only another six times with most coming at my insistence.

I finally gave up keeping track and gave up on her caring enough to change. Short of divorce, how do I relieve my sexual tension without compromising my beliefs and myself?[3]

4.3.3

In Europe, a woman was near death from a special kind of cancer. There was one drug that the doctors thought might save her. It was a form of radium that a druggist in the same town had recently discovered. The drug was expensive to make, but the druggist was charging ten times what the drug cost him to make. He paid $400 for the radium and charged $4,000 for a small dose of the drug. The sick woman's husband, Heinz, went to everyone he knew to borrow the money and tried every legal means, but he could only get together about $2,000, which is half of what it cost. He told the druggist that his wife was dying, and asked him to sell it cheaper or let him pay later. But the druggist said, "No, I discovered the drug and I'm going to make money from it." So, having tried every legal means, Heinz gets desperate and considers breaking into the man's store to steal the drug for his wife.[4]

---

1. American Bar Association, *Model Rules of Professional Conduct*, Rule 3.3(a)(3).
2. From Elliot D. Cohen, "Lawyers' Liberation," in *Ethics in the Legal Profession*, ed. Elliot D. Cohen and Michael Davis, 2nd ed. (Amherst, N.Y.: Prometheus Books, 2009).
3. Anonymous blogger, Street Directory.com. Retrieved online on April 10, 2009, from www.streetdirectory.com/travel_guide/9171/self_improvement_and_motivation/mitigating_factors.html.
4. Lawrence Kohlberg, "Heinz's Dilemma," About.com: Psychology. Retrieved online on April 2, 2009, at http://psychology.about.com/od/developmentalpsychology/a/kohlberg.htm.

Negative versus Positive Dilemmas

It is generally a good idea to avoid framing situations in terms of *negative* dilemma arguments—that is, dilemma arguments both of whose alternatives are perceived to have unpalatable consequences. This is because they place the focus on these negative consequences and not on looking for a reasonable solution to the problem at hand. As a result, such dilemma thinking tends to lead to *decision by indecision*: that is, allowing the changing tide of events over time to dictate the outcome rather than the exercise of sound reasoning. For example,

> Either I accept the job offer, or I don't accept it.
> If I accept it, I'll be stuck in a low-paying job; if I don't accept it, I'll risk not finding anything better.
> Therefore, either I'll be stuck in a low-paying job, or I'll risk not finding anything better.

Unfortunately, if I think about the negative possibilities of the above conclusion long enough, the job in question might be filled when I finally decide to take it.

Notice, however, that the same set of facts can be cast in terms of a *positive dilemma*—that is, an argument that takes the form of a dilemma, except that each of its two options have *positive* (instead of negative) consequences. For example,

> Either I accept the job offer, or I don't accept it.
> If I accept it, I won't risk not finding anything better; and if I don't accept it, I won't be stuck in a low-paying job.
> Therefore, either I won't risk not finding anything better, or I won't be stuck in a low-paying job.

Here, a negative dilemma was turned into the above positive dilemma simply by negating and switching the two consequents of its minor premise. Table 4.2 shows

Table 4.2

	Negative Dilemma	Positive Dilemma
Form	Either p or q If p then r; and if q then s Therefore, either r or s	Either p or q If p then not s; and if q then not r Therefore, not s or not r
Example	Either I accept the job offer (p) or I don't accept it (q). If I accept it (p), I'll be stuck in a low-paying job (r); and, if I don't accept it (q), I'll risk not finding anything better(s). Therefore, either I'll be stuck in a low-paying job (r) or I'll risk not finding anything better (s).	Either I accept the job offer (p) or I don't accept it (q). If I accept it (p), I won't risk not finding anything better (not r); and if I don't accept it (q), I won't be stuck in a low-paying job (not s). Therefore, either I won't risk not finding anything better (not r) or I won't be stuck in a low-paying job (not s).

how a set of statements (p, q, r, and s) in a negative dilemma can be transformed into a positive dilemma according to the rule of negating and switching the two consequents of the minor premise.[9]

This shows that dilemma thinking can be a function of how we choose to "construct" reality. That is, we can choose to focus on the negative aspects of reality (metaphorically speaking, looking at the glass half empty) and to construct negative dilemmas. Contrarily, we can choose to focus on the positive aspects of reality (looking at the glass half full) and to construct positive dilemmas.[10]

Such constructions of reality can have direct bearing on our *emotional* life. For example, extreme negative dilemma thinking (an outlook of hopelessness no matter what option is taken) is commonplace in depression.[11] Consider the following example of the "depressed thinking" of a twenty-eight-year-old male who hasn't yet found a life partner:

> Either I will remain single, or I'll have to settle for someone.
> If I remain single, I will be alone the rest of my life; if I have to settle for someone, I'll be stuck in a loveless marriage.
> Therefore, either I will be alone the rest of my life, or I'll be stuck in a loveless marriage.

Here, both options identified lead to negative consequences, thereby allowing the depressed person to sustain his bleak outlook on his own life. However, notice that the range of possibilities (disjuncts) leaves out more favorable possibilities, such as eventually finding a "true love."

One way to show that such negative dilemma thinking is not the only way to construct reality is to use the same set of facts to construct a *positive* dilemma. Thus, in response to the depressed single man, we could say,

> Either you will remain single, or you will have to settle for someone.
> If you remain single, you won't get stuck in a loveless marriage; if you have to settle for someone, at least you won't be alone!
> Therefore, either you won't get stuck in a loveless marriage, or at least you won't be alone.

While construction of this positive dilemma does not prove that the negative dilemma is false,[12] it can serve the useful therapeutic function of helping a person to look on the brighter side of reality. It can also prove that a person has no more reason to accept the negative dilemma than he or she has to accept the positive dilemma; therefore, the bleak outlook on reality is at best only part of the truth.

---

9. This rule of transforming a negative dilemma into a positive dilemma assumes that the two alternatives in the major premise are mutually exclusive—that is, that they can't both be true at once.
10. We can also choose to avoid dilemma thinking altogether.
11. This and other emotions will be examined more closely in chapter 16 on emotional reasoning.
12. To show it to be false, we would have to either break a horn or escape between the horns of the dilemma.

Exercise Set 4.4

Express each of the following dilemma arguments in standard (negative) dilemma form, and consider whether any of the premises can be shown to be false. Then, turn the dilemma into a positive dilemma by negating and switching the consequents. What value, if any, do you think casting the argument in such a positive mode has in helping to solve the problem? In your estimation, does negative dilemma thinking in the case in question promote decision by indecision?

4.4.1

What do you do when you are really good at something—something that very few others excel at, even—and you kind of hate it? Worse, what happens when you are good at something that few others are, and it is something that could benefit the public? Do you sacrifice your own happiness for the greater good? Also, aren't you supposed to be happy when you do things that you are good at?

This is a big problem that has been plaguing me of late. OK, more than of late—I've probably been struggling with this issue for about two or three years. For as long as I can remember, I have been committed to working towards a better America for low-income kids. I dropped out of Fordham Law School after only two days and attended grad school at Columbia instead to further my progress along this path. Ever since grad school, I worked to create more quality, affordable child care in New York City. Along the way, I developed highly specialized knowledge in child care facilities development and finance. People respect my thinking and ideas on the topic, my expertise. It is nice to be only 30 and be seen as an expert. At the same time, I also discovered that I really hate child care facilities and finance for a variety of reasons.

Sure, there are days and times when I am excited by what is going on and all the opportunities that seem to be cropping up of late. More often, however, I am just depressed by the moronic decisions, bureaucratic inertia, and general fear of change. Yet, every time I am on the verge of walking away from it all, I find myself distraught. Who else will do this? I'm good at it, damn it, and these kids need all the support they can get, even if they never know that people like me are out there for them. There are some great people out there that I would miss working with, and what else could I do anyway? It's not like I have a back-up career. The guilt and doubt kick in, and it kills me just as much as my general unhappiness in my field does.

Damned if you do, and damned if you don't.[1]

4.4.2

This particular problem has me in a bit of a bind, and I can't decide what to do. There are two people involved in my story. The girl, we shall call Sue. The guy, we shall call George.

Sue I've known for most of my life. Always been somewhat good friends. George I've only known for the past year or so. He comes off as an alright guy I guess. These two have been dating for the past year. From what I can tell, it isn't a very good relationship. Very heated arguments over nothing, sometimes they go days without talking to each other.

One month ago we were all at a party with friends of ours. George got too drunk, got in a heated argument with Sue, and ended up violently throwing her into a wall. I had to be physically restrained at this point, because I was ready to snap his neck. George was "escorted" out by the other guys at the party.

She breaks up with him at this point. And I think to myself, finally the girl is starting to show some sense and will get into a better relationship. It's been a month now, and she's had a fling or two in the meantime. But, she has been talking to George again. She's thinking about getting back together with him.

(continued)

_____

1. "A Personal Dilemma," *Campaign for Unshaved Snatch and Other Rants*, August 23, 2006. Retrieved online on April 18, 2009, from www.cussandotherrants.com/2006/08/personal-dilemma.html.

There are two things I can do here. Option one, stay out of it, since its "none of my business" according to Sue. Or, I could start dating Sue. She has always had a thing for me, but we just never actually got around to seeing each other.

The problem is, I'm not ready for anything yet. I got out of something kind of big a little while ago, and I really can't fathom being with another woman yet. If anything, dating Sue will probably end up not working and might compromise our friendship.

Should I leave the issue alone? Or should I man up and date the girl, preventing her from getting back with George?[2]

---

2. Seraphim, "[Help Me TW] Personal Dilemma," Tribal War, August 9, 2007. Retrieved online on April 18, 2009, from www.tribalwar.com/forums/archive/t-500471.html.

5

Truth-Functional Logic

THE MEANING OF TRUTH-FUNCTIONAL LOGIC

Words like "and," "or," and "if-then" can be used to connect statements to form more complex statements whose truth values depend on the truth values of the individual statements that are connected. These more complex statements thus formed are said to be *truth-functional* because their truth depends on the individual statements they connect. For example, the statement "It is raining, and the street is wet" is truth-functional because its truth value is a function of the truth values of the two statements that compose it—namely "It is raining" and "The street is wet." These component statements are referred to as *simple* statements because they are not themselves composed of other statements. Now, if both of these statements are true, then the complex (or "compound") statement "It is raining, *and* the street is wet" will be true. But if one of these component statements is false, then the complex statement that conjoins them will be false.

The validity of some arguments depends on truth-functional connections between the statements composing them. For example, hypothetical syllogisms and disjunctive syllogisms, examined in chapters 3 and 4 of this book, respectively, are truth-functional in this way. *The methods used to symbolize and analyze truth-functional statements and to determine the validity of truth-functional arguments is called truth-functional logic.*

SYMBOLIZING TRUTH-FUNCTIONAL CONNECTIVES

Testing the validity of truth-functional arguments is facilitated by introducing special symbols to represent truth-functional connectives. Table 5.1 symbolizes and provides illustrations of five major truth-functional connectives. As you can see, the five symbols given in table 5.1 can be useful in symbolizing the logical form of statements in ordinary language. For example, the form of the complex

Table 5.1

Connective	Symbol	Name of Logical Relationship	Sample of Truth-Functional Statement Using Connective	Logical Form of Sample Statement
and	& (ampersand)	conjunction	It is night **and** the sun is below the horizon.	p & q
not	~ (tilde)	negation	**It is not both the case that** it is night and the sun is **not** below the horizon.	~ (p & ~q)
or	∨ (wedge)	disjunction	It is **not** night **or** the sun is below the horizon.	~p ∨ q
if . . . then . . .	⊃ (horseshoe)	material implication	**If** it is night then the sun is below the horizon.	p ⊃ q
if and only if	≡ (tribar)	material equivalence	It is night if and only if the sun is below the horizon.	p ≡ q

English statement "It is not the case both that it is night and that the sun is not below the horizon" can be clearly articulated as ~ (p & ~q).

Each of the relationships expressed by the five connectives has a formal name: negation, conjunction, disjunction, material implication, and material equivalence. In conjunction (p & q), each individual statement is referred to as a *conjunct*. Thus, in p & q, p is a conjunct, as is q. In disjunction (p ∨ q), each individual statement is referred to as a *disjunct*.

CONSTRUCTING TRUTH TABLES TO DEFINE TRUTH-FUNCTIONAL CONNECTIVES

Since the symbols that represent these five relationships represent truth-functional connectives, they can be defined entirely in terms of truth and falsehood. The tables that provide such truth-functional definitions are called *truth tables*. Table 5.2 presents truth-table definitions of our five symbols.[1] Notice that the first two columns of the truth table given in table 5.2 provide all possible truth combinations of statements that could be substituted for the two variables, p and q. Each row of the truth table represents a different set of truth combination. The number of rows the truth table will have is determined by applying the formula 2^n, where n equals the number of different statement variables. Thus, the truth table has four rows (2^2).

Look at the column that provides the truth-table definition for negation (~p). When p is true, ~p is false; when p is false, ~p is true. Thus, "~" is a *truth-value reverser*.

Look now at the column that provides the truth-table definition for conjunction (p & q). *Notice that the only time conjunction is true is in the first row, where p and q are both true.* For example, the conjunction "It is night & the sun is below the horizon" would not be true if either conjunct were false. Thus, "&" is said to be a strong operator; that is, it requires that both conjuncts be true in order for the conjunction itself to be true.

Look now at the column that provides the truth-table definition for disjunction (p ∨ q). *Notice that the only time disjunction is false is in the fourth row where p and q are both false.* This means that a disjunction is true only when at least one disjunct is true. For example, the disjunction "It's not night ∨ the sun is below the horizon" is true if *at least one* of these disjuncts is true.

Next, look at the column that defines material implication (p ⊃ q). *Notice that the only time material implication is false is in the second row, where p is true, and q is*

Table 5.2

p	*q*	*~p*	*p & q*	*p ∨ q*	*p ⊃ q*	*p ≡ q*
T	T	F	T	T	T	T
T	F	F	F	T	F	F
F	T	T	F	T	T	F
F	F	T	F	F	T	T

---

1. T = true and F = false.

false. Thus, p can be said to materially imply q when ~ (p & ~q). For example, "It's night" materially implies "The sun is below the horizon" because ~ (It's night & ~ The sun is below the horizon).

Finally, look at the column that defines material equivalence (p ≡ q). Notice that whenever p and q are both true, the material equivalence is true, and whenever p and q are both false, the material equivalence is true. *Thus, two statements can be said to be materially equivalent when each has the same truth value.* For example, "It's night" is materially equivalent to "The sun is below the horizon" because when one is true, the other is true, and when one is false, so too is the other.

USING TRUTH TABLES TO DETERMINE THE VALIDITY OF TRUTH-FUNCTIONAL ARGUMENTS

Truth tables may be used to determine the validity of truth-functional arguments. As discussed in chapter 2, a valid argument is one that has a valid form, and a valid form is one such that any consistent substitution instance of the variables that makes all of the premises true will also make the conclusion true. Accordingly, in a valid argument, we must not be able to find a single row of a truth table in which all of the premises are true and the conclusion false. If such a row is found, then not all consistent substitution instances of the variables in the argument that make the premises true will make the conclusion true; therefore, the argument will not be valid.

Consider, for example, the fallacies of *affirming the consequent* and *denying the antecedent* discussed in chapter 3:

- Fallacy of affirming the consequent:

    p ⊃ q
    q
    _____
    ∴ p[2]

- Fallacy of denying the antecedent:

    p ⊃ q
    ~p
    _____
    ∴ ~q

Both of these argument forms are invalid, which can easily be seen by examining row 3 of the truth table in table 5.3. Notice that the third row provides instances in which all premises of the given arguments are true but their conclusions false. This clearly proves that any argument that denies the antecedent or affirms the consequent is indeed invalid. On the other hand, notice that there are no substitu-

---

2. The three dots arranged in the form of a pyramid in front of the conclusion symbolize "therefore."

Table 5.3

p	*q*	*~p*	*~q*	*p ⊃ q*
T	T	F	F	T
T	F	F	T	F
F	**T**	**T**	**F**	**T**
F	F	T	T	T

tion instances in which the premises p ⊃ q and p are true, but the conclusion q is false. This clearly shows that *affirming the antecedent* is valid.[3]

Argument forms with more than two variables will require larger truth tables to test for validity. Thus, an argument form with three statement variables will have eight rows (2^3), and one with four variables will have sixteen rows (2^4). For example, consider this argument form:

p ⊃ (q & r)
p
_____
. ˙ . **r**

The truth table in table 5.4 can be constructed to test the validity of the above argument form.

Notice that the first row is the only one in which all of the premises are true. However, notice also that the conclusion (r) is also true. Therefore, since there are no substitution instances in which all the premises are true and the conclusion false, the given argument form is valid.

With respect to the design of table 5.4, observe that the truth value of the complex statement p ⊃ (q & r) is determined by first determining its simplest components—p, q, and r—and then proceeding to more complex components composed of these simpler components, such as the conjunction q & r.

Parentheses, such as those surrounding "(q & r)" in the complex statement p ⊃ (q & r), are used to punctuate a complex statement so that it can be interpreted as intended. For example, without parentheses, p ⊃ q & r would be ambiguous and

Table 5.4

p	*q*	*r*	*q & r*	*p ⊃ (q & r)*
T	**T**	**T**	**T**	**T**
T	T	F	F	F
T	F	T	F	F
T	F	F	F	F
F	T	T	T	T
F	T	F	F	T
F	F	T	F	T
F	F	F	F	T

3. See chapter 3 for a discussion of affirming the antecedent.

could mean p ⊃ (q & r), but it could also mean (p ⊃ q) & r. While the former is a material implication with a complex consequent, the latter is a conjunction with a complex first conjunct, and these statement forms do not have the same truth values.

Constructing a Crucial Row of a Truth Table

To avoid lengthy truth tables in testing the validity of an argument, an abbreviated truth-table process is possible in which one attempts to produce one crucial row of a truth table. Such a row would be one that shows the truth conditions under which all premises are true and the conclusion false. If such a row can be produced, then the argument is invalid. On the other hand, if it is not possible to produce such a row, then the argument is valid. The complete proof that the argument is valid often requires the production of an entire truth table. If, however, the truth values necessary to make the conclusion false also make at least one premise false, then the argument must be valid because no case can possibly be produced in which all premises are true and the conclusion false. Sometimes trial and error is necessary to find a crucial row that invalidates the argument.

   This process may constructively begin by attempting to assign values to the conclusion that make it false and then working backwards to consistently assign values to the premises that make them true. For example, consider the following argument:

   p ⊃ q
   q ⊃ r
   ~p
   ∴ ~r

As you can see, by assigning a value of true to r, the conclusion will be false. Then, we can assign the value of false to q, which would make the premise q ⊃ r true. Then, by assigning the value of false to p, the premise ~p and the premise p ⊃ q will also be true:

   p (F) ⊃ q (F)
   q (F) ⊃ r (T)
   ~p (F)
   ∴ ~r (T)

As you can see from table 5.5, these values will accordingly produce one crucial row of a truth table that clearly shows that the argument in question is invalid.

Table 5.5

p	*q*	*r*	*~p*	*~r*	*p ⊃ q*	*q ⊃ r*
F	F	T	T	F	T	T

Exercise Set 5.1

Construct a truth table or a crucial row of a truth table to determine the validity of each of the below argument forms. If you cannot provide a single row that invalidates the argument form, then provide the entire truth table.

5.1.1
p ∨ q
p
_____
∴ ~q

5.1.2
(p & q) ⊃ ~q
p
_____
∴ ~q

5.1.3
p ≡ q
~p
_____
∴ ~q

5.1.4
~ (p & q)
_____
∴ ~p ∨ ~q

5.1.5
p
_____
∴ ~p

5.1.6
p ∨ (q & r)
∴ p ∨ r

5.1.7
(p ⊃ q) & (~q ∨ r)
r
_____
∴ p

5.1.8
p & (q ∨ r)
~ (p & r)
~p
_____
∴ s

(*continued*)

5.1.9
p & q
q ≡ r
~r ∨ s
_____

∴ ~s

5.1.10
p ⊃ q
q
_____

∴ p ∨ r

5.1.11
~p ⊃ (~q ∨ r)
~p
_____

∴ r ⊃ q

5.1.12
(p ≡ q) & s
(q ⊃ r) & (s ⊃ ~r)
_____

∴ ~p & q

Exercise Set 5.2

Translate each of the argument forms in Exercise Set 2.1 into symbolic form (using the symbols introduced in this chapter) and test each for validity by constructing a truth table.

SYMBOLIZING AND ANALYZING ARGUMENTS IN ORDINARY LANGUAGE

Since arguments in real-life contexts do not already come symbolized and ready for truth-table analysis, one must do this on one's own. Consider, for example, the following argument by author Eugene F. Rogers Jr., which attempts to show that a popular, conservative anti–gay marriage argument based on the sanctity of marriage leads to a contradiction:

> I want to consider gay marriage by first reflecting on the theology of marriage, and I want to reflect on the theology of marriage under the rubric of sanctification. This approach is consistent with the tradition of the Orthodox Church, which regards marriage as a way of participating in the divine life not by way of sexual satisfaction but by way of ascetic self-denial for the sake of more desirable goods. Theologically understood, marriage is not primarily for the control of lust or for procreation. It is a

discipline whereby we give ourselves to another for the sake of growing in holiness— for, more precisely, the sake of God. . . . If this account is correct, then it turns out that conservatives wish to deprive same-sex couples not so much of satisfaction as of sanctification. But that is contradictory, because so far as I know no conservative has ever seriously argued that same-sex couples need sanctification any less than cross-sex couples do. It is at least contradictory to attempt in the name of holiness to deprive people of the means of their own sanctification.[4]

The conclusion of this argument occurs in the last line: "It is at least contradictory to attempt in the name of holiness to deprive people of the means of their own sanctification." In other words, Rogers is saying that the argument opposing same-sex marriage based on the sanctity of marriage leads to a statement of the form p & ~p—namely that it is both true and false that same-sex couples should be prevented from marrying.

This method of attempting to refute an argument by showing that it leads to a contradiction is known as the method of reductio ad absurdum ("reduction to the absurd").[5] Cast in terms of five premises and a conclusion, Rogers's reductio ad absurdum argument appears to be as follows:

1. If same-sex marriages are unholy, then same-sex couples should be prevented from marrying.
2. Same-sex marriages are unholy.
3. If the purpose of marriage is sanctification, and a couple needs sanctification, then it is false that the couple should be prevented from marrying.
4. The purpose of marriage is sanctification.
5. Same-sex couples need sanctification.
6. Therefore, same-sex couples should be prevented from marrying, and it's false that same-sex couples should be prevented from marrying.

To perform a truth-table analysis of an argument in ordinary language such as the above one, we will need to express the logical form of the argument. This is done by formulating the argument purely in terms of statement variables and symbols of logical connectives. However, when an argument has several premises of considerable length such as the above one, it can be useful first to create a dictionary in which each *statement* of the argument is assigned a different letter to represent it. Conventionally, these letters are *capital* letters in order to distinguish them from statement variables, which are expressed as lower-case letters. The following is an example of such a dictionary:

U = same-sex marriages are unholy.
P = same-sex couples should be prevented from marrying.
S = the purpose of marriage is sanctification.
N = same-sex couples need sanctification.

---

4. Eugene F. Rogers Jr., "An Argument for Gay Marriage," religion-online.org. Retrieved online on April 20, 2009, from www.religion-online.org/showarticle.asp?title=3069.
5. See chapter 15 for further discussion of this approach.

These letters can now be used to express the argument as follows:

U ⊃ P
U
(S & N) ⊃ ~P
S
N
_____
∴ P & ~P

It is important to notice that the above expression is not the *form* of the argument since each of the capital letters that occur in it are not statement *variables* but statements. To express the form of the above argument, we may now use lower-case letters such as in the following:

u ⊃ p
u
(s & n) ⊃ ~p
s
n
_____
∴ p & ~p

We may now say that the argument expressed in capital letters is a substitution instance of the logical form expressed in lower-case letters. Notice that for each different variable in the argument form, there is a *simple* statement that is substituted for it. For example, the simple statement U is a substitution instance of the statement variable u, the simple statement P is a substitution instance of the statement variable p, and so on. A form that has this one-to-one correspondence between each different variable and a simple statement is sometimes referred to as the *specific form* of the argument.

Specific forms need to be distinguished from *general* forms. For example, the following is a general form of Rogers's argument:

v
w
x
y
z
_____
∴ t

Notice that by respectively substituting the premises and conclusion of Rogers's argument for each of the above statement variables, we can get Rogers's argument. Thus, by substituting U ⊃ P for v, U for w, (S & N) ⊃ ~P for x, S for y, N for z, and P & ~P for t, we get Rogers's argument. However, in making these substitution instances, we must substitute *complex* statements (such as U ⊃ P for v) for

Table 5.6

u	p	s	n	u ⊃ p	s & n	~p	(s & n) ⊃ ~p	p & ~p
T	T	T	T	T	T	F	F	F
T	T	T	F	T	F	F	T	F
T	T	F	T	T	F	F	T	F
T	T	F	F	T	F	F	T	F
T	F	T	T	F	T	T	T	F
T	F	T	F	F	F	T	T	F
T	F	F	T	F	F	T	T	F
T	F	F	F	F	F	T	T	F
F	T	T	T	T	T	F	F	F
F	T	T	F	T	F	F	T	F
F	T	F	T	T	F	F	T	F
F	T	F	F	T	F	F	T	F
F	F	T	T	T	T	T	T	F
F	F	T	F	T	F	T	T	F
F	F	F	T	T	F	T	T	F
F	F	F	F	T	F	T	T	F

some of the variables. This distinguishes a general form from a specific form. In contrast to the specific form of an argument, in a general form there is no one-to-one correspondence between each *simple* statement and each distinct variable.

The distinction between general and specific forms is important because truth-table analysis of arguments must test the specific form of an argument, not a general one. For example, the truth table in table 5.6 tests the specific form of Rogers's argument. As you can see, there is no row in which all of the premises are true and the conclusion false. Therefore, Rogers's argument is valid.

But is this argument also sound? If it is, then critics of same-sex marriage who base their case on the sanctity of marriage contradict themselves.

The orthodox theological view Rogers is attacking might take issue with some of his premises, however. In particular, they might deny the fifth premise, which states that the purpose of marriage is sanctification. Indeed, such opponents of same-sex marriage might insist that this premise must be qualified to apply only to heterosexual marriages, and they might claim that while same-sex couples need sanctification, the route to their sanctification is not through marriage. Such a strategy, however, leaves opponents of same-sex marriage who base their rejection on the sanctity of marriage in need of an independent, rational argument for why same-sex marriage fails to sanctify same-sex couples. But can a rational argument be made for such differential treatment of human beings?

Exercise Set 5.3

For each of the following arguments, (1) create a statement dictionary by assigning a capital letter to each of the statements in the argument, (2) express the argument using these capital letters, (3) symbolize the specific form of the argument using small-case letters, and

(continued)

(4) construct a truth table or a crucial row of a truth table to determine the validity of the argument form. If you cannot provide a single row that invalidates the argument, then provide the entire truth table.

5.3.1
Obama can either attempt to exercise diplomacy with the Taliban in Afghanistan or commit increasing numbers of U.S. forces to the region. If he attempts to exercise diplomacy, then the Taliban will continue to escalate its reign of oppression. If he commits increasing numbers of U.S. forces to the region, then he will involve the United States in another costly war that will never be won. Therefore, the Taliban will continue to escalate its reign of oppression, or Obama will involve the United States in another costly war that will never be won.

5.3.2
A person is clinically dead if and only if the person's brain is totally and irreversibly nonfunctional. If a person is in a persistent vegetative state, then his or her brain is not totally and irreversibly nonfunctional. Therefore, if a person is in a persistent vegetative state, then the person is not clinically dead.

5.3.3
If we someday clone entire human beings and use them for spare parts, then human clones will be treated like mere things. However, we cannot both treat human clones like mere things and treat them ethically. We will someday clone entire human beings. But we will not use them for spare parts. Therefore, we will treat human clones ethically.

5.3.4
If a person has a right to die with dignity, then physicians should be allowed to assist terminally ill patients in dying. If this is the case, then state and federal laws should be passed protecting from civil and criminal liability physicians who assist the suicide of a terminally ill patient. A person has the right to die with dignity. Therefore, such laws should be passed.

5.3.5
When you look at the comparison between herbivores and humans, we compare much more closely to herbivores than meat-eating animals. Humans are clearly not designed to digest and ingest meat. Clearly, if humans were meant to eat meat we wouldn't have so many crucial ingestive/digestive similarities with animals that are herbivores. —Atma Jyoti Ashram[1]

5.3.6
We cannot both protect free speech on the Internet and protect children from the dangers of exposure to pornography. But we must protect children from the dangers of exposure to pornography. Therefore, we cannot protect free speech on the Internet.

5.3.7
The United States should allow sixteen-year-olds to drink under adult supervision. In Belgium, most of Canada, Italy, and Spain, sixteen-year-olds can drink in restaurants under adult supervision, and there is less of an alcohol-abuse problem in these countries than in the United States. If this is the case, then the United States should allow sixteen-year-olds to drink under adult supervision.

5.3.8
Sex outside of marriage is ethical only if both partners give fully informed and free (uncoerced) consent to the sex. Therefore, sex outside of marriage is ethical if and only if both partners give fully informed and free consent to the sex.

---

1. Atma Jyoti Ashram, "Humans: Are We Carnivores or Vegetarians by Nature?" Atma Jyoti blog, April 29, 2008. Retrieved online on February 26, 2008, at http://blog.atmajyoti.org/2008/04/humans-are-we-carnivores-or-vegetarians-by-nature.

> **5.3.9**
> Homosexuality is either genetic or a choice. Homosexuality is genetic. But if it is not a choice, then homosexuals cannot be held responsible for their sexual preference. Therefore, they cannot be held responsible for their sexual preference.
>
> **5.3.10**
> If the war on terrorism is really a war, then terrorists are prisoners of war, and they are entitled to the rights of prisoners of war under the Geneva Conventions. But the war on terrorism is not really a war. After all, unlike other wars, it has no temporal or geographical limits nor need the enemy wear the uniform of a recognized state. Therefore, terrorists are not both prisoners of war and entitled to the rights of prisoners of war under the Geneva Conventions.

STATEMENT FORMS

Tautologies

Truth-functional statements resemble arguments insofar as they also have a form. Some truth-functional statements are true by virtue of their forms. That is, the forms of these statements are such that any consistent substitution instances of their variables will produce a true statement. Such statement forms (as well as their substitution instances) are called *tautologies*. For example, consider the statement form p ∨ ~p. Table 5.7 provides its truth table. Notice that p ∨ ~p will be true under all possible truth conditions. This makes it a tautology. In fact, this is a so-called law of logic known as the *law of excluded middle*. In essence, it says that for any statement, it is either true or false. For example, "Abraham Lincoln was an American president ∨ ~ Abraham Lincoln was an American president."

Another law of logic is the *law of noncontradiction*, which says that a statement cannot be both true and false. That is, ~ (p & ~p). Still, another such law is the *law of identity*, which states that for any statement, if it is true, then it is true; that is, p ⊃ p. Table 5.8 provides the truth tables for all three laws of logic. Notice that each of these laws always turns out to be true. Each, therefore, is a tautology.

Table 5.7

p	*~p*	*p ∨ ~p*
T	F	T
F	T	T

Table 5.8

p	*~p*	*p & ~p*	*~ (p & ~p)*	*p ⊃ p*	*p ∨ ~p*
T	F	F	T	T	T
F	T	F	T	T	T

Contradictory Statement Forms

Some statement forms may also be *contradictory*: that is, all consistent substitution instances of their variables are always false. The negation of a tautology is always a contradiction. For example, the negation of ~ (p & ~p) is p & ~p, which in essence says that a statement is both true and false. As you can see from table 5.8, this is always false.

Contingent Statement Forms

Finally, some statement forms may be *contingent*—that is, some consistent substitution instances of their variables are true while others are false. For example, consider the statement form p & q. A substitution instance of this form is "George Washington was the first American president & George W. Bush was the forty-third American president." Since both conjuncts are true, the conjunction is also true. However, consider another substitution instance of p & q, which states, "George Washington was the forty-third American president & George W. Bush was the first American president." Since both conjuncts are false, the conjunction is false. Thus, the statement form p & q has both true and false substitution instances and is therefore contingent.

Accordingly, its truth table looks as shown in table 5.9. Notice that the first row shows a value of true, while the other three rows show a value of false. So, as you can clearly see from this table, p & q has both true and false substitution instances and is therefore a contingent statement form.

THE PRACTICAL IMPORT OF DISTINGUISHING BETWEEN TAUTOLOGOUS, CONTINGENT, AND CONTRADICTORY STATEMENT FORMS

There is practical import in distinguishing between tautologies, contradictions, and contingent statements. Tautologies have the awe-inspiring status of being necessary truths. Indeed, as you have seen, it is always true that a statement implies itself, that it is either true or false, and that it is not both true and false. However, these truths are empty in the sense that they do not convey anything factual about the world. Thus, knowing that a statement is either true or false will not tell you whether the statement in question is in fact true.

In contrast, contingent statements (statements that are substitution instances of contingent forms) tell us something about the world, but they are not necessarily true. For example, the statement "George W. Bush invaded Iraq primarily to

Table 5.9

p	*q*	*p & q*
T	T	**T**
T	F	**F**
F	T	**F**
F	F	**F**

Table 5.10

p	*q*	*p ⊃ q*	*~ q*	*(p ⊃ q) & p*	*[(p ⊃ q) & p] & ~ q*
T	T	T	F	T	**F**
T	F	F	F	F	**F**
F	T	T	T	F	**F**
F	F	T	T	F	**F**

gain control of its oil reserves" is a contingent statement and therefore cannot be deemed true by virtue of its form. Yet, if it is true, it does indeed tell us something (disconcerting) about the world. To find out if such a contingent statement is true, we need independent evidence. That is, we simply cannot make such a claim unless we can provide a rational argument for it. This book is largely devoted to showing how to effectively argue for contingent statements.

Being able to identify contradictions is also important because, if a statement is a substitution instance of a contradictory statement form, then we can safely conclude that it is false. For example, suppose someone told you that anything the Bible forbids is wrong, then admitted that the Bible forbids adultery but claimed that he did nothing wrong in having an affair. In such a case, you could safely discount this person's statement. Why? Because this person's statement is a substitution instance of [(p ⊃ q) & p] & ~ q. Table 5.10 presents its truth table. As you can see, any statement of this form is always false and therefore a contradiction.

Exercise Set 5.4

For each of the following statement forms, construct a truth table to determine whether it is tautologous, contingent, or contradictory:

5.4.1
p

5.4.2
(p ∨ p) ⊃ p

5.4.3
(p ⊃ q) ≡ (~p ∨ q)

5.4.4
(p & q) & ~ (p & q)

5.4.5
(p ⊃ q) & (q ⊃ p)

5.4.6
p ≡ ~ ~ p

5.4.7
~ (p ∨ ~p)

(continued)

5.4.8

$\sim (p \lor q) \equiv (\sim p \,\&\, \sim q)$

5.4.9

$\sim (p \,\&\, q) \equiv (\sim p \lor \sim q)$

5.4.10

$[(p \supset q) \,\&\, p] \supset q$

5.4.11

$[(p \supset q) \,\&\, \sim p] \supset \sim q$

5.4.12

$[(p \supset q) \,\&\, (q \supset r)] \supset (p \supset r)$

MATERIAL VERSUS LOGICAL EQUIVALENCE

As you have seen, two statements are materially equivalent when each has the same truth value. For example, it was an ancient discovery that the morning star was also the evening star and that both referred to the planet Venus. Hence, the statements "Venus is the morning star" and "Venus is the evening star" are both true, and the statement of their material equivalence would therefore also be true. But even though both "morning star" and "evening star" refer to Venus, it is still possible to imagine that they refer to two different things. That is, it is logically possible (it is not contradictory to say) that the morning star is *not* the evening star. This is why they are said to be *materially* equivalent. It is a contingent feature of the material world, a matter of empirical fact arrived at through sense perception, that the morning star and the evening star have the same referent.

In contrast, some statements are *logically* equivalent. Two statements are said to be logically equivalent if the statement of their material equivalence is a tautology. That is, it is of a form that is true under all possible truth conditions and therefore cannot possibly be false. For example, the statement "It is raining" is logically equivalent to "It is not the case that it is not raining." The form of the first is p, while the form of the second is $\sim \sim$ p. The statement of the material equivalence of these two forms is $p \equiv \sim \sim p$, which, as you may have already seen in constructing the truth table in exercise 5.4.6, is a tautology. Table 5.11 provides its truth table.

THREE LOGICAL EQUIVALENCES

Table 5.12 presents three logical equivalences along with their traditional names. While the above logical equivalences (in conjunction with several others) can be used as transformation rules for the construction of formal proofs,[6] they are also relevant to transformations that we commonly make in ordinary life contexts.

---

6. See, for example, Irving M. Copi and Carl Cohen, *Introduction to Logic* (Upper Saddle River, NJ: Prentice Hall, 2009), ch. 9.

Table 5.11

p	$\sim p$	$\sim \sim p$	$p \equiv \sim \sim p$
T	F	T	T
F	T	F	T

Table 5.12

Name	Logical Equivalence
Material Implication	$(p \supset q) \equiv (\sim p \vee q)$
De Morgan's Law	$\sim (p \vee q) \equiv (\sim p \,\&\, \sim q)$
	$\sim (p \,\&\, q) \equiv (\sim p \vee \sim q)$
Double Negation	$p \equiv \sim \sim p$

For example, by material implication, the statement "If I don't get an A on the exam, then I might as well fail" is logically equivalent to "Either I get an A on the exam, or I might as well fail." Thus, this rule enables us to transform a conditional statement into a disjunction. In some instances, being able to make this transformation can have important practical significance. For example, in translating the conditional "If I don't get an A on the exam, then I might as well fail" into a disjunction, I may be able to see more clearly the black-and-white nature of my thinking.

Consider De Morgan's law, so named after the mathematician and logician Augustus De Morgan. This equivalence allows us to transform a negated disjunction into a conjunction and a negated conjunction into a disjunction. In this way, it can help clear up some common confusions. Thus, knowing that a disjunction is false is different from knowing that each individual disjunct is false. For example, from the fact that it is false that either the economy will improve or the stock market will crash, it does not follow that either the economy will not improve or the stock market will not crash. Rather, by De Morgan's Law, it means that the economy will not improve *and* the stock market will not crash. These are indeed different statements. The first would be true if the economy did not improve and the stock market crashed. The second would be true only if the stock market did *not* crash.

Some misunderstandings in ordinary life might accordingly be cleared up by the ability to validly make transformations from one form of truth-functional statement to another.

Exercise Set 5.5

Each of the following arguments is either a valid or an invalid application of double negation, material implication, or De Morgan's law. Determine which are valid and which are invalid applications. If the inference is valid, indicate which of these three logical equivalences was used to deduce the conclusion. If the inference is invalid, then explain what went wrong in making the deduction.

(*continued*)

5.5.1
It is not the case that it is not the case that today is Friday.
Therefore, today is not Friday.

5.5.2
If I go to the concert, then I will not be able to study.
Therefore, either I will not go to the concert or I will not be able to study.

5.5.3
It is not the case both that the Nixon administration broke into Democratic National Headquarters and that it was a moral administration.
Therefore, the Nixon administration did not break into Democratic National Headquarters, and it was not a moral administration.

5.5.4
It is not the case that it is not the case that it is not the case that George W. Bush was the most popular American president.
Therefore, George W. Bush was not the most popular American president.

5.5.5
Either Roe v. Wade will not be overturned, or abortion will not be an option.
Therefore, if *Roe v. Wade* is overturned, then abortion will be an option.

5.5.6
It is not the case that either there is no life in other galaxies or it will not contact us.
Therefore, there is life in other galaxies, and it will contact us.

5.5.7
If human cloning is permitted, then the value of human life will be degraded.
Therefore, either human cloning is not permitted, or the value of human life will be degraded.

5.5.8
If it is not the case that the Bush Doctrine violates international law, then the high officials in the former Bush administration should not be prosecuted for war crimes.
Therefore, either the Bush Doctrine violates international law, or the high officials in the former Bush administration should not be prosecuted for war crimes.

5.5.9
It is neither a federal holiday nor a weekend day.
Therefore, it is either a federal holiday or a weekend day.

5.5.10
The economy will improve, or the unemployment rate will continue to rise.
Therefore, it is not the case both that the economy will not improve and the unemployment rate will not continue to rise.

6

✢

Categorical Statements

In chapter 2 we introduced the categorical syllogism as a deductive argument composed of statements that relate classes, or "categories," and uses quantifiers to relate these classes. Such statements are known as categorical statements.

All categorical statements have two terms, a subject term and a predicate term, which are connected by a *copula*, that is, by a form of the verb "to be" (such as "is," "is not," "are," "are not," "will be," and "will not be"). A *term* is a string of symbols that refers to a class. The *subject term* is the first term, and the predicate term is the term that comes after the copula. "All men are created equal," which is contained in the Declaration of Independence, is a famous example of a categorical statement. In this statement, "men" is the subject term, "created equal" is the predicate term, and "are" is the copula.

The word "all" in this statement is called a quantifier because it tells you *how much* of the first class is included in the second class. Thus, the quantifier "all" in this statement says that each and every member of the first class (men) is included in the second class (those who are created equal).

UNIVERSAL AND PARTICULAR QUANTIFIERS

There are two types of quantifiers: universal and particular. A *universal* quantifier refers to all members of a class. Therefore, if the statement "All men are created equal" is true, it must be true of each and every man—past, present, and future.

To better grasp the meaning and import of this statement, take a look at the context in which Thomas Jefferson, the drafter of the Declaration of Independence, asserted it:

> We hold these truths to be self-evident, that all men are created equal, that they are endowed by their Creator with certain unalienable Rights, that among these are Life, Liberty and the Pursuit of Happiness.

Jefferson is clearly saying that *all* men have "unalienable rights to life, liberty, and the pursuit of happiness." Notice, however, that this entails that black men also have these rights. So why did Jefferson himself keep black slaves? This also does not address whether, for the purposes of recognizing such "unalienable" rights, women too were to be regarded as "men." Unfortunately, in 1776 the avenues for pursuing one's own happiness through freely forging and aspiring to career goals, attaining an education, and partaking in the political franchise were not open to women.

So, perhaps Jefferson was really drafting a declaration of independence not for all but *some* human beings—in particular, for white males. This would have changed his universally quantified statement to a *particular* statement—that is, a categorical statement that uses a particular quantifier.

A *particular quantifier* refers to *some* members of a class, as in, "Some men have unalienable rights to life, liberty, and the pursuit of happiness."[1] This statement would be true if only white males had such unalienable rights. This point of view has the scent of unfair discrimination. Unfortunately, the history of oppression of women and minorities in the United States is consistent with it.

QUANTITY AND QUALITY

Categorical statements have both quantity and quality. The *quantity* of a categorical statement pertains to the type of quantifier it has—that is, to whether it is universal or particular. The *quality* of the statement pertains to whether it is negative or affirmative—that is, whether it asserts class inclusion or exclusion. For example, the statement "No man is an island" contained in John Donne's famous poem "For Whom the Bell Tolls" is universal in quantity because it refers to *all* men, and it is negative in quality because it says that all men are *not* included in the class of islands.[2] On the other hand, in his poem Donne follows this statement with the statement "Every man is a piece of the continent," which is universal in quantity because it refers to all men; however, it is affirmative in quality because it says that every man *is* included in the class of pieces of the continent.

Compare this with the statement "Some politicians are libertarians," which is *particular* (it says that *some* politicians are libertarians) and affirmative in quality (it asserts that the politicians in question *are* included in the class of libertarians).

STANDARD CATEGORICAL FORM STATEMENTS

Since there are two types of quantity (universal and particular) and two types of quality (affirmative and negative), we can therefore distinguish four different types of categorical statements based on their quality and quantity: (1) universal

---

1. *Some* means *at least one*. Thus, the claim that some men have such rights would be true even if there were just one man who did.
2. Note that the quantifier "no" therefore does double duty, providing both the (universal) quantity and the (negative) quality of a categorical statement.

Table 6.1

Type	Quantity	Quality	Standard Form
A	Universal	Affirmative	All S is P
E	Universal	Negative	No S is P
I	Particular	Affirmative	Some S is P
O	Particular	Negative	Some S is not P

affirmative, (2) universal negative, (3) particular affirmative, and (4) particular negative.

Let S be a variable (placeholder) to stand for the subject term of a categorical statement, and let P be a variable to stand for its predicate term. Using this symbolism we can express the *standard form* of each of the four different types of categorical statements as follows:

Universal affirmative: All S is P.
Universal negative: No S is P.
Particular affirmative: Some S is P.
Particular negative: Some S is not P.

It is also customary to refer to these four forms of categorical statements, respectively, by the first four vowels of the English language, that is, A, E, I, and O. Table 6.1 summarizes the nature of each of these four types of categorical statements.

Each of the four categorical statements given in table 6.1 can be represented diagrammatically by two intersecting circles standing for the subject (S) and predicate (P) classes. These diagrams are called Venn diagrams after the logician and mathematician John Venn. For example the A-form statement can be represented as shown in figure 6.1. Notice that the section of the diagram that contains things that are S and not P is shaded out, and the part of S that is not shaded out is the section of S that is also P. Thus, the diagram tells us that all S is P.

In a like manner, the E-form can be represented as shown in figure 6.2. Notice that the intersection of S and P is shaded out to indicate that no S is P.

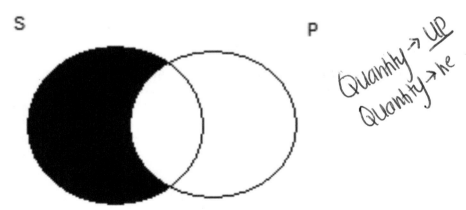

Figure 6.1.   A-Form Statement

S   P

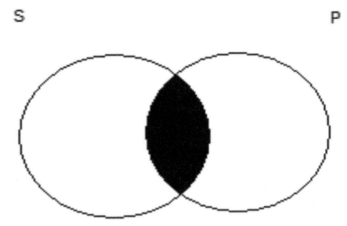

Figure 6.2.   E-Form Statement

S   P

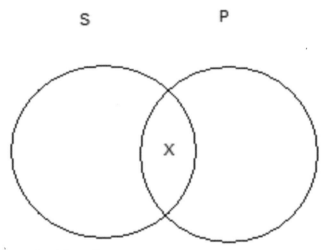

Figure 6.3.   I-Form Statement

I- and O-forms can also be represented by Venn diagrams that use an *x* to stand for a class member. Thus, the I-form can be represented as shown in figure 6.3. Notice that the *x* is placed at the intersection of S and P to indicate that there is something that is both S and P.

Finally, the O-form can be represented by placing an *x* in the section that is S and not P, indicating that there is something that is S and not P (figure 6.4).

These diagrams can thus provide a visual means of seeing what is being asserted by a categorical statement. For example, the O-form statement "Some presidents who attended Yale are not members of Skull and Bones" can accordingly be represented as shown in figure 6.5.

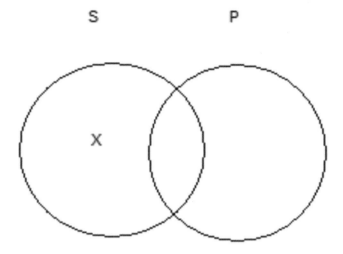

Figure 6.4. O-Form Statement

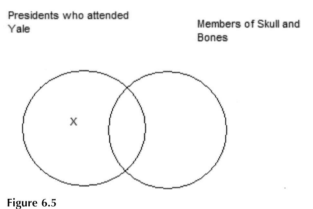

Figure 6.5

What is more, when the third term of a categorical syllogism is diagrammed alongside the S and P terms, Venn diagrams can also be used to test the validity of categorical syllogisms.[3]

Exercise Set 6.1

For each of the following categorical statements, determine the form, and construct a Venn diagram to symbolize it.

6.1.1
"No person is a copy of another person." —Blogger

(continued)

_____

3. Venn diagramming of categorical syllogisms is discussed in the appendix of this book

6.1.2
Some governors are not former actors who are bodybuilders.

6.1.3
"Some editors are failed writers." —T. S. Eliot

6.1.4
"Some of the worst mistakes of my life have been haircuts." —Jim Morrison

6.1.5
"All war is deception." —Sun Tzu

6.1.6
"No excellent soul is exempt from a mixture of madness." —Aristotle

TRANSLATING ORDINARY LANGUAGE STATEMENTS INTO STANDARD CATEGORICAL FORM

Expressing statements in standard categorical form can be useful for purposes of testing the validity of deductive inferences made from categorical statements. However, the reasoning we do in ordinary language contexts does not usually come in standard form. Instead, we must translate it into standard form.

Editing Categorical Statements Using Parameters

For one, as you have seen, the terms of a categorical statement refer to classes. But categorical statements expressed in ordinary language often do not speak in the language of classes. Sometimes we may have to edit these statements using *parameters*, which are words that help us to speak consistently in the language of classes. For example, we might more naturally state that Socrates drank hemlock rather than that Socrates is a *person* who drank hemlock. Yet, the latter statement, unlike the former, contains the copula "is" that relates Socrates to the *class* of persons who drank hemlock. In this case we use "person" as a parameter for recasting an ordinary language statement into a standard categorical form statement.

Since the purpose of translating statements in ordinary language is to assess *the author's thinking*, it is important that editing proceed in a manner that remains true to the author's intended meaning. Consider, for example, Albert Einstein's statement that "force always attracts men of low morality." Here "always" indicates universality of time, so an appropriate parameter for interpreting this statement would be that of time along with the use of the universal quantifier "all." This manner of translation would yield the universal affirmative (A-form) statement "All times when force attracts men are times when force attracts men of low morality."

Another constructive example is philosopher Friedrich Nietzsche's claim that "profound suffering makes noble and separates the sufferer from the uninitiated." Here it would make sense to interpret Nietzsche as speaking of *experiences* of suffering. And since he appears to be affirming something of all such experiences, it would appear that his statement is universal affirmative (A-form). So interpreted, we would translate Nietzsche as stating, "All experiences of profound suffering are experiences that make sufferers noble and separate them from the uninitiated."

As this last example suggests, sometimes (and not uncommonly), a quantifier may not be explicitly stated, and we may therefore have to glean from the context whether the quantity of the statement is universal or particular. For example, consider the following title of an Associated Press article posted to Yahoo! News:

After scandal, students are leaving Oral Roberts University.[4]

Notice it simply says "students" and not "some students." However, it is doubtful that it meant to imply that *all* students were leaving the university. This is confirmed in the first paragraph of the article, which mentions by name only one student, who was "among many students having second thoughts about staying at Oral Roberts after six months of scandal at the evangelical Christian university." Accordingly, the title of the article is really an implicit I-form statement, which could be edited and set in standard form as "Some students are students leaving Oral Roberts University after a scandal."

Now consider the following report of a study conducted about marijuana smokers:

Young people who do not smoke marijuana end up with a better quality of life and higher levels of educational achievement than their peers who do smoke marijuana. Those who do smoke pot early in life have lower incomes and greater health problems later in life, according to a study. Dr. Phyllis Ellickson, of the Rand Corporation's Drug Policy Research Center, and her colleagues analyzed survey data from 5,833 California and Oregon middle school students.[5]

Look carefully at the first statement: "Young people who do not smoke marijuana end up with a better quality of life and higher levels of educational achievement than their peers who do smoke marijuana." Treating this as an A-form statement would yield an obviously false statement. This is because it is not true that *all* young non–marijuana users end up better off than peer marijuana users. This would be to assume that no other factors besides marijuana smoking can affect quality of life and educational achievement, which is an unreasonable assumption.

Indeed, the study itself had to adjust for gender, race-ethnicity, household composition, and parental education. Having adjusted for these variables, the study ultimately concluded that those in the class of young non–marijuana users ("abstainers") had a *greater probability* of ending up with a better quality of life and level of educational achievement than peer users.[6] This yields the A-form

4. Associated Press, "After Scandal, Students Are Leaving Oral Roberts University," Yahoo! News, May 2, 2008. Retrieved online on August 2, 2008, from news.yahoo.com/s/ap/20080502/ap_on_re_us/oral_roberts_scandal.

5. Buddy T., "Smokers Underestimate Marijuana's Harm," About.com, March 23, 2009. Retrieved online on April 8, 2009, from alcoholism.about.com/od/pot/a/blnida050110.htm.

6. Phyllis L. Ellickson, Steven C. Martino, and Rebecca L. Collins, "Marijuana Use from Adolescence to Young Adulthood: Multiple Developmental Trajectories and Their Associated Outcomes," Rand Corporation Reprint Series. Retrieved online on April 8, 2009, from rand.org/pubs/reprints/2006/RAND_RP1192.pdf.

statement "All persons in the class of young abstainers are persons with a greater probability of ending up with a better quality of life and level of educational achievement than peer users of like gender, race-ethnicity, household composition, and parental education." Notice that being in the subject class does not necessarily mean that one will end up better off in the stated ways. According to the study, it just places one in a class that makes this more probable relative to the class of peer marijuana users.

As this example shows, once you quantify a statement, you may find that the terms themselves need to be edited to reflect accurately the claim being made. Thus, a cursory reading of the first statement may have led to the misconception that just by abstaining from smoking marijuana, you will end up being better off than your peers who do smoke it.

Exercise Set 6.2

Translate each of the following statements into standard categorical form using suitable parameters, as needed, and indicate the form of the statement.

6.2.1
"All you need is love." —John Lennon

6.2.2
"No man has a good enough memory to be a successful liar." —Abraham Lincoln

6.2.3
"Nothing gives us courage more readily than the desire to avoid looking like a damn fool." —Dean Koontz

6.2.4
"It is wrong always, everywhere, and for everyone, to believe anything upon insufficient evidence." —William James (Hint: translate this with three statements.)

6.2.5
"I stand by all the misstatements that I've made." —Dan Quayle

6.2.6
"Nothing great in the world has ever been accomplished without passion." —Georg Wilhelm Friedrich Hegel

6.2.7
"No rational argument will have a rational effect on a man who does not want to adopt a rational attitude." —Karl Popper

6.2.8
"No man is free who is not master of himself." —Epictetus

6.2.9
"Take the course opposite to custom and you will almost always do well." —Jean Jacques Rousseau

6.2.10
"All we are saying is give peace a chance." —John Lennon

Translating Universal Statements

The statements of ordinary language often contain a variety of words that serve as quantifiers. Table 6.2 is a partial list of words that commonly function as *universal* quantifiers. For example, consider the following opening paragraphs from an article about a victim of sexual abuse whose psychological trauma went largely ignored by the medical community:

> It was not until Emma was on the verge of killing herself that she realised that the crippling despair with which she had lived since she was 11 was not normal. "It was a bit like when there's snow on the ground," she said. *"Everything was really muffled.* But when I was a kid, I just thought that was what life was like."
>
> Triggered by a childhood of sexual abuse and compounded by a lack of medical support, Emma, now 22 and living in Leeds, spent more than a decade struggling under the blanket of depression. *"None of the doctors took it seriously,"* she said. *"All I got were antidepressants."* (Emphasis added.)[7]

In this context, Emma describes her depression in terms of the statement "Everything was really muffled," which appears to indicate a sort of detachment from reality and forlornness that she had come to accept as "normal." Notice this statement is universal and affirmative: she is saying that "all things were really muffled." This universality is an earmark of depression. When one is depressed, *all* reality (not just some of it) looks bleak ("muffled").

In the second paragraph, Emma states that "none of the doctors took it [her depression] seriously." Note that the word "none" indicates both a universal quality and a negative quantity. Translated into standard form, this statement therefore says, "No doctors are people who took my depression seriously." She then goes on to defend (argue for) this universal negative statement with the further statement "All I got were antidepressants." Interestingly, this defense does not appear to support the conclusion adequately that no doctor took her depression seriously. Instead, it raises a serious question about the efficacy of antidepressants in the treatment of depression.

Table 6.2

Universal Quantifiers
All
Every
Each
None
No
Not any

---

7. Hannah Fletcher, "None of the Doctors Took Me Seriously," *Times Online*, April 24, 2008. Retrieved online on April 8, 2009, from www.timesonline.co.uk/tol/news/uk/health/article3803380 .ece.

In fact, in chapter 18 we will discuss the involvement of *faulty thinking* in depression. While this is not to disavow the potential value of antidepressants in at least some cases of depression, as you will see, depression is not merely a medical problem. It is also one about thinking. This may well be what Emma was primarily reacting to when she said that no doctors took her depression seriously.

Translating Singular Statements

A singular statement states that a particular individual has or does not have a certain attribute or property. For example, consider the statement "Elvis Presley is the king of rock 'n' roll." Most musicologists would agree that Elvis Presley exerted a profound influence on the rise and development of rock 'n' roll music, although not to the exclusion of other greats such as Chuck Berry, Buddy Holly, and the Beatles. Yet to call Elvis the king of rock 'n' roll says that *only* he has this title. It means that if *anyone* is king of rock 'n' roll, it is Elvis; conversely, if *anyone* is Elvis Presley, then he is king of rock 'n' roll. The statement is therefore a universal statement even though it is a singular statement.

A singular statement can be translated as a universal statement. The universality stems from the fact that any individual can be treated as a class having one member. Thus, the class of Elvis Presleys has only one member—namely Elvis himself—not including any of his impersonators. Similarly, definite descriptions like "the king of rock 'n' roll," "the current president of the United States," "the author of Huckleberry Finn," and so on are classes having just one member. For example, the singular statement "Richard Nixon was involved in the Watergate cover-up" is a universal affirmative statement, and its form is therefore "All S is P." With some artificiality, it can be translated into standard form as "All individuals identical to Richard Nixon were involved in the Watergate cover-up." Similarly, the statement "Gerald Ford was not a person involved in the Watergate cover-up" is a universal *negative* statement, and its form is therefore "No S is P." Again, with some artificiality, it can be translated into standard form as "No individual identical to Gerald Ford was involved in the Watergate cover-up."

As you can see from the above examples, singular statements can be translated into standard categorical form as either universal affirmative or universal negative statements. As you will also see, being able to so translate singular statements is important because it will allow you to assess the validity of deductions that contain singular statements.

Translating Particular Statements

Table 6.3 provides a partial list of words that commonly function as *particular* quantifiers. Consider, for example, the title and first paragraph of the following article about the acceptance of gays into the Catholic priesthood:

Vatican to Accept *a Few* Gay Priests
Active Homosexuals Will Not Be Allowed

ROME: A new Vatican document excludes from the priesthood most gay men, with few exceptions, banning in strong and specific language candidates "who are actively homosexual, have deep-seated homosexual tendencies, or support the so-called 'gay culture.'"[8]

The title says that *a few* gay men are accepted into the priesthood—namely those that are not "active homosexuals." But it also says that *most* gay men, with *few* exceptions, are excluded from the priesthood. Thus, three categorical statements are being asserted:

1. A few gay men are accepted into the priesthood.
2. Few gay men are accepted into the priesthood.
3. Most gay men are not accepted into the priesthood.

Can you see the difference between the use of "a few" in (1) and "few" in (2)? "A few" means that "some are," while "few" means "most are not." Table 6.4 illustrates how each of the said quantifying words ("a few," "few," and "most"), as used in each of the above categorical statements, can be translated into standard categorical form.

Notice that "a few" translates into an I-form statement, and "few" translates into the O-form. Notice also that the "most" statement says the same thing as the "few" statement and therefore has the same standard categorical form translation.

Table 6.3

Particular Quantifiers

Some
A few
A couple
Most
Not all
Almost all

Table 6.4

Quantity Indicating Word	Example	Translation into Standard Categorical Form
a few	A few gay men are accepted into the priesthood.	Some gay men are accepted into the priesthood.
few	Few gay men are accepted into the priesthood.	Some gay men are not accepted into the priesthood.
most	Most gay men are not accepted into the priesthood.	Some gay men are not accepted into the priesthood.

8. Ian Fisher and Lauri Goodstein, "Vatican to Accept a Few Gay Priests," *International Herald Tribune*, November 24, 2005. Retrieved online on April 9, 2009, from www.highbeam.com/doc/1P1-115611202.html.

Translating Only Statements

One frequently occurring word in categorical statements is the word "only." As a rule, only statements are translated as universal affirmative statements. For example, consider former president Dwight D. Eisenhower's statement that "only Americans can ever hurt America," which he made in a library dedication speech in Abilene, Kansas, on May 1, 1962. Eisenhower stated,

> Now, America today is just as strong as it needs to be. America is the strongest nation in the world and she will never be defeated or damaged seriously by anyone from the outside. Only Americans can ever hurt America.[9]

Presumably Eisenhower was talking about people (or nations of people) in this context and not, for instance, natural disasters. Accordingly, his statement could be translated as "All people who can ever hurt America are Americans." Notice how the order of the subject ("Americans") and predicate ("can hurt America") are switched in this translation. As a rule, any statement of the form "Only S is P" can be translated by switching the subject (S) and predicate (P) and using the A-form (universal affirmative).

Once this translation is made of an only statement, it can also be easier to assess its truth. Do you really believe that *all* people who can ever hurt America are Americans? This would mean that other nations or foreign organizations could never present a threat to American security. It would require that we must somehow always blame ourselves for any breach in our security. But perhaps it is closer to the truth to say that "most people who can hurt America are Americans." This would be an I-form statement, a particular affirmative, and therefore no longer a *universal* claim.

"Only" statements also need to be distinguished from statements using the phrase "the only." Consider, for example, the following statement:

> Since 1964 the only Democrats who have won the presidency are white Protestant males from the South who appeared to be moderates rather than liberals and whom white working-class voters could envision as "one of us."[10]

Here the translation also takes the A-form; however, the subject and predicate terms are not switched. Thus, "all Democrats who have won the presidency are white Protestant males from the South who appeared to be moderates rather than liberals and whom white working-class voters could envision as 'one of us.'" Accordingly, as a rule, statements of the form "The only S is P" translate as "All S is P."

However, in some cases, the words "the only" do not appear at the beginning of the statement. Consider, for example, this statement made by pundit Will Rogers:

---

9. "Only Americans Can Ever Hurt America." Eisenhower Library Dedication, Abilene, Kansas, May 1, 1962.

10. John B. Judis and Ruy Teixeira, "Back to the Future: The Re-emergence of the Emerging Democratic Majority," *American Prospect*, June 19, 2007. Retrieved online on April 8, 2009, from www.prospect .org/cs/articles?article=back_to_the_future061807.

On account of being a democracy and run by the people, we are the only nation in the world that has to keep a government four years, no matter what it does.

Presumably, the "we" here refers to America. Thus, Rogers is advancing the following argument:

America is a democracy and run by the people.
Therefore, America is the only nation in the world that has to keep a government four years, no matter what it does.

Notice that the above conclusion can also be understood as "The only nation in the world that has to keep a government four years, no matter what, is America." Since this statement is of the form "The only S is P," it can now be translated into standard form as follows: "All nations in the world that have to keep a government four years, no matter what, is America." Notice that this is a universal affirmative (A-form) statement. That is, it is of the form "All S is P." *Accordingly, in translating "the only" statements, the term immediately following "the only" will be the subject (S) of an A-form statement.* As you can see, the term that came immediately after "the only" (namely, "nation in the world that has to keep a government four years, no matter what") turns out to be the subject term (S).

Exercise Set 6.3

Translate each of the following statements into standard categorical form, and indicate the form of the statement.

6.3.1
"No one can earn a million dollars honestly." —William Jennings Bryan

6.3.2
"Most people would rather give than get affection." —Aristotle

6.3.3
"A lot of people think Christianity is about always being perfect." —Billy Ray Cyrus

6.3.4
"Each person has their own calling on this Earth." —Billy Ray Cyrus

6.3.5
"A friend is someone who gives you total freedom to be yourself." —Jim Morrison

6.3.6
"The only purpose for which power can be rightfully exercised over any member of a civilized community against his will is to prevent harm to others." —John Stuart Mill

6.3.7
"Almost all of our sorrows spring out of our relations with other people." —Arthur Schopenhauer

6.3.8
"The only true wisdom is in knowing you know nothing." —Socrates

(continued)

6.3.9
"Only the dead have seen the end of the war." —Plato

6.3.10
"Many a man will have the courage to die gallantly, but will not have the courage to say, or even to think, that the cause for which he is asked to die is an unworthy one." —Bertrand Russell

6.3.11
"A few philosophers really do important work." —Alfred Korzybski

6.3.12
"Few men have the virtue to withstand the highest bidder." —George Washington

6.3.13
"Patriotism is the virtue of the vicious." —Oscar Wilde

6.3.14
"A woman is the only thing I am afraid of that I know will not hurt me." —Abraham Lincoln

6.3.15
"Almost no one is foolish enough to imagine that he automatically deserves great success in any field of activity." —Sidney J. Harris

6.3.16
"Everybody likes a compliment." —Abraham Lincoln

6.3.17
"An expectation is a future object, recognized as belonging to me." —Samuel Alexander

6.3.18
"The real secret of magic lies in the performance." —David Copperfield

6.3.19
"Only one man ever understood me, and he didn't understand me." —Georg Wilhelm Friedrich Hegel

6.3.20
"Important principles may, and must, be inflexible." —Abraham Lincoln

6.3.21
Rupert Murdoch is the CEO of News Corporation.

6.3.22
News Corporation is the parent company of Fox News.

6.3.23
"War is an ugly thing, but not the ugliest of things." —John Stuart Mill (Hint: translate as two statements.)

6.3.24
"An eye for an eye makes the whole world blind." —Mahatma Gandhi

6.3.25
"Nothing you can't spell will ever work." —Will Rogers

EXISTENTIAL IMPORT

In contrast to universal statements, particular statements always have what logicians call *existential import*. This means that such statements entail the existence of individuals in the classes to which they refer. For example, the statement "Some men are beings with unalienable rights to life, liberty, and the pursuit of happiness" entails the existence of men and of beings with the said unalienable rights. Thus, it would be self-contradictory to say that some men have these rights but that men or beings with these rights do not exist.

I- and O-form statements therefore make existential claims. More formally, "Some S is P" claims the following:

There is at least one x such that x is S and x is P.

And "Some S is not P" claims the following:

There is at least one x such that x is S and x is not P.

For example, "Some politicians are corrupt" claims that there is at least one thing such that it is a politician *and* it is corrupt. Given the existence of a being that is both a politician and corrupt, this statement will be true. However, if one of these conjuncts is false, the existential claim will also be false. For example, "Some politicians are from Mars" is false because there are no Martians and therefore, of course, none that are politicians. *Hence, any I- or O-form statement that refers to an empty class will be false.*

In contrast, compare saying that "all unicorns are creatures with one horn." There is, indeed, a sense in which this statement is true because it correctly describes a feature of a unicorn. However, if this statement had existential import, then it would be false because unicorns are mythological creatures and therefore do not exist. More generally, if universal statements necessarily had existential import, then it would be impossible to make true universal statements that referred to classes without members (for example, mythological creatures, fictional characters, perfectly rigid physical bodies, and perfect geometrical shapes, lines, and points).

In fact, the father of deductive logic, Aristotle, did not have a problem with this because he did not believe that there was such a thing as an empty class in the first place. For him, a class was simply a collection of concrete particular things. For example, we can now speak meaningfully about the class of automobiles, which consists of all particular automobiles in existence. On the other hand, on this understanding of classes, there was no such class in Aristotle's own day since there were then no automobiles.

Yet, this seems at odds with the fact that we do make intelligible (and true) statements about empty classes. For example, novelist H. G. Wells made sense when, in his famous novel *The Time Machine*, his main character (the Time Traveller") spoke of time travel using a time machine:

"Long ago I had a vague inkling of a machine—"
"To travel through Time!" exclaimed the Very Young Man.

"That shall travel indifferently in any direction of Space and Time, as the driver determines."

Filby contented himself with laughter.

"But I have experimental verification," said the Time Traveller.

"It would be remarkably convenient for the historian," the Psychologist suggested. "One might travel back and verify the accepted account of the Battle of Hastings, for instance!"

Indeed, it appears to be true that a time machine could help us to verify historical accounts. Further, this statement about the utility of time machines seems to be true even if there never was nor ever will be such a machine. And, indeed, from airplanes to cyberspace, so much of what used to be science fiction has now become part of science and everyday life. Are we therefore to dismiss talk about empty classes as nonsense?

Of course, most discourse in the course of our daily lives does not refer to empty classes but rather to classes with members since these are what ordinarily affect us. Thus, we talk about BMWs, not time machines, and Fido, not unicorns. In the world of practical realities, the Aristotelian *assumption* that classes have members generally holds true.

Nevertheless, there are still at least some practical, everyday contexts in which it would not even be reasonable to assume existential import. For example, a statement on a course syllabus that "all students in this class who are found to have plagiarized will fail the course" does *not* assume that there are, or will be, any students in the class found to have plagiarized; it says only that *if* there are any, they will fail the course. Indeed, the point of including such a statement on a syllabus would be to try to ensure that there are not any students in the class who turn to plagiarism.

So Aristotle's theory of classes can be restrictive, and many logicians today do not accept it. Instead, they have taken a "Boolean interpretation of universal statements," so named after George Boole, one of the founders of modern logic. According to this interpretation, universal statements do not, themselves, have existential import. For example, we can interpret "All unicorns are creatures with one horn" as a universal *conditional* statement that says,

If anything is a unicorn, then it is a one-horned creature.

So interpreted, this statement is true but does not entail that there actually are any unicorns. Accordingly, a Boolean interpretation allows for the assertion of universal statements that refer to empty classes.

Since the issue of existential import will come up in the next two chapters, it is helpful to have a precise account of what it means for us to *assume* existential import of a universal statement: *to assume existential import of an A- or E-form statement means to assume that the subject class (S) of the given statement has at least one member.* Thus, in stating, "All S is P" or "No S is P," we assume existential import when we assume that there is at least one S.

This existential statement can be added to a Boolean interpretation of a universal statement in order to give an interpretation of a universal statement with existential import. Thus, any universal affirmative statement with existential import, "All S is P," can be interpreted as follows:

(1) "If anything is S, then it is P," *and* (2) "there is at least one S."

For example, the statement "All dogs are mammals" can be interpreted as (1) "If anything is a dog, then it is a mammal," and (2) "There is at least one dog."

Similarly, any universal negative statement with existential import, "No S is P," can be interpreted as follows:

(1) "If anything is S, then it is not P," *and* (2) "There is at least one S."

For example, the statement "No dogs are cats" can be interpreted as (1) "If anything is a dog, then it is not a cat," and (2) "There is at least one dog."

In contrast, an interpretation of a universal statement that does not assume existential import is a Boolean interpretation, which therefore includes (1) but not (2). For example, such an interpretation of the statement "All students in this class who are found to have plagiarized are students who will fail the course" will simply be "If anyone is a student in this class found to have plagiarized, then he or she is a student who will fail the course."

Whether such a Boolean interpretation is used or existential import is assumed for an A- or E-form statement will depend on the context. Thus, there will be some universal statements for which a Boolean interpretation is reasonable and others for which it is reasonable to assume existential import and unreasonable *not* to assume it. As you will see, there will also be some contexts in which assuming existential import is at least not unreasonable and in which reasonable people can agree to disagree. This is in contrast to I- and O-form statements, which *always* make existential claims and therefore always have existential import.

Exercise Set 6.4

Each of the following statements can be translated into a standard A- or E-form statement. (1) Translate each into a standard A- or E-form statement. (2) Determine whether the statement, in your judgment, should assume existential import. (3) If you judge that it does not assume existential import, provide a Boolean interpretation. If you judge that it does assume existential import, translate it by adding the additional existential statement.

Note that to make your decision, you may need to Google the terms of the statement if you are not familiar with them.

6.4.1
Othello loves Desdemona.

6.4.2
God is the creator of the universe.

6.4.3
Big Foot is afoot.

(continued)

6.4.4
None of the alleged Elvis sightings has proven to be authentic.

6.4.5
The only state in the United States that has legalized assisted suicide is Oregon.

6.4.6
Iago is most honest (spoken by Shakespeare's Othello).

6.4.7
The Beatles are a 1960s rock group that came out of Liverpool.

6.4.8
No Martians are overweight couch potatoes who gorge on McDonald's fries.

7

Immediate Deductions

In the last chapter, we discussed categorical statements. In this chapter, we will look at several types of deductions from categorical statements, called *immediate deductions*. The sense in which these deductions are "immediate" can be illustrated by comparing the form of such an inference to that of a categorical syllogism.

Consider the following examples of valid categorical deductive forms:

Form 1 (syllogistic form):
   All M is P.
   All S is M.
   Therefore, all S is P.
Form 2 (immediate deductive form):
   Some S is P.
   Therefore, some P is S.

Notice that in form 1, there are three terms (S, P, and M), whereas in form 2, there are only two (S and P). In form 1, the conclusion, all S is P, is deduced because the subject term (S) in the minor premise is linked to the predicate term (P) in the major premise by means of a middle term (M). Schematically, S → M → P; therefore, S → P. In contrast, in form 2, no middle term (M) links S and P.[1] The connection between S and P in the conclusion is therefore not "mediated" by a third term. This is the sense in which immediate deductions can appropriately be called "immediate."

THE SQUARE OF OPPOSITION

Immediate deductions were first identified and studied by the ancient philosopher Aristotle. As mentioned in the previous chapter, Aristotle did not believe

---

1. As you will see later in this chapter, form 2 is an example of a valid conversion of an I-form statement.

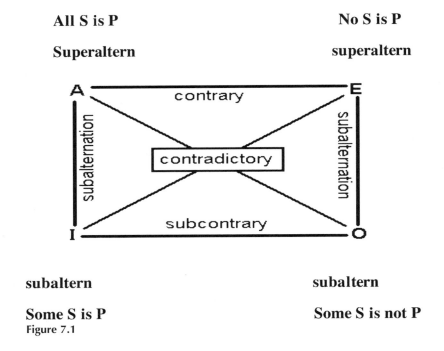

All S is P   **No S is P**

Superaltern   **superaltern**

subaltern   **subaltern**

Some S is P   **Some S is not P**
Figure 7.1

that there was any such thing as empty classes. Consequently, he assumed that all universal statements (A- and E-statements) had existential import. Based largely on this assumption, he was able to plot deductive relationships between A-, E-, I-, and O-form statements on a diagram that has come to be called the traditional square of opposition. Figure 7.1 presents Aristotle's square.

Subalternation

As displayed, the relationship of *subalternation* exists between A- and I-statements (left side of square) and E- and O-statements (right side of square). In subalternation, the A-statement is said to be the *superaltern* of the I-statement, which is its corresponding *subaltern*. Similarly, the E-statement is said to be the superaltern of the O-statement, which is its corresponding subaltern. According to subalternation, each subaltern can be deduced from its corresponding superaltern.

Thus, from the A-statement "All S is P," the I-statement "Some S is P" can be deduced, and from the E-statement "No S is P," the O-statement "Some S is not P" can be deduced. For example, from "All senators are politicians" you can deduce "Some senators are politicians." That is, if all senators are politicians, then surely *some* of them are. And from "No senators are angels" you can deduce "Some senators are not angels." That is, if no senators are angels, then surely *some* of them aren't.

Notice, however, that these deductive inferences assume existential import of the universal statements, A and E. The subalternation relationship between these universal statements and their corresponding particular statements would simply not hold if the class in question was empty. For example, from the truth of "All unicorns are one-horned creatures" you could not deduce "Some unicorns are one-horned creatures" because the latter statement entails that there are unicorns, which is false. Nevertheless, subalternation is still valid when classes have members, which is quite often the case in practical life situations.

Contradictories

Take a look at the diagonal axes of the square of opposition. Notice that the two pairs of statements, A and O and E and I, are called *contradictories*. Contradictories are statements that cannot both be true and cannot both be false. For example, the statements "All surgeons are physicians" and "Some surgeons are not physicians" cannot both be true, nor can they both be false. In other words, if one is true, the other is false; if one is false, the other is true.

Notice that if A- and E-statements are assumed to have existential import, the relationship of contradiction will be invalidated in the case of statements that refer to empty classes. For example, consider again the respective A- and O-statements "All unicorns are one-horned creatures" and "Some unicorns are not one-horned creatures." Since there are no unicorns, the A-statement will be false if it is taken to have existential import. But the O-statement will also be false since there are no unicorns. Therefore, both A- and O-statements will be false. But then they could not be contradictories because, by definition, A- and O-statements cannot both be false.

The way around this problem is to take a Boolean interpretation of A- and E-statements and therefore not to assume that these universal statements have existential import. In that case the statement pairs, A and O and E and I, will remain contradictories even when they refer to empty classes. However, on this interpretation, subalternation (and, as you will see, contrariety) will no longer hold.

Contraries

Now look at the top axis of the Square of Opposition. Notice that the statements, A and E, are called *contraries*. Contraries are statements that both cannot be true but both *can* be false. For example, the statements "All psychologists are neurotic" and "No psychologists are neurotic" cannot both be true, but both can be false, as when (which seems to be the case) just some of them are neurotic. Thus, if one contrary is true, then the other is false since both cannot be true. So, if "All psychologists are neurotic" is true, then "No psychologists are neurotic" must be false. However, if one contrary is false, the other can be either true or false. Thus, if "All psychologists are neurotic" is false, then it can be true that "no psychologists are neurotic," but it can also be false. The relationship of contrariety assumes existential import in order to be valid. In other words, it breaks down, along with subalternation, in the case of statements that refer to empty classes. For example, the corresponding subalterns of the statements "All Vulcans are part human" and "No Vulcans are part human" are false since Vulcans are fictional creatures in the classic TV show *Star Trek* and therefore do not exist.[2] This means that "Some

---

2. While it might be claimed that they exist in the TV show, it is false that they exist in reality, outside the show.

Vulcans are part human" and "Some Vulcans are not part human" are both false. But then their corresponding contradictories, "All Vulcans are part human" and "No Vulcans are part human," have to be true. (Remember that if one contradictory is false, then the other must be true.) But if "All Vulcans are part human" and "No Vulcans are part human" are both true, then they cannot be contraries because contraries, by definition, cannot both be true. Nevertheless, in the case of statements whose terms refer to classes that have members, the relationship of contrariety between A- and E-statements remains intact.

Subcontraries

Now look at the bottom axis of the square of opposition. Notice that the statements I and O are called *subcontraries*. Subcontraries are statements that can both be true but cannot both be false. For example, the statements "Some priests are Jesuits" and "Some priests are not Jesuits" are subcontraries because while both can be true, both cannot be false. Therefore, if "Some priests are not Jesuits" is false, then "Some priests are Jesuits" is true; conversely, if "Some priests are Jesuits" is false, then "Some priests are not Jesuits" is true.

It is easy to see that both of these statements can be true but perhaps a little harder to see that both cannot be false. So, why can't these statements both be false? Here is the proof. Any given priest will either be a Jesuit or not. If the given priest is a Jesuit then the statement "Some priests are Jesuits" will be true. On the other hand, if the given priest is not a Jesuit then the statement "Some priests are not Jesuits" will be true. Therefore, at least one of these subcontraries will have to be true; therefore, both cannot be false.

Table 7.1

When:	A-Form is:	E-Form is:	I-Form is:	O-Form is:
A-Form is True		False (Contrar.)	True (Subalt.)	False (Contradict.)
E-Form is True	False (Contrar.)		False (Contradict.)	True
I-Form is True	True or False (Subalt.)	False (Contradict.)		True or False (Subcontrar.)
O-Form is True	False (Contradict.)	True or False (Subalt.)	True or False (Subcontrar.)	
A-Form is False		True or False (Contrar.)	True or False (Subalt.)	True (Contradict.)
E-Form is False	True or False (Contrar.)		True (Contradict.)	True or False (Subalt.)
I-Form is False	False (Subalt.)	True (Contradict)		True (Subcontrar.)
O-Form is False	True (Contradict.)	False (Subalt.)	True (Subcontrar.)	

It should now be evident that subcontrariety also assumes existential import in order to be valid. That is, it breaks down in the case of I- and O-statements whose terms refer to empty classes. For example, consider again the statements "Some Vulcans are part human" and "Some Vulcans are not part human." Since Vulcans do not exist, both statements are false. But if both are false, then they cannot be subcontraries because, by definition, both subcontraries cannot be false.

Inferences on the Square

Table 7.1 shows the truth values of A-, E-, I-, and O-forms when one of these forms is given as true/false. The rationale for the inference is also provided in parentheses. If the case is indeterminate and no valid deduction can be made, "true or false" is indicated. *Note that table 7.1 assumes existential import of A- and E-statements.*

Exercise Set 7.1

Following are sets of categorical statements. (1) Assume the first statement of each set to be true. Given this assumption, what can you deduce about the truth status (true, false, or indeterminate) of each of the other statements in the set? (2) Now assume the first statement of each set to be false. Given this assumption, what can you deduce about the truth status (true, false, or indeterminate) of each of the other statements in the set? In all cases, assume existential import holds for A- and E-statements. Justify each response by referencing the corresponding relationship on the square of opposition.

7.1.1
"No man has a good enough memory to be a successful liar." —Abraham Lincoln
a. All men have a good enough memory to be a successful liar.
b. Some men have a good enough memory to be a successful liar.
c. Some men do not have a good enough memory to be a successful liar.

7.1.2
"All men are created equal." —Declaration of Independence
a. No man is created equal.
b. Some men are not created equal.
c. Some men are created equal.

7.1.3
"Some people wonder all their lives if they've made a difference." —Ronald Reagan
a. Some people do not wonder all their lives if they've made a difference.
b. No people wonder all their lives if they've made a difference.
c. All people wonder all their lives if they've made a difference.

7.1.4
"Some men do not know when to quit while they are ahead." —Blogger
a. All men know when to quit while they are ahead.
b. Some men know when to quit while they are ahead.
c. No men know when to quit while they are ahead.

The Boolean Interpretation of the Square of Opposition

As you have seen, subalternation, contrariety, and subcontrariety are valid only if these inferences involve classes that have members. When they do involve empty classes, however, these inferences will be invalid. For example, from "All Vulcans are part human," you cannot infer that "Some Vulcans are part human." From the truth of "All Vulcans are part human," you cannot infer that "No Vulcans are part human" is false. And from the falsehood of "Some Vulcans are part human," you cannot infer that "Some Vulcans are not part human" is true.

Taking a Boolean interpretation of the universal statements, A and E, will not save these inferences when they involve empty classes, but it will permit valid inferences based on contradiction. For example, the Boolean interpretation[3] of the statement "All Vulcans are part human" is that "If anything is a Vulcan, then it is part human." Clearly, if this statement is true, then its contradictory, "Some Vulcans are not part human," will necessarily be false.

Assuming Existential Import:
The Case of Trying to Prove God's Existence

If you are working with statements that involve empty classes, then the Boolean interpretation allows you to interpret universal statements without giving them existential import and therefore allows you to draw only inferences that are valid. On the other hand, when you are working with classes with members (as is most often the case), then you can interpret the universal statements, A and E, as having existential import and therefore allowing you to draw valid inferences based on subalternation, contrariety, and contradiction.

The decision to grant a universal statement existential import will depend on one's judgment about whether the terms of the statement refer to classes with members. About this, however, there may sometimes be disagreement. For example, consider the following deduction by subalternation:

> God is almighty.
> Therefore, some being that is identical with God is almighty.

At least some theists (believers in God's existence) might be eager to give the premise in this argument existential import and to pronounce it valid. On the other hand, a Boolean interpretation would keep this assumption out of the premises. For, on a Boolean interpretation, this argument would look as follows:

> If any being is identical to God then it is almighty.
> Therefore, some being that is identical to God is almighty.

This inference is clearly invalid since the premise does not have existential import while the conclusion does. To make this argument valid requires addition of the existential assumption that there is at least one being identical to God:

---

3. See chapter 6.

If any being is identical to God then it is almighty.
There is at least one being that is identical to God.
Therefore, some being that is identical to God is almighty.

This argument is indeed valid, but is it sound? Clearly, the soundness of the argument will depend on whether the existential assumption is true. Interestingly, this seems to be the same problem that at least sometimes arises when one tries to construct a rational argument to prove God's existence. In order to prove that God exists, you have to assume God's existence!

Consider, for example, the so-called ontological proof for God's existence offered by eleventh-century Benedictine monk Saint Anselm. Anselm argued,

> If that, than which nothing greater can be conceived, exists in the understanding alone, the very being, than which nothing greater can be conceived, is one, than which a greater can be conceived. But obviously this is impossible. Hence, there is no doubt that there exists a being, than which nothing greater can be conceived, and it exists both in the understanding and in reality.

In these winding statements, Anselm makes the argument that God must exist (not just as a concept in the mind but in reality) because God is, by definition, a perfect being ("that than which nothing greater can be conceived"), and since a being that didn't exist would not be perfect, God has to exist. The argument is essentially this:

> God is a perfect being.
> Therefore, God exists.

The most famous criticism of this argument came from philosopher Immanuel Kant in the eighteenth century. According to Kant, "Existence is not a predicate," by which he meant existence is not itself a property that can be added to a thing in order to embellish it. To give you an idea of what Kant meant, imagine I told you that my car is a red Ford Mustang convertible with a Pioneer custom stereo, fifteen thousand miles, and a V8 turbo-charged engine. And then imagine I added, "Oh, I almost forgot to mention that it also exists." Indeed, this would be a strange thing to add because, as Kant admonished, existence is not itself a property of a thing. Instead, to say that the car exists is to say that something in the world matches its description. It is not to add another property to that description. Analogously, one can't add existence to God in order to perfect him because existence is not part of the description of God in the first place.

But there is another criticism of this argument that may be more fundamental to any proof for God's existence (not just Anselm's), and it concerns the issue of assuming existential import. Consider the following Boolean interpretation of Anselm's argument:

> If there is anything satisfying the description of God, then it is a perfect being.
> Therefore, there is something that satisfies the description of God.

Clearly, this argument is invalid unless we add the existential assumption that there is something that satisfies the description of God. Thus, the following argument would surely be valid:

> If there is anything satisfying the description of God, then it is a perfect being.
> There is something that satisfies the description of God.
> Therefore, there is something that satisfies the description of God.

But notice that this argument assumes just what it tries to prove—namely that God exists: that is, that there is something that satisfies the description of God. This argument therefore goes in a circle and proves nothing.[4]

Philosopher Søren Kierkegaard thought that such circularity was an unavoidable consequence of *any* attempt to prove God's existence. He put this point concisely when he stated,

> The idea of demonstrating that this unknown something (God) exists could scarcely suggest itself to Reason. For if God does not exist it would of course be impossible to prove it; and if he does exist it would be folly to attempt it. For at the very outset, in beginning my proof, I will have presupposed it, not as doubtful but as certain (a presupposition is never doubtful, for the very reason that it is a presupposition).[5]

Nevertheless, Kierkegaard did not himself end with nonbelief. Rather, he claimed that belief in God required a "leap of faith" and that rational argument could not prove God's existence without the circularity of assuming it in the first place.

As you can see from this discussion of Anselm's argument, it can at least sometimes be the judgment of whether to assume existential import of singular statements about God that determines whether an argument for God's existence is valid. But, as Kierkegaard maintained, it may also be this assumption that trivializes the argument by making it circular.

Exercise Set 7.2

If you are a theist (believe in God), respond to question set 7.2.1; if an atheist (disbelieve in God), respond to 7.2.2; if an agnostic (neither believe nor disbelieve in God), respond to 7.2.3.

7.2.1
Can you prove your belief in God?
   If not, why should you take the "leap of faith"? Are you blindly leaping, or is there some good reason that justifies this faith, which does not itself assume God's existence? (Don't

---

4. Notice that once the existential assumption is added to the premises, the argument is valid without the first premise about God's being a perfect being. This is because you can certainly deduce the existential assumption from itself. That is, the following inference is valid:

There is something that satisfies the description of God.
Therefore, there is something that satisfies the description of God.

5. Søren Kierkegaard, "Why God's Existence Cannot Be Proven," in *Philosophers at Work: Issues and Practice of Philosophy*, ed. Elliot D. Cohen (Belmont, Calif.: Wadsworth Publishing Co., 2000), 530–31.

say the Bible proves it because it is the word of God. This is to assume already that God exists.)

If you think you can prove God's existence, what is your argument, and does it already assume that God exists? That is, if you were not already convinced that God exists, would you still think your argument proves that God exists?

7.2.2
What argument do you have to support your belief that God does not exist? (Do not appeal to the lack of evidence to prove the affirmative statement that God exists as this would be a fallacy.[1]) If you were not already assuming it false that God exists, would you still think your argument proves that God does not exist? Is it still at least possible that God exists in spite of your argument to the contrary?

7.2.3
Why do you neither believe nor disbelieve in God? That is, why are you not convinced either way by any arguments? Why do you not believe on faith that God exists? Is there anything else in which you have faith but cannot prove—for example, the existence of a physical world outside your own sense experiences of it?

How do you know this sense experience is veridical and correctly corresponds to the existence of external objects? Is this a form of faith—an assumption of existential import about your statements about the external world? For example, "I see a table" assumes that there is a table. Why not just say, "I am having tablelike sensations" instead?

So, in dismissing faith in God's existence should you also be dismissing faith in the external world?

---

1. This would be the fallacy of appeal to ignorance. See chapter 21.

The Contextual Approach to Determining Existential Import

To eliminate any variation in the interpretation of A- and E-form statements, it may be tempting to formulate a strict rule that A- and E-form statements never assume existential import; therefore, inferences like subalternation and contrariety that assume existential import are always invalid. Indeed, this is how some approaches have attempted to solve the problem.[6] However, to do this is to throw the baby out with the bath water, for the assumption of existential import is clearly in order in many contexts in life.

On the other hand, some approaches tend to go in the opposite direction and assume existential import always.[7] While this approach is likely to adequately capture the lion's share of statements in the practical contexts of life, it also fails to accommodate situations in which the classes in question are empty or in which there is room for disagreement.

---

6. See, for example, Irving Copi and Carl Cohen, *Introduction to Logic,* 13th ed. (Upper Saddle River, N.J.: Prentice Hall, 2008).

7. This appears to be the approach taken by Moore and Parker. In a note they state, "It is quite possible to interpret categorical claims this way. By allowing both the A- and the E-claims to be true and both the I- and the O-claims to be false, this interpretation reduces the square to contradiction alone. We're going to interpret the claims differently; however, at the level at which we're operating, it seems much more natural to see 'All Cs are Ds' as conflicting with 'No Cs are Ds.'" Brooke Noel Moore and Richard Parker, *Critical Thinking,* 8th ed. (New York: McGraw-Hill, 2007), 257.

In contrast, the approach taken here avoids both extremes and instead assesses existential import contextually. Thus, in some situations, it may be unreasonable not to assume existential import (for example, when speaking about classes that obviously have members, such as humans, dogs, trees, cars, and so on). In some situations it may be unreasonable to assume existential import (as when speaking about mythological creatures or fictional characters, for example). And in some situations it may be debatable as to whether one should assume existential import, as when speaking about classes whose members' existence is in dispute (for example, life in other galaxies, the big bang theory, evolution, machines that can think, and God).

Of course, the fact that it is debatable whether a class has members does not give one the right to assume that it does. For this, one would need a rational argument, even if it didn't convince everyone. For example, as we have already seen, one cannot prove God's existence by assuming that God exists. Similarly, one cannot simply assume that the theory of evolution is true without having a rational argument for it.[8]

Exercise Set 7.3

Each of the following immediate deductions is valid if it is assumed that A- and E-forms have existential import. For each argument, briefly explain why or why not you think this assumption should be made. For example, in 7.3.1, you will need to decide whether the class of clairvoyants should be assumed to have at least one member.

7.3.1
All clairvoyants are potentially helpful in solving crimes.
Therefore, some clairvoyants are potentially helpful in solving crimes.

7.3.2
No unidentified flying object (UFO) is from another planet.
Therefore, some UFOs are not from another planet.

7.3.3
All government officials convicted of treason will be executed.
Therefore, some government officials convicted of treason will be executed.

7.3.4
No weapons of mass destruction (WMD) are in Iraq.
Therefore, some WMD are not in Iraq.

7.3.5
All hobbits are inhabitants of Middle Earth.
Therefore, it is false that no hobbits are inhabitants of Middle Earth.

7.3.6
All ghosts are invisible beings.
Therefore, some ghosts are invisible beings.

7.3.7
No philosophy professors are creatures from the planet Uranus.
Therefore, some philosophy professors are not creatures from the planet Uranus.

---

8. The argument for evolution will be examined in chapter 8.

7.3.8
All polar bears are on the endangered species list.
Therefore, it is false that no polar bears are on the endangered species list.

7.3.9
All apples are fruit.
Therefore, it is false that no apples are fruit.

7.3.10
No creatures with hearts are creatures without kidneys.
Therefore, some creatures with hearts are not creatures without kidneys.

OTHER IMMEDIATE INFERENCES

Other immediate deductions using categorical statements are possible that are not on the square of opposition. These include conversion, contraposition, and obversion.

Conversion

The *converse* of a categorical statement is formed by switching the positions of the subject and predicate terms. Table 7.2 indicates which conversions are valid. Notice that E- and I-statements can validly be converted. As tables 7.3 and 7.4 show, the converses of these forms are *logically equivalent*. This means that these statements and their converses will always have the same truth value.

For example, if "No honest people are liars" is true, then its converse, "No liars are honest people," is true; if "No liars are honest people" is true, then its converse,

Table 7.2

Premise	Converse	Status
(A) All S is P	Some P is S	Valid (if existential import is assumed)
(E) No S is P	No P is S	Valid
(I) Some S is P	Some P is S	Valid
(O) Some S is not P	Some P is not S	Invalid

Table 7.3

No S is P	No P is S
True	True
False	False

Table 7.4

Some S is P	Some P is S
True	True
False	False

"No honest people are liars," is true. Likewise, if "No honest people are liars" is *false*, then its converse, "No liars are honest people," is false; if "No liars are honest people" is false, then its converse, "No honest people are liars," is false.

The same thing can be said of I-form statements. The converse of an I-form statement is always logically equivalent to the statement. However, this is not equally true of A- and O-form statements. The converse of an A-statement is not logically equivalent to the A-statement, nor is it deducible from it. For example, the statement "All gays are human" and its converse, "All humans are gays," are not equivalent, nor can "All humans are gays" be deduced from "All gays are human." In fact, as you can see, while "All gays are human" is true, its converse is false.

However, the converse of an A-statement can validly be deduced from the A-statement *by limitation*. This means that the converse is deducible only if the quantity is also changed to particular. For example, the converse by limitation of "All senators are politicians" is "Some politicians are senators." Thus, the following deduction is valid:

> All senators are politicians.
> Therefore, some politicians are senators.

Notice that the subject and predicate are switched in the conclusion and that the quantity is also changed from universal to particular. This inference is valid.

However, notice also that in this inference a particular statement is deduced from a universal statement. As you have seen, while particular statements have existential import, universal statements do not necessarily have it. This means that this inference is valid only if the A-form is assumed to have existential import. Since it is true that there is at least one senator, this existential assumption can be made.

In contrast, consider the following conversion inference:

> All perfect circles are geometrical figures.
> Therefore, some geometrical figures are perfect circles.

Since perfect circles do not exist, the A-form premise cannot reasonably be assumed to have existential import, whereas the conclusion is a particular statement and therefore does have existential import (it entails the existence of at least one perfect circle). The inference is therefore invalid.

Finally, as you can see from table 7.2, in the case of O-statements, no conversion is valid. For example, from the O-statement "Some illegal acts are not felonies," you cannot deduce its converse, "Some felonies are not illegal acts."

Exercise Set 7.4

For each of the following statements, (1) translate it into standard categorical form, (2) state its converse, and (3) indicate whether this converse can be validly deduced from its original statement. In any case in which you need to assess existential import, apply the contextual approach as discussed in the previous section of this chapter.

7.4.1
"A banker is a fellow who lends you his umbrella when the sun is shining, but wants it back the minute it begins to rain." —Mark Twain

7.4.2
"Not a few things about friendship are matters of debate." —Aristotle

7.4.3
"It is never too late to give up your prejudices." —Henry David Thoreau

7.4.4
"Very few facts are able to tell their own story, without comments to bring out their meaning." —John Stuart Mill

7.4.5
The tyrannosaurus is a carnivore.

Obversion

Obversion changes the form of a statement to a logically equivalent form. All standard categorical form statements can be validly obverted. Table 7.5 displays the obverse of each of the standard categorical form statements. Each of the obverses given in the table is formed by mechanically following two steps:

1. *Change the quality of the statement without changing its quantity.* Thus, A-form will change to E-form, and E-form to A-form. And I-form will change to O-form, and O-form to I-form.
2. *Replace the predicate term (P) with its complement.* The complement of P (non-P) is the class of all things that do not belong to P. For example, the complement of humans is the class of nonhumans, which includes *everything in the world that is not human*—all other living things and all other naturally occurring or created things.

For example, consider Seneca's claim that "all cruelty springs from weakness," which, in standard categorical form, is the A-form statement "All acts of cruelty are acts that spring from weakness." The obverse of this statement is "No acts of cruelty are non–*acts that spring from weakness.*" Or consider Shakespeare's line from *Twelfth Night* that "some men are born great,"[9] which, in standard categorical form,

Table 7.5

Premise	Obverse
(A) All S is P	No S is non-P
(E) No S is P	All S is non-P
(I) Some S is P	Some S is not non-P
(O) Some S is not P	Some S is non-P

---

9. The complete quote is, "Be not afraid of greatness: some men are born great, some achieve greatness, and some have greatness thrust upon them."

is the I-form statement "Some men are persons who are born great." The obverse of this statement is "Some men are not non–*persons who are born great.*"

Note that the entire predicate term of each of these obverses has been italicized. When a term is complex and has modifiers, as in the above case, there can be some ambiguity as to the scope of the prefix "non." The purpose of the italics is to make clear that the prefix "non" applies to the entire term and not just to part of it. For example, the complement of "persons who are born great" is not *nonpersons* who are born great but rather the much broader class that includes everything except persons who are born great. Italicizing the entire term eliminates such ambiguity when the prefix "non" is used to designate the complement of a complex term.

A categorical statement and its obverse are always logically equivalent, which means if the one is true, then the other is also true; if the one is false, then the other is also false. For example, if "Some men are persons who are born great" is true, then its obverse, "Some men are not non–*persons who are born great*" is also true, and vice versa; if "Some men are persons who are born great" is false, then its obverse is also false, and vice versa.

Exercise Set 7.5

For each of the following categorical statements, translate it into standard categorical form, and state its logically equivalent obverse.

7.5.1
"He that can have patience can have what he will." —Benjamin Franklin

7.5.2
"No man is good enough to govern another man without that other's consent." —Abraham Lincoln

7.5.3
A few nonsmokers are spokespersons for the tobacco industry.

7.5.4
"Few people are capable of expressing with equanimity opinions which differ from the prejudices of their social environment. Most people are even incapable of forming such opinions." —Albert Einstein

7.5.5
Naprozine is a noncortical steroid.

Contraposition

The *contrapositive* of a categorical statement is formed by switching around the subject and predicate terms, then taking the complement of each. Table 7.6 displays the contrapositives of each form and their validity status. Consider, for example, Andre Malraus's thought-provoking A-statement that "All art is a revolt against man's fate." Switching the subject and predicate and replacing them with their complements, we get, "All non–*revolts against man's fate* are nonart," which is the valid contrapositive of Malraus's original statement.

Table 7.6

Premise	Contrapositive	Status
(A) All S is P	All non-P is non-S	Valid
(E) No S is P	Some non-P is not non-S	Valid by limitation only (Assumes existential import)
(I) Some S is P	Some non-P is non-S	Invalid
(O) Some S is not P	Some non-P is not non-S	Valid

Notice that since an A-form statement is logically equivalent to its contrapositive, Malraus's original statement and its contrapositive are logically equivalent. Therefore, if one of these statements is true, then the other is also true; if one is false, then the other is also false.

However, the case is otherwise in regard to the contrapositive of an *E-form* statement. In this case, the premise changes quantity from universal to particular:

No S is P.
Therefore, *some* non-P is not non-S.

For example, consider the following inference:

No Democrats are Republicans.
Therefore, no non-Republicans are non-Democrats.

Clearly, *this inference is invalid*. For example, members of the Libertarian Party are both non-Republicans and non-Democrats. Therefore, the conclusion is false, even though the premise is true. However, this inference can be made valid by changing the quantity in the conclusion from universal to particular as follows:[10]

No Democrats are Republicans.
Therefore, *some* non-Republicans are not non-Democrats.

The above inference is known as contraposition *by limitation* because it restricts the conclusion to "some." Notice, however, that this inference is valid only if we assume that the E-form premise has existential import. This is because the conclusion is now a particular statement, which therefore has existential import. In the present example, there is no problem with assuming existential import of the premise because the class of Democrats is not empty. However, in cases where the premise refers to an empty class, contraposition by limitation is invalid.

Further, a statement and its contrapositive by limitation are not logically equivalent. Thus, while you can deduce "Some non-Republicans are not non-Democrats" from "No Democrats are Republicans," you cannot deduce "No Democrats are

---

10. That the following inference is valid can be proved by a series of immediate deductions as follows:

No Democrats are Republicans.
Therefore, some Democrats are not Republicans (by subalternation).
Therefore, some Democrats are non-Republicans (by obversion).
Therefore, some non-Republicans are Democrats (by conversion).
Therefore, some non-Republicans are not non-Democrats (by obversion).

Republicans" from "Some non-Republicans are not non-Democrats." This is because you cannot in general validly deduce "all" from "some."

As you can see from table 7.6, contraposition of an I-form statement is never valid, whereas contraposition of the O-form is valid. Consider, for example, the following statement made by Thomas Jefferson:

> Some men are not born with saddles on their backs, nor are others born booted and spurred to ride them.

It would appear from the context that Jefferson is denying that some men, presumably black people, are animals.[11] Thus, as expressed in standard form, the first part of this compound statement appears to assert the O-form statement "Some men are not animals born with saddles on their back." Its valid contrapositive would accordingly be "Some non–*animals born with saddles on their back* are not nonmen."

Notice that by obverting this statement, we can validly eliminate the double negation "not non" so that it states the following: "Some non–*animals born with saddles on their back* are men." This statement no longer expresses the contrapositive of Jefferson's original statement, but since it is a valid obversion of its contrapositive, it is still logically equivalent to it.

Exercise Set 7.6

For each of the following categorical statements that can be validly contraposed, state its logically equivalent contrapositive. If the statement cannot validly be contraposed, then indicate this. For cases that involve existential import, take the contextual approach discussed earlier in this chapter.

7.6.1
All generic drugs are drugs that cost less than brand-name drugs.

7.6.2
Some telecommunications companies that conduct illegal spying operations for the government are companies with retroactive legal immunity against criminal and civil prosecution.

7.6.3
Some ethicists who work for the government are not freethinkers.

7.6.4
No psychotropic medications are drugs that should be taken with alcoholic beverages.

7.6.5
All over-the-counter drugs are nonprescription drugs.

MAKING MULTIPLE IMMEDIATE DEDUCTIONS

Consider again Jefferson's original statement that "some men are not animals born with saddles on their back." Can you see how, given the truth of this state-

---

11. It is interesting that he should have said this in light of the fact that he was a slave owner.

ment, you can deduce the falsehood of the statement "No non–*animals born with saddles on their back* are men"? Here is the proof:

"Some men are not animals born with saddles on their back" (premise).

1. Therefore, "Some men are non–*animals born with saddles on their back*" (by obversion).
2. Therefore, "Some non–*animals born with saddles on their back* are men" (by conversion).
3. Therefore, it is false that "no non–*animals born with saddles on their back* are men" (by contradiction).

Notice that in step 1, the O-form premise is changed to the I-form by obverting it (changing its quality and taking the complement of its predicate term). Then in step 2, the I-form is validly converted by switching around the subject and predicate terms. Finally, notice that the converted I-form statement in step 2 is the contradictory of the E-form statement in step 3; therefore, this E-form statement must be false.

It is thus possible to combine the various kinds of immediate inferences—those both on and off the square of opposition—to make a series of deductions. Once you have a clear idea of how each of these forms of deduction works, it becomes easier to see your away around these more complex sets of deductions.

Exercise Set 7.7

For each of the following sets of statements, what can you infer about the other statement in the set (1) if you assume that the first statement is true, and (2) if you assume that the first statement is false. That is, given these respective assumptions, state whether the second statement in each set is true, false, or indeterminate. Also provide proof for your evaluation. That is, state the immediate deductions you made in order to reach your answer.

Note that you may need to make multiple immediate deductions to get your answer, including some immediate inferences contained on the square of opposition.

Apply the contextual method for assuming existential import discussed earlier in this chapter.

7.7.1
Some former soldiers are Iraq veterans.
No Iraq veterans are former soldiers.

7.7.2
No just wars are wars undertaken for economic gain.
Some wars undertaken for economic gain are just wars.

7.7.3
All pink elephants are delusions.
Some nondelusions are non–pink elephants.

7.7.4
Some neoconservatives are proponents of unitary executive authority.
Some non–proponents of unitary executive authority are non-neoconservatives.

(continued)

7.7.5
Some foreign advisors are board members of multinational corporations.
No board members of multinational corporations are foreign advisors.

7.7.6
Some professors are not progressives.
Some nonprogressives are professors.

7.7.7
Some Fender guitars are Telecasters.
No Telecasters are Fender guitars.

7.7.8
Some Fender guitars are not Stratacasters.
No non-Stratacasters are Fender guitars.

7.7.9
All freethinkers are critical thinkers.
Some critical thinkers are not nonfreethinkers.

7.7.10
All chain smokers are nicotine addicts.
Some non–nicotine addicts are not non–chain smokers.

8

Categorical Syllogisms

Acategorical syllogism is one whose major premise, minor premise, and conclusion are all categorical statements. In contrast to immediate deductive
arguments, which have only a subject term (S) and a predicate term (P), a categorical syllogism also has a middle term (M). The job of the middle term is to link the
subject term to the predicate term in the conclusion.

THE BASIC PARTS OF A CATEGORICAL SYLLOGISM

For purposes of illustration, take a look at the following common form of categorical syllogism:

Major premise: All M is P.
Minor premise: All S is M.
Conclusion: All S is P.

Notice this form contains three A-form statements. As you will see, there are
many other forms of categorical syllogisms, some valid and some not, which
contain various combinations of the four standard forms of categorical statements
(A, E, I, and O).

Any syllogism that consists of three premises in standard categorical form is
itself said to be in *standard form.* As you will see, it is helpful to put a categorical
syllogism into standard form in order to check it carefully for validity.

The above form is a valid form because *any substitution instances of its three terms
that make the premises true will also make the conclusion true.* For example, let S = humans, P = mammals, and M = primates. Substituting these values for S, P, and M,
respectively, in the given form will yield the following argument:

All primates are mammals.
All humans are primates.
Therefore, all humans are mammals.

Clearly, the conclusion is true and necessarily follows from the premises, which are also true. Try as you may, it will not be possible to find any substitution instances of this form that would make the premises true and the conclusion false.

All valid categorical syllogisms such as this one have exactly three terms, each used exactly twice. Notice also how the middle term "primates" appears in both major and minor premises but not in the conclusion. Once the middle term links the subject term (S) to the predicate term (P) in the conclusion, its logical job is done.

You can also distinguish the major premise from the minor premise by the terms each contains. In particular, the major premise contains the predicate term (P) of the conclusion, which is appropriately called the *major term*, whereas the minor premise contains the subject term (S) of the conclusion, which is appropriately called the *minor term.*

As you can see, knowing this taxonomy can be useful for finding the basic parts of a categorical syllogism. Once you know what the conclusion of a categorical syllogism is, you already know what one term of the major premise is (the major term) and what one term of the minor premise is (the minor term). Since the third term, the middle term (M), appears in both major and minor premises, if you know that term, then you know *all* terms of the syllogism in question. Table 8.1 provides a summation of this basic taxonomy.

Table 8.1

Part of Syllogism	Definition	Example
middle term (M)	term that is in both premises but not the conclusion	"primates"
minor term (S)	term that is the subject of the conclusion	"humans"
major term (P)	term that is the predicate of the conclusion	"mammals"
major premise	premise that contains the major term (P)	"All primates are mammals"
minor premise	premise that contains the minor term (S)	"All humans are primates"
conclusion	premise that contains both major and minor terms	"All humans are mammals"

Exercise Set 8.1

For each of the following categorical syllogisms, indicate whether the term set in bold type is the major, minor, or middle term. Also indicate which premise is the major premise and which is the minor premise. Note that for the purposes of this exercise, the major premise is not necessarily the premise that is listed first.

8.1.1
All **senators** are congresspersons.
All Senate majority leaders are senators.
Therefore, all Senate majority leaders are congresspersons.

8.1.2
Some propagandists are haters of truth.
No **lovers of wisdom** are haters of truth.
Therefore, some propagandists are not lovers of wisdom.

8.1.3
All freethinkers are critical thinkers.
Some **freethinkers** are academicians.
Therefore, some academicians are critical thinkers.

8.1.4
All signatories to the U.S. Constitution are believers in democracy.
No dictators are believers in democracy.
Therefore, no **signatories to the U.S. Constitution** are dictators.

DISTRIBUTION OF TERMS

One way to check categorical syllogisms for validity is by constructing Venn diagrams, which use circles to diagrammatically represent categorical statements. This method is discussed in the appendix. Another method is by evaluating a given syllogism against a relatively small set of rules (just five), the violation of which invalidates the syllogism. Since the rule method does not require the construction of diagrams, it tends to be tidier and can yield faster results. This is the method discussed in this chapter.

Construction of a set of rules for testing the validity of standard categorical form syllogisms requires the application of a technical concept known as *distribution*. Each term in the categorical statements comprising a categorical syllogism will either refer to *all* members of a class or to just *some* members of a class. When the term refers to all members of the class, it is said to be *distributed*; when it refers to just some members, it is said to be *undistributed*.

Table 8.2 shows the distribution status of each term in each of the four standard categorical form statements. Notice that the distribution status of the subject term (S) can be determined by the *quantity* of a categorical form statement. If the quantity is universal (A- and E-forms), then the subject term is distributed; if the quantity is particular (I- and O-forms), then the subject term is undistributed.

In contrast, notice that the distribution status of the predicate term (P) can be determined by the *quality* of a categorical form statement. If the quality is affirmative (A- and I-forms), then the predicate term is undistributed; if the quality is negative (E- and O-forms), then the predicate term is distributed.

For example, consider the A-form statement "All oncologists are physicians." Since this statement refers to *all* oncologists, its subject term ("oncologists") is distributed. However, the statement only refers to *some* physicians—namely those who are oncologists. Indeed, it says that all oncologists are physicians, but it

Table 8.2

Statement Form	Subject Term (S)	Predicate Term (P)
All S is P	Distributed	Undistributed
(E) No S is P	Distributed	Distributed
Some S is P	Undistributed	Undistributed
(O) Some S is not P	Undistributed	Distributed

does not also say that all physicians are oncologists. Therefore, its predicate term ("physicians") is undistributed.

In contrast to the A-form, both terms of an E-form statement are distributed. For example, the statement "No atheists are Christians" says that all atheists are excluded from being Christians; it also says that all Christians are excluded from being atheists.

In contrast to E-form statements, both terms of an I-form statement are undistributed. For example, the statement "Some professors are logicians" says both that some professors are logicians and that some logicians are professors, but it says neither that all professors are logicians nor that all logicians are professors. Therefore, both of its terms are undistributed.

Finally, in an O-form statement, the subject term is undistributed, while the predicate term is distributed. For example, the subject term ("criminals") in the O-statement "Some criminals are not career criminals" only refers to some criminals—namely the ones that are not career criminals. Therefore, this term is undistributed. Let's call this subclass of criminals to which the subject term of this statement refers the class of noncareer criminals. Now notice that the predicate term of this statement refers to *all* career criminals because the statement says that all career criminals are excluded from the class of noncareer criminals. Therefore, the predicate term "career criminals" is distributed.

Exercise Set 8.2

Translate each of the following statements into standard categorical form, state its form, and indicate the distribution of its subject and predicate terms.

8.2.1
"A good marriage would be between a blind wife and a deaf husband." —Honoré de Balzac

8.2.2
"The only time people dislike gossip is when you gossip about them." —Will Rogers

8.2.3
"Most rock journalism is people who can't write, interviewing people who can't talk, for people who can't read." —Frank Zappa

8.2.4
"Nothing happens to any thing which that thing is not made by nature to bear." —Marcus Aurelius

8.2.5
"Few people think more than two or three times a year." —George Bernard Shaw

---

FIVE RULES FOR TESTING THE VALIDITY OF CATEGORICAL SYLLOGISMS

The quantification of terms (whether a term refers to some or all members of a class) is one essential aspect of the formal validity of categorical syllogisms. For example, consider the following syllogism:

Table 8.3

Rule	Fallacy	Example
Rule 1: The syllogism must have exactly three terms each used in the same sense.	Four Terms Fallacy	All pigs have tails. All fascists are pigs. So, all fascists have tails.
Rule 2: The middle term must be distributed in at least one premise.	Fallacy of Undistributed Middle	Some mammals are cows. All humans are mammals. So, some humans are cows.
Rule 3: Whatever term is distributed in the conclusion must also be distributed in the premise in which it appears.	Fallacy of Illicit Distribution	All monkeys are primates. No humans are monkeys. So, no humans are primates.
Rule 4: Between the major premise, minor premise, and conclusion, there must be either no negative statements or exactly two, one of which is in the conclusion.	Faulty Negative Fallacy	No males are females. No women are males. So, no women are females.
Rule 5: The syllogism cannot have a particular conclusion and two universal premises unless the minor premise has existential import.	Existential Fallacy	No pets are mythical creatures. All centaurs are mythical creatures. So, some centaurs are not pets.

Dogs have fleas.
Ike is a dog.
Therefore, Ike has fleas.

The major premise in this argument is ambiguous because it is not clear whether "dogs" is distributed or undistributed. If "dogs" is distributed in the major premise and thus refers to *all* dogs, then the argument is valid. On the other hand, if "dogs" in the major premise is undistributed and therefore refers to only *some* dogs, then the argument is invalid. Therefore, the validity of this syllogism necessarily depends on the distribution of its terms.

Accordingly, any set of rules adequate for testing the validity of categorical syllogisms must take account of distribution. Such a rule base against which to test a categorical syllogism for validity is provided in table 8.3. This table includes the rule, the name of the fallacy committed when the rule in question is violated, and a simple example of a syllogism that commits the fallacy.

FALLACIES IN CATEGORICAL SYLLOGISMS

The Four Terms Fallacy

As you can see from table 8.3, the *four terms fallacy* is committed when the syllogism violates rule 1. One common version of this fallacy is called the *fallacy of equivocation*. This involves using the same term in two different senses. As you can see from the somewhat humorous example, the word "pig" is used in two different senses. In one sense, that in which the term is used in the minor premise, "pig" refers to a gross person. In the sense of the term employed in the major premise, "pig" refers to the farm animal. While this example is blatant, the fallacy can be more subtle and much more dangerous.

The word "terrorist" is a good example of a term that has often been equivocated on in political contexts, sometimes to gain political advantage. Especially since the September 11, 2001, attacks, this term has become associated with non-state-sponsored "terrorism" of the sort propagated by such groups as al-Qaeda, Hamas, and Hezbollah. Consider, for example, the following excerpt from a speech given by President George W. Bush on May 15, 2008, before the Israeli Knesset:[1]

> No one who prays to the God of Abraham could strap a suicide vest to an innocent child, or blow up guiltless guests at a Passover Seder, or fly planes into office buildings filled with unsuspecting workers. In truth, the men who carry out these savage acts serve no higher goal than their own desire for power. They accept no God before themselves. . . . And that is why the founding charter of Hamas calls for the "elimination" of Israel. And that is why the followers of Hezbollah chant, "Death to Israel, Death to America!" That is why Osama bin Laden teaches that "the killing of Jews and Americans is one of the biggest duties." And that is why the president of Iran dreams of returning the Middle East to the Middle Ages and calls for Israel to be wiped off the map. . . . Some seem to believe that we should negotiate with the terrorists and radicals, as if some ingenious argument will persuade them they have been wrong all along. We have heard this foolish delusion before. As Nazi tanks crossed into Poland in 1939, an American senator declared: "Lord, if I could only have talked to Hitler, all this might have been avoided." We have an obligation to call this what it is—the false comfort of appeasement, which has been repeatedly discredited by history. . . . America stands with you in breaking up terrorist networks and denying the extremists sanctuary. America stands with you in firmly opposing Iran's nuclear weapons ambitions.

While Bush did not mention anyone's name in this speech (he stated that "some seem to believe"), his remarks appear to have been aimed at then Democratic presidential candidate hopeful Barack Obama, who had said he would be willing to speak to the president of Iran but had also explicitly denied that he would do the same regarding groups like Hezbollah, Hamas, and al-Qaeda. Bush seems to have wanted his audience to draw the following inference about Obama:

Major premise: All persons who would *negotiate with terrorists* are persons who would negotiate with Hamas, Hezbollah, and al-Qaeda.
Minor premise: Obama is a person who would *negotiate with terrorists*.
Conclusion: Obama is a person who would negotiate with Hamas, Hezbollah, and al-Qaeda.

1. George W. Bush, speech to Israeli Knesset, May 15, 2008. Retrieved online on April 8, 2009, from newsbusters.org/blogs/noel-sheppard/2008/05/15/text-video-president-bushs-speech-israeli-knesset.

But notice that the phrase "negotiate with terrorists" as it appears in the minor premise refers to "negotiating with nations such as Iran," and assuming that the word "terrorists" even applies to Iran in the first place, this is the only possible sense in which Obama was willing to negotiate with terrorists. However, this is not the same sense in which the phrase "negotiate with terrorists" is used in the major premise, for there this term refers to persons who would negotiate with groups such as Hamas, Hezbollah, and al-Qaeda, which, again, Obama had explicitly disavowed.

Equivocations such as this one are subtle. Because Bush did not mention names, it could not be proven that he was drawing any inferences about Obama, and while the press posed the question, Bush's press secretary did not confirm that Bush was referring to Obama. So anyone else (other than Bush) who drew the above inference that Obama supports negotiating with extremist groups like Hamas, Hezbollah, and al-Qaeda will have committed the fallacy of equivocation. This is why, in a free society, we the people must be vigilant in inspecting our inferences before we allow ourselves to be "set up" for fallacious reasoning by government officials or by others who have vested interests in what we believe.[2]

As you can see, committing the four terms fallacy can be a serious mistake. In fact, it has even been behind the murder of innocent people. An instructive example of such a case is the murder of members of the Sikh religion. Sikhs wear beards and turbans and have been confused with persons of Middle Eastern descent, even though they are Indians. On September 15, 2001, four days after the attacks on the World Trade Center in New York City, Balbir Singh, a gas station owner, was shot and killed outside his gas station in Mesa, Arizona. The gunman had mistaken him for a terrorist because of his beard and turban. The logic here is elementary and fatally flawed:

> All Middle Easterners are terrorists.
> Balbir Singh is a person who has a beard and turban.
> Therefore, Balbir Singh is a terrorist.

The major premise is an example of a stereotype that increased in popularity after the 9/11 attacks. A stereotype is a kind of fallacious thinking involving the oversimplification of reality. Stereotypes are discussed in chapter 9. However, there is obviously more wrong with this argument than its blatant stereotype (not to mention the vagueness of the word "terrorist" in the major premise). The stereotype in the major premise means that the argument cannot be sound because one of its premises is not acceptable.

But, clearly, the argument is also invalid, for it has four terms, whereas validity requires three. "Middle Easterners" is not the same as "persons who have beards and turbans." Regretfully, this four terms fallacy and conceptual muddle appears

---

2. It is noteworthy that any implicit comparison Bush made between attempting to negotiate with Iran and negotiating with the Nazis was a false one. At the time Bush made the comparison, the latest national intelligence estimate had maintained with a high degree of probability that Iran had discontinued its nuclear weapons program in 2005 and therefore posed no immediate threat to American national security. Bush fails even to address this point.

to have been responsible for over seven hundred further crimes (including other murders and attempted murders) since the murder of Balbir Singh.[3]

Fallacy of Undistributed Middle Term

As you can see from table 8.3, this fallacy is committed when the syllogism in question violates rule 2, which requires that the middle term be distributed in at least one of the premises. As discussed earlier in this chapter, a term is said to be distributed when it refers to all members of the class in question; it is undistributed when it refers to just *some* members. For instance, consider the example provided in table 8.3:

Some mammals are cows.
All humans are mammals.
So, some humans are cows.

The middle term here is "mammals," which is undistributed in both major and minor premises. As a result, these premises only refer to some mammals. The major premise refers to cows, which are mammals, and the minor premise refers to humans, which are also mammals. But, obviously, the conclusion is invalid because the middle term in each of its occurrences refers to distinct classes of mammals but never to *all* mammals. For example, the syllogism would indeed be valid (but needless to say not sound) if the major premise said that *all* mammals are cows.

One popular version of this fallacy is committed when it is concluded that because two distinct classes are included in a broader class, one of these classes must be included in the other. This version of the fallacy takes the following form:

All P is M.
All S is M.
Therefore, all S is P.

Notice that the middle term (M) is undistributed in both of its occurrences. This is because it is the predicate term of an A-form statement in both premises, and the predicate term of an A-form statement is always undistributed. Therefore, any argument of this form commits the fallacy of undistributed middle and is therefore invalid.

For example, on October 8, 2007, the popular mainstream media pundit Ann Coulter appeared on CNBC's *The Big Idea* hosted by Donny Deutsch, who happens to be Jewish. The topic of her interview was her vision of a "perfect" America. At one point, she said that Jews would be Christian in such an America. She stated, "Jews need to be perfected." "We should all be Christian?" asked Deutsch. "Yes," responded Coulter. "It's a lot easier. It's a kind of fast track. . . . You have to obey." She went on to say,

---

3. "The Turban Question," Global Wire, April 20, 2008. Retrieved on May 18, 2008, from globalwire.blogspot.com/2008/04/turban-question.html.

Do you know what Christianity is? We believe your religion, but you have to obey.
. . . We just want Jews to be perfected, as they say. . . . That is what Christianity is. We
believe the Old Testament, but ours is more like Federal Express. You have to obey
laws. We know we're all sinners. . . . That is what Christians consider themselves:
perfected Jews. We believe the Old Testament. As you know from the Old Testament,
God was constantly getting fed up with humans for not being able to, you know, live
up to all the laws. What Christians believe—this is just a statement of what the New
Testament is—is that that's why Christ came and died for our sins. Christians believe
the Old Testament. You don't believe our testament. . . . This is what Christians consider themselves, because our testament is the continuation of your testament.

According to Coulter, what makes Christians *perfected* Jews is the fact that they
subscribe to the New Testament, which, for Christians, is the final word of God.
Coulter, therefore, accepts the idea that Christians are a kind of Jew, albeit "perfected." Thus, according to Coulter, whether one is a Christian or Jew is purely
a matter of which bible one follows, but since Christians still follow the Old
Testament, they are still also Jews. She therefore appears to accept the following
argument:

> All Jews are followers of the Old Testament.
> All Christians are followers of the Old Testament.
> Therefore, all Christians are Jews.

Indeed, this argument appears to be the basis for her argument that Christians are
"perfected" Jews since they would have to be Jews before they could be perfected
Jews. But notice that the middle term, which is "Old Testament," is undistributed
in both premises. Just because Christians and Jews both subscribe to the Old
Testament does not mean that Christians are Jews or, conversely, that Jews are
Christians.[4] In fact, while Coulter views Christianity as a "Federal Express" to
salvation, Jews, she says, "have to obey laws." Coulter's idea of Christianity is
thus at odds, and therefore appears to be inconsistent, with what she says the Old
Testament and Judaism require.

Coulter's argument is not in kind different from the statement that since all
Muslims have a bible, and all Christians have a bible, all Christians must therefore be Muslims. On this logic, we might even say that Muslims are "perfected"
Christians since they believe that their bible (the Qur'an) is the correct interpretation of Jesus's teachings. But this logic is flawed because it commits the fallacy of
undistributed middle term.

This fallacy is often at the root of personal attacks on a disfavored group. For
example, versions of this argument were in vogue during the 1960s:

> All pot-smoking, free-sex hippies are peaceniks.
> Most students are peaceniks.
> Most students are pot-smoking, free-sex hippies.

---

4. In fact, in a footnote in her book *Godless: The Church of Liberalism*, she states, "Throughout this
book I often refer to Christian and Christianity . . . but the term is intended to include anyone who
subscribes to the Bible of the God of Abraham, including Jews and others." This flawed logic suggests
that she would also call all Jews Christians.

It didn't matter that the thousands of students protesting the Vietnam War had legitimate reasons for doing so, not the least of which was the fact that the war was based on the false premise that "the communists would come here" unless we stopped them in Southeast Asia.

Ann Coulter is also well-known for her negative attacks on so-called liberals. For example, in an article titled "Liberalism and Terrorism: Two States of the Same Disease," Coulter states,

> No matter what defeatist tack liberals take, real Americans are behind our troops 100 percent, behind John Ashcroft 100 percent, behind locking up suspected terrorists 100 percent, behind surveillance of Arabs 100 percent. Liberals become indignant when you question their patriotism, but simultaneously work overtime to give terrorists a cushion for the next attack and laugh at dumb Americans who love their country and hate the enemy. . . . In this war [the Iraq War], those who cannot stay focused on fighting the enemy are objectively "pro-terrorist."[5]

Here is Coulter's argument cast in standard categorical form:

> Pro-terrorists are persons who cannot stay focused on fighting the enemy.[6]
> Liberals are persons who cannot stay focused on fighting the enemy.
> Therefore, liberals are pro-terrorists.

Among the liberals whom Coulter says cannot stay focused on fighting the enemy, she mentions Senator Patrick Leahy (D-VT), whom she calls "Sen. Patrick Do-Nothing Leahy." If Leahy's fault, in Coulter's estimation, were failure to act, this would make Leahy inept but not "pro-terrorist," for to be "pro-terrorist" means having a favorable attitude toward terrorists. But Coulter provides no empirical evidence that this senator harbored such an attitude.

Even if it is true that both liberals and pro-terrorists do not (or "cannot") stay focused on fighting "the enemy," that does not make liberals pro-terrorists or pro-terrorists liberals. To try to claim this is again to commit the fallacy of undistributed middle.

Fallacy of Illicit Distribution

As you can see from table 8.3, this fallacy is committed when the syllogism in question violates rule 3, which requires that whatever term is distributed in the conclusion be distributed in the premise. For instance, consider the example provided in table 8.3:

> All monkeys are primates.
> No humans are monkeys.
> So, no humans are primates.

5. Ann Coulter, "Liberalism and Terrorism: Different Stages of the Same Disease," Worldnet Daily, July 3, 2002. Retrieved online on April 8, 2009, from www.worldnetdaily.com/news/article.asp?ARTICLE_ID=28177.

6. The argument could be made valid by converting this major premise so that it reads "All persons who cannot stay focused on fighting the enemy are pro-terrorists," but then this premise would be false, and the argument would therefore be unsound.

Here, the major term "primates" is distributed in the conclusion but not in the major premise. This means that the conclusion is saying something about *all* primates while the major premise is saying something about only some primates—namely those that are monkeys. Indeed, the fact that all humans are excluded from the class of monkeys does not necessarily mean that they must be excluded from the class of *all* primates. The conclusion of this syllogism is therefore invalid.

Illicit distribution may also occur in the minor term of the conclusion. For example, consider the following syllogism:

No giraffes are humans.
All giraffes are animals.
Therefore, no animals are humans.

Notice that the minor term, namely "animals," is distributed in the conclusion but not in the minor premise. Clearly, the minor premise is talking about only some animals, namely giraffes, whereas the conclusion is talking about *all* animals— that is, it says that all animals are excluded from the class of humans.

Now, let's take a look at an example of how the fallacy of illicit distribution can be committed in an ordinary language context. On December 6, 2005, Kirk Caraway, Internet editor of the *Nevada Appeal*, published a provocative editorial titled "If It's Not Torture, Then It's OK to Use It on Cheney." Here are some excerpts:

"We do not torture."
   That's what President George W. Bush said, and we can believe him, right? After all, that whole water boarding thing is just a walk in the park. . . . Here is how CIA sources described this technique to ABC News: "The prisoner is bound to an inclined board, feet raised and head slightly below the feet. Cellophane is wrapped over the prisoner's face and water is poured over him. Unavoidably, the gag reflex kicks in and a terrifying fear of drowning leads to almost instant pleas to bring the treatment to a halt."
   Perhaps the Justice Department could use this to speed up some investigations that are taking forever. How about that two-year investigation into who leaked Valerie Plame's CIA status? Stick Karl Rove on the water board and we can see who really leaked what in just a couple of minutes. *That would be fair, wouldn't it? After all, his boss says it's not torture, right?* And how about this whole question about whether we were lied into the war in Iraq. I bet Dick Cheney would have the answer for that one. . . . Just for fun, we could strap Bill Clinton to the water board and find out a whole lot on what happened during his term in the White House. . . . Think of all the situations this could be used for. Hook up Tom DeLay, see if he really did break Texas campaign laws. Get the Halliburton executives in there and ask what happened to all our money. Stick O. J. Simpson on the water board and find out if he killed his ex-wife. Remember, it's not torture. Bush says so. (Emphasis added)[7]

Clearly, Caraway is attempting to reduce to the absurd President Bush's claim that "We do not torture," despite the fact that under his administration at least three individuals had been waterboarded.[8] Presumably, he does not truly believe

---

7. Kirk Caraway, "If It's Not Torture, Then It's OK to Use It on Cheney," Common Dreams.org, December 6, 2005. Retrieved online on April 9, 2009, from www.commondreams.org/views05/1206-29 .htm.
8. See also chapter 3 for discussion of waterboarding.

that Dick Cheney, Bill Clinton, Karl Rove, Tom Delay, and O. J. Simpson should be waterboarded. He is attempting to prove that once we accept that waterboarding is not torture, it is not unfair to apply it freely. Cast in standard form, the basic syllogism is as follows:

All torture is unfair treatment.[9]
No waterboarding is torture.
Therefore, no waterboarding is unfair treatment.

As you can see, the major term, namely "unfair treatment," is distributed in the conclusion but not in the major premise, which means that the syllogism commits the fallacy of illicit distribution. Indeed, even if it is given that waterboarding is not torture, that does exclude it from *all* unfair treatment.

For example, it has sometimes been claimed that waterboarding is not torture because torture necessarily causes severe physical pain, whereas waterboarding only occasions extreme fear.[10] It has also sometimes been claimed that torture must cause lasting physical damage, whereas waterboarding does not do this.[11] However, even if these claims are accepted, this does not mean that waterboarding is not an unfair kind of treatment. Thus, it may still be unfair to occasion extreme fear in someone or to provoke emotional trauma, even if this does not have any lasting bodily consequences. The mere fact (if, indeed, it is a fact) that waterboarding does not constitute torture in these said ways does not mean that it is excluded from all other egregious or unfair forms of treatment. Therefore, the conclusion of Caraway's argument does not follow from its premises because these premises talk only about some kinds of unfair treatment (namely torture), whereas the conclusion makes a claim about *all* kinds of unfair treatment.

The failure of Caraway's argument is nevertheless instructive. Much of the debate about whether waterboarding is really torture may have skated across the point that even if it is not, it can still be unfair treatment. Article 3 of the Geneva Conventions, which establishes international conventions for the "protection of victims of war," forbids not only torture but also "outrages on personal dignity, in particular, humiliating and degrading treatment" as well as "cruel treatment."[12] Even *if* waterboarding is not torture, it would be a stretch to deny that it is humiliating, degrading, or cruel.

Faulty Negative Fallacy

As you can see from table 8.3, this fallacy is committed when the syllogism in question violates rule 4, which states the conditions for the use of negative statements in categorical syllogisms. It says that in a valid syllogism, as between its

9. This major premise is assumed rather than explicitly stated, but it seems clear that the point of the claim "We don't torture" is to convey that torturing someone would be wrong.
10. Serge Wing, "Waterboarding Doesn't Fit Torture's Severe Pain Criteria," *USA Today*. Retrieved online on May 22, 2008, from http://blogs.usatoday.com/oped/2007/11/waterboarding-d.html.
11. Joseph Farah, "Waterboarding Is Not Torture," *Worldnet Daily*, May 22, 2008. Retrieved online on May 22, 2008, from www.worldnetdaily.com/news/article.asp?ARTICLE_ID=59481.
12. Article 3 of the Geneva Conventions (1949). Retrieved online on May 22, 2008, from www.unhchr.ch/html/menu3/b/91.htm.

major premise, minor premise, and conclusion, there can be either no statements with *negative quality* or exactly two, one of which must be in the conclusion. For instance, consider the example provided in table 8.3:

> No males are females.
> No women are males.
> So, no women are females.

This syllogism violates rule 4 and thus commits the faulty negative fallacy because it consists of three negative statements—namely three E-form statements comprising both the major and minor premises and the conclusion. Indeed, just because women are excluded from males, and males from females, it does not follow that women are excluded from females.

In one common version of this fallacy, there are two exclusive (negative) premises and an affirmative conclusion. Consider, for example, the following question posted to Yahoo! Answers:

> If you're not a Christian would you have no problem lying in court after swearing with your hand on the bible?
> I was just thinking since not everyone who takes the stand in court is a Christian, the people who put their hands on the bibles and swear to tell the truth, if they don't follow and believe in Christian teachings and history, then wouldn't they have no problem lying in the courtroom since the bible and Christ mean nothing to them?[13]

Cast in standard categorical form, the argument that perplexes this questioner appears to be as follows:

> No believers in the teachings of the Bible/Christ are persons who would lie under oath.
> No non-Christians are believers in the teachings of the Bible/Christ.
> Therefore, all non-Christians are persons who would lie under oath.

As you can see, this argument commits the faulty negative fallacy because it has two negative (E-form) premises and an affirmative (A-form) conclusion. Indeed, just because no non-Christians are believers in the teachings of the Bible/ Christ does not mean that they would lie under oath, *even if* it is supposed that no believers would so lie. For example, the nonbeliever could be an atheist with a strong conviction in the immorality of lying under oath. Or, the nonbeliever could be a Jew, a Buddhist, a Hindu, or a member of another religious group that also teaches against lying. Or, the nonbeliever could simply be afraid to be caught in a lie and therefore risk being charged with the crime of perjury (lying under oath).

On the Yahoo! Answers website, visitors are given the opportunity to respond to the questions that are posed, and the one posing the question ("the Asker") is then allowed to choose what he or she believes to be the "best answer" to

---

13. "If You're Not a Christian Would You Have No Problem Lying in Court after Swearing with Your Hand on the Bible?" Yahoo! Answers. Retrieved online on April 8, 2009, from answers.yahoo .com/question/index?qid=20080516204323AAHFrJe.

the question he or she has posed. Here is the answer that the Asker in this case choose:

> Best Answer—Chosen by Asker
> I know a so called "Christian" that placed his hand on the Bible to get his son out of jail and it was a lie. I was there in court. This man goes to church every Sunday and pretends to be a Christian singing and praying in church. So I don't think anybody has a problem lying when it comes to getting what they want. Christian or not.

As you can see, neither the Asker nor the person who gave this answer ("the Answerer") realized that the argument was invalid to begin with. Instead the Answerer attempted to show that the major premise of the Asker's argument was false by giving an example of a Christian who lied under oath. But the truth of this premise did not matter because the argument was invalid. So what was truly the best answer to the Asker's query? Just this: From the fact that non-Christians do not believe the teachings of the Bible/Christ, it does not follow that they would lie under oath, even if you assume that Christians would never lie under oath.

Existential Fallacy

As you can see from table 8.3, this fallacy is committed when the syllogism in question violates rule 5, which states that the syllogism cannot have a particular conclusion and two universal premises *unless the minor premise has existential import*. This proviso about existential import is important. Without it, many sound arguments would need to be called invalid. For example, consider the following syllogism,

> *Syllogism A:*
> All mammals are mortal.
> All porpoises are mammals.
> Therefore, some porpoises are mortal.

In syllogism A, both premises are universal, and the conclusion is particular. However, since the subject term "porpoises" in the minor premise can be assumed to have members, the particular statement in the conclusion, which also entails the existence of porpoises, can be validly deduced.

In contrast, consider the example given in table 8.3, where the conclusion has existential import but the minor premise does not:

> *Syllogism B:*
> No pets are mythical creatures.
> All centaurs are mythical creatures.
> So, some centaurs are not pets.

Notice that in syllogism B, the minor premise talks about "centaurs" (creatures in Greek mythology with the head, arms, and torso of a man and the body and legs of a horse), which is obviously an empty class. Therefore, the particular conclusion "Some centaurs are not pets" cannot validly be deduced because it implies the existence of centaurs, whereas the minor premise does not.

Rule 5 is intended to invalidate arguments with particular conclusions like syllogism B that have two universal premises and a minor premise with no existential import. In contrast, rule 5 permits arguments with particular conclusions like syllogism A that have two universal premises and a minor premise that does have existential import.

As discussed in chapter 6, determining whether existential import can be ascribed to a statement can be contentious. One example includes statements about evolution and, consequently, inferences made from them. While evolutionists think that there are actual instances of evolutionary processes in which one species evolves into another, many nonevolutionists, including creationists, believe that this class of evolutionary processes is empty, or at least that there is no convincing evidence for the existence of instances of evolution. Consider, for example, the following popular argument advanced by some nonevolutionists:

> Despite the bright promise that paleontology provides a means of "seeing" evolution, it has presented some nasty difficulties for evolutionists the most notorious of which is the presence of "gaps" in the fossil record. Evolution requires intermediate forms between species and paleontology does not provide them. The gaps must therefore be a contingent feature of the record.[14]

This argument can be cast as a valid standard form categorical syllogism as follows:

> No process having intermediate species is a process proven by paleontology.
> All evolution is a process having intermediate species.
> Therefore, no evolution is a process proven by paleontology.

Clearly, the author of this argument does not intend to give existential import to the minor premise in this syllogism because he is not committed to the existence of evolution. In fact, the point of the argument is to show that no instances of evolution have been proven by paleontology. Therefore, no particular statements entailing the existence of evolution can be validly deduced from the premises in this argument.

In contrast, consider the following rebuttal to the above argument advanced by the National Academy of Sciences (NAS):

> Creationists argue that the theory of evolution is faulty because of gaps in the fossil record (creationists identify as gaps those situations where intermediate fossil forms between two related species are as yet undiscovered). But an increasing number of intermediate forms have been and continue to be found. . . .
>
> Evolutionary theory predicts that there would be one or more creatures with characteristics of both the ancient fish and the later land-dwellers. A team of scientists decided to look in sedimentary rock in northern Canada that was deposited about 375 million years ago, about the time these intermediate species were thought to have lived, based on other evidence from the fossil record. In 2004, the team found what they had predicted: the fossil of a creature with features of fish (scales and fins) and

---

14. David B. Kitts, "Paleontology and Evolutionary Theory," *Evolution* 28 (1974): 467. Retrieved online on May 27, 2008, from www.anointed-one.net/quotes.html.

features of land-dwellers (simple lungs, flexible neck, and fins modified to support its weight). The bones in the limbs of this fossil, named *Tiktaalik*, resemble the bones in the limbs of land-dwelling animals today.[15]

Accordingly, here is a standard form categorical syllogism that the NAS seems to accept as a rebuttal to the nonevolutionist/creationist argument:

> All fossils of intermediate species are proof of evolution.
> All *Tiktaalik* fossils are fossils of intermediate species.
> Therefore, all *Tiktaalik* fossils are proof of evolution.

Clearly, the NAS takes the subject term "*Tiktaalik* fossils" to refer to a class with members inasmuch as it believes that scientists have actually discovered the fossils they have so named. Therefore, for the NAS, the minor premise of the above argument has existential import and would therefore support a particular conclusion. Thus, the NAS would apparently also accept the following argument:

> All fossils of intermediate species are proof of evolution.
> All *Tiktaalik* fossils are fossils of intermediate species.
> Therefore, some *Tiktaalik* fossils are proof of evolution.

This syllogism is valid if the class of *Tiktaalik* fossils is assumed to have members. Given this assumption, the minor premise has existential import and in turn commits us to the existence of fossils of intermediate species, which would mean that intermediate species did in fact roam the earth at one time (according to the NAS, about 375 million years ago).

In this regard, consider this teaser:

> When the assumed evolutionary processes did not match the pattern of fossils that they were supposed to have generated, the pattern was judged to be "wrong." A circular argument arises: interpret the fossil record in terms of a particular theory of evolution, inspect the interpretation, and note that it confirms the theory. Well, it would, wouldn't it?[16]

Do evolutionists engage in such intellectual cheating or card stacking by interpreting the fossil record (for example, *Tiktaalik* fossils) as fossils of intermediate species in order to prove that the theory of evolution is correct? Evolutionists, of course, would deny this accusation. For example, as the NAS noted, the scientists who discovered the *Tiktaalik* fossils used the theory of evolution along with prior fossil records to predict the finding of a creature with features of both fish and land dwellers. This is where *inductive* logic comes in—namely at the level of lending *probability* to an interpretation of reality—in this case that *Tiktaalik* fossils signify intermediary species in a gradual evolution from fish to land dwellers. In the next chapters we will examine inductive logic.

---

15. National Academy of Sciences, *Science, Evolution, and Creationism*, 2008. Adapted from full-length version. Retrieved online on May 27, 2008, from books.nap.edu/html/11876/SECbrochure.pdf.
16. Tom S. Kemp, "A Fresh Look at the Fossil Record," *New Scientist* 108 (1985): 66–67. Retrieved online on May 27, 2008, from www.anointed-one.net/quotes.html.

Exercise Set 8.3

Using the five rules discussed in this chapter, determine whether each of the following categorical syllogisms is valid or invalid. If it is invalid, state the fallacy it commits.

8.3.1
No gay people are heterosexuals.
All homophobes are gay people.
Therefore, some homophobes are not heterosexuals.

8.3.2
No fictional villains in the Batman movies who endanger the residents of Gotham City are characters who make good role models.
All characters identical with the Joker are fictional villains in the Batman movies who endanger the residents of Gotham City.
Therefore, some characters identical with the Joker are not characters who make good role models.

8.3.3
All valid syllogisms are syllogisms that are free of formal fallacies.
No invalid syllogism is a valid syllogism.
Therefore, no invalid syllogisms are syllogisms that are free of formal fallacies.

8.3.4
All unmarried men are bachelors.
All bachelors are single men.
Therefore, all single men are unmarried men.

8.3.5
Some nurses are nurse practitioners.
All registered nurses are nurses.
Therefore, all registered nurses are nurse practitioners.

8.3.6
No acts of gender discrimination are legal acts.
All acts of sexual harassment are acts of gender discrimination.
Therefore, no acts of sexual harassment are legal acts.

8.3.7
All cases of lying under oath are cases of perjury.
All cases of saying something false under oath are cases of not telling the truth under oath.
Therefore, all cases of saying something false under oath are cases of perjury.

8.3.8
All physicians are medical practitioners.
All psychiatrists are medical practitioners.
Therefore, all psychiatrists are physicians.

8.3.9
No poor people are millionaires.
No corporate CEOs are poor people.
Therefore, all corporate CEOs are millionaires.

8.3.10
All space aliens are creatures from another planet.
All Martians are space aliens.
Therefore, all Martians are creatures from another planet.

FORMULATING AND ASSESSING CATEGORICAL SYLLOGISMS IN ORDINARY LANGUAGE: THE CASE FOR "ALL WARS ARE CIVIL WARS"

Categorical syllogisms do not typically come "set up" and ready to evaluate. Like other arguments in ordinary language, they are often *enthymematic*.[17] That is, some parts are explicitly stated, while others are assumed. Consider, for example, the following argument about the nature of war, which was advanced by François Fénelon, a seventeenth-century French Roman Catholic priest and archbishop:

> All wars are civil wars, because all men are brothers. . . . Each one owes infinitely more to the human race than to the particular country in which he was born.

The conclusion of this argument is clearly the A-form statement "All wars are civil wars." The word "wars" is the minor term (S), and "civil wars" is the major term (P). This means that the word "war" will be one of the terms of the minor premise, and that "civil wars" will be one of the terms of the major premise. So, in order to construct the complete categorical syllogism, we need to find the middle term (M), which will provide the other term of both the major and minor premises.

Fénelon defends his conclusion that all wars are civil wars by *explicitly* stating just one premise, namely, that *all men are brothers*. Now, given that Fénelon intends this premise to apply to warfare, he seems to be saying that all wars fought by men are wars fought by brothers. Presumably he is also *assuming*, but not explicitly stating, that all wars are fought by men, from which it now follows that all wars are fought by brothers. More formally laid out, here is at least part of Fénelon's thinking in categorical form:

> *Major premise:* All wars fought by men are wars fought by brothers.
> *Minor premise:* All wars are wars fought by men.
> *Conclusion:* All wars are wars fought by brothers.

Since this syllogism satisfies all five rules for testing validity, it is valid. The conclusion of this syllogism brings into clearer focus Fénelon's rationale for his conclusion that all wars are civil wars. All wars are civil wars because they are fought by brothers:

> All wars are wars fought by brothers.
> Therefore, all wars are civil wars.

However, as you can see, the major premise is missing from this syllogism. The premise "All wars are wars fought by brothers" is clearly the minor premise because it contains the minor term "wars." But it is now possible to formulate the major premise because it is the premise containing the major term and the middle term, and we now know what both of these terms are. The major term is "civil wars" because this term is the predicate of the conclusion. The middle term is "wars fought by brothers" because we know that the middle term is contained in both premises but not the conclusion, and "wars fought by brothers" is in the

---

17. See chapter 3 for a discussion of enthymemes in hypothetical syllogisms.

minor premise but not in the conclusion. So we now know that the missing major premise contains the terms "wars fought by brothers" and "civil wars." Moreover, if Fénelon's argument is to succeed, this missing premise must at least make the argument valid. The question of whether the argument is sound (that is, whether all the premises are true) would then still be an open question.

When supplying an argument's missing premise, and the author has not given any reason to do differently, it is sound policy to supply the premise that *validates* the argument. Otherwise, you will end up attacking a straw man—that is, deliberately setting the argument up in such a way that allows you to defeat it, blowing it over as though it were made of straw. This is not intellectually honest, nor does it advance the goals of knowledge and pedagogy.

Accordingly, here is Fénelon's argument, including the major premise that validates the argument:

> *Major premise:* All wars fought by brothers are civil wars.
> *Minor premise:* All wars are wars fought by brothers.
> *Conclusion:* All wars are civil wars.

Since this argument satisfies all five rules for testing the validity of categorical syllogisms, it is valid. Notice that if the order of the terms in the major premise were reversed so that "wars fought by brothers" was the predicate term and "civil wars" was the subject term, the argument would commit the fallacy of undistributed middle and therefore be invalid. But the author has not given us any reason to interpret his major premise in this manner so as to invalidate his argument.

Given the validity of the argument as presented, the next step in the assessment process is to check for soundness—that is, to examine the premises to see if they are true. Recall that Fénelon said, "Each one owes infinitely more to the human race than to the particular country in which he was born." This expresses the idea that human beings have a common bond and kinship that transcends national boundaries and to which we all owe our allegiance. Eighteenth-century philosopher Immanuel Kant expressed a related idea when he stated that all human beings belong to the same "community of ends," which enjoins respect for the individual dignity of our fellow citizens of this world community.

Are all wars, then, really wars fought by brothers, as Fénelon suggests? When viewed in this light, this premise has a point. Fénelon's views on the brotherhood of humankind were inspired and infused by his religiosity and belief in the human potential for spiritual unity with God, but as Kant's secular stance reveals, the idea of a bond of solidarity between human beings as such is not necessarily tied to God or religion.

In *An Enquiry Concerning the Principles of Morals*, agnostic philosopher David Hume emphasized the grounds of morality in sympathy for others, stating,

> No qualities are more entitled to the general good will and approbation of mankind than beneficence and humanity, friendship and gratitude, natural affection and public spirit, or whatever proceeds from a tender sympathy with others and a generous concern for our kind and species.[18]

---

18. David Hume, *An Enquiry concerning the Principles of Morals*, sec. 2, pt. 1, retrieved June 15, 2009, from www.gutenberg.org/dirs/etext03/nqpmr10.txt.

For Hume, this feeling of "tender sympathy with others" and "generous concern for our kind and species" sets the grounds of all other human virtues. For him, it is this caring for other human beings that cultivates friendship, leads us to help others in time of need, makes us appreciative of the goodwill of others, promotes love, and nullifies narrow self-interest in favor of public concern.

In contrast, basic military training attempts to break down such human regard and to recast the other as the enemy and as less than human. Seen from this angle, war is indeed the turning away, indeed the dehumanization, of one's fellow human beings, of one's brothers—and sisters.

Of course, from a narrower biogenetic perspective, human beings of different ancestry are not to be called one's brothers and sisters. Still, for Fénelon (as for Kant), these are only accidental, nonessential features of humankind, which is instead bound by a common human heritage that transcends variables such as culture, gender, race, religion, ethnic origin, and even sexual preference. It is at this juncture that logic must rest its case on the question of whether Fénelon has presented a sound argument.

Exercise Set 8.4

Translate each of the following arguments into a standard form categorical syllogism and determine its validity. If you think that it is invalid, then state the name of the fallacy it commits.

8.4.1
No fruits and vegetables grown with conventional pesticides are healthy, but organic fruits and vegetables are not grown with conventional pesticides. Therefore, organic foods are healthy.

8.4.2
All fish that contain high levels of mercury are unsafe to eat, but wild Alaskan salmon does not contain high levels of mercury. Therefore, wild Alaskan salmon is not unsafe to eat.

8.4.3
Fruits and vegetables imported from Mexico and Guatemala are sometimes contaminated with human feces. However, some fruits and vegetables contaminated with human feces have been linked to typhoid fever. So, some fruits and vegetables imported from Mexico and Guatemala have been linked to typhoid fever.

8.4.4
All socialists believe in a democratic government; however, since all Democrats believe in taxing the wealthy while reducing the tax burden for the middle class, it follows that all socialists are Democrats.

8.4.5
All Democrats are opposed to giving special tax breaks to the wealthy, but since all communists are also opposed to giving such tax breaks to the wealthy, it follows that all Democrats are communists.

8.4.6
No free-market capitalists are communists. However, all libertarians are free-market capitalists. Therefore, libertarians cannot be communists.

8.4.7

Militaristic governments have always emphasized defense spending over education, health care, and the needs of the poor. Since all Republican administrations are militaristic governments, it follows that some Republican administrations are militaristic governments.

8.4.8

All Jehovah's Witnesses reject blood transfusions, and since anyone who rejects medical treatment has no business seeking medical attention at a hospital, all Jehovah's Witnesses have no business seeking medical attention at a hospital.

8.4.9

No creature that can only be killed with a silver bullet through the heart can be human. All werewolves can only be killed with a silver bullet through the heart. Quite obviously, therefore, at least some werewolves cannot be human.

8.4.10

Any laws that permit racial profiling violate the equal protection clause of the Fourteenth Amendment to the U.S. Constitution. A few laws that permit racial profiling target Middle Easterners. Therefore, some laws that target Middle Easterners violate the equal protection clause of the Fourteenth Amendment to the U.S. Constitution.

Exercise Set 8.5

Set each of the following arguments up as a standard form categorical syllogism, and briefly discuss its validity and soundness.

8.5.1

"I cannot conceive of a God without the property of existence. Therefore, God exists." —Rene Descartes[1]

8.5.2

"Things which lack knowledge, such as natural bodies, act for an end. . . . Now whatever lacks knowledge cannot move toward an end, unless it be directed by some being endowed with knowledge and intelligence. . . . Therefore, some intelligent being exists by whom all natural things are directed to their end; and this being we call God." —St. Thomas Aquinas, *Summa Theologica*

8.5.3

"It is sufficient that I am able clearly and distinctly to conceive one thing apart from another, in order to be certain that the one is different from the other. . . . On the one hand, I have a clear and distinct idea of myself, insofar as I am only a thinking and unextended thing, and as on the other hand, I possess a distinct idea of body, in so far as it is only an extended and unthinking thing, it is certain that I am entirely and truly distinct from my body, and may exist without it." —Rene Descartes, *Meditation VI*

(*continued*)

---

1. This is Robert Solomon's translation of Descartes' version of St. Anselm's ontological argument for God's existence, which Descartes presents in his *Meditation III*. See Robert C. Solomon, *Philosophy: Problems and Perspectives* (New York: Harcourt Brace, 1977), 217.

8.5.4

"An idea is always a generalization, and generalization is a property of thinking. To generalize means to think." —Georg Wilhelm Friedrich Hegel

8.5.5

"Any group with Arab in its name has GOT to have SOMETHING to do with terrorism, right? Therefore . . . [because] Obama knows someone who . . . is in any way affiliated with any organization with Arab in its name, why that just proves that he is connected with terrorism—or worse!" —Blogger[2]

8.5.6

"Since all knowledge comes from sensory impressions and since there's no sensory impression of substance itself, it follows logically that there is no knowledge of substance." —Robert M. Pirsig, *Zen and the Art of Motorcycle Maintenance*

8.5.7

"If then virtue is an attribute of the spirit, and one which cannot fail to be beneficial, it must be wisdom; for all spiritual qualities in and by themselves are neither advantageous nor harmful, but become advantageous or harmful by the presence with them of wisdom or folly. If we accept this argument, then virtue, to be something advantageous, must be a sort of wisdom." —Socrates, *Meno*

8.5.8

"Death is nothing to us; for what has been dissolved has no sensation, and what has no sensation is nothing to us." —Epicurus, *Principal Doctrines*

8.5.9

"And, indeed, it is plain that no conceivable observation, or series of observations, could have any tendency to show that the world revealed to us by sense-experience was unreal. Consequently, anyone who condemns the sensible world as a world of mere appearance, as opposed to reality, is saying something which . . . is literally nonsensical." —Alfred Jules Ayer, *Language, Truth and Logic*.

8.5.10

"The moral vacuity of dogmatic libertarianism is poisonous to public life. By teaching that 'greed is good,' strict free-market ideology holds out the promise that private vices can be public virtues." —Benjamin Storey and Jenna Silber Storey, *Weekly Standard*, January 24, 2008

8.5.11

"The fact is that by definition, marriage is the union between one man and one woman, because men and women are the only categories of human beings that can bring forth the next generation. Limiting marriage to one man and one woman cannot, therefore, be construed to be discriminatory. It is a necessary condition for marriage." —Pastor Errol Naidoo, *Behind the Mask*

8.5.12

"So if only Christians have a moral compass, wouldn't non-Christian nations fall into a pit of immorality?

People love to argue that Atheists and Eastern belief systems have no moral compass. And that Christianity seems to be the only way to develop this moral compass.

---

2. This blogger is actually attacking this type of "guilt by association" argument made by some during the 2008 presidential race to try to connect then presidential candidate Barack Obama with terrorism. See blog entries on "No Quarter." Retrieved online on November 1, 2008, from www.noquarterusa.net/blog/2008/10/10/obamas-terrorist-ties.

So with that said, shouldn't places like Asia where there is less than a 1% Christian population be devoid of morals? And things like Buddhism be full of evil and immoral codes?" —Blogger

8.5.13
"Liberals are traitors—at least the self-conscious ones are. And it is not because they hate Bush or disagree with the Iraq war. Their treason stems from their behavior—from the way they go around telling everyone that they hate Bush and disagree with the war—even to the extent that they sympathize with and give material aid to the enemy." —Posting, "Liberals are Traitors," EclectEcon.com. Retrieved online on April 21, 2009, from www.eclectecon .com/posts/1188437538.shtml.

9

Generalization

So far we have examined deductive reasoning. It is now time to turn to a careful inspection of *inductive* reasoning. Inductive reasoning is the chief supplier of the content (premises) of deductive reasoning. It typically puts the flesh on the bare bones of a valid deductive form. In (valid) deductive reasoning, the conclusion necessarily follows from the premises, while in inductive reasoning, the conclusion follows from the premises with probability.

INDUCTION AS PROBABILISTIC REASONING

Probability is itself an estimate of how possible some event or state of affairs is. It is sometimes possible to calculate this rating of possibility mathematically. For example, without knowing anything else about a coin or the circumstances under which it will be tossed, the probability of coming up heads on a single toss is 50 percent because there are only two possibilities (heads or tails), each of which is assumed to be equally possible.

Mathematical probability ratings can go beyond the flip of a coin, the role of a die, and the dealing of cards and enter into practical life decisions. For example, it is possible to calculate the risks of a certain kind of surgery based on the outcomes of past cases. Pragmatically, mathematical ratings tell you how reasonable it is to believe in a certain outcome when you know nothing else that distinguishes your particular case from others. For example, your case of surgery may be complicated by other factors (such as other illnesses) that might present other risk factors not taken into account in previous studies. In the end, assessments of probability in practical life situations often involve factors that cannot easily be quantified and assigned mathematical values—for example, your level of confidence in a physician as based not only on his or her past track record and training but on your personal assessment of the physician's beside manner and your ability to work successfully with this individual in confronting your health problem.

155

Chapter 9

THE DEFEASIBILITY OF INDUCTION

A statement is always more or less probable *in relation to the evidence provided by a set of premises.* Probability assessments always involve an inference from a set of premises, and this probability can increase or decrease depending upon what evidence is provided in these premises.

This raises an important difference between inductive and deductive inferences. Inductive inferences are *defeasible,* whereas deductive inferences are not. An inference is defeasible when its conclusion can be probable to a certain degree in relation to a set of evidence but not probable to that same degree in relation to a wider body of evidence. More formally, a conclusion h can be probable in relation to a set of evidence e, whereas h may not be probable in relation to the conjunction of e and some further evidence e.

Since the conclusion of a valid deductive inference necessarily follows from its premises, no additional premise can be added to invalidate the inference. For example, if all humans are mortal, and Socrates is mortal, then it will follow that Socrates is mortal regardless of whatever else might be true of Socrates. In contrast, the addition of further premises can, in principle, always defeat the conclusions of inductive inferences.

This property of inductive inferences can be illustrated by the not-infrequent case of a criminal trial, where a legal argument used to convict an innocent person is later defeated (sometimes even decades later) by the introduction of new evidence. For example, DNA testing in forensic examinations has been used successfully as evidence to defeat prior legal arguments, even ones in which defendants have been put to death for crimes they did not commit. So the conclusion (h) that a given defendant committed a murder might have been probable in relation to the original body of evidence e (say, eyewitness testimony, the defendant's fingerprints found on the murder weapon, a clear motive for the crime, or inconsistencies in the defendant's testimony), whereas this same body of evidence conjoined with new DNA evidence from skin, blood, and hair samples taken from the exhumed body of the victim might defeat the conclusion h (by virtue of not matching the defendant's DNA).

Indeed, the history of scientific advancement can be understood in terms of the defeasibility of inductive inferences in this sense. Thus, the arguments by which Isaac Newton defended his ideas about absolute space and time were subsequently defeated and superseded by the growing body of evidence to support Albert Einstein's special theory of relativity. Most advances in medical science have similarly been achieved by challenging and defeating old arguments by adducing new evidence. For example, in 1983 Australian pathologist Robin Warren successfully isolated the bacterium (*helicobacter pylori*) that causes stomach ulcers. Before then, it was argued that stomach ulcers were caused by emotional stress.

PROBABILITY AS RELATIVE TO BEARERS OF EVIDENCE

In this context, it should be noted that probability is also *relative to those who possess the evidence that makes a given conclusion probable.* For example, for the ancient Babylonians, it was probable that the world was flat in relation to the evidence of the senses because when a ship sailed out to sea, it did indeed appear as though the ship dropped off the face of the earth. However, when explorers sailed around the world, the evidence provided by the completion of this journey defeated the perceptual evidence for the earth's flatness. Today, with astronomical evidence that reaches light years beyond that of the ancient Babylonians, what is probable for us was at most science fiction for them. And, indeed, it is likely that what is probable for us today will be defeated by new evidence possessed by generations to come. Thus, the possibilities of crossing over into parallel universes and traveling through time, which are for us only science fiction, may for future generations be confirmed scientific hypotheses.

Exercise Set 9.1

Provide two examples of a conclusion that was once probable relative to previous evidence but is now no longer probable relative to the current body of evidence. One of these examples should be of something you personally used to believe (or disbelieve) but now no longer believe (disbelieve). Discuss the reasons for your change of mind.

INDUCTION AS REASONING BEYOND DIRECT EXPERIENCE

Inductive reasoning is *empirical* reasoning—that is, reasoning from experience. Were it not for such reasoning from experience, our knowledge of the world would be restricted to what we experienced directly. For example, even if you could know that *this* particular fire is hot, you could not know that all fire is hot because you do not directly experience all fire. You could not know the causes of things, physical laws, or even whether the food in your refrigerator was still there after you closed the refrigerator door because all statements that describe these claims about the world go beyond your immediate experience.

Eighteenth-century philosopher David Hume succinctly expressed the import of inductive reasoning:

> It is certain that the most ignorant and stupid peasants—nay infants, nay even brute beasts—improve by experience, and learn the qualities of natural objects, by observing the effects which result from them. When a child has felt the sensation of pain from touching the flame of a candle, he will be careful not to put his hand near any candle; but will expect a similar effect from a cause which is similar in its sensible qualities and appearance.[1]

However, while Hume is correct that all of us do indeed "improve by experience," it is doubtful that all of us benefit equally from our experiences. To a great extent, this disparity can be due to how well we are able to draw conclusions from our experiences. For example, one person may learn from past failures, while another may continue to repeat the same mistakes. Philosopher George Santayana reminded us of this challenge of learning from our past mistakes when he famously stated, "Those who cannot learn from history are doomed to repeat it."

---

1. David Hume, *An Enquiry Concerning Human Understanding*, in *Philosophic Classics: From Plato to Derrida*, ed. Forrest E. Baird and Walter Kaufmann (Upper Saddle River, N.J.: Prentice Hall, 2007), 731.

So it is that inductive reasoning can expand our horizons, help us to see beyond what is now before us, and open up new avenues for our success in the material world. But this reasoning needs to be adequate to the occasion. Like deductive reasoning, it can mislead as well as provide a tool for attaining truth. It can be fallacious and unsound. The present section of this text (chapters 9 to 13) will examine different types of inductive reasoning and the key fallacies connected with each of these different types of induction.

GENERALIZATION

We should at the outset distinguish between generalization and *a* generalization. Generalization (without the preceding "a") is a process of reasoning in which one attempts to justify or prove a statement about all or most members of a class by appealing to a sampling of *some* members in the given class. In contrast, *a* generalization is simply a statement about all or most members of a given class, whether or not it has been arrived at through the said process of reasoning. In this latter sense, universal affirmative (A-form) statements ("All S is P") and universal negative (E-form) statements ("No S is P") are generalizations. To avoid confusion, we will refer to the latter statements as *universal statements* instead of calling them "generalizations." This also follows the usage we have employed in preceding chapters.

As you saw in chapter 6, statements about *most* members of a class are particular statements that are translatable into standard categorical form as "Some S is P" or "Some S is not P." Thus, while such particular statements have also been called generalizations, they are strictly speaking not universal statements. However, because they approach but do not attain universality, we will refer to these statements as *quasi-universal statements.* Accordingly, we will only use the word "generalization" to refer to the reasoning process by which one infers universal or quasi-universal statements about a given class from just some members of the class.

Now, most of us are familiar with the expression "That is only a generalization," which is ordinarily used to advocate against acceptance of a given universal or quasi-universal statement. However, not all universal and quasi-universal statements are created equal. While some are worthy of belief, others are not. Whether it is reasonable to believe such statements will depend on the process by which they are reached.

Let's look at the basic structure of the generalization process. Accounting for quantity and quality of the conclusion, there are four possible inference types:

1. Universal affirmative generalization:
   Some S is P.
   Therefore, all S is P.
2. Universal negative generalization:
   Some S is not P.
   Therefore, no S is P.
3. Quasi-universal affirmative generalization:
   Some S is P.
   Therefore, most S is P.

4. Quasi-universal negative generalization:
   Some S is not P.
   Therefore, most S is not P.

By deductive standards, all four generalization types are invalid because the conclusion contains information that is not contained in the premises. Specifically, in the universal affirmative and universal negative cases (inference types 1 and 2 above), the subject term of the conclusion (S) is distributed, whereas it is undistributed in the premise. That is, in the conclusion S refers to all members of the class, whereas in the premise it only refers to some members. Similarly, in the quasi-universal affirmative and quasi-universal negative cases (inference types 3 and 4 above), in the conclusion S refers to most members of the class, whereas in the premise it only refers to some members.

As a result, the conclusion of each of these four inference types does not *necessarily* follow from its premise. For example, let S = humans and P = geniuses. Given these substitution instances, inferences 1 and 2 have true premises and false conclusions. Now, let S = dogs and P = Cairn terriers. Given *these* substitution instances, inference 3 has a true premise but a false conclusion. Finally, let S = humans and P = heterosexuals. Given these substitution instances, inference 4 has a true premise but a false conclusion. Therefore, all four inference types are formally invalid.

The Fallacy of Unrepresentative Sample:
The Case of the Women's Health Initiative Study

To say that each of the above four inference types is formally invalid does not necessarily mean that its conclusion does not follow from its premise with some degree of *probability*. The degree to which the conclusion is probable, however, depends on whether the sample of individuals from which the generalization is reached is *representative* of the class of individuals about which we are generalizing. Generalizations from unrepresentative samples may be said to commit the *fallacy of unrepresentative sample*.

Consider, for example, the study conducted in 2002 by the Women's Health Initiative (WHI), a branch of the National Institutes of Health (NIH), to assess the major health benefits and risks of hormone replacement therapy (HRT) for menopausal women. In this study, 16,608 women ages fifty to seventy-nine were randomized into experimental and control groups: 8,506 women were given HRT (a combination of estrogen and progestin), while 8,102 women were given a placebo. After a mean follow-up period of 5.2 years, the NIH stopped the experiment due to adverse effects. Among other risks (including breast cancer and strokes), the subjects who were given HRT were at a 29 percent higher risk of having heart attacks than those given placebos.

The NIH concluded that these risks could be generalized to women of the same age in the general population. It stated,

> The WHI enrolled a cohort of mostly healthy, ethnically diverse women, spanning a
> large age range (50–79 years at baseline). It is noteworthy that the increased risks for

cardiovascular disease . . . were present across racial/ethnic and age strata and were not influenced by the antecedent risk status or prior disease. *Hence, the results are likely to be generally applicable to healthy women in this age range.* (Emphasis added)[2]

Accordingly, the WHI made the following inductive generalization:

> *Premise:* The 8,602 mostly healthy women (ages fifty to seventy-nine) given HRT were at a 29 percent increased risk of having heart attacks as compared to the 8,102 women not given HRT.
>
> *Conclusion:* All healthy women in this age range taking HRT are at a 29 percent increased risk of having heart attacks as compared to those not on HRT.[3]

Notice that this argument generalizes from a sample of 16,608 subjects to all (healthy) women in the general population who are between the ages of fifty and seventy-nine and on HRT. In fact, this group consists of millions of women. Therefore, if true, the WHI's conclusion has serious implications for millions of women. But does the WHI's generalization hold up under closer scrutiny?

On March 29 and 30, 2008, forty menopause specialists convened in Zurich to examine the evidence for the risks of HRT.[4] The committee argued that the WHI study was not *completely representative of women taking HRT* because the sample included disproportionate percentages of several significant risk factors for heart disease.

First, the average age of women in the study was sixty-three, which is about ten years older than most women beginning HRT. In addition, of the 16,608 women randomly assigned in the WHI study, 36 percent had high blood pressure, 49 percent were current or past smokers, and 34 percent were clinically obese. This additional evidence therefore called into question whether the women sampled in the study were sufficiently healthy and young enough to be *representative* of the general population of healthy, younger women on HRT.

Ordinarily, the more *diversified* a sample, the more representative it is. Diversity refers to the proportion of different subgroups included in a sample. For example, if you are generalizing about all dogs, then you would need to sample the different breeds of dogs and not just, say, beagles.

Arguably, the sample in the 2002 WHI study was not diversified enough because it did not include enough younger women. (As mentioned, the average age of women taking HRT was about ten years younger than the average age of women in the study.) And there were disproportionate numbers of women who had high blood pressure (36 percent), who were current or past smokers (49 percent), and who were clinically obese (34 percent). Insofar as this sample failed to be diversified enough to be representative of the general population of

---

2. Women's Health Initiative, "Risks and Benefits of Estrogen Plus Progestin in Healthy Menopausal Women," *JAMA* 288 (2002): 321–33. Retrieved online on June 2, 2008, from jama.ama-assn.org/cgi/content/full/288/3/321.

3. According to the WHI, this meant that "over 1 year, 10,000 women taking estrogen plus progestin compared with placebo might experience 7 more CHD events." WHI, "Risks and Benefits."

4. "Global Menopause Summit Concludes That HRT Is Safe for Healthy Women Entering Menopause," Drugs.com, May 20, 2008. Retrieved on June 3, 2008, from www.drugs.com/news/global-menopause-summit-concludes-hrt-safe-healthy-women-entering-menopause-8215.html.

healthy, younger women taking HRT, it committed the fallacy of unrepresentative sample.

In May 2008, the WHI itself conducted a follow-up study to its 2002 study.[5] This follow-up study examined 271 subjects from the 2002 study who had heart attacks and compared them with over 700 subjects in the control group. This new study looked at the subjects' ratios of good to bad cholesterol and found that subjects who entered the study with favorable cholesterol levels were not at increased risk of developing heart problems while taking HRT (estrogen alone or estrogen plus progestin), while women with unfavorable cholesterol levels were at a greater risk of having heart-related complications. This study therefore concluded that it was not HRT alone that placed women at a higher risk of heart disease but rather the *conjunction* of taking HRT and having a poor good-to-bad cholesterol rating.

Assuming we accept this conclusion, does this mean that menopausal women who do *not* have a poor good-to-bad cholesterol ratio can safely take HRT? The answer to this question is no. First, even if taking HRT and having a poor good-to-bad ratio implies being at risk of having a heart attack, and you do not have a poor ratio, it still does not follow that you are not at risk.[6] You might still have some other health factor that predisposes you to heart disease in taking HRT. Second, there are still other possible health risks of HRT, such as breast cancer and strokes. Third, a more careful future study might corroborate the conclusion of the 2002 WHI study.[7] Ironically, it used to be thought that HRT actually prevented heart attacks, a conclusion reversed in light of the 2002 WHI study, which held that HRT increased the risk of heart attack. This nicely illustrates the defeasible, thus tentative, nature of inductive logic.

Exercise Set 9.2

For each of the following arguments, discuss whether the conclusions drawn are based on a representative sample.

9.2.1
This fire is hot, so all fire will be hot.

9.2.2
Several studies have shown that the artificial sweetener saccharin caused bladder tumors in rats. So it will do the same in human beings who receive it in relatively similar amounts.

9.2.3
Between 1971 and 1976, the Ford Motor Company produced one of America's first compact cars called the Pinto. Crash tests of this car resulted in ruptured fuel tanks in eight out of

(continued)

---

5. Amanda Gardner, "Cholesterol Test Spots When HRT Raises Heart Risks," *Washington Post*, May 22, 2008. Retrieved online on June 3, 2008, from www.washingtonpost.com/wp-dyn/content/article/2008/05/22/AR2008052201608.html.

6. This would be to commit the fallacy of denying the antecedent. See chapter 3.

7. See "WHI Follow-up Study Confirms Health Risks of Long-Term Combination Hormone Therapy Outweigh Benefits for Postmenopausal Women," *NIH News*, March 4, 2008. Retrieved online on June 2, 2008, from public.nhlbi.nih.gov/newsroom/home/GetPressRelease.aspx?id=2554.

eleven tests at speeds averaging 31 mph. But Ford released the car anyway, resulting in the deaths of at least five hundred people from gas-tank explosions due to Pinto rear-end collisions. Therefore, it is safe to say that Ford could have inferred in advance that the fuel tanks of most Pintos would rupture upon impact at speeds averaging 31 mph.

9.2.4
My son was responsible for causing several accidents when he was a teenager, so this goes to show that most male teenagers are high-risk drivers.

9.2.5
Nixon had Watergate scandal, Reagan had Iran-Contra, and Bush had the outing of covert CIA agent Valerie Plame, the firing of several federal prosecutors for political reasons, and the illegal warrantless surveillance program, among other scandals. All of these presidents were Republicans. So, it is not hard to see that Republican administrations tend to be corrupt.

9.2.6
My father chain-smoked cigarettes all his adult life and developed coronary artery disease. So, it is clear that most people who chain-smoke cigarettes for many years are at high risk of developing heart disease.

9.2.7
My dog was not protected by any flea preventative and caught fleas when left out in the flea-infested yard. So, all or most dogs without flea preventative will catch fleas if left out, under similar conditions, in a flea-infested yard.

9.2.8
Among adults, the rate of infection with human papillomavirus type 16 (HPV-16) is about 20 percent. Most infections are benign; however, some lead to cervical cancer. A vaccine for this virus was tested on 2,392 women, ages sixteen to twenty-three, who were randomly assigned to receive the drug or a placebo. The primary analysis of results was limited to those who were negative for the virus at registration and after seven months of tracking. At 17.4 months after completing the vaccine regime, nine cases of the virus were detected in those assigned placebos, and no cases were found in the group that received the vaccine.[1] Therefore, it would it be reasonable to suppose that these results could be generalized to the general population of women between these same ages.

---

1. L. A. Koutsky et al., "A Controlled Trial of a Human Papillomavirus Type 16 Vaccine," *N. Engl. J. Med.* 347, no. 21 (2002): 1645–51. Abstract retrieved online on November 1, 2008, from www.ncbi.nlm.nih.gov/pubmed/12444178?dopt=Abstract.

Hasty Generalization

But should the conclusion of the 2008 WHI study be accepted in the first place? Notice that this study was based on only 271 subjects who had heart attacks. This seems a relatively small sample from which to generalize about all menopausal women with a poor good-to-bad cholesterol ratio. As you have seen, the larger group of women from which these subjects were taken included an inordinate number of women who had high blood pressure, were past or present smokers, or were obese. These factors have also been linked to heart disease, and it is not clear how many women in the 2008 study sample also had one or more of these health risks.

One way to guard against such an unrepresentative sample is to increase the number of subjects it contains. Had the sample included several thousand otherwise healthy women who had a poor good-to-bad cholesterol ratio, the results of the study would have been more impressive. The relative smallness of the sample increased the likelihood that it was not truly representative of the broad population of women it was supposed to represent. Insofar as the sample in the 2008 WHI study was too small to be representative of all women or most menopausal women with poor cholesterol ratios, the WHI can be said to have committed the *fallacy of hasty generalization*, which consists of *drawing a conclusion about all or most members of a class on the basis of an insufficient number of members.*

When is a sample large enough to constitute a *sufficient* number of members? There is no formula here. However, a number of cases can be called sufficient to support a conclusion about all or most members of a class if and only if it is large enough to be representative of that class.

This is not to say that a small sample cannot ever be representative. For example, if you left a single ice cube at room temperature and it melted, you would ordinarily be justified in concluding that *all* ice cubes melt at room temperature. There would be no need to increase your sample, at least as long as you *assumed* that this ice cube was representative of all ice cubes.

However, the assumption of uniformity among class members is often not reasonable to make. In the case of generalizations about health risks posed to human beings by a therapy, it is not defensible because, unlike ice cubes and the temperature at which they melt, human beings are not quite so uniform when it comes to factors affecting their health. For example, some human beings can eat fatty foods and remain relatively healthy, whereas others develop coronary artery disease—and some do so even when they rigorously watch their diets.

Unfortunately, in everyday life we humans tend to generalize hastily about our own species without taking into account the great variability among us. This includes making generalizations about human behavior. For example, a woman whose husband has been unfaithful may come to believe that all men are unfaithful. And this universal affirmative statement may, in turn, become the major premise of a categorical syllogism that summarily brands each individual man she subsequently meets as being unfaithful.

A statement of this latter sort is called a *stereotype*.

Exercise Set 9.3

Provide at least three actual examples of hasty generalization. These may be inferences you have personally made, or they may be inferences made by others. You might consider surfing Internet blogs to find instructive examples.

Stereotypes

A *stereotype* is a universal or quasi-universal statement that (negatively or positively) rates a class of people without regard to individual differences among class members. We are all familiar with popular stereotypes. Some involve ethnic ratings: all Italians are in the mob, all blacks have rhythm, and all Jews are rich. Some involve gender ratings: all women are fickle, all men are after just one thing, and all poor people are lazy. Some involve sexual preference: all gay men are flamboyant, and all straight men are masculine. In fact, it is hard to find a class of people for which some stereotype has not been created.

The tendency to think in terms of stereotypes—that is, to use them as major premises from which to *prejudge* others—may well have originated as a survival mechanism. We live in a world of uncertainty, a complex world in which we cannot easily predict how others might act to affect our own interests. Thus, being able to boil down reality to a set of universal or quasi-universal statements about other human beings could make this precarious and complex world of ours much more manageable.

In fact, the word "stereotype" itself originally referred to a printing stamp, a device that simplified the task of printing by allowing us to mass-produce copies with just one mold. The journalist Walter Lippmann was the first to apply this word to the "stamping out" of multiple responses to human behavior through the use of a single universal or quasi-universal statement that rates a given class of human beings. This does indeed simplify things. But at what cost?

The virtue of stereotypes—the ability to make prejudgments—is also its vice. This is because stereotypical thinking prevents us from judging individuals on their own merits. This type of thinking treats everyone in a given class as the same despite individual differences. This creates a *mind-set*—that is, a perception in advance of evidence—that remains unshaken even in the face of evidence to the contrary. In subscribing to a stereotype, we close our minds to the possibility of contrary evidence. For those who wonder how mass exploitation and destruction of human life, as in institutionalized slavery and mass genocide, have been possible, the answer lies in the ability to systematically treat human beings not as individuals but as stereotypes. If black people are not really people but more like farm animals to be used for a select purpose, then it becomes easier to exploit them without feeling guilty. If Jewish people are not really human beings but instead evil demons responsible for all social and economic ills, then it becomes easier to "exterminate" them, as though they were insects or vermin.

Hitler used this stereotypical thinking to scapegoat Jewish people. Unfortunately, the same stereotype is still being propagated. For example, observe what one recent Web blog says about Jewish people:

> They are charged with mixing this blood [of "white Christian adults"] into their masses (unleavened bread) and using it to practice superstitious magic. They are charged with torturing their victims, especially the children; and during this torture they shout threats, curses, and cast spells against non-Jews. This systematic murder has a special name, it is called ritual murder.

What is the evidence that Jews perform such "ritualistic murder"? There is none, only the stereotype itself of Jews as evil demons. Jewish demonic activities such as those described are constructed to support the stereotype, but the only thing that supports the belief in these activities is the stereotype itself.

In this way stereotypes are a primary cultural means of arousing, transmitting, and sustaining false ideas along with dangerous emotions, such as blind hatred and irrational fear. They involve the absence of critical and free thinking. They enslave and chain us to gross misconceptions rather than liberate us to think for ourselves; they alienate rather than unite.

Exercise Set 9.4

9.4.1
List and briefly discuss five stereotypes that you think have had a serious negative impact on human relations.

9.4.2
List and discuss at least one stereotype that you personally hold or have held in the past.

The Fallacy of Biased Sample

While it is arguable that most stereotypes are originally the product of hasty generalization, this is by no means the only way by which they are propagated. They are also socially transmitted from one generation to another as part of a social program of indoctrination. In fact, in everyday contexts, people often draw hasty generalizations about a group of people in order to corroborate or support a stereotype that they already have about that group. For example, consider the following post taken from a news community website:

> Every homosexual that I have known or have had the unfortunate occasion to cross paths with have been mentally unstable. Gay men especially, their actions are all motivated by sex. They are promiscuous and have brought AIDS into our Society. I am so sick of "gay rights." The thought of gays adopting or raising children should be against the law. Gays are causing a huge breakdown in the morality of our Society. Children need to be raised in a stable and heterosexual environment. And yes, I agree that gays are pedophiles. There are some prominent Gays in Bisbee who you would be surprised about their actions.[8]

Clearly, this blogger (pseudonym Jack) harbors several antigay stereotypes—that gay people are unstable, care only about sex, are promiscuous, brought about the AIDS epidemic, are responsible for moral decline in society, and are pedophiles. In the last two sentences, Jack is attempting to prove or justify that "gays are pedophiles" by pointing out that some prominent gays in his community of Bisbee, Arizona, are gay. However, it is doubtful that Jack has inferred that (all or most) gays are pedophiles from the (alleged) fact that there are some prominent gays in his community who are pedophiles. Rather, Jack is using these individuals, if they exist at all, to bolster the stereotype to which he has already subscribed. In this way, hasty generalizations are frequently used to support stereotypes that have already been accepted.

The obvious problem with such a verification process is that it is biased. The process recognizes only those instances that support one's generalization and

---

8. Jack, "Gays Are Pedophiles—Promote Youth Promiscuity," topix.com, March 25, 2007. Retrieved online on April 18, 2009, from www.topix.com/forum/city/bisbee-az/TKHCJQJKH37GF27NE.

ignores any instances that contradict it. It is not merely that the sample from which Jack is generalizing (a few prominent citizens of Bisbee) is too small. It is not merely that the sample is not representative of all gay men. It also suffers from the further problem of being biased. Let us call this the *fallacy of biased sample*, which involves the (conscious or unconscious) inclusion in a sample of only those instances that confirm an already accepted universal or quasi-universal statement.

Consider this further example of the fallacy of biased sample, which trades on the stereotype that all (or most) old people are senile. During the last presidential race, Republican presidential candidate John McCain erred by saying publicly, while in Jordan, that Iran (a Shiite nation) was supporting al-Qaeda in Iraq (a Sunni group); he was quietly corrected by Senator Joseph Lieberman, who was by his side. A day later, when McCain was in Israel, he erred a second time by referring to the Jewish holiday of Purim as "their version of Halloween here."[9] Again, Senator Lieberman was on hand to correct McCain. This time, Lieberman himself took the blame for McCain's error, claiming that he had earlier explained the holiday to McCain by using the analogy with Halloween. Here is a comment that appeared on an MSNBC news site that reported the story:

> Mc Cains verbal mistakes only proves that he is senile. . . . The repubs have an old man for a candidate who is advised by another old man. What a joke.[10]

Notice that the commenter (pseudonym VI from Wisconsin) uses McCain's mistakes to "prove" that he is senile. But McCain's errors do not prove that he is senile—only that he is not adequately informed on the issues he is discussing. Indeed, if a younger person made the same errors, the question of senility or mental competence would never come up. It was raised only because McCain was almost seventy-two years old. That is, VI already assumed that all people McCain's age must be senile. He (or she) already held the ageist stereotype and simply used McCain's mistakes (and Lieberman's misguidance) as proof of the very same stereotype: since McCain himself was an old man, he in particular was senile.

The fallacy of biased sample is vicious because it excludes the possibility of refuting a stereotype. In considering only those cases that corroborate the stereotype, evidence to the contrary is summarily dismissed. Thus, for example, if presented with an example of an old person who is mentally competent or a gay person who is not a pedophile, the person doing the biased sampling will dismiss the contradictory evidence as not really being contradictory: "Well, you don't really know what he does behind closed doors." Or a universal statement might be replaced with a quasi-universal statement: "Well, maybe all old people aren't senile, but most of them are." The person doing the biased sampling might then try to shift the focus back on cases he or she thinks do fit the stereotype: "What about that guy in Texas who just abducted that little boy?" Or, "Look at how

---

9. While a festive holiday, Purim celebrates the deliverance of the Jews from massacre by Haman.

10. Mark Murray, "McCain: Purim = Halloween?" MSNBC, March 20, 2008. Retrieved online on April 8, 2009, from firstread.msnbc.msn.com/archive/2008/03/20/787720.aspx.

many traffic accidents are caused by these old people who just don't know what they're doing!"

Exercise Set 9.5

Provide at least two actual examples of the fallacy of biased sampling. These may be biased samplings you have made in attempting to defend your own stereotypes, or they may be the biased samplings of others. You might consider surfing Internet blogs to find instructive examples.

Falsifying Inductive Generalizations

The conclusions of inductive generalizations are always probable in relation to the evidence. That is, no matter how large and representative your sample is, the conclusion is still subject to the possibility of disconfirmation in the future. For example, all past and present creatures we have known that have had hearts have also had kidneys. This makes probable the conclusion "All creatures with hearts are creatures with kidneys." Nevertheless, it is still possible for a creature with a heart to happen along someday that somehow gets by without any kidneys. This is always possible, even though, relative to the evidence of our past observations, it is not probable.

Thus, the conclusion of an inductive generalization never follows *necessarily* from a sample, no matter how representative that sample is. In contrast, the conclusion of an inductive generalization can, with certainty, be falsified. That is, for any universal affirmative statement "All S is P," if there is even one instance of an S that is not P, then it will necessarily follow that the universal statement is false. Likewise, for any universal negative statement "No S is P," if there is one instance of an S that is P, then it will necessarily follow that the universal negative statement is false.

For example, consider the universal affirmative statement "All swans are white." This was believed to be true in pre-seventeenth-century Europe until black swans were discovered in Australia in 1697. Even one black swan would have been sufficient to falsify the statement, no matter how many swans were consistently observed to be white prior to the discovery of black swans in Australia.

Notice that if at least one swan is not white, then *some* swans are not white. But as you can see from the discussion of categorical statements in chapter 6, the particular negative statement "Some swans are not white" is the contradictory of the universal affirmative statement "All swans are white." And, if the contradictory of a statement is true, then the statement itself must be false. Therefore, if there is at least one swan that is not white, then it necessarily follows that the statement "All swans are white" is false.

In this manner you can (deductively) show a universal statement to be false. Notice, however, that this mode of falsification doesn't work for quasi-universal statements: that is, statements of the form "Most S is P" or "Most S is not P." For example, the fact that some Americans are not theists (believers in God) does not necessarily mean that it is false that *most* Americans are theists. In fact, according to a recent survey, 73 percent of Americans say they believe in God—although only 58 percent are "absolutely certain" that there is a God.[11]

Exercise Set 9.6

Find a survey, study, or case example on the Internet that serves to falsify each of the following universal statements:

9.6.1
No heterosexuals are child molesters.

9.6.2
All U.S. senators voted (in 2002) to authorize the use of military force in Iraq.

9.6.3
All Arabs support the destruction of Israel.

9.6.4
All mainstream TV news show hosts who do not work for Fox News are liberals.

9.6.5
No Germans in Nazi Germany opposed the Nazis.

---

11. Harris Interactive, "While Most Americans Believe in God, Only 56% Are 'Absolutely Certain,'" Harris Poll 80, October 31, 2006. Retrieved online on June 26, 2008, from www.harrisinteractive.com/harris_poll/index.asp?PID=707.

10

Predictions

Inductive inferences that make predictions resemble inductive generalizations insofar as they draw a conclusion from a set of observed cases. However, in predictive inductions, the conclusion is not a universal or quasi-universal statement. Instead, it is a *singular statement about the future*. The general structure of such an inference is as follows:

a is S and is P; b is S and is P; c is S and is P.
d is S and is P; e is S and is P . . . z is S and is P.
This is S.
Therefore, this will also be P.

For example, the sun has risen every day from the beginning of recorded history. Therefore, just as was true for all other days in the past, the sun will rise tomorrow. This does not mean that it *necessarily* follows that the sun will rise tomorrow. As philosopher David Hume tells us, "That the sun will not rise tomorrow is no less intelligible a proposition, and implies no more contradiction, than the affirmation, that it will rise."[1] This means that even though it has consistently risen on past days, it is still conceivable for the sun *not* to rise tomorrow, which means it does not necessarily follow from the fact of its having consistently risen in the past that it will rise tomorrow.

Nevertheless, it is highly probable, given its consistent record of having risen in the past. That is, as long as the sample from which the prediction is made is representative of the past, the prediction is probable. Thus, the same standards that apply to inductive generalization apply to predictive inductions. The sample must have a sufficient number of cases and must be sufficiently diverse to make it representative of the class being used to ground the prediction. Quite obviously, the scope of all recorded history is both sufficient in number and diversity of days

1. David Hume, *An Enquiry Concerning Human Understanding*, Harvard Classics 37 (P. F. Collier & Son, 1910). Retrieved online on April 17, 2009, from 18th.eserver.org/hume-enquiry.html.

to warrant the prediction. Nevertheless, as Hume rightly reminds us, it is still possible for the sun not to rise tomorrow. For example, the earth could be destroyed by a cosmic accident!

Despite the fact that predictive inductions are not certain, we cannot rationally avoid making them. While time travel is not impossible, it is presently not something we are able to accomplish. Thus, we have no reasonable alternative to basing our decisions about the future on the past. Before we act, we cannot fast-forward to the future to see what will happen if we perform a certain action, then rewind and make our decision about whether to perform the act or not. Thus, you have discovered past uniformities and expect that they will continue into the future. For example, you have learned that touching the hot stove causes a burn, and you believe that it will do the same in the future should you happen to touch it. Indeed, it is unlikely that you would live a single day if you did not rely on the evidence of the past to make predictions about the future.

Unfortunately, in everyday life, we humans not uncommonly misapply the evidence of the past in dealing with future possibilities. There are four commonplace ways in which this can happen: (1) magnifying risks, (2) insisting on the past, (3) ignoring the past, and (4) insufficient analogy. This chapter examines each of these fallacies.

MAGNIFYING RISKS

Most of us have heard mention of Murphy's law, so-named after the aerospace engineer Edward Murphy, who worked on safety-critical systems (systems whose failure could result in death or serious injury). In 1949, Murphy was working for McDonnell Douglas on a U.S. Air Force rocket-sled project testing the human ability to tolerate acceleration. One such experiment involved attaching sixteen meters that measured acceleration to a subject's body. There were two ways to attach the meters, one correct and the other incorrect, and someone selected the wrong way. Murphy then responded to the error by stating, "If there are two or more ways to do something, and one of those ways can result in a catastrophe, then someone will do it." This was the original version of Murphy's law.[2]

This principle makes sense if it is interpreted as a practical guide for someone like Murphy whose job it is to guard against dangerous mistakes in designing products. For example, it was a good idea to design an electrical plug in such a way that you cannot plug it into an electrical outlet backwards and shock yourself. This is because there was a good chance that unless this dangerous option was designed out, someone, amid the hundreds of thousands of diverse users in the general population, would have eventually chosen it. This is also why toy manufacturers are not supposed to make products for children out of toxic materials (for example, lead paint) or objects that can be dangerous if swallowed (for example, marbles). Our past experience with children is that they put things in

---

2. "Murphy's Law," The Jargon File. Retrieved online on April 8, 2009, from www.catb.org/jargon/html/M/Murphys-Law.html.

their mouths. Thus, we can predict with a high degree of probability that eventually some subset of children will ingest the toxic or dangerous substance.

But not all interpretations of Murphy's law are this rational. A few days after Murphy stated his principle, Maj. John Paul Stapp (the test subject of the above mentioned acceleration-tolerance experiment) gave a press conference in which he is said to have misquoted Murphy as saying, "If something *can* go wrong, then it will."[3] This is the formulation of Murphy's law with which most of us are familiar. It has also been called Finagle's law, as it is referred to by science fiction writer Larry Niven in several of his stories about asteroid miners who worship the dead god Finagle and his "mad" prophet, Murphy.[4]

Clearly, Finagle's law is fallacious because it fails to base predictions about the future on a sample that is sufficient in number and diversity to justify the prediction. The mere fact that something can go wrong does not itself mean that it will. Thus, the mere fact that the bridge you are crossing can collapse does not mean that it will. Indeed, in the course of a day, numerous things that can go wrong simply do not. Let us call this fallacy the *fallacy of magnifying risks*, which involves turning smaller risks of something undesirable happening into much larger risks.

Another somewhat attenuated formulation of Finagle's law that commits this fallacy states, "If there is any chance of something's going wrong, then it *probably* will." This version, which we might call "softened Finagle's law," at least recognizes that predictions are probabilistic rather than definite. However, just because there's a chance of something's going wrong does not make it a probability. If this inference were acceptable, then it would be probable that the sun will not rise tomorrow since, as you have seen, its rising tomorrow is not certain. Clearly, however, based on our past experience, we are indeed justified in thinking that the sun will rise tomorrow.

Unfortunately, it is not uncommon for people to commit the fallacy of magnifying risks by relying on a version of Finagle's law as a reason not to pursue desired goals. Thus, a person commits this fallacy when he or she refuses to travel by air because if an airplane can crash, it will, or because since plane crashes have happened before, a particular plane will probably crash. Indeed, by the same logic, people would be advised not to travel by motor vehicles because these too can crash.

In fact, recent statistics suggest that cars are more likely to crash than airplanes. According to a comparative-risk study conducted by the U.S. Department of Transportation, for the years between 1999 and 2003, the average fatality rate for motor vehicles was 36,667 (1 out of 7,700), whereas for air carriers, it was 138 (1 out of 2,067,000). And while the fatality rate was 1.3 deaths per 100 million vehicle miles and 1.9 deaths per 100 million aircraft miles, "Since the average number of passengers in an aircraft far exceeds the average number of passengers in a motor vehicle, the passenger mile risk of air carrier transportation is significantly less than that of motor vehicle transportation."[5] Unfortunately, in driving under the

---

3. "Murphy's Law," The Jargon File.

4. "Finagle's Law," The Jargon File. Retrieved online on April 8, 2009, from www.catb.org/jargon/html/F/Finagles-Law.html.

5. U.S. Department of Transportation, "A Comparison of Risk: Accidental Deaths—United States 1999–2003," January 1, 2004. Retrieved online on July 1, 2008, from hazmat.dot.gov/riskmgmt/riskcompare.htm.

influence of Finagle's law, many people tend to overlook or discount such hard data.

Exercise Set 10.1

Discuss the rationality of each of the following perspectives in light of the above discussion on magnifying risks:

10.1.1
"Ever have one of those weeks where everything goes wrong? Argh! It just seems it's been one thing after another. I try not to be negative but it just seems that this week has been filled with more bad than good. Have you ever noticed that if something's going to happen it all seems to come at once? I wonder if it's better that way." —Blogger

10.1.2
"It is possible to fail in many ways (for evil belongs to the class of the unlimited . . . and good to that of the limited), while to succeed is possible only in one way (for which reason also one is easy and the other difficult—to miss the mark easy, to hit it difficult)." —Aristotle, *Nicomachean Ethics*

10.1.3
"You're going to die. You can stop worrying about that. It's going to happen. But how you will die is the great mystery of your life. Suspenseful, chalkboard-grating music. Or is it? While there's a chance you'll die in mysterious or unexpected circumstances, there's a far better chance you'll die of heart disease in a hospital bed decades from now. While you could be murdered, it's way more likely you'll kill yourself, unless you're black. In that case, you're slightly more likely to die from assault. We're all more likely to die in a car accident than by any sort of cide. But here's the sad truth: You probably don't need to worry about heights, snakes, Arabs, Crack addicts, vengeful women or men with mustaches who drive generic vans. They won't get you, because they and you will probably die of some sort of painful ailment first. If not heart disease, cancer. If not cancer, stroke. If not stroke, then emphysema."[1]

10.1.4
You will always find something in the last place you look.

10.1.5
"Plan for things to go wrong. We've heard it before, and it's still true: if something can go wrong, it will. Figure out ahead of time where your problem-solving effort is vulnerable and develop appropriate contingency plans. Start on this as soon as you begin the problem-solving effort, making it a normal part of defining a problem."[2]

---

1. Peter Nicely, "How You'll Probably Die," TenCarTrain.com. Retrieved online on November 3, 2008, from http://tencartrain.com/?p=646.
2. Jeanne Sawyer, "Problem-Solving Success Tip: Plan for Things to Go Wrong," Articlesbase.com. Retrieved online on November 3, 2008, from www.articlesbase.com/management-articles/problemsolving-success-tip-plan-for-things-to-go-wrong-527761.html.

THE FALLACY OF INSISTING ON THE PAST

While adherents of Finagle's law magnify risks, those who commit the fallacy of insisting on the past go further by *fatalistically* seeing the past as an indelible blight on the future. That is, according to the latter way of thinking, if anything has gone wrong in the past, then it *must*, as a matter of *lawful necessity*, continue to do so in the future; therefore, there is nothing whatsoever anyone can do about it. Thus, whatever has happened in the past is set in stone for the future. An airline that has had a plane crash cannot therefore improve its safety record in the future, for it is doomed to have more of the same. A student who has earned failing grades in the past cannot improve his performance in the future. A failed marriage means not just that this marriage was unsuccessful but that any future marriage will likely end up on the rocks. Getting fired from a job unavoidably and irrevocably portends the same for the future. Human beings have since the beginning of recorded history been at war with one another. Therefore, we *must* always settle our disputes through war in the future, and a state of enduring peace on earth is a fiction that cannot and will not ever be attained. Crime, poverty, racial discrimination, and a host of other social problems have been persistent fixtures of past history; therefore, it is impossible for things to be otherwise in the future. As such, moral progress is not just improbable but impossible.

The fallacy here lies in failing to realize that what happened in the past is a fallible and contingent basis for predicting what will happen in the future. The future is probable *in relation to* the evidence of the past, but the evidence of the past is subject to change; therefore, so too are the probabilities about the future. Thus, the student who changes his study habits can increase his probability of improved academic performance. In future relationships, a person who has had an unsuccessful marriage can avoid making some of the same mistakes. The loss of a job might mean enlisting in new training, correcting skill deficiencies, seeking out an employer with different expectations, or making other changes that could alter the probable future outcome. War is not necessarily the only option, and a world without crime, poverty, and racial discrimination is not a contradiction in terms.

A prime danger of insisting on the past is that one will not make constructive changes in order to increase the probability of a brighter future. If the past is fatalistically destined to repeat, then there is simply no point in trying to change things for the future. Thus, this fallacy portends acquiescence and complacency rather than a foreword-moving openness to change.

As the philosopher Plato made clear, the world that we perceive through our senses is not one that gives us certainty. While you can have reasonable belief (be "reasonably certain") that things will or will not go the way you want them to go, you cannot have *absolute certainty*. There is some measure of risk in whatever we do. While this does not mean that we should take unnecessary and unreasonable risks with our lives or those of others, it does mean that we will accomplish little or nothing if we are not prepared to assume some amount of risk.

Exercise Set 10.2

In the light of the above discussion of insisting on the past, assess the rationality of each of the following views about our ability to change or control the future:

(continued)

10.2.1
"Jews and Arabs have always been at war, they will never stop, it's in their nature and blood. And they have been fighting each other since the beginning of time, it's even recorded in the Bible." —Blogger

10.2.2
"Man Dies When Lawn Mower Overturns on Top of Him
When your time is up, it's up! He could have been anywhere else, and he still would have passed." —Blogger

10.2.3
"First, the eternal predestination of God, by which before the fall of Adam He decreed what should take place concerning the whole human race and every individual, was fixed and determined." —John Calvin, *Concerning the Eternal Predestination of God*

10.2.4
"Hardly anyone can remain entirely optimistic after reading the confession of the murderer at Brockton the other day: how, to get rid of the wife whose continued existence bored him, he inveigled her into a desert spot, shot her four times, and then, as she lay on the ground and said to him, 'You didn't do it on purpose, did you, dear?' replied, 'No, I didn't do it on purpose,' as he raised a rock and smashed her skull. . . . If this Brockton murder was called for by the rest of the universe, if it had to come at its preappointed hour, and if nothing else would have been consistent with the sense of the whole, what are we to think of the universe? Are we stubbornly to stick to our judgment of regret, and say, though it couldn't be, yet it would have been a better universe with something different from this Brockton murder in it? That, of course, seems the natural and spontaneous thing for us to do; and yet it is nothing short of deliberately espousing a kind of pessimism. The judgment of regret calls the murder bad. Calling a thing bad means, if it means anything at all, that the thing ought not to be, that something else ought to be in its stead. Determinism, in denying that anything else can be in its stead, virtually defines the universe as a place in which what ought to be is impossible—in other words, as an organism whose constitution is afflicted with an incurable taint, an irremediable flaw." —William James, *The Dilemma of Determinism*

10.2.5
"Neither will an existentialist think that a man can find help through some sign being vouchsafed upon earth for his orientation: for he thinks that the man himself interprets the sign as he chooses. He thinks that every man, without any support or help whatever, is condemned at every instant to invent man. As Ponge has written in a very fine article, 'Man is the future of man.' That is exactly true. Only, if one took this to mean that the future is laid up in Heaven, that God knows what it is, it would be false, for then it would no longer even be a future. If, however, it means that, whatever man may now appear to be, there is a future to be fashioned, a virgin future that awaits him—then it is a true saying. But in the present one is forsaken." —Jean-Paul Sartre, *Existentialism Is a Humanism*

THE FALLACY OF IGNORING THE PAST

The flip side of insisting on the past (fatalistic thinking) is ignoring the past. This is "wishful thinking"—that is, believing that things will be different in the future than they were in the past, even though nothing has changed to warrant such optimism. Thus, it is wishful thinking to suppose that a nation with a consistent history of oppressing its citizens and acting in violation of their human rights will suddenly change its ways and become democratic. This is not probable *relative to its past history*. Of course, things could change and increase the probability. A leader could have an epiphany, or a new, progressive leadership could take the reins of government. But in the absence of any reason for doing so, expecting things to be different is wishful thinking.

A commonplace example of this fallacy arises in cases of domestic violence. In such cases, there is typically a cycle of abuse that moves in stages. For example, in an abusive couple's relationship, there is a stage characterized by aggressive behavior, which may include beatings, emotionally degrading verbal attacks, and/or sexual assault. After this stage, there is a period of relative calm in which the abusive spouse may express remorse, attempt to make excuses for the behavior, or make up for it, for example with gifts. After this stage, there is a period of "walking on eggshells," where tension builds and the abusive spouse becomes increasingly volatile, until there is a repeat of aggressive behavior, which completes the cycle. Thus, the cycle begins again.[6]

In the stage of relative calm, it is not uncommon for the victim of the abuse to commit the fallacy of ignoring the past by believing that "things will be different" in the future, even though the cycle of abuse may have repeated hundreds of times. By ignoring the past, the victim remains in this perpetual cycle of abuse. Unless there is professional intervention, there is no rational basis for the belief that "things will be different," and it is therefore probable that the cycle of abuse will continue.

As you can see, the fallacies of ignoring and insisting on the past, while opposites, have similar outcomes. In both cases, one fails to take actions that could improve the probability of a brighter future. Thus, the victim of abuse does not seek help and remains locked in the cycle of abuse by ignoring the past, and the person who has had an unsuccessful marital stint concludes that the future must resemble the past and therefore gives up on finding a suitable mate.

Exercise Set 10.3

Philosopher George Santayana is well-known for having stated, "Those who do not remember the past are condemned to repeat it." Provide at least three examples of how ignoring the past has actually led to its being repeated. You may use historically significant events as well as personal experiences.

SEEKING PROBABILITY AS AN ANTIDOTE TO INSISTING ON AND IGNORING THE PAST

Aristotle made the keen observation that extremes tend to lead to vice, whereas virtue tends to lie in the mean between the extremes. This also appears to be true with regard to the ethics of belief. Neither a fatalistic nor a wishful outlook about

---

6. University Health Services, "Domestic Violence," University of Massachusetts, Amherst. Retrieved online on April 8, 2009, from www.umass.edu/fsap/issues/violence.html.

the past appears to be constructive. Both insisting on and ignoring the past tend to be self-defeating and destructive. So what lies between them?

The answer is probability. The past is not irrelevant to the future, nor does it determine the future. Rather, it affords us evidence from which we can make *probabilistic* predictions. In his classic book, *The Problems of Philosophy*, philosopher Bertrand Russell succinctly expressed this "golden mean" between insisting on and ignoring the past:

> It must be conceded, to begin with, that the fact that two things have been found often together and never apart does not, by itself, suffice to prove demonstratively that they will be found together in the next case we examine. The most we can hope is that the oftener things are found together, the more probable it becomes that they will be found together another time, and that, if they have been found together often enough, the probability will amount *almost* to certainty. It can never quite reach certainty, because we know that in spite of frequent repetitions there sometimes is failure at the last, as in the case of the chicken [who has become accustomed to being fed] whose neck is wrung. Thus, probability is all we ought to seek.[7]

Seeking probability is flexible and adaptive. When we find that a manner of attacking a problem consistently fails, this gives us reason for thinking that it will probably continue to fail in the future. It therefore provides a reason to change our strategy. Unlike the abuse victim who says, "Things will be different," when there is no reason to think so, and unlike the fatalist who says that he is doomed to repeat the past, the probability seeker knows when it is reasonable to make suitable changes or to try something new. Such flexible adaptability can make the difference between a stagnant existence and one that is prosperous.

Exercise Set 10.4

The following appeared on a Yahoo! Answers blog:

Why do I keep messing up??

They say to err is to be human, but I keep on making errors and do not seem to be doing much else. And on top of that, I seem to always hurt the people around me. How can I change? For example, the other night, I was at my sister's wedding and my husband came with me, but he spent the entire night outside and I had to keep making excuses for him. When he finally did come in I told him that if he did not want to be here why did he even come? He said that he is not comfortable there, but he wanted to be there for me. Well I was mad, I said to him that he was not there for me if he was outside. I stormed out of the wedding and had a huge fight with him, thus hurting my sister and making a huge *** out of myself. Then we went back to his mom's house (staying there for weekend because it was close to the wedding) and continued to fight because he said I made him angry by not understanding his point. So my question is why do I keep messing up and how do I fix it?

If this person ignores the past, she will make the same mistakes and continue to wonder why she keeps "messing up." If she insists on the past, she will also keep making the same mistakes and not try anything different. If she takes a probability-seeking approach, how will she go about addressing her problem?

---

7. Bertrand Russell, *The Problems of Philosophy* (New York: Oxford University Press, 1972), 65–66.

INDUCTION BY ANALOGY:
THE CASE OF ANIMAL EXPERIMENTATION

Another type of predictive inference is by way of analogy—that is, comparison. In this kind of induction, one observes that two (or more) things have a certain set of features *F* in common; then, observing that one (or more) of these things have a certain further feature *G* in common, one infers that the other thing(s) will also have *G*.

One example of induction by analogy is in the use of animals in medical research in order to draw inferences about human beings. For example, because a certain chemical agent causes cancer in laboratory mice, it may be inferred that it will do the same in human beings.

Like all inductions, the conclusions of analogical inductions are more or less probable, depending on the evidentiary basis from which they are drawn. In analogical inferences, the probability of the conclusion depends on the number of relevant similarities between the things compared and the number of relevant differences between them. Any similarity or difference can be said to be *relevant* if it can affect the probability of a conclusion inferred from analogical reasoning.

For example, there are some similarities between humans and mice that appear to be relevant for purposes of cancer research. Thus mice, like humans, exhibit low rates of cancer in youth, increased rates until old age, and decreased rates in very old age. Several infectious diseases that are carcinogenic (cancer causing) in mice are also carcinogenic in human beings. We have already seen how studies suggest that hormone replacement therapy (estrogens) increase the risk of cancer in women. In mice, estrogens are also carcinogenic when administered in old age. Both species have tumor-suppressing genes. In both species there are sex differences in the risk of cancer. Cancer risk varies from place to place—from nation to nation in humans and from lab to lab in mice.[8]

Insofar as these similarities are *relevant* to cancer research, they increase the probability that a cancer finding in mice also applies to humans. However, there also appear to be some relevant *dissimilarities* between humans and mice, which tend to reduce the probability of such cross-species inferences. For example, quite obviously, humans are much larger than mice. This fact could have a bearing on whether a relatively small amount of a chemical agent, such as the sugar substitute saccharin, could cause cancer in mice but not in humans. Humans live a lot longer than mice too. Mice tend to develop different types of cancers than humans. Most cancers in humans tend to occur in epithelial cell tissue, whereas in mice cancers tend to occur in connective and lymphatic tissues as well as blood vessels. Mice require fewer tumor-suppressing genes to suppress tumor growth than do humans. Humans require more cancer-causing genes to affect mutations than do mice.[9] Such differences as these can decrease the probability that a finding in mice applies to humans.

Therefore, quite obviously, the analogy between mice and humans can only take us so far, and the results of such findings need in the end to be observed in

---

8. "Mouse Models in Cancer Research," Suite101.com. Retrieved online on April 8, 2009, from www.suite101.com/article.cfm/new_cancer_treatments/118883/2.
9. "Mouse Models in Cancer Research," Suite101.com.

humans to be confirmed. Thus, we do not know that a cancer drug with a degree of effectiveness in shrinking tumors in mice will in fact work to shrink tumors in humans. In fact, in 2004 the Food and Drug Administration (FDA) reported that 92 percent of new medicines passing animal tests ultimately fail to have the same effects in humans.[10]

The main reason for conducting research on animals before humans is to safeguard the well-being of humans. However, any measure of success such experimentation may have had in the past has been bought at the expense of great pain and suffering to animals. A promising new frontier intended to circumvent the ethical problems raised by animal experimentation is the use of computers to simulate the physiology of animals and hence track the reactions of drugs, chemicals, infectious diseases, and so forth onscreen rather than in vivo.

For example, based on research data from the past thirty years, scientists at Johns Hopkins have developed a computer simulation of the hearts of dogs, guinea pigs, rats, and mice. While such simulations have proven useful in educational contexts to teach what is already known about animal and human physiology, a major challenge for such simulations has been to predict answers to questions that are not already known from prior research.[11]

It does appear possible, however, to construct analogical arguments from computer simulations that actually make predictions about things not already known from prior research. For example, recent work on the construction of physiologically based pharmacokinetic (PBPK) models has had a significant measure of success in predicting drug or chemical absorption, distribution, metabolism and excretion, and toxicity.[12]

The success of such simulations will depend on our ability to construct computer programs that permit us to examine the relevant similarities and differences between animal physiology and human physiology as the basis for drawing predictive conclusions. As stated, the extent of relevant similarities and differences determines the probability of the conclusion of such analogical induction.

However, the determination of whether a similarity or difference is *relevant* is itself a finding that will need to have been gleaned from prior testing and observation. For example, how do we know that the age of a mouse is a risk factor in developing cancer? This cannot be answered without prior knowledge. Just how all such knowledge of relevant factors in making analogical inferences can be acquired without some kind of advanced animal experimentation is not entirely clear.

In any event, computer simulations must accurately reflect the actual physiology of animals in order to provide a useful substitute for animal experiments. However, given the low rate of predicting the effects of new medicines on humans based on animal experimentation—according to the FDA, it's only 8 percent—it

---

10. Medical Research Modernization Committee, "A Critical Look at Animal Experimentation: Contemporary Animal Experimentation." Retrieved online on April 8, 2009, from www.mrmcmed .org/crit2.html.
11. Medical Research Modernization Committee, "A Critical Look at Animal Experimentation."
12. Dr. Hadwen Trust, "Science Review 2006: Showcasing Successes in Non-Animal Research," Politics.co.uk. Retrieved online on April 8, 2009, from www.politics.co.uk/opinion-formers/Dr -Hadwen-Trust-for-Humane-Research/reports-and-briefings-$447630$4.htm.

appears that the probabilities of conclusions of cross-species analogical arguments, whether based on actual or simulated animal experimentation, tend to be low. Perhaps this is because the relevant differences between animal and human physiology are substantial, such that the analogy between them is often *insufficient* to support reasonable inferences about humans.

The Fallacy of Insufficient Analogy

An induction by analogy can be said to commit a *fallacy of insufficient analogy* when the things being compared are not (relevantly) similar enough to justify the conclusion or dissimilarities between these things defeat the probability of the conclusion.[13] For example, consider the following induction by analogy made in a speech delivered by former secretary of defense Donald Rumsfeld at the Eighty-eighth Annual American Legion National Convention in 2006:

> When those who warned about a coming crisis, the rise of fascism and Nazism, they were ridiculed or ignored. Indeed, in the decades before World War II, a great many argued that the fascist threat was exaggerated or that it was someone else's problem. Some nations tried to negotiate a separate peace, even as the enemy made its deadly ambitions crystal clear. It was, as Winston Churchill observed, a bit like feeding a crocodile, hoping it would eat you last.
>
> There was a strange innocence about the world. Someone recently recalled one U.S. senator's reaction in September of 1939 upon hearing that Hitler had invaded Poland to start World War II. He exclaimed:
>
> "Lord, if only I had talked to Hitler, all of this might have been avoided!"
>
> I recount that history because once again we face similar challenges in efforts to confront the rising threat of a new type of fascism. Today, another enemy—a different kind of enemy—has made clear its intentions with attacks in places like New York and Washington, D.C., Bali, London, Madrid, Moscow and so many other places. But some seem not to have learned history's lessons.[14]

In the above-cited passage of the speech, Rumsfeld draws an analogy between those who, in the years leading up to World War II, did not take the threat of Nazism seriously and those who in 2006 were criticizing the Bush administration for its policies on terrorism. Rumsfeld also states, "Some nations tried to negotiate a separate peace, even as the enemy made its deadly ambitions crystal clear." In this statement, he refers to British Prime Minister Neville Chamberlain's attempt in 1938 to appease Adolph Hitler by signing the Munich Agreement, which conceded parts of Czechoslovakia to Nazi Germany. Rumsfeld accordingly argues that a policy of appeasement with respect to current-day terrorists, or one of not taking the threat seriously, will have the same adverse consequence that

---

13. The term *defeat* in this context does not mean "reduces the probability to zero." This would make such (defeated) conclusions necessarily false, whereas (as Hume rightly saw) conclusions derived from experience are never necessarily true or false. Rather, in this context, "defeat" means that the conclusion would no longer be reasonably believed based on the available evidence.

14. "A Transcript of the Address Delivered at the 88th Annual American Legion National Convention by Secretary of Defense Donald H. Rumsfeld, Salt Lake City, Utah, Tuesday, August 29, 2006," *Stars and Stripes*. Retrieved online on July 7, 2008, from www.stripes.com/article.asp?section=104&article=38796&archive=true.

appeasement of Hitler had in 1938—namely it will empower them to commit widespread atrocities.[15]

However, as Rumsfeld himself admits, this time the enemy is a "different kind of enemy." The enemy to which Rumsfeld refers is not a nation but rather terrorist groups such as al-Qaeda. Because such terrorist groups are not uniformed soldiers fighting under the flag of a given nation, some have argued that they should be treated as criminals rather than as enemy combatants, which means that the manner of confronting such a threat may not be the same as fighting a war against a nation that can easily be identified, located, and retaliated against. Hitler was such a national threat; al-Qaeda is not. This distinction in turn raises questions about the legitimacy of referring to a "war on terror" fought against such terrorist groups. This is because wars typically have definite beginnings and ends and are fought against identifiable nations. The so-called war on terrorism is more like a war on drugs. It is ubiquitous and has no geographical or temporal boundaries. Comparing World War II to the war on terrorism is therefore a stretch.

Further, Rumsfeld was particularly critical of Americans, especially journalists, who criticized the Bush administration for its invasion and occupation of Iraq and for its use of torture on detainees in such prisons as Guantánamo Bay and Abu Ghraib. But most progressive media that were critical of the Bush administration's handling of terrorism did not advocate that America negotiate with terrorist groups such as al-Qaeda. Nor did they object to putting suspected terrorists in detention facilities as long as they were treated humanely and accorded due process. Thus, Rumsfeld seems to have missed the mark by trying to compare criticism of the Bush administration's policy on terrorism to Neville Chamberlain's attempt to appease the Nazis through negotiation or to the failure, prior to World War II, to take the threat of Nazism seriously.

Therefore, it would appear that Rumsfeld's analogy is a false one. Chamberlain tried to *negotiate* with Hitler. Critics of the Bush administration have not generally advocated negotiating with terrorist groups like al-Qaeda. True, they disagreed with the Bush administration's particular tactics in confronting this threat: for example, torturing detainees, depriving them of due process, invading and occupying sovereign nations, and spying on American citizens without a court order. However, only by making the very controversial and questionable assumption that anyone who did not advocate these things was "soft" on terrorism could Rumsfeld compare these critics to those who, during the buildup to World War II, did not take the threat of Nazism seriously.

Exercise Set 10.5

In his March 2003 speech giving Saddam Hussein forty-eight hours to leave Iraq, President George W. Bush stated,

---

15. Rumsfeld assumes, but does not argue, that Chamberlain's failed negotiations with Hitler did in fact contribute to these negative results. Whether or not this assumption is true to begin with is a complication we will ignore.

In the twentieth century, some chose to appease murderous dictators, whose threats were allowed to grow into genocide and global war. In this century, when evil men plot chemical, biological and nuclear terror, a policy of appeasement could bring destruction of a kind never before seen on this earth.

In the above, Bush analogizes appeasement of Hitler with appeasement of Saddam Hussein, the former dictator of Iraq. Is Bush's argument any more or less convincing than Rumsfeld's? Defend your answer.

Exercise Set 10.6

Determine whether each of the following predictive arguments contains any of the predictive fallacies discussed in this chapter. If it does, indicate the fallacy, and explain why it commits this fallacy.

10.6.1
My husband has had several affairs. At first I was going to leave him, but this time he's sworn to me on his knees that he won't ever do it again.

10.6.2
"Penicillins and cephalosporins have similar chemical configurations. Both classes of antibiotic are of low molecular weight, are highly substituted, and possess a ß-lactam ring, on which antimicrobial activity depends. Cephalosporins and penicillins differ in that the 5-membered thiazolidine ring of penicillin is replaced with a 6-membered dihydrothiazine ring in the cephalosporins. However, after degradation, penicillin forms a stable penicilloate ring, with preservation of the thiazolidine ring, whereas cephalosporins undergo rapid fragmentation of the ß-lactam and dihydrothiazine rings. On the basis of these differences in degradation, immunologic cross-reactivity between ß-lactam rings of these compounds might be minimal, a finding supported by clinical and monoclonal antibody analysis."[1]

10.6.3
I am twenty-five, and I haven't been able to find anyone yet to share my life with. If I haven't found anyone at this point, I'm sure I never will.

10.6.4
"Monday, I took a short day at work to help serve at a funeral reception at church. . . . As I've written here before, I enjoy serving at these receptions even though I don't have a domestic bone in my body. . . . Part of it is . . . my fear as a childless woman; I will probably end up dying alone, with no one to grieve or show up for the funeral. Admittedly, this freaks me the hell out." —Blogger

10.6.5
When I was your age, I was short too, and then suddenly I had a growth spurt. So, believe me, the same thing will happen to you.

10.6.6
A nurse I know stuck herself with a needle from an HIV-infected patient. So she is almost certain to become infected with the HIV virus. (Suggestion: Google a reliable study of occupationally acquired HIV infections before evaluating this prediction.)

---

1. Michael E. Pichichero, MD, "A Review of Evidence Supporting the American Academy of Pediatrics Recommendation for Prescribing Cephalosporin Antibiotics for Penicillin-Allergic Patients," *Pediatrics* 115, no. 4 (April 2005): 1048–57. Retrieved online on November 5, 2008, from http://pediatrics.aappublications.org/cgi/content/full/115/4/1048#SEC6.

11

Testimonials

A further common variety of induction is the testimonial, in which one draws conclusions based on what other people say. Were it not for the testimony of others, our knowledge would be quite limited indeed, since the lion's share of what we can claim to know we learn from what others tell us. Without countenancing the testimony of others, there would be no history to learn and teach, no scientific knowledge accessible to us through the volumes amassed and recorded by scientists, no wisdom of the ages passed on through philosophical treatises. Medical, legal, engineering, and other professional opinions would fall on deaf ears were it not for testimonials.

The structure of inferences based on testimony is roughly this:

Person S stated that p.
S is a reliable source.
Therefore, p is true.

The phrase "reliable source" in the second premise means essentially that S has a consistent track record of speaking truth. This does not mean that S must always be correct. However, the probability of the conclusion that p is true is a direct function of the extent that S has been reliable in the past. Accordingly, unless you were justified in believing S to be reliable, you would not be justified in believing that p.

The judgment that S is reliable may be gleaned from one's own experience with S, but it may also itself be based on the testimony of some further person(s). In the latter case, the further person(s) must also be reliable; otherwise, one would not have grounds for believing that S is a reliable source and therefore p is true. Quite obviously, we must stop somewhere in this regress of trusted sources.

Many of us often select a professional such as a medical doctor or a lawyer on the basis of a referral from a trusted friend. However, friendship is not per se a basis for taking the word of another about a technical matter. True, the friend might be able to provide some evidence about the reliability of the physician based on his or her own personal experience as a patient. However, the lack of technical expertise of laypersons, coupled with the complexity of problems in a technical field, tends to make trusting the opinion of a friend (or friends) a provisional and questionable basis for reliability claims. This is where *credentialing* typically comes in.

Having documentation that the professional in question has successfully completed training in an accredited professional program that qualifies him to address problems of the sort for which professional help is sought can serve to establish a justified claim to reliability. However, credentials, as most of us know, are not everything. Further evidence could be obtained by checking to see whether the professional has had malpractice suits filed against him and whether he has been subject to state disciplinary action for questionable practices. Further, getting second, third, and sometimes even fourth corroborating opinions from other professionals satisfying the same rigorous standards can help to justify a claim to reliability.

SURFING THE INTERNET TO KEEP INFORMED

A serious challenge in our digital information age is how to determine if an *Internet source* is reliable. The Web is a vast sea of interconnected data consisting of both true and false claims, with no internal central authority to strain the veridical from the sludge, thus leaving it to the consumer of information to distinguish between the two.

The Internet is also the greatest bastion of democracy ever conceived by humankind. On the Internet, anyone is free to post his or her ideas and opinions. Thus, any attempt to regulate this dynamic flow of data by means of a central regulating authority (such as the federal government) would mean the demise of its free architecture. Under the control of a central governing authority, we would be told what to think. There would be censorship—not freedom of speech and inquiry. But this also means that we must be competent consumers of information so that we do not fill our minds with false sludge instead of truth. We must be discrete about what we commit to belief.

So what should we look for before accepting something as truth on the Net? Answer: look for documents (news items, technical and scientific articles, historical treatises, editorials, ethical and philosophical essays, and so forth) that use the methods of free and critical thinking discussed throughout this book to impart information or make a case. In particular, look for sources that back up what they claim with evidence and provide sound arguments rather than ones that contain fallacies, use stereotypes, or appeal to hatred, prejudice, or other forms of irrationality. Look for sources that tend to get the facts straight, provide sufficient detail to get an accurate view of reality, and offer insightful connections between facts. Like mainstream media, some news websites have been instrumental in breaking stories that have not appeared elsewhere. For example, alternative online news sources such as Salon, Raw Story, Truthdig, and the Alternet specialize in covering stories ignored or downplayed by mainstream media. The news webzine Buzzflash touts itself as providing "progressive news and commentary with an attitude," and while left-leaning, its editor works diligently to see that its authors back up their claims with verifiable fact and rational argument.

One should also be wary of self-styled experts who speak on technical subjects without credentials that qualify them to do so. For instance, blogs consist of posts by persons who often have little or no formal training in the subject matter about which they are commenting. Thus, someone with a health problem might post a well-meaning comment about her experience with a particular illness. While the post might prove useful to others confronting the same illness, it can also be misleading about medical facts. It therefore cannot suffice as a substitute for medical expertise.

One can also not assume that an author has the facts straight even if the article in question appears on a reliable website. It is therefore a good idea to look for other reliable, independent sources that corroborate the author's fact claims before forming a belief.

In some cases, international news sources can provide eye-opening perspectives not found in domestic media. For example, in May 2003, the Arab news agency Al Jazeera showed pictures of war casualties against the wishes of British and American governments. Responding to criticisms, editor in chief Ibrahim Hilal stated, "What we are doing is showing the reality. We didn't invent the bodies, we didn't make them in the graphics unit. They are shots coming in from the field. This is the war." Thus, while mainstream American media did not permit Americans to view these images, Al Jazeera took a different perspective that despite the horrors of war, people had a right to see its ravages. "If I hide shots of British or American people being killed, it is misleading to the British and American audience," said Hilal.

As an Arab news agency, Al Jazeera may arguably be said to have a pro-Arab, anti-Israeli, and anti-American perspective. On the other hand, it would be disingenuous to suppose that American media don't likewise harbor their own biases. This is why it is important to consider alternative media sources; otherwise, we run the serious risk of locking ourselves into a set of media biases without even realizing it.

Human beings always perceive reality through a set of social, cultural, and personal beliefs and values that influence their perception. Expecting an "objective" account of reality that transcends these cognitive filters is therefore asking too much of any source of information. Nevertheless, as you have seen in this book, logical standards set limits on what can count as a rational argument. Thus, it is misleading to claim that all "biases" are created equal. For example, the neo-Nazis, the American Civil Liberties Union (ACLU), and the National Rifle Association (NRA) all have their own sets of organizational biases. The neo-Nazis harbor biases in favor of the white Arian race and against anyone who is of a different race. The ACLU is for liberal democracy. The NRA is against gun control. But only the neo-Nazis accept dangerous stereotypes and irrational prejudices based on blind hatred and fear. The critical and free thinker is open to alternative interpretations of reality so long as they are rational.

Exercise Set 11.1

11.1.1
Provide an example of an online item that is supposed to be informative in some way (for example, it gives advice or makes factual claims) but is not, in your estimation, from a reliable source—that is, a trustworthy author or website. Explain why you believe the source should not be trusted.

11.1.2
Provide an example of an online item that is, in your estimation, from a reliable source. Explain why the source should be trusted.

11.1.3
Select a news story and find two different perspectives on it. For example, you could contrast a mainstream newspaper such as the *Washington Post* or the *New York Times* with the *New York Post* or the *New York Daily News*, or you could compare a mainstream news source with an independent media source such as the *Huffington Post* or *Mother Jones*.

MAINSTREAM MEDIA AS AN INFORMATION SOURCE

Mainstream corporate media also has its organizational biases, which stem chiefly from their primary motivation: maximizing the bottom line. For companies like General Electric (which owns NBC), News Corporation (which owns Fox News), Disney (which owns ABC), Time Warner (which owns CNN), and Viacom (which owns CBS), the end game is increasing profits and paying dividends to stockholders. These giant corporations depend on the federal government for lucrative contracts, tax breaks, subsidies, access to White House officials for cost-effective news feeds, industry deregulation (media ownership and cross-ownership rules), and other perks. These companies also have assembled powerful lobbies in Congress and the Federal Communications Commission to influence the legislative process in their favor. This means that they cannot afford to bite the governmental hand that feeds them. After all, the government can either permit them to grow and prosper or regulate them out of existence. Given their core bottom-line interests, it is obvious why these companies might fail to be reliable sources in reporting on the activities of their government beneficiaries. For example, during the lead-up to the Iraq War, the mainstream corporate media did very little to dispel and much to propagate the myth that there were weapons of mass destruction in Iraq. When one learns that media monoliths such as GE/NBC were engaged in supplying jet engines to Lockheed Martin to produce military aircraft on lucrative national defense contracts, it becomes even clearer why the NBC newsroom might have been constrained by corporate pressure from blowing the lid on the myth of weapons of mass destruction (WMD) in Iraq.

This means that as consumers of information, we must tread carefully in assuming that the mainstream media outlets will always be reliable sources. We cannot assume that as profit-seeking corporations above all, these giant news organizations will simply promulgate "the truth, the whole truth, and nothing but the truth." This does not mean that mainstream corporate media cannot be part of a news package that keeps us informed. It means that such outlets cannot be our *only* source of news if we are to be adequately informed about matters of state. So long as the Internet architecture remains open (and not also controlled by giant corporations), we may still turn to independent online news sources, as well as online international news sources, to give us a more balanced and informed news perspective.

Exercise Set 11.2

Assemble your own news package that you think would likely give you a balanced view of news. Include both mainstream media and independent media sources as well as online, broadcast and/or cable TV, radio, and print sources.

PARROTING: THE CASE OF JUDITH MILLER
AND THE *NEW YORK TIMES*

The most basic fallacy of testimonials is *blind acceptance (and repeating) of what another states as fact.* The danger of such parroting is that one is then capable of believing groundless and destructive testimony. The *New York Times*'s reporting about WMD in Iraq is a case in point. One of the *Times*'s reporters, Judith Miller, was among the most influential in propagating the WMD myth. In 2001 and 2002, prior to the invasion of Iraq, Miller wrote several stories about the WMD program that Iraq's dictator, Saddam Hussein, was allegedly conducting. Unfortunately, these stories were based largely on false testimony provided by the now notorious U.S. informant Almed Chalabi and his Iraqi National Congress (INC), a group of anti-Hussein Iraqi militants whose purpose was to instigate a national uprising against Hussein. In fact, in 1998 under the Clinton administration, a bill was passed (the so-called Iraq Liberation Act) that appropriated $97 million in U.S. military aid to the INC.

In 2003, after the invasion of Iraq, Miller was also "embedded" on assignment to cover a U.S. military unit in search of WMD. She later revealed that she was given "secret information" by the Pentagon, which she was "not permitted to discuss" with *Times* editors.[1]

The above profile paints Miller more as a spokesperson for the U.S. government than a member of the fourth estate tasked with keeping a watchful eye on government and keeping us informed. In the end, Miller "retired" from her post at the *Times*, but she never accepted responsibility for having gotten things so wrong. "WMD—I got it totally wrong," she said in a 2005 interview. "The analysts, the experts and the journalists who covered them—we were all wrong. If your sources are wrong, you are wrong."[2]

The problem, however, was that Miller's sources were not reliable: Chalabi was on the payroll of the U.S. government, and the Pentagon, which she was supposed

---

1. Norman Solomon, "Judith Miller, the Fourth Estate and the Warfare State," Common Dreams, October 17, 2005. Retrieved online on April 8, 2009, from www.commondreams.org/views05/1017-22 .htm.
2. Solomon, "Judith Miller."

to be keeping a watchful eye on, had muzzled her. Miller also failed to consult other potentially credible sources who challenged the White House's claims—for example, experienced weapons inspectors such as Hans Blix and Scott Ritter. And there appears to have been a number of other analysts she could have consulted prior to the invasion who disagreed with the U.S. government's claims about WMD in Iraq.[3]

But it was not entirely Miller's fault that the *Times* got it wrong. The editors printed Miller's stories, and they also failed to take seriously other potential sources who disagreed with government officials and those working for them. Had Miller and her editors been less eager to believe government officials and more vigilant in seeking out sources that disagreed with them, the *Times* might never have gotten it so wrong.

An instructive example of how the *New York Times* might have proceeded is the manner in which national Canadian newspaper *The Globe and Mail* more recently handled the question of whether there had been increased violence in Afghanistan by the Muslim extremist group known as the Taliban. In a July 14, 2008, front-page article titled "Top Soldier Denies Significant Increase in Violence" with the subtitle "Assertion Contradicts Data Showing Rise in Taliban Attacks," *Globe and Mail* reporter Graeme Smith stated,

> Canada's top soldier [Chief of the Defense Staff Walter Natynczyk] has dismissed the growing violence in Kandahar as "insignificant," contradicting all public data and highlighting the growing gap between Canada's upbeat view of the war and the sober analysis from other NATO countries.

The article went on to cite statistics compiled by an independent security-consulting agency, Vigilant Strategic Services Afghanistan (VSSA), and to point to corroboration from the United Nations and the Afghan NGO Safety Office. "For the year to date," it stated, "VSSA counted 532 insurgent attacks as of July 6, up 77 percent from 300 last year."

Natynczyk was also quoted as saying, "Kandaharans have returned to their normal pattern of life," and characterized the city as "bustling"; another official, Lt. Gen. Michel Gauthier, was quoted as saying, "We drove through Kandahar city today. In fact, we drove through Kandahar city, I think, more than once in the last few days, and it doesn't look like a city that's in shock." These remarks were then juxtaposed with the reaction of a roomful of Afghan businessmen in Kandahar City, who were reported to have "laughed raucously when informed that the Canadian military believes the city has returned to normal." One of these businessmen was quoted as saying, "There is panic now in Kandahar. Everybody is wondering what will happen next."

While such eyewitness testimony was obtained from a relatively small number of businessmen in Kandahar City, this testimony was arguably still more credible than that of a Canadian officer who did not seem to know whether he had driven through the city more than once in the past few days. The residents of this war zone did not have to guess about such matters.

---

3. Solomon, "Judith Miller."

The *Globe and Mail* accordingly did its job in attempting to key into such alternative sources and to expose contradictions with officialdom. Had the *New York Times* done the same in its reporting on WMD in Iraq (for example, taking seriously the testimony of weapons inspectors), then more American citizens might have been better informed about the issue, and perhaps more of us would have been reluctant to support the Bush administration in its invasion of Iraq.

The fact that the *Times* chose to parrot officialdom did not, however, exempt any of us from the responsibility to keep informed. Being a critical and free thinker requires more than simply believing something because it is printed in the *New York Times*. We also had a responsibility to consult other, independent media sources.

Exercise Set 11.3

Provide at least three examples of parroting. You may find these in the media or in your personal encounters; however, at least one of these examples must come from the media. Explain why you believe your examples reflect parroting, and discuss how the parroting could have been avoided—for example, other sources that could have been consulted.

12

Inductive Hypothesis

While eyewitness testimony from reliable sources can be useful, much of what we know is not *directly* observed but inferred from effects. For example, while we can observe the ravaging effects of a nuclear explosion, we cannot directly observe the subatomic event that caused it. A physician may diagnose a patient as having HIV (the human immunodeficiency virus known to cause AIDS) on the basis of a series of tests that confirm the existence of HIV *antibodies*, which are not the virus itself but rather an immunological response to it. In criminal cases, an accused may be found guilty of a crime without anyone's having seen the crime committed, largely on the basis of indirect evidence such as that obtained from DNA testing. The study of history offers explanations of events, for example the assassination of President John F. Kennedy, that may be speculative and not themselves directly observable. Even the existence of other minds besides one's own is not directly observable and can only be inferred, for instance, from outward manifestations like goal-directed behavior.

INDUCTIVE HYPOTHESES

Inferences that involve such indirect observation form the basis of hypotheses. A *hypothesis* is a statement or group of statements used to explain a fact or facts perceived as needing explanation. A statement or group of statements H (hypothesis) can be said to explain a fact F when F can be inferred from H. A fact F is perceived as needing explanation when it is perceived (by some person) as problematic. For example, we often want an explanation for the death of a person, especially when it occurs under unusual circumstances. What was the cause of Smith's death? The hypothesis "a lethal poison was in Smith's drink" explains the fact that Smith died immediately after finishing his drink because this fact can be inferred from it.

This does not mean that the lethal-poison-in-the-drink hypothesis is the correct one. It still could have been a coincidence that Smith finished his drink and then

191

died, and there could have been some other cause—for example, a massive heart attack—that was unrelated to the consumption of the drink. As you will see, it is a fallacy to assume that just because one event follows another, the first must be the cause of the second. Nevertheless, this hypothesis does explain the fact of Smith's having died after finishing his drink, and for this reason, it can be said to be a *relevant* hypothesis: that is, a statement from which this fact can be inferred. But to say that a hypothesis is relevant does not mean it is correct. The hypothesis still needs to be tested along with all other relevant, competing hypotheses.

Testability distinguishes a scientific hypothesis from a dogmatic one. For example, the statement that there are invisible, undetectable gremlins in your gas tank may well be counted as a relevant explanation as to why your car is stalling out. But there is absolutely no way to disconfirm this hypothesis. If the car stops stalling out, you can say that the gremlins have gone away, and if the car begins stalling out again, you can simply say they have returned. And since these gremlins are invisible and undetectable, there is absolutely no observation you can make that will prove you wrong. Critical and free thinkers reject such dogmatic explanations in favor of scientific ones, which can be tested.

A scientific hypothesis can be tested by inferring statements from it, then seeing if they are true or false. The form of such testing inferences is as follows:

> If h, then f.
> f.
> Therefore, h.

For example, consider the manner in which a person is tested for HIV. The standard testing regimen involves two different indirect enzyme tests: the enzyme-linked immunosorbent assay (ELISA) and the more complex test known as the western blot. Typically, a person must have two positive ELISA tests and a confirmatory positive western blot test in order to be diagnosed with HIV. This battery of tests provides an accuracy rate of greater than 99 percent. Of course, this still is not certain, and it is possible, though extremely unlikely, that a person will have two positive ELISA tests and a positive western blot. Some studies place these combined false-positive rates between 0.0004 and 0.0007 percent.[1] Typically, after getting a negative ELISA result, a person is not tested further. However, there is about a 0.001 percent chance of getting a false negative on an ELISA: that is, the test could miss about ten true positives in ten thousand HIV-infected people.[2]

Given this background information, let h be the hypothesis "Jones has HIV," and let f be the fact that "Jones tested positive for HIV antibodies on two ELISA tests and one western blot test." Inserting these substitution instances into the above form, we get the following argument:

> If Jones has HIV, then he will test positive for HIV antibodies on two ELISA tests and one western blot test.

---

1. "HIV Test," Wikipedia. Retrieved online on April 17, 2009, from en.wikipedia.org/wiki/HIV_test#Accuracy_of_HIV_testing.
2. Medical University of South Carolina, "Sensitivity and Specificity." Retrieved online on April 8, 2009, from www.musc.edu/dc/icrebm/sensitivity.html.

Jones tested positive for HIV antibodies on two ELISA tests and one western blot test.
Therefore, Jones has HIV.

As you saw in chapter 3, this argument is formally invalid, an instance of affirming the consequent. This means that the hypothesis, "Jones has HIV," does not *necessarily* follow from the premise that Jones has tested positive for HIV antibodies on the stated testing regimen. For example, Jones could have had a false positive. But while the probability of the conclusion is not 100 percent, it is still very impressive, greater than 99 percent.

However, suppose that Jones gets a negative on an ELISA test. We are then left with the following inference:

If Jones has HIV, then he will test positive for HIV antibodies on two ELISA tests and one western blot.
Jones did not test positive for HIV antibodies on one ELISA test.
Therefore, Jones does not have HIV.

This inference is valid because it is a substitution instance of the below valid form:

If h, then f.
Not f.
Therefore, not h.

However, recall that there is still a 0.001 percent chance that the ELISA test is a false negative and Jones really has HIV. Since this is still a possibility (even if a very remote one), the conclusion is still not 100 percent probable. But since there is a 99.999 percent probability that the negative ELISA test is accurate, this test lowers the probability of the hypothesis that Jones has HIV to 0.001 percent.

Therefore, as you can see, some test results (such as positive results on the battery of HIV tests) can raise the probability of the HIV hypothesis, while other test results (such as a negative ELISA test) can defeat or substantially diminish it. Generally speaking, a fact that confirms a hypothesis (that is, raises its probability) is called a *convergent fact*. A fact that disconfirms a hypothesis (that is, lowers its probability) is called a *divergent fact*. In the end, a hypothesis worthy of acceptance will be one that has, on balance, the greatest probability of being true relative to any alternative hypotheses that might be accepted.

Exercise Set 12.1

For each of the following sets of facts f, (1) formulate a relevant hypothesis h that is confirmed by f, and (2) construct the hypothetical syllogism that confirms h. In some cases, you might consider researching the matter (for instance, on the Internet) before formulating your hypothesis.

(continued)

12.1.1
John, a thirteen-year-old, has suddenly developed acne.

12.1.2
The size of the polar icecap is shrinking. Arctic ice is getting thinner and is rupturing.

12.1.3
In the United States, the unemployment rate is increasing, wages are falling, the stock market is spiraling downward, banks are failing, the cost of living is increasing, the rate of home foreclosures is rising, and major industries such as the automotive industry are reporting billions in lost revenues.

12.1.4
Bob has pain in the center of his chest radiating into his left arm and jaw. He has nausea, shortness of breath, and is sweating.

12.1.5
Sarah has lost interest in daily activities; she has problems concentrating, is irritable, and has unexplained physical problems.

12.1.6
You receive an e-mail message at your company e-mail address from "the mail administrator" saying that your e-mail account is about to be terminated unless you go to a certain website and enter your password and username to confirm your user information.

THE SCIENTIFIC METHOD: THE CASE OF O. J. SIMPSON

Formulating, testing, and evaluating hypotheses make up the core ingredients of what is commonly called the *scientific method*. This method consists of seven basic steps: (1) defining the problem, (2) formulating preliminary hypotheses, (3) gathering further evidence, (4) formulating a leading hypothesis, (5) testing the leading hypothesis and its competitors, (6) evaluating hypotheses, and (7) choosing and acting on a hypothesis. Each of these seven steps is discussed and illustrated below using the well-known criminal case of former football player Orenthal James "O. J." Simpson.

Step 1: Defining the Problem

As was discussed above, we hypothesize about, and attempt to explain, facts when we perceive them to be problematic—that is, to pose a problem. A fact raises a problem when it raises a question for which we desire an answer. There are two sorts of problems: practical and intellectual. A practical problem raises a question of the sort "What should I do?" whereas an intellectual problem raises a question of the sort "What should I think?" In chapter 14 we will discuss moral problems as a species of practical problems.

Broadly speaking, scientific problems are intellectual problems. They raise a question about what to think or believe. For example, what is heat? what is matter? and what is energy? are all scientific questions that philosophers and scientists have attempted to answer since the beginning of recorded history. This is not to say that answers to scientific questions do not have practical application: Einstein's special theory of relativity provided an answer to questions about the nature of matter and energy, leading to the production of nuclear reactors and (unfortunately) atomic bombs.

In the well-known case of O. J. Simpson, the problem involved explaining the deaths of two individuals, Simpson's ex-wife, Nicole Brown, and her friend, Ronald Goldman. On June 12, 1994, before midnight, the bodies of Brown and Goldman were found outside Brown's townhouse at 875 South Bundy Drive in the Brentwood section of Los Angeles, California. A couple living in the neighborhood had been led by a dog to Brown's body lying in a pool of blood at the bottom of the steps leading into the townhouse.[3] The Los Angeles police were notified and subsequently found Goldman's body also on the premises. Nicole Brown lay face down. Her short black dress was drenched in blood. A few inches from her body were a set of keys; a dark-blue knit cap; a beeper; a white, blood-spattered envelope; and a bloodstained, left-hand leather glove. To her right, against a garden fence, lay the body of Ronald Goldman. His eyes were open, and his light-brown shirt and blue jeans were drenched in blood. A trail of bloody footprints led away from the bodies toward the back of the property. Alongside these footprints, drops of blood trailed in the same direction.[4]

How did Brown and Goldman end up dead under the conditions just described? This question defined the problem confronting the Los Angeles Police Department (LAPD). Obviously, answering this question was more than an academic exercise. For example, if the two were murdered, then the perpetrator or perpetrators needed to be apprehended and brought to justice.

The point of a definition is not to assume an answer to a problem but rather to help guide the search for relevant evidence. If the definition is too broad, then it will not adequately fulfill this function. For example, in the Simpson case, defining the problem at hand as "What causes people to die?" would have been too broad to guide the police in their investigation into the deaths of Brown and Goldman.

In this case, defining the problem in terms of how these two individuals died under the conditions described was adequate for the purposes of guiding the police investigation because it focused their inquiry on evidence relevant to the deaths of Brown and Goldman. Moreover, as will become clear, keeping the hypothesis that Brown and Goldman were murdered separate from the definition of the problem to be solved made it less likely that the investigation would be biased by preconceptions of what really happened on the night of June 12, 1994.

Step 2: Formulating Preliminary Hypotheses

Locking down the crime scene, the police began a search of the premises and found Nicole and O. J.'s children safe in an upstairs bedroom. The police also observed that there were multiple stab wounds to both victims' bodies. Brown had

3. In fact, it was Brown's dog who led them to the body. The dog, which had bloody paws, had been wandering about the neighborhood barking.
4. Thomas L. Jones, "Notorious Murders: O. J. Simpson," truTV.com. Retrieved online on April 8, 2009, from www.trutv.com/library/crime/notorious_murders/famous/simpson/brentwood_2.html.

almost been decapitated by these wounds, and Goldman had several puncture wounds associated with "taunting," or torture.

Taking in this evidence, the police began, at this early stage, to formulate preliminary hypotheses to answer the question posed by the facts they had already ascertained: the blood-drenched bodies, the bloody trail of footprints, and so forth. The most obvious was that this would be a *criminal* investigation, not merely one into the deaths of two people. Indeed, the presenting evidence raised the clear possibility of a double homicide—the death of two human beings caused by another human being or beings.

Notice, however, that there were several possible homicide hypotheses. For example, perhaps Brown and Goldman were killed by just one other human being. Perhaps they were killed by two or more other human beings. Or perhaps they killed each other.

A further hypothesis was that Brown and Goldman were *murdered*. It appears that the LAPD took this hypothesis to be the most probable, even at this early stage of the investigation. The gravity of the wounds was, after all, consistent with a vicious attack. Still, other possible, relevant hypotheses did not involve murder, such as killing in self-defense or under other mitigating conditions, and the answers to these questions could not to be assumed away; they had to be answered by a court.

Moreover, the hypothesis that Brown and Goldman had been murdered was very general and needed to be narrowed down to one or more suspects. Thus, another hypothesis was that O. J. Simpson murdered Brown and Goldman.

Obviously, at this early point in the police investigation, there was no concrete evidence to support the hypothesis that Simpson had committed double murder. Nevertheless, the stage at which preliminary hypotheses are formulated is a creative one in which the investigator is free to imagine hypotheses that explain the problematic facts at hand. Since Simpson was, after all, Brown's ex-husband, and since it is not uncommon for one spouse or former spouse to seriously harm or kill another in a jealous rage, the Simpson double-murder hypothesis was, even at the very beginning of the police investigation, a possibility worth considering.

Step 3: Gathering Further Evidence

True, after their preliminary walk-through of the Bundy Drive residence, the police did not have evidence against O. J. Simpson to link him to the homicides or to support the hypothesis that he had committed double murder. Still, the police officers at the scene, among them Detective Mark Fuhrman, were asked by their chief of operations to drive to O. J. Simpson's nearby home on 360 North Rockingham Avenue. At least part of their official reason for doing so was to let Simpson know that his children were in police custody. However, since Simpson was Nicole's ex-husband and therefore closely connected to her, the possibility that he was involved in the homicides might also have been part of the reason for driving to his house that night.[5]

---

5. Jones, "Notorious Murders," www.trutv.com/library/crime/notorious_murders/famous/simpson/brentwood_2.html.

When the police arrived at Simpson's Rockingham estate, they found a white Ford Bronco parked outside the gate. Upon inspection of the vehicle, they noticed a blood spot on its exterior near the door handle. On the grounds that an emergency situation existed (preempting the need for a search warrant), the officers entered the premises. They rang the doorbell, but no one answered. They spoke with two individuals, Simpson's daughter Arnelle and his friend Kato Kaelin, both of whom resided in guesthouses at the back of the property. They were told that Simpson had been picked up at his Rockingham residence by a limousine at around 10:45 p.m. to catch a "red-eye" (midnight) flight to Chicago.[6]

On inspecting the grounds, Fuhrman informed the other officers of a discovery he had made in the garden and led them to a glove located behind the guesthouse occupied by Kato Kaelin. It appeared to be the right-hand mate to the glove found next to Brown's body.[7]

In addition, another officer discovered what looked like blood drops near two cars parked in the Rockingham estate driveway. These red spots formed a trail to the rear of the white Ford Bronco. The officer also saw what looked to be other blood spots on the driver's door and on the console close to the Bronco's passenger's side. He further discovered that the red spots led to the front door of Simpson's Rockingham estate.[8]

When one of the officers contacted Brown's parents to inform them of their daughter's death, a voice could be heard in the background, screaming, "O. J. did it! O. J. killed her! I knew that son of a bitch was going to kill her!" It was the voice of Nicole's sister, who apparently had some cause to suspect that Simpson would harm her sister.[9]

When the officers located Simpson in Chicago and phoned him, he did not ask for details surrounding the death of his ex-wife but said that he would book a flight back to Los Angeles. When Simpson returned, he had a bandage on his hand, which he alleged covered a wound that had reopened when he broke a glass in his Chicago hotel room.[10]

Step 4: Formulating a Leading Hypothesis

At some point during the collection of evidence, one preliminary hypothesis will tend to "fit the facts" more than any of the others. This then becomes the leading hypothesis. In Simpson's case, prior to careful forensic evaluation, the evidence linking him to the double homicide was not strong enough to arrest him on the charge of murder. Yet, it clearly supported the hypothesis that he did commit a double murder. For example, if Simpson had committed such brutal and bloody

---

6. Jones, "Notorious Murders," www.trutv.com/library/crime/notorious_murders/famous/simpson/night_3.html.

7. Jones, "Notorious Murders," www.trutv.com/library/crime/notorious_murders/famous/simpson/night_3.html.

8. Jones, "Notorious Murders," www.trutv.com/library/crime/notorious_murders/famous/simpson/night_3.html.

9. Jones, "Notorious Murders," www.trutv.com/library/crime/notorious_murders/famous/simpson/night_3.html.

10. Jones, "Notorious Murders," www.trutv.com/library/crime/notorious_murders/famous/simpson/serve_4.html.

murders, then he would probably have gotten some blood on the car he used immediately afterward. The Simpson double-murder hypothesis accordingly became the LAPD's leading hypothesis. However, without testing the blood to see if it contained traces of Brown's blood, the evidence was not sufficient to charge him with the murders. Therefore, the hypothesis still needed to be tested.

But there were also other possible explanations for the facts in question. For example, someone other than Simpson could have committed double murder, or someone could have tried to frame Simpson for the murders. Moreover, as more evidence was gathered through the process of testing the leading hypothesis, another hypothesis might suggest itself as more reasonable. For example, as you will see, the defense team for O. J. Simpson relied substantially on the hypothesis that the blood specimens gathered from the crime scene were cross-contaminated as a result of shoddy forensic practices.

Step 5: Testing the Leading Hypothesis and Its Competitors

A strong hypothesis will have considerable *predictive and explanatory power*. That is, one will be able to infer many other facts from it that accordingly converge on the hypothesis. The Simpson double-murder hypothesis turned out to have such predictive power. Forensic analysis subsequently conducted on the evidence collected from both the Bundy and Rockingham scenes converged on this hypothesis:

- DNA analysis of the blood found in and around Brown's townhouse matched Simpson's blood.[11]
- DNA analysis of the blood found in, around, and on Simpson's white Bronco revealed traces of blood from Brown, Goldman, and Simpson.[12]
- On June 13, 1994, the investigators also collected a pair of socks from Simpson's bedroom at his Rockingham estate. The socks were subsequently found to have a bloodstain on them. DNA analysis showed the blood on these socks to be Brown's.[13]
- The left-hand glove found at Brown's residence and the right-hand glove found at Simpson's home proved to match. DNA analysis showed that the blood on the glove found on Simpson's property contained blood from Simpson and both victims. Moreover, these gloves, Aris Isotoners, were dark-brown leather, cashmere lined, and extra large. In 1990, Brown had purchased two pairs of these gloves for Simpson. Between 1989 and 1992, only 240 pairs had been sold exclusively by Bloomingdale's New York department store location on Third Avenue. Simpson testified under oath that he did not own a pair of Aris Isotoner gloves, but the prosecution presented press releases of Simpson wearing such gloves during football games in 1993 and 1994.[14]

---

11. Associated Press, "O. J. Simpson Civil Trial," *USA Today*, October 18, 1996. Retrieved online on April 8, 2009, from www.usatoday.com/news/index/nns25.htm.
12. Associated Press, "O. J. Simpson Civil Trial."
13. Associated Press, "O. J. Simpson Civil Trial."
14. Jones, "Notorious Murders: O. J. Simpson," www.trutv.com/library/crime/notorious_murders/famous/simpson/hairs_14.html.

- The trail of bloody footprints on Brown's property were shown to have been made by a pair of size 12 Bruno Magli shoes, an extremely rare, expensive Italian shoe. Simpson's shoe size was size 12. Despite Simpson's claiming under oath that he did not own such shoes, the prosecution offered photographs into evidence showing Simpson wearing such shoes on two different occasions at two different football games.[15]
- Hair apparently from Simpson was found in the dark-blue knit cap found near Brown's body. Dark-blue fibers apparently from the cap were found on Goldman's shirt.[16]
- Two cuts on Simpson's left middle finger[17] could have accounted for the trail of blood left at the Brown residence as well as in the Bronco and at Simpson's Rockingham estate.[18]

Other converging evidence in favor of the Simpson double-murder hypothesis included an arrest record, which stated that in 1989 Simpson had been charged with beating Nicole while they were still married. He had hit and kicked her while threatening to kill her, according to police. After pleading no contest, Simpson was placed on two years' probation and ordered to undergo psychiatric counseling and to perform community service.[19]

Simpson's former girlfriend Paula Barbieri had also broken up with him on the day of the murders. According to Barbieri he was disturbed about this, and phone records showed that Simpson had attempted to contact her shortly before the murders.[20] Friends and family claimed that Brown had repeatedly told them that Simpson had been stalking her and had threatened to kill her if he found her with another man.[21] Although the latter was hearsay and therefore not legally admissible to establish motive, taken together all of these facts suggest background conditions quite common in domestic murder cases that consistently support the Simpson double-murder hypothesis and might well have been inferred from it with a high degree of probability.

As for the murder weapon, a cutlery store produced a receipt showing that six weeks prior to the murder, Simpson had purchased a twelve-inch stiletto knife. Investigators were able to show that such a knife created wounds matching those found on Brown and Goldman.[22]

The divergent evidence adduced by the defense to disprove the Simpson double-murder hypothesis included attorney Johnny Cochran's famous attempt

15. Jones, "Notorious Murders: O. J. Simpson," www.trutv.com/library/crime/notorious_murders/famous/simpson/hairs_14.html.

16. Associated Press, "O. J. Simpson Civil Trial."

17. William C. Thompson, "Proving the Case: The Science of DNA: DNA Evidence in the O. J. Simpson Trial," 67 U. Colo. L. Rev. 827. Retrieved online on April 8, 2009, from phobos.ramapo.edu/~jweiss/laws131/unit3/simpson.htm.

18. Associated Press, "O. J. Simpson Civil Trial."

19. Larry Schwartz, "Before Trial, Simpson Charmed America," ESPN.com. Retrieved online on April 8, 2009, from espn.go.com/sportscentury/features/00016472.html.

20. "O. J. Simpson Murder Case," Wikipedia. Retrieved online on April 17, 2009, from en.wikipedia.org/wiki/O._J._Simpson_murder_case.

21. "O. J. Simpson Murders," Altered Dimensions. Retrieved online on April 8, 2009, from www.altereddimensions.net/crime/OJSimpsonMurders.htm.

22. "O. J. Simpson Murders," Altered Dimensions.

to show that the gloves allegedly worn by Simpson as he committed the murder did not fit. Said Cochran to the jury, "If it doesn't fit, you must acquit."[23] However, the prosecution argued that the gloves had shrunk because they had been soaked in blood. In fact, the prosecution proved that a new pair of the same gloves of the same size that had not been soaked in blood fit quite well.[24] Thus, in the end, the evidence of the gloves' not fitting was not all that impressive.

The defense also argued that Simpson didn't have enough time, roughly from 9:45 p.m. to 11 p.m., to commit the murders and be ready for the limo driver to take him to the airport for a flight to Chicago. If this were true, then Simpson would have had an *alibi*, a fact that *falsifies* a hypothesis—in this case, the Simpson double-murder hypothesis. Simply put, if Simpson did not have enough time to commit the murders, then he couldn't have committed them.

However, the prosecution had placed the time of the murders at about 10:15 p.m., which would have given Simpson time to commit them and make the five-minute trip home in time to catch a limousine to the airport.[25] Moreover, the limo driver, Allan Parks, testified that he arrived at Simpson's house at 10:22 p.m. on the night of the murders and didn't see Simpson's Bronco parked outside when he was looking for street numbers. Parks maintained that at 10:55 p.m. he saw "a large, shadowy figure of an African-American person at the front door of Simpson's Rockingham estate." Moments later Simpson answered the intercom that Parks said he had previously been sounding for fifteen minutes.[26]

As you have seen, the Simpson double-murder hypothesis had strong predictive and explanatory power. Reality forms a coherent system. When a hypothesis is correct, it tends to fit the facts. When it is false, it tends to run up against contradicting facts. The Simpson double-murder hypothesis appeared to fit the facts as they emerged. Nevertheless, Simpson was acquitted. Why?

The Planting Hypothesis

The defense, which consisted of some of the most renowned lawyers in the country, claimed that two other *competing hypotheses* had enough evidentiary support to create a reasonable doubt about whether Simpson committed the double murder. One of these hypotheses was that the forensic evidence supporting the murder hypothesis had been *planted*.

The defense argued the following points:[27]

- DNA analysis of the blood found in and around Brown's townhouse matched Simpson's blood only because Simpson's blood was planted. The blood sam-

23. "'If It Doesn't Fit, You Must Acquit' Defense Attacks Prosecution's Case; Says Simpson Was Framed," CNN.com, September 28, 1995. Retrieved online on April 8, 2009, from www.cnn.com/US/OJ/daily/9-27/8pm.

24. "O. J. Simpson: Week-by-Week: Week 22, June 19–23," Court TV News, June 5, 2004. Retrieved online on April 8, 2009, from www.courttv.com/trials/ojsimpson/weekly/22.html.

25. "O. J. Simpson: Week-by-Week: Week 25," www.courttv.com/trials/ojsimpson/weekly/25.html.

26. "O. J. Simpson: Week-by-Week: Week 37," www.courttv.com/trials/ojsimpson/weekly/37.html.

27. Thompson, "Proving the Case: The Science of DNA."

ples from the Brown residence were wet when they were transferred from test tubes to plastic bags. A "transfer stain," or smear, on the bag was consistent with the blood's being wet when it was transferred. But the blood samples should not have been wet because it only takes about three hours to dry, and according to the laboratory report, the samples were air-dried in open test tubes for fourteen hours before being bagged. Therefore, the bag containing the transfer stain could not have been the original blood sample.

- Blood was missing from Simpson's sample tube. The nurse who drew the blood testified that he had drawn about 8 ml of blood from Simpson. However, according to LAPD Crime Laboratory records, the tube contained only 6.5 ml when it reached the lab.

- The DNA in the blood samples found on the rear gate of the Brown residence contained high concentrations of undegraded DNA. These samples were collected at the same time and should have been exposed to the same environmental conditions as the other samples collected at the crime scene, including those from the front gate, yet these other samples were highly degraded and contained little identifiable DNA. Therefore, the sample from the rear gate was planted.

- Detective Mark Fuhrman planted the bloody glove he found behind the guesthouse at the Rockingham estate in order to frame Simpson. The defense argued that Fuhrman was a racist, which established a motive for framing Simpson, a black man. According to the testimony of one defense witness, Fuhrman told her he used false pretexts to pull over interracial couples. She also said he told her he would like to put "niggers in a pile and burn them." Another defense witness testified that Fuhrman said, "The only good nigger is a dead nigger."[28]

- Detective Fuhrman planted the victims' blood in the Bronco. Fuhrman reported seeing bloodstains on the lower sill of the Bronco's door. Photographs of the Bronco showed that there were indeed stains where Fuhrman reported them, but they could be seen only when the door of the Bronco was open. This meant that Fuhrman must have gained access to the car even though the detectives testified that the doors were locked.

- Brown's blood was planted on the sock collected from Simpson's bedroom. The blood matching Brown's was about the size of a quarter and stiffened the fabric underneath it. Yet when the sock was collected on June 13, 1994, by LAPD criminalist Dennis Fong, he had not noticed the stain. On June 22, 1994, the socks were examined by LAPD laboratory supervisor Michelle Kestler and two experts for the defense, Michael Baden and Barbara Wolf, none of whom noticed the bloodstain. On June 29, 1994, the socks were reexamined at the request of Judge Lance Ito, and still no bloodstain was noticed. However, the bloodstain was discovered on August 4, 1994. Therefore, the blood must have been planted on the sock sometime after June 29, 1994.

- The chemical preservative ethylenediaminetetraacetic acid (EDTA) was found in the sock stain. This preservative was contained in the test tubes that

28. David Margolick, "Simpson Jury Hears of Racist Incidents," *New York Times*, September 6, 1995. Retrieved online on April 8, 2009, from query.nytimes.com/gst/fullpage.html?res=990CEED91E3DF 935A3575AC0A963958260.

contained Brown's and Goldman's blood samples. This suggests that the blood on the socks came from the laboratory test tubes.

As stated, the defense did not intend for the above evidence to establish the planting hypothesis, just to create a reasonable belief that it might be true. However, can the facts the defense gave to support the planting hypothesis be accounted for in a way that renders them consistent with the Simpson double-murder hypothesis? If so, then such alternative explanations could diminish the persuasiveness of the defense's case and further support the prosecution's case. Here are some possible explanations for the facts at hand:

- The wet transfer could still have been an LAPD error committed in the haste of making the samples available, and the official records might not have reflected the truth about how the blood sample was prepared.
- The fact that the blood at the back gate was not as degraded as elsewhere might also have been explained by the fact that it was in a more shaded area or otherwise not similarly exposed to the elements. In other words, the assumption that the blood located in different physical locations had to degrade at exactly the same rate was itself questionable.
- Even if Fuhrman was a racist, as the defense argued, there is still a large evidentiary gap between this fact and his having planted the glove. Indeed, if he was responsible for planting the glove, then he would probably have been behind the planting of the other evidence against Simpson. This would have been quite difficult to do, especially in a way that completely eliminated all other suspects except Simpson.
- The doors to the Bronco were reported to have been locked, but even if Fuhrman had access to the Bronco, that did not mean he planted the blood inside it. The defense provided no evidence establishing this claim.
- While the failure to notice the bloodstain on the sock does seem to be grounds for concern, this might still have been an oversight, especially if the LAPD was as incompetent as the defense tried to make it out to be.
- As the prosecution made clear, the nurse who drew Simpson's blood could have been mistaken about how much blood was drawn.
- As for the EDTA found on the sock, the person who tested the sock for this preservative did not think the quantity of the chemical found was consistent with blood from the test tube. The defense then produced an expert who believed that the quantity found was consistent with the blood from the test tube. So the experts did not agree on this point. When two experts disagree, it makes sense to call in a third and maybe a fourth or fifth expert. This was not done.

The Cross-Contamination Hypothesis

The defense had another hypothesis that competed with the Simpson double-murder hypothesis. It was that the blood samples were *cross-contaminated*. The defense made the following points in support of this hypothesis:[29]

---

29. Thompson, "Proving the Case: The Science of DNA."

- The blood collected at the Brown residence may have been contaminated with Simpson's DNA at the LAPD laboratory. The LAPD's forensic scientist admitted to spilling some of Simpson's blood from a test tube and shortly thereafter handling the samples containing the blood from the Brown residence. Some of Simpson's blood may have been inadvertently transferred to the samples by way of the scientist's gloves or instruments.
- The DNA of the person who really left the blood drops could not be detected because it was degraded and destroyed due to mishandling of the blood samples from the Brown residence. The blood samples had been left for several hours in a hot truck, causing them to degrade. As a result, the subsequent cross-contamination of the sample caused it to match Simpson's DNA falsely.
- The small quantity of DNA found was consistent with the cross-contamination hypothesis. On the blood sample from the glove, Simpson's DNA was found only on the area where the forensic scientist wrote his initials. In the blood samples collected from the Brown residence, the first sample the forensic scientist handled had the most DNA from Simpson, while the later samples contained much less, a pattern also consistent with the cross-contamination hypothesis.
- The LAPD laboratory had a documented history of problems with cross-contamination due to poor sample-handling procedures, such as failure to follow written protocols and to take precautionary measures such as changing gloves. In addition, an expert for the defense claimed to have found that test tubes containing the blood of Brown and Goldman had been contaminated with Simpson's DNA.

Against Simpson's defense team, the prosecution argued that cross-contamination of the blood found at the Brown residence was not likely because test samples taken from clear areas next to the bloodstains did not contain DNA. The prosecution's logic was that if the blood samples were contaminated with Simpson's DNA, then the test samples would also probably (although not necessarily) be contaminated.

The defense rejected this logic, claiming it was still possible that the test samples had not been exposed when the cross-contamination occurred. However, while this is true, the fact that the test samples came up negative for DNA does significantly diverge from, and lower the probability of, the cross-contamination hypothesis.

Step 6: Evaluating Hypotheses

As discussed, the main standard for assessing the acceptability of a hypothesis is its predictive and explanatory power. In the Simpson case, the *single* hypothesis with the most predictive and explanatory power appeared to be the Simpson double-murder hypothesis.

But predictive and explanatory power is not the only standard for evaluating hypotheses. Another secondary standard is *simplicity*. This standard has sometimes been called Ockham's razor after the fourteenth-century English logician,

William of Ockham. It states that "entities must not be multiplied beyond necessity." That is, if you have a choice between two or more competing hypotheses
that otherwise have the same predictive and explanatory power, then you should
choose the one that makes the fewest assumptions or includes the fewest provisos
or conditions.

Now, it appeared that the defense had to rely on both cross-contamination
and the planting of evidence in order to explain the facts at hand. For example,
the cross-contamination hypothesis doesn't explain why the mate to the bloody
glove found at the Brown residence was found at Simpson's Rockingham residence. To explain this, the defense had also to rely on the planting hypothesis.
Conversely, the planting hypothesis did not explain certain facts, such as why
there was no evidence linking anyone else except Simpson to the crimes. For
this, the defense had to rely on the cross-contamination hypothesis. On the
other hand, neither of these hypotheses managed to successfully explain why
the bloody footprints at the crime scene matched those made by a pair of size
12 Bruno Magli shoes. Only the Simpson double-murder hypothesis managed
to adequately explain this fact. Accordingly, since Simpson's defense team had
to make claims *both* about cross-contamination *and* the planting of evidence in
order to defend its client against very incriminating evidence, its defense was a
lot more complicated than the prosecution's hypothesis that Simpson committed the double murders.

Because truth forms a coherent system, the true hypothesis is likely to contain
a lesser number of conditions, provisos, or assumptions than one that is false. As
most of us have experienced firsthand, if we are on the wrong track, we may end
up making a lot of excuses before we confront the truth. For example, we might
make excuses for the misconduct of a friend or family member. "Oh, he's probably being falsely accused. He would never molest a child." At some point, when
our attempt to save our pet hypothesis has to swim upstream against a tide of divergent facts, reason tells us to relinquish it in favor of the simpler explanation.

In the Simpson case, the double-murder hypothesis explained the most facts,
had the greatest predictive power, and provided the simplest explanation. It
therefore had the greatest probability of being the correct explanation.

Step 7: Choosing and Acting on a Hypothesis

Even if Simpson's defense team could account for all the facts—an assumption
that does not appear to be true—it would have done so at the expense of mount-
ing proviso upon proviso. This is not to say that the more complicated hypothesis
is necessarily false. It is, however, a matter of probability, and the least complicated way of explaining the same set of facts tends more often to be the true one.

So, did the jury err when it acquitted Simpson? Within the rules set by our
criminal justice system, it is arguable that the jury reached the correct verdict—
not because Simpson was, as a matter of fact, innocent of committing the double
murder but because the defense had successfully created reasonable doubt in the
mind of the jury as to whether he was guilty of the crime. Here, it is important to
avoid the fallacious assumption that the verdict "not guilty" means "innocent."
The fact that the state did not succeed in proving its case beyond a reasonable

doubt does not mean that Simpson was innocent of the crimes with which he was charged.

From the perspective of choosing the more probable hypothesis, the answer seems clear. The Simpson double-murder hypothesis was the strongest of the competing hypotheses based on its greater ability to explain and predict the facts and its greater simplicity. In fact, on February 4, 2007, in a civil trial, the jury reached a unanimous decision to hold Simpson liable for the deaths of Nicole Brown and Ronald Goldman and awarded $8.5 million in compensatory damages to the Goldman family and Ron Goldman's biological mother.

The evidence given to support the Simpson double-murder hypothesis in the criminal trial was also introduced in the civil trial. However, the standard of proof in a civil trial is lower than that in a criminal trial. In a civil trial, jurors are asked to reach a decision based on "the preponderance of evidence," which means a greater than 50 percent probability, and only nine out of twelve jurors must concur in order for a verdict to be reached. In contrast, in a criminal trial the state has to prove the charges "beyond a reasonable doubt," and all twelve jurors have to agree on the verdict. Effectively, in the civil trial, the jury chose the most probable hypothesis based on the evidence. In the murder trial, the jury based its decision on the fact that there was a least some reasonable possibility that the alternative hypotheses were true.

In this regard, probability is like a pie, and each competing hypothesis is a piece carrying some finite amount of probability. The larger one slices one piece, the smaller the other pieces must become. Thus, the extent to which a competing hypothesis to the Simpson double-murder hypothesis was supported by the facts was the extent to which the probability of the latter hypothesis was diminished.

The Fallacy of Unsupported Hypothesis

Let's grant that the hypotheses competing with the double-murder hypothesis presented by O. J. Simpson's defense team in the criminal trial—namely the planting hypothesis and the cross-contamination hypothesis—had enough support to create a reasonable doubt in the minds of the jurors. As the civil trial suggests, this does not mean that it would be reasonable to accept either of the competing hypotheses over the Simpson double-murder hypothesis. As you have seen, neither of the competing hypotheses, taken singly or together, adequately explained or squared with the facts. For example, in the planting hypothesis, the person who planted the evidence—say, Fuhrman—would have to have had access to the size 12 rare and extremely expensive Bruno Magli shoes worn by Simpson, or at least to have gone to the trouble of finding out what type of shoes Simpson wore and then purchased them. And he would have to have done this and planted the footprints made by these shoes even before he found out about the homicides. This is rather far-fetched. Similarly, the cross-contamination theory alone does not explain the shoe prints; nor does it alone explain the fact that the bloody Aris Isotoner glove found at Simpson's Rockingham estate had the blood of the victims on it.

Accordingly, it would arguably have been unreasonable for the jury to accept either of the competing hypotheses. Let us say that the acceptance of such a hypothesis commits the *fallacy of unsupported hypothesis*. This fallacy involves accepting a hypothesis that either has (1) too much divergent evidence against it, or (2) not enough convergent evidence to support it. Accepting either of the competing hypotheses to the Simpson double-murder hypothesis, as put forth by Simpson's defense team, would have involved commission of this fallacy. But, as we have seen, the use of either of these hypotheses to create a reasonable doubt did not require the acceptance of either. Thus, Simpson's defense team did not itself commit these fallacies. It is not clear, however, whether any of the jurors committed it.

One does not have to look far to discover clear cases in which people commit the fallacy of unsupported hypothesis. This fallacy is quite prevalent in ordinary life. One commonplace context for its occurrence is situations of extreme fear. Motivated by intense fear, people often jump to conclusions and think the worst has happened when there are more probable explanations. For example, in cases where a loved one has not returned (say, from work or school) at the usual time, it is not uncommon for many of us to think the worst. Thus, hypotheses like "He must have gotten into a terrible automobile accident or he is having an affair" may come to mind before more probable explanations like "He stopped off to shop, he is working late, or he is stuck in traffic." Of course, the dreaded hypotheses are not impossible, and the gathering of subsequent evidence can later bear them out. However, in the absence of such evidence, it is unreasonable to think the worst. There is an important logical difference between what is most probable and what is most feared. While the former always depends on evidence, the latter does not.

In emotionally stressful situations, it is often hard to think rationally. But, as we shall see in chapter 16, much of this stress is often of our own creating. By jumping to conclusions, we help to perpetuate our emotional stress. By being scientific and following the seven steps of the scientific method discussed in this chapter, you can avoid much of this self-induced stress and accordingly perform more competently.

Thus, one can start by adequately defining one's problem. The problem is not why does he have to do this to me? or how could such a terrible thing (a terrible accident) have happened? These already assume an unproven hypothesis. Rather ask, why is he late? Then, the second step is to formulate as many relevant preliminary hypotheses you can think of: He is working late; he stopped off after work to have a drink with friends; he's stuck in traffic; he was in an accident; he had a flat tire; he went to the gym; and so on.

Once you see that there are so many other relevant competing hypotheses besides the feared ones that could also be true, you may be less apt to jump to conclusions and think the worst. Then, by gathering further evidence, you can begin to get a better picture as to which of these hypotheses to take more seriously. For example, by calling his office mate, you might learn that he mentioned possibly going to the gym after work, thereby lowering the probability of the accident hypothesis and raising the probability that he is at the gym. And, of course, one way to test the latter hypothesis is simply to wait a while longer to see if he returns home, safe and sound. In this way, many and sundry everyday problems can be managed by applying the scientific method instead of irrationally jumping to conclusions.

Exercise Set 12.2

Provide responses to each of the following questions about the Simpson murder case. Defend each response.

12.2.1
If you were on the jury of the Simpson murder trial, would you have found him "not guilty"?

12.2.2
Was either the planting hypothesis or the cross-contamination hypothesis or both sufficient to create a reasonable doubt?

12.2.3
Do you think the fact that Mark Fuhrman appeared to harbor racial prejudice toward blacks should have been a factor in creating a reasonable doubt in the minds of the jurors?

12.2.4
What, in your estimation, was the simplest explanation of the facts of the case?

Exercise Set 12.3

12.3.1
On May 30, 2006, eighteen-year-old Natalie Holloway disappeared while on a high school graduation trip to Aruba, never to be found. The case was well publicized in the media, and there are many factual accounts of the case to be found on the Internet. For this case, construct each of the seven steps of the scientific method discussed in this chapter, beginning with the formulation of a definition of the problem and ending with choosing and acting on a hypothesis.

12.3.2
In 1947 materials associated with the crash of a flying object were recovered in Roswell, New Mexico. The event has been the subject of much debate, including the claim that what crashed was an alien craft containing beings from another planet. For this case, construct each of the seven steps of the scientific method discussed in this chapter, beginning with the formulation of a definition of the problem and ending with choosing and acting on a hypothesis. In choosing a hypothesis, be sure to consider what you think is the simplest explanation of the facts. Factual accounts can be found on the Internet.

13

Causation

Knowing the causes and effects of things is a major aspect of human survival. If you know that fire can burn your flesh if you touch it, then you can avoid the flames. If you know that MRSA is a highly contagious form of bacteria, then you can take precautions against contracting it. Indeed, from pathogens to the hazards of crossing a busy street, we must apply our fundamental knowledge of causation in order to survive intact even for a single day.

But just what is causation anyway?

THE MEANING OF CAUSATION

Causation is a relation between a cause and an effect. The cause can be a state or condition (for example, the presence of oxygen) or an event (for example, the act of striking a match). The effect is an event that typically occurs after (but sometimes simultaneously with) the cause (for example, the igniting of the match).

In some cases, we can speak of *agent* causation—that is, a *person's* causing something, as in John's causing an automobile accident. Here, however, we typically speak elliptically about something that John did (or failed to do) that caused the accident. For example, John's *going through a red light* caused a second vehicle to broadside John's car. In this case, we can understand agent causation in terms of a relationship between two events: John's going through a red light (the cause) and the second vehicle's broadsiding John's car (the effect).

Causes as Necessary and/or Sufficient Conditions

The relationship between a given cause and effect can be interpreted differently in different contexts. In some cases, the cause of an event is a necessary condition for its occurrence. A *necessary condition* for the occurrence of an event is an event, state, or condition without which the event cannot occur. For example, in this sense, a certain virus, say the HIV virus, causes AIDS. Exposure to the HIV virus (typically by way of sexual or needle-sharing activities) is a necessary condition of getting AIDS because one cannot get AIDS without being exposed to this virus.

Notice, however, that being exposed to the HIV virus is not a sufficient condition of getting AIDS. A *sufficient condition* for the occurrence of an event is an event, state, or condition in the presence of which the event must occur. Being exposed to the HIV virus is not a sufficient condition for getting AIDS because it is possible to be exposed to the virus and still not get AIDS. For example, not all exposure contains enough of the virus to infect one with the HIV virus.

There are, however, contexts in which the relation between cause and effect is one of sufficient condition. For example, consuming an alcoholic beverage can be said to cause an increase in one's blood alcohol because it is a sufficient condition of increasing one's blood alcohol.

There are also contexts in which the relation between cause and effect is one of *both necessary and sufficient condition*. For example, consider Isaac Newton's third law of thermodynamics, according to which for every action there is always an opposite equal reaction. Thus, if you push on a wall, the wall pushes back with equal force. The force exerted on the wall (Fw) at the same time (t) causes the force exerted on you (Fy); conversely, Fy at t causes Fw.[1] Since Fy is a sufficient condition of Fw, and Fw is a sufficient condition of Fy, the relationship can be represented in terms of two conditions: (if Fy then Fw) and (if Fw then Fy). As you have seen in chapter 3, this means that Fy is both a necessary and sufficient condition of Fw.

A sufficient condition consists of a set of conditions that are jointly sufficient for a certain effect. For example, striking a match is not sufficient to ignite it. This act must occur under other conditions, such as the presence of oxygen, the absence of moisture, and the application of surface friction. In this respect, each of these other conditions can be said to be a necessary condition of igniting the match.

However, in ordinary contexts, we typically single out one of these conditions and call it *the cause*, while we relegate all the other conditions to mere *causal conditions*. Thus, we would ordinarily refer to the act of striking the match as the cause but refer to the presence of oxygen as a *causal condition*.

Causes versus Causal Conditions

The standards by which we judge and distinguish causes from mere causal conditions appear to be variable and typically depend on the purpose for which a causal judgment is being made. For example, in the practical context of determining the cause of an accident, we are ordinarily concerned with identifying an act perpetrated by a person for purposes of assigning blame or responsibility. Thus, John's going through a red light can be designated as the cause of the accident because John can legally be held accountable for the act and made to pay.

In medical contexts, the distinction between active and passive euthanasia depends on the assignment of causation and has practical implications for the as-

---

1. Newton's third law of thermodynamics accordingly also provides an example of *simultaneous causation*: that is, where cause and effect occur simultaneously (at the same time).

signment of criminal responsibility. Active euthanasia, sometimes called "mercy killing," is the killing of a patient for humanitarian reasons related to the patient's illness, such as to end pain and suffering due to a progressed cancer. For example, active euthanasia may involve administration of a lethal medication. In such contexts, the medication is said to cause the death of the patient.

In contrast, passive euthanasia involves allowing a patient to die for humanitarian reasons related to the patient's illness. For example, withdrawing a respirator is said to be passive euthanasia because it allows the patient to die of natural causes—namely the disease.

Notice, however, that the withdrawal of a respirator is one among several conditions that must be present, which are jointly sufficient for the patient to die. For example, upon withdrawal of the respirator, the patent will not die if she can breathe on her own. In such contexts, the withdrawal of the respirator is relegated to a condition of the patient's death, whereas the disease is considered the cause of death. In this way, physicians are able to withdraw respirators without being held criminally liable for killing (causing the death of) the patient.

There are, however, medical contexts in which the distinction between causes and conditions is not so clear-cut. For example, decades ago it was permissible to "allow" newborns with Down syndrome who had intestinal blockages to starve to death, even though the intestinal blockages could easily be repaired surgically. Thus, the illness (the intestinal blockages) became a pretext for "allowing" the patient to die when the true reason for not saving the child was the fact that he or she had Down syndrome.

Currently, medical law and practice no longer permit physicians and the infants' families to stand by while these newborn patients starve to death. In fact, it does not stretch language very far to say that in such cases, failing to perform the routine surgery necessary to save these patients is to *kill* them. That is, the omission of the routine surgery itself could arguably be considered not merely a causal condition of the patient's death but rather its *cause*.

Notice that acts of omission can also be causes in some contexts. For example, a driver who fails to put his foot on the brake in approaching a pedestrian cannot correctly claim not to have caused the death of the pedestrian because he "simply" *omitted* to put his foot on the break.

Exercise Set 13.1

The following is a description of the tragic circumstances of Karen Ann Quinlan, whose landmark legal case in 1976 set the precedent for the legalization of passive euthanasia in the United States. Read it, and respond to each of the questions that follow. Defend your responses.

In April 1975, Quinlan went on a radical diet, reportedly in order to fit into a dress that she had recently bought. On April 15, having eaten nothing but a few slices of bread over a period of roughly forty-eight hours, she attended a party at a friend's house. After consuming alcohol (and allegedly Valium tranquilizers, although this has been disputed by her family), Quinlan told her friends that she was feeling dizzy and went off to lie down on her friend's bed. She was found a while later by partygoers, unconscious and not breathing. She suffered irreversible brain damage

(continued)

after experiencing an extended period of respiratory failure and subsequently was placed on a respirator in a hospital. No precise cause of her respiratory failure has been given, although her mother has said that the doctors' best guess was that she fell asleep or passed out and choked on her own vomit. This could have been caused by the combination of alcohol and the weakness caused by her self-imposed deprivation of food.

Her parents wanted to have her taken off the respirator that was sustaining her, but hospital officials refused. In 1976, the Quinlans took their case to the New Jersey Supreme Court, which sided with them in its decision. When she was taken off the respirator, Quinlan surprised many by continuing to breathe unaided and was fed by artificial nutrition for nine more years. She lived in a persistent vegetative state until her death from pneumonia in 1985.

13.1.1
List all possible necessary conditions of Karen Ann Quinlan's brain damage.

13.1.2
List any possible sufficient conditions of Quinlan's brain damage.

13.1.3
Were all of the conditions you listed in 13.2.1 jointly sufficient for Quinlan's brain damage?

13.1.4
List any possible sufficient condition of Quinlan's death.

13.1.5
If Quinlan had died in a matter of minutes after the respirator was disconnected, what would the likely "cause" of death have been?

CONSTANT CONJUNCTION

All causal relationships defined as sufficient conditions assume a conjunction between cause and effect. That is, if one thing is the cause of a second thing, then whenever the first thing occurs, the second thing also occurs. Thus, if fire causes heat (that is, it is a sufficient condition of heat), then it follows that whenever there is fire, there is heat.

In fact, according to eighteenth-century British philosopher David Hume, the relationship of causation can be defined in terms of such a "constant conjunction." According to Hume, a cause is "an object followed by another, and where all objects similar to the first are followed by objects similar to the second."[2] Hume's account of causation underscores the idea that the relationship of causation is established empirically: that is, through experiencing the constant junction of events. Thus, to use Hume's example, no matter how much you analyzed the concept of water a priori (that is, without consulting experience), you would not be able to divine that it could suffocate a person submerged in it. This property of water to suffocate could only be discovered through the experience of this property as

---

2. David Hume, *An Enquiry Concerning Human Understanding*, in *Enquiries Concerning Human Understanding and Concerning the Principles of Morals*, ed. L. A. Selby-Bigge, third ed. rev. (Oxford: Clarendon Press, 1975), 76. Hume also gives a *psychological* version of his definition: "An object followed by another, and whose appearance always conveys the thought to that other" (77).

constantly conjoined with water. This means that causal relationships are arrived at through the process of inductive generalization (see chapter 9).

Unfortunately, inductive generalization cannot by itself establish a causal relationship. The fact that two things have always been observed to be joined with one another does not necessarily mean that they are *causally* related. As John Stuart Mill made clear, if this were all there was to causality, then you might as well say that night causes day or that day causes night since one has always been observed to follow the other.[3] But night does not cause day, nor does day cause night. These are caused by the position of the earth in relation to the sun. Thus, the mere fact that one thing consistently follows another does not mean they are causally related.

The Post Hoc Fallacy

The Latin phrase *post hoc ergo propter hoc* ("after this therefore because of this") captures the fallacy inherent in Hume's analysis. The fact that one event follows another, even if this sequence is constant, does not give us satisfactory grounds for concluding that the sequence is one of causation. Let us call this fallacy the *post hoc fallacy*.

A popular form of this fallacy is assuming a causal relationship between two events after observing a single instance in which the first is followed by the second. For example, you walk under a ladder, have bad luck, and straightaway conclude that walking under the ladder is what caused your bad luck. You eat in a restaurant, come down with the flu, and straightaway conclude that eating in the restaurant caused the illness. Soon after having boasted about not having gotten into an automobile accident for quite some time, a car backs into yours, so you straightaway conclude that your boasting caused the accident. Indeed, the myriad of ways in which such fallacious reasoning can be—and is—committed in practical life contexts is extensive.

Consider the following example of the post hoc fallacy as contained in an excerpt from a speech given by George W. Bush on September 6, 2006:

> In the early days and weeks after 9/11, I directed our government's senior national security officials to do everything in their power, within our laws, to prevent another attack. Nearly five years have passed since these—those initial days of shock and sadness—and we are thankful that the terrorists have not succeeded in launching another attack on our soil. . . . One reason the terrorists have not succeeded is because of the hard work of thousands of dedicated men and women in our government, who have toiled day and night, along with our allies, to stop the enemy from carrying out their plans. And we are grateful for these hardworking citizens of ours. Another reason the terrorists have not succeeded is because our government has changed its policies— and given our military, intelligence, and law enforcement personnel the tools they need to fight this enemy and protect our people and preserve our freedoms.[4]

---

3. John Stuart Mill, *A System of Logic, Ratiocinative and Inductive: Being a Connected View of the Principles of Evidence and the Methods of Scientific Investigation* (London: Longmans, Green, 1865), 337–38.

4. White House Briefing Room, retrieved online from www.whitehouse.gov/news/releases/2006/09/20060906-3.html.

In the above, Bush explicitly gives his administration credit for there not having been another terrorist attack on America in the five years between September 11, 2001, and September 6, 2006. According to Bush, this was the result of the work and policy changes of his administration.

Among these policy changes were increased security measures at airports. But these changes also included warrantless spying on American citizens, torture of detainees in Guantánamo and Abu Ghraib, and the invasion of Iraq. So, Bush claimed that because there hadn't been any subsequent terrorist attacks since the time these policies were implemented, the latter must have been causally related to the former.

However, this observed conjunction alone proves nothing. We might as well claim that there were no more terrorist attacks on American soil up to September 6, 2006, because in 2004 a Democratic Congress replaced a Republican one. This, however, would be just as groundless as Bush's claim. The mere fact that the policy changes in question were followed by no more terrorist attacks does not mean that the first was the cause of the second.

Exercise Set 13.2

Provide five actual examples of the post hoc fallacy. You may use your own fallacious causal claims or causal claims made by others as examples.

FEAR AND SUPERSTITION AS
THE BASIS OF CAUSAL JUDGMENT

Unfortunately, fear and superstition instead of critical and free thinking frequently shape causal judgment. An instructive example of this usurpation of rationality can be found in the history of diagnosing the causal etiology of diseases. The history of medicine is a testament to how human beings have allowed fear and superstition instead of critical and free thinking to determine the causes of human maladies. This has resulted in the maltreatment, social ostracizing, and persecution of hundreds of thousands of disease sufferers throughout history.

For example, epilepsy, a disease caused by brain lesions that cause seizures, was once thought to be caused by evil spirits, and medical treatment consisted of attempting to exorcise them. In the eighteenth century, epilepsy was thought to be contagious, and epileptics were locked away in solitude in mental institutions. In the early twentieth century epileptics were prevented from marrying and having children. Fear and superstition thus took the place of careful scientific investigation, and as a result innocent persons were denigrated and made to suffer.

In the nineteenth century, a new disease was "discovered." This so-called disease was said to arise out of the "unnatural" and debilitating act of masturbation. This disease was said to cause

> dyspepsia, constrictions of the urethra, epilepsy, blindness, vertigo, loss of hearing, headache, impotency, loss of memory, irregular action of the heart, general loss of health and strength, rickets, leucorrhea in women, and chronic catarrhal conjunctivitis

... elongation of the clitoris, reddening and congestion of the labia majora, elongation of the labia minora, and thinning and decrease in size of the penis ... enlargement of the superficial veins of the hands and feet, moist and clammy hands, stooped shoulders, pale sallow face with heavy dark circles around the eyes, a "draggy" gait, and acne ... and evidence indicated it was a cause of hereditary insanity ... an hereditary predisposition toward consumption ... [and] general disability.[5]

In this case, the causal relationship between masturbation and these "symptoms" was fueled by a religious perspective that condemned this form of sexual activity. A religious value was accordingly transformed into the language of disease: a litany of symptoms caused by the forbidden act.[6] Critical and free thinking was again rejected in favor of dogmatic and blind conviction.

In 1981, when cases of AIDS first began to appear in the United States among the gay population, these individuals were ostracized and discriminated against. Religious extremists saw the disease as a punishment brought down by God on gay persons for their "sinful" sexual practices. Again, fear and superstition shaped causal judgment instead of critical thinking.

Exercise Set 13.3

Provide at least one other historical example of a disease whose causal etiology or treatment was based largely on fear, superstition, or other irrational grounds. Explain why the causal judgments involved in diagnosing or treating this disease were irrational.

MILL'S METHODS OF ESTABLISHING CAUSAL RELATIONSHIPS

So how do we go about using critical thinking to establish causal relationships? In 1843 John Stuart Mill set forth several inductive "methods" for confirming causal relationships in *A System of Logic*. These methods include the following: (1) agreement, (2) difference, (3) joint method of agreement and difference, and (4) concomitant variation. In what follows we will use the disease of AIDS to illustrate how these methods work.

The Method of Agreement

According to Mill,

> If two or more instances of the phenomenon under investigation have only one circumstance in common, the circumstance in which alone all the instances agree is the cause of the given phenomenon.[7]

---

5. H. Tristram Engelhardt Jr., "The Disease of Masturbation: Values and the Concept of Disease," in *Contemporary Issues in Bioethics*, ed. Tom L. Beauchamp and Leroy Walters, 3rd ed. (Belmont, Calif.: Wadsworth, 1989), 86.

6. Engelhardt, "The Disease of Masturbation."

7. John Stuart Mill, *A System of Logic: Ratiocinative and Inductive*, chapter 8, sec. 1. Retrieved online on June 15, 2009, from mirror.pacific.net.au/gutenberg/2/7/9/4/27942/27942.txt.

Table 13.1

Case	Antecedent Conditions	Phenomenon Under Investigation
1	A **B** C D E	e
2	A **B** F G H	e
3	**B** F G	e
4	**B** F H	e

That is, you should look for the cause of something in that condition which is present in all instances of that for which you are seeking the cause. This method can be illustrated by table 13.1.

For example, let cases 1–4 comprise a list of dogs and cats that died from kidney disease; let antecedent conditions A–H be a list of ingredients in the food each of these animals was fed prior to its death; and let the phenomenon under investigation (e) be death by kidney disease. Clearly, B would be a prime suspect since it was "the circumstance in which alone all the instances agree."[8] While this does not *necessarily* mean that B was the culprit, the Food and Drug Administration, charged with protecting consumer safety, would be remiss in its duty if it overlooked B.

Applying Mill's method of agreement to discovering the cause of AIDS presented a special challenge because at first it was not clear what this common condition might be. For example, in the above application of the method to the deaths of animals, there was a reasonable belief that the offending agent was a food ingredient. In contrast, it was not clear whether the cause of AIDS was a chemical that was being ingested, an infectious agent, or even an activity.

AIDS (acquired immune deficiency syndrome) is a disease characterized by a severely compromised immune system[9] that makes one vulnerable to opportunistic infections. The diagnosis of AIDS is made when a patient with a compromised immune system has one or more of a complex, or "syndrome," of approximately twenty-six "indicator diseases," for example, pneumocystis carinii pneumonia, Kaposi's sarcoma, and candidiasis (yeastlike fungal infection).[10] Because the causal etiology of AIDS was unknown when cases of the disease began to emerge in 1981, the disease could not then be defined in terms of any specific cause. Instead it was defined in terms of such opportunistic infections.

At first, cases were restricted to gay persons, and the disease earned the status of "gay disease." However, as many more cases of the disease continued to be reported to the Centers for Disease Control (CDC), it became apparent that there were a few major possible avenues of transmission that did not exclude transmission to and from heterosexuals. Based on its demographic studies, the CDC drew the conditional conclusion that if AIDS had an infectious cause, then it was trans-

---

8. This is based on an actual case. The common ingredient (B) in the deaths of the animals was wheat gluten imported from China. See Lisa Wade McCormick, "American Importer Recalls All Wheat Gluten," ConsumerAffairs.com, April 4, 2007. Retrieved online on March 25, 2009, from www.consumeraffairs.com/news04/2007/04/pet_food_recall15.html.

9. This is determined by an immune system cell count known as a CD4 cell count that is below two hundred cells per cubic millimeter of blood.

10. Centers for Disease Control, "AIDS Definition," *MMWR* 36 (suppl. 1S) (1987). Retrieved online on July 28, 2008, from www.rightto.com/theories/aidsdef.html.

mitted by blood (hemophiliacs and intravenous drug users were affected), intimate sexual contact, and mother-to-infant contact (for instance, breast feeding).[11]

The CDC's inference appeared to have squared with other independent research going on at the time. In May 1983, a French researcher, Luc Montagnier, reported having isolated a virus he called LAV, which he claimed caused AIDS. One year later, American researcher Robert Gallo reported having isolated a virus he called HTLV-III, which he claimed caused AIDS. These two viruses were later determined to be the same virus, and they were renamed HIV.[12]

While the research of Montagnier and Gallo laid the foundation for further testing, neither of these pioneers in AIDS research appeared to have adequately confirmed that HIV was the cause of AIDS. Unfortunately, Montagnier derived his findings by isolating the virus from *just one* individual who had AIDS. Gallo's tests also appeared to have been procedurally flawed. For example, instead of finding the HIV virus in the blood samples taken from each of his subjects who had AIDS, as Mill's method of agreement would have required, he apparently pooled the blood of several subjects (as many as ten) in order to attain his results.[13]

Nevertheless, the findings of Montagnier and Gallo have been borne out by subsequent, more extensive studies. For example, in 1993, a CDC task force published the results of a survey in which it had reviewed 230,179 AIDS-like cases reported since 1983. As table 13.2 reflects, there were 47 cases of apparent HIV-free AIDS and 127 uncertain cases. All other cases (230,005) had received a positive HIV test. While this certainly raised questions about the forty-seven subjects who had AIDS and appeared to be HIV-free, the vast number of subjects who had AIDS did also test positive for HIV.[14]

The Method of Difference

According to Mill's method of difference,

> If an instance in which a phenomenon under investigation occurs and an instance in which it does not occur, have every circumstance in common save one, that one

Table 13.2

All Subjects Surveyed Who Had AIDS	Subjects Having Positive HIV Tests	Indeterminant Cases	Subjects Having AIDS Who Did Not Have a Positive HIV Test
230,179	230,005	127	47

---

11. Robert C. Gallo, "A Brief History of AIDS," Student BMJ, December 2006. Retrieved online on March 25, 2009, from student.bmj.com/issues/06/12/education/450.php.

12. A unique feature of the HIV virus is that it is a *retrovirus*. A retrovirus is a virus made up of RNA instead of DNA. It also contains an enzyme known as transcriptase, which allows it, once in a host cell, to translate its RNA into DNA and to inject itself into the cell's chromosomes. In this way, the virus takes over the host cell and duplicates itself.

13. Eleni Papadopulos-Eleopulos, Valendar F. Turner, and John M. Papadimitriou, "Has Gallo Proven the Role of HIV in AIDS?" *Emergency Medicine* 5 (1993). Retrieved online on March 25, 2009, from www.virusmyth.com/aids/hiv/epgallo.htm.

14. Avert, "Evidence that HIV Causes AIDS," Avert.org, March 20, 2009. Retrieved online on March 25, 2009, from Retrieved online on March 25, 2009, from www.avert.org/evidence.htm.

Table 13.3

Cases That Are Identical Except for Circumstance A	Phenomenon Under Investigation Present	Circumstance A Present
Case 1	Yes	Yes
Case 2	No	No

occurring only in the former, the circumstance in which alone the two instances differ, is . . . the cause, or an indispensable part of the cause, of the phenomenon.[15]

This method is represented in table 13.3.

For example, let case 1 be a dog that has eaten dog food that contains ingredient A, and let case 2 be a dog that has eaten the same dog food without ingredient A. And let the phenomenon under investigation be kidney disease. According to Mill's method of difference, if the dog that has eaten A develops kidney disease and the dog that has not eaten A does not develop kidney disease, then the cause, or an indispensable part of the cause, of the kidney disease in case 1 is ingredient A.

Clearly, it is not always easy to find cases that "have every circumstance in common save one." Indeed, there are likely to be some variations between instances. However, it is appropriate to suppose that some circumstances will be relevant whereas some are not. For example, each of the dog foods in question might have a different name on the can. That would clearly be irrelevant to the food's causal relation to kidney disease.

Regarding the question of what causes AIDS, some researchers have made twins the subjects of their investigations. Indeed, given the close fit between the environmental and genetic circumstances of twins, it would seem reasonable to suppose that twins are relevantly similar enough to accommodate Mill's method of difference.

In one such study, monozygotic (identical) twin girls were compared. The subjects were born to HIV-positive parents. One twin showed clinical evidence of AIDS and tested positive for HIV; the other at the age of three showed no clinical signs of AIDS and was HIV negative.[16] Similar findings were noted in the case of dizygotic (nonidentical) twins.[17] Table 13.4 summarizes the use of the method of difference in these studies.

The Joint Method of Agreement and Difference

Mill's joint method of agreement and difference is simply the use of both the method of agreement and the method of difference to investigate the same phe-

15. Mill, *A System of Logic*, chapter 8, sec. 2.
16. R. Menez-Bautista et al., "Monozygotic Twins Discordant for the Acquired Immunodeficiency Syndrome," *American Journal of Diseases of Children* 140, no. 7 (July 1986): 678–79. Abstract retrieved online on July 31, 2008, from www.ncbi.nlm.nih.gov/pubmed/3012996?dopt=Abstract.
17. C. L. Park, "Transmission of Human Immunodeficiency Virus from Parents to Only One Dizygotic Twin," *Journal of Clinical Microbiology* 25, no. 6 (June 1987): 1119–21. Abstract retrieved online on July 31, 2008, from www.ncbi.nlm.nih.gov/pubmed/3597757?dopt=Abstract. For other corroborative studies, see also U.S. Department of Health and Human Services, "The Evidence That HIV Causes AIDS," February 27, 2003. Retrieved online on July 31, 2008, from www.niaid.nih.gov/Factsheets/evidhiv.htm.

Table 13.4

Cases That Are Relevantly Similar Except for HIV Status	Develops AIDS	Tests Positive for HIV
Twin 1	Yes	Yes
Twin 2	No	No

nomenon. Thus, for example, as you have seen, each of these methods by itself gives some probability to the claim that the cause of AIDS is the HIV virus. When both of these methods are used to investigate the cause of AIDS, as we have illustrated in this chapter, then the probability of the claim about causation can be even greater.

The Method of Concomitant Variation

According to Mill's method of concomitant variation,

> Whatever phenomenon varies in any manner whenever another phenomenon varies in some particular manner is either a cause or an effect of that phenomenon or is connected with it through some fact of causation.[18]

The basic idea here is that in cases where a cause or effect admits of gradations, when you increase or decrease the cause, the phenomenon under investigation also increases or decreases.

This method has clearly been applied to showing that the cause of AIDS is HIV. More specifically, it is possible to predict the probability of someone's developing AIDS by measuring "viral load," or the quantity of virus in one's blood.[19]

For example, table 13.5[20] is based on a ten-year study of 1,604 HIV-positive men. Here, viral load can be seen as a function of RNA copies per milliliter of blood plasma. RNA is the basic building block of HIV.[21] As you can see from the table, the greater or smaller the amount of virus in one's bloodstream, the greater or smaller the chance of one's developing AIDS. According to the method of

Table 13.5

Viral Load (RNA Copies per Milliliter of Blood Plasma)	Proportion of Patients Developing AIDS Within Six Years
less than 500	5.4%
501–3,000	16.6%
3,001–10,000	31.7%
10,001–30,000	55.2%
more than 30,000	80.0%

18. Mill, *A System of Logic*, chapter 8, sec. 6.
19. J. W. Mellor et al., "Plasma Viral Load and CD4+ Lymphocytes As Prognostic Markers of HIV-1 Infection," *Annals of Internal Medicine* 126, no. 12 (June 1997): 946–54. Abstract retrieved online on July 31, 2008, from www.ncbi.nlm.nih.gov/pubmed/9182471?dopt=Abstract.
20. Avert, "Evidence that HIV Causes AIDS."
21. See note 11.

concomitant variation, this further increases the probability that there is a causal relationship between HIV and AIDS.

Practical Implications of Applying Mill's Methods

As you can see from our study of Mill's methods of finding causal relationships, they are useful bases for scientifically addressing the question of causation. In the case of AIDS, the practical significance of these methods in helping scientists to find what was, at first, an elusive disease cannot be overstated.

By providing a scientific edifice on which to address causation, these methods can help us short-circuit many of the self-defeating and often dangerous consequences of basing our judgments on fear, superstition, and other forms of antiscientific, irrational thinking and emoting.

Thus, before the cause of AIDS was proven, there was much discrimination against persons with AIDS in the areas of employment, housing, and education. Media coverage about AIDS waned until the disease emerged in the heterosexual population, proving that it affected not just gays and drug addicts but everyone. People with AIDS were socially ostracized and rejected by both relatives and friends. At a time when they needed support and love, they found themselves living as social outcasts, alone in their suffering.

Much of the social stigma that propelled these discriminatory and unkind practices stemmed from fear of catching AIDS through casual contact. People viewed shaking the hand of a person with AIDS with trepidation. To have hugged or kissed someone with AIDS was thought a death sentence by many. These fears were not based on evidence because there was none. And they would have persisted were it not for the discovery that the virus that causes AIDS cannot be transmitted through casual contact. This knowledge, however, was gained by a careful, objective, and methodical investigation using the tools of reasoning discussed in this chapter.

Mill's methods for determining causal relations are another important contribution to the toolbox of critical and free thinkers. They are open to use in combating one's own personal fears and superstitions, which scuttle rational judgment and thwart personal and interpersonal happiness. They should accordingly be taken out of the textbook and put to work in the arena of daily living.

Exercise Set 13.4

For each of the following, were any of Mill's methods for establishing causal relations used? If so, which? If not, what basis was used for attempting to establish a causal relation? In your estimation, was sufficient evidence provided to establish a causal relation? Defend your answer.

13.4.1

May 23, 2006—People who smoke marijuana do not appear to be at increased risk for developing lung cancer, new research suggests.

While a clear increase in cancer risk was seen among cigarette smokers in the study, no such association was seen for regular cannabis users. . . .

A total of 611 lung cancer patients living in Los Angeles County, and 601 patients with other cancers of the head and neck were compared with 1,040 people without cancer matched for age, sex, and the neighborhood they lived in.

All the participants were asked about lifetime use of marijuana, tobacco, and alcohol, as well as other drugs, their diets, occupation, family history of lung cancer, and socioeconomic status.

The heaviest marijuana users in the study had smoked more than 22,000 joints, while moderately heavy smokers had smoked between 11,000 and 22,000 joints.

While two-pack-a-day or more cigarette smokers were found to have a 20-fold increase in lung cancer risk, no elevation in risk was seen for even the very heaviest marijuana smokers.

The more tobacco a person smoked, the greater their risk of developing lung cancer and other cancers of the head and neck. But people who smoked more marijuana were not at increased risk compared with people who smoked less and people who didn't smoke at all.[1]

13.4.2

In July 1976, the American Legion held a convention at the Bellevue-Stratford Hotel in Philadelphia to celebrate the country's bicentennial. Within two days after the start of the event, one veteran after another became ill with an acute pneumonia illness. Ultimately, 221 patients were stricken, and 34 patients eventually died of this mysterious epidemic which came to be known as Legionnaires' Disease. . . .

During the Fall of 1976, imaginations soared with proposed etiologies from scientists, physicians, media personnel, and the public. Theories ranged from nickel carbonyl intoxication and viral pneumonia to communist or pharmaceutical company conspiracies against the American veterans. The CDC investigation soon expanded—all the disease survivors and their available relatives, and over 4,400 Legionnaires and their families were questioned, and cadavers were autopsied at the microscopic level.

By September 1976, the focus of the investigation shifted entirely to the Bellevue-Stratford Hotel. The CDC team collected numerous samples from the air, water, soil, dirt and materials from the hotel and its surroundings. However, these samples tested negative for a questionable microbe or toxic chemical. Finally, on January 18, 1977, it was announced that Joseph McDade and his team had isolated the bacterium that causes Legionnaires' Disease. McDade couldn't grow the bacteria for reasons to be discovered, yet he succeeded in obtaining evidence of its existence and pathogenesis through a series of experiments.

Further analysis revealed that the bacteria thrived in the Bellevue-Stratford hotel's cooling tower. From that water supply the hotel derived its air conditioning and the bacteria were actively pumped into the hotel.[2]

13.4.3

The AIDS epidemic is caused by fornicators and adulterers. This does not mean that all people who have AIDS are immoral. A moral husband or wife can be given AIDS by an immoral marriage partner. Children can contract aids before birth from a mother who is either immoral or was given the virus by someone who was immoral. A moral person can contract AIDS by means of injection or transfusion, but in that case also, the disease ultimately comes from someone who is immoral. . . . Yes, the real cause of the AIDS epidemic is rejection of God, sin and immorality. Fornicators and adulterers are the cause of the AIDS epidemic. They are angels of death, servants of the devil, and murderers.[3]

13.4.4

Professor Adrian Raine, a leading psychologist at the University of California, will outline a growing body of evidence showing that violent offenders have physical defects in a part of the brain linked to decision-making and self-control—which may make them more likely to lash out.

(*continued*)

---

1. Salynn Boyles, "Pot Smoking Not Linked to Lung Cancer," WebMD, May 23, 2006. Retrieved online on April 10, 2009, from www.webmd.com/lung-cancer/news/20060523/pot-smoking-not-linked-to-lung-cancer.

2. "History of Legionnaires' Disease," justice.loyola.edu. Retrieved online on August 10, 2008, from http://justice.loyola.edu/~klc/BL472/Legionnaire/history.html.

3. Roy Davison, "What Is the Real Cause of the AIDS Pandemic," OldPaths.com. Retrieved online on November 23, 2008, from www.oldpaths.com/Archive/Davison/Roy/Allen/1940/aids.html.

Raine's latest research, to be unveiled this week in Sheffield, looked at whether brain deficits could be avoided by action in the early years when the tissue is still developing.

A group of three-year-olds from Mauritius were given an intensive programme of enriched diet, exercise and cognitive stimulation, which included being read to and involved in conversation. By the age of 11 they demonstrated increased brain activity on brain scan read-outs, and by 23 they were 64 percent less likely than a control group of children not on the programme to have criminal records.

"This is not the silver bullet to solving crime and violence, but I think it's certainly one of the ingredients," said Raine, a former prison psychologist.[4]

13.4.5

Recently, it has been reported that a serious adverse reaction called nephrogenic systemic fibrosis (NSF) may occur after exposure to the extracellular nonionic low osmolar gadolinium-based contrast agent gadodiamide. . . . Most patients, but not all, are on regular dialysis treatment. The typical course begins with subacute swelling of distal parts of the extremities followed during subsequent weeks by severe skin induration and sometimes anatomical extension involving thighs, antebrachium, and lower abdomen. The skin induration may be aggressive and associated with constant pain, muscle restlessness, and loss of skin flexibility. In some cases, NSF leads to serious physical disability including wheelchair requirement. . . .

Grobner was the first to propose that . . . contrast media containing Gd might be a trigger of NSF. Marckmann reported 13 patients who had been exposed to gadodiamide prior to the development of NSF. The authors could not identify any other common exposure/event. . . .

In August 2006, all members of the European Society of Urogenital Radiology (ESUR) received an electronic mail asking them to report cases of NSF to the chairman of the ESUR contrast media safety committee in request for material for the upcoming meeting of the committee. . . . Based on the obtained information, it seems appropriate to draw the following conclusions:

More than 150 patients have developed NSF after exposure to a Gd-based contrast medium. The overwhelming majority (~90%) had had gadodiamide with certainty. . . .

NSF after exposure to gadodiamide has been seen in Caucasian and Afro-Americans. It has been observed also in the United Kingdom, USA, the Netherlands, France, Belgium, Austria and Denmark. The patients were either on dialysis or had reduced renal function. . . .

There are no reports of NSF in patients with normal kidney function. Around 200 million patients have had injections of a gadolinium-based contrast agent since the early 1980s. A population of more than 30 million patients has received gadodiamide. So, in patients without ESRD [end-stage renal disease], all gadolinium-based contrast agents seem to be safe.[5]

13.4.6

I haven't been sick a single day since I began your program. Georgia is a 37-year-old mother of two who dreaded the coming of each winter because it brought seasonal depression and chronic sinusitis for her. After pushing through her symptoms for several years, which left her completely fatigued, she finally decided to take matters into her own hands this fall. After six illness-free months, she wrote to tell us how good she's feeling.

I started having problems after the birth of my second child. It was a hard birth and I lost a lot of blood. Even though I received transfusions, it still took me a while to get back to my old self. That first winter was a bear. I think I caught every flu, every stomach virus that was going around. I just couldn't get on top of it. . . .

Then the next winter I got sick again—with bronchitis—and stayed sick through most of January and February. I began to feel so tired that I just didn't want to get out of bed in the mornings. . . .

Then last fall, a friend of mine recommended your website and vitamins, so I took a look for myself. I ordered the Personal Program and began taking the nutrients daily. After just a few weeks,

4. Gabby Hinsliff, "Diet of Fish 'Can Prevent' Teen Violence," Guardian.co.uk, September 14, 2003. Retrieved online on April 10, 2009, from www.guardian.co.uk/politics/2003/sep/14/science.health.

5. Henrik S. Thomsen, "Nephrogenic Systemic Fibrosis: A Serious Late Adverse Reaction to Gadodiamide," *European Radiology* 16, no. 12 (December 2006). Retrieved online on November 13, 2008, from www.pubmedcentral.nih.gov/articlerender.fcgi?artid=1705479.

my hair, nails and skin looked so much better! I had more energy and less moodiness around my period. But the real test was yet to come: four long months of winter.

Now I'm happy to say that after six months on your program, I haven't been sick a single day and my periods have been totally regular and symptom-free! My husband couldn't believe it. He's taking a multivitamin now, too, and so are the kids.[6]

13.4.7

In a study published in the April 9 issue of the journal *Neurology*, this trial is the first in humans to show that recovering memory after brain injury is harder for people who have the E4 type of the apolipoprotein E (APOE) gene, which is already known to influence Alzheimer's disease. . . . The study looked at 110 head injury patients who were rated for level of traumatic brain injury, assessed for memory function and genotyped at the APOE gene. Although participants with the E4 form of the APOE gene matched those without the E4 form in terms of age, gender and severity of injury, there were clear differences in memory function between the two groups. The E4 group showed worse recovery of general memory function after injury.[7]

---

6. "I Haven't Been Sick a Single Day Since I Began Your Program," "Women's Stories," Women to Women. Retrieved online on November 23, 2008, from www.womentowomen.com/womens-stories/notsickasingleday.aspx.
7. "Memory Loss after Brain Injury Worse When Alzheimer's Gene Present," Prohealth.com, April 26, 2002. Retrieved online on January 26, 2009, at www.prohealth.com/library/showarticle.cfm?id=1680&t=Alzheimers.

CONTRARY-TO-FACT CONDITIONALS

One further way to understand causal relationships is in terms of *contrary-to-fact conditionals*, statements that assert what would (or probably would have) happened if something else, which did not in fact happen, had happened. On this approach, we may say that an event C caused an event E if E would not (or probably would not) have happened if C did not happen. For example, in saying that the cow kicking over the lantern caused the barn to catch fire, we understand that the barn would not (or probably would not) have caught fire if the cow had not kicked over the lantern.

However, since contrary-to-fact conditionals refer to conditions that do not in fact happen, care should be taken not to make unwarranted speculations about what would have happened under different circumstances. Indeed, in many contexts in which causal ascriptions are made, we may be less than objective in the search for causes.

In some cases, we may be hard put to admit responsibility for our actions, especially when they lead to an undesirable result. We might accordingly rationalize the result by blaming it on circumstances beyond our control. For example, after getting into an automobile accident, a person might argue that if a passenger had not distracted him by talking to him, then he would not have rear-ended the car in front of him. In other cases, people may be willing to take the blame for actions that are more realistically the fault of others. For example, a woman might blame herself for having been sexually assaulted. She might tell herself that if she had not worn her low-cut, red dress, then her date would not have raped her.

Of course, this does not mean that contrary-to-fact conditionals are never justified. For example, it is quite justified to say that if you are struck by a Mack truck traveling 100 miles per hour while you are crossing the highway, then you will (or probably will) be killed. How then can we distinguish justified contrary-to-fact conditionals from unjustified ones?

Contrary-to-fact conditionals can be thought of as enthymematic (incomplete) deductive arguments.[22] In such arguments, the consequent of the conditional in question is the conclusion, while the antecedent is a contrary-to-fact premise (a supposition) from which this conclusion is being inferred.[23] Consider the case presented by the first of the above examples: I would not have rear-ended the car in front of me if you had not distracted me while I was driving. Here, the argument in question would be along the following lines: If we suppose for the sake of argument that you do not distract me while I am driving, then we can conclude that I do not rear-end the car in front of me. Thus,

> *Supposition:* You do not distract me while I am driving.
> *Conclusion:* I do not rear-end the car in front of me.

Notice, however, that the conclusion in this argument does not follow from the supposition unless at least one other premise is assumed. For example, we must assume that there are no other conditions that impair my (timely) ability to brake. Thus,

> *Supposition:* You do not distract me while I am driving.
> *Additional assumption:* No other conditions are present that impair my ability to brake before hitting the car in front of me.
> *Conclusion:* I do not rear-end the car in front of me.[24]

However, the question is now whether the additional assumption is itself justified. Indeed, other possible conditions might have been present. For example, perhaps I did not get enough sleep the night before the accident; maybe the alcoholic beverage I drank at dinner slowed up my reflexes (even if I was not intoxicated); maybe someone or something else distracted me. In short, unless I can show that no other such condition was present, my argument is not a sound one. Accordingly, my contrary-to-fact conditional is also unjustified because it makes an unjustified assumption.

Consider the case of the second example provided above: If I had not worn that low-cut, red dress, then my date would not have raped me.

> *Supposition:* I do not wear my low-cut, red dress.
> *Conclusion:* My date does not rape me.

However, this inference requires at least two additional assumptions:

---

22. See chapter 3.
23. See chapter 2.
24. Strictly speaking, this conclusion does not validly follow from the above premises unless an additional premise is also added—namely, "If you do not distract me, and no other conditions are present that impair my ability to brake before hitting the car in front of me, then I do not rear-end the car in front of me."

Assumption 1: My date is sexually aroused by me only if I wear my low-cut, red dress.

Assumption 2: My date is motivated to rape someone only if sexually aroused by that person.

But, as is well documented, rape is typically a crime of power and control rather than sex. This is why elderly women wearing housedresses are sometimes raped. Moreover, even if some date rapes are a result of sexual arousal, this does not mean that a necessary condition of such sexual arousal is that the victim wears a low-cut, red dress. Hence, both of the above assumptions are unjustified, and therefore the original contrary-to-fact conditional is unjustified.

As you can see, being able to distinguish between justified contrary-to-fact conditions and unjustified ones has substantial practical importance. Indeed, failure to make such a distinction has led victims of rape to senselessly blame themselves for their victimization. Failure to make this distinction also frequently leads to self-destructive rationalizations. Thus, if I construct unjustified contrary-to-fact conditionals to blame others for my own mistakes, I will fail to learn from these mistakes. For example, I might continue to get into automobile accidents.

Exercise Set 13.5

For each of the following contrary-to-fact conditionals, (1) set it up as an argument with a supposition and a conclusion; (2) state its additional assumptions; (3) examine each additional assumption, and indicate whether it is justified; and (4) on the basis of steps 1–3, state whether the original contrary-to-fact conditional is justified.

13.5.1
If I had gotten the flu vaccine this year, then I wouldn't have gotten the flu this year.

13.5.2
If I had been home instead of out clothes shopping when my husband had the heart attack, then he would still be alive today.

13.5.3
If Al Gore had become president in 2000 rather than George W. Bush, then the United States would probably not have invaded Iraq.`

13.5.4
If the United States had not been involved in a costly war in Iraq, then the U.S. economy would not have entered a depression in 2009.

13.5.5
If Franklin Roosevelt had not put his New Deal into effect between 1933 and 1939, the United States would not have recovered from the Great Depression.

13.5.6
If machines could think and were self-aware, then they would have a right to life.

13.5.7
If space aliens were human, then they would have hearts and kidneys.

(continued)

13.5.8
John Lennon would have written more great songs had he not been killed at age forty by Mark Chapman.

13.5.9
If Elvis Presley had not abused drugs, he wouldn't have died of a sudden heart attack at age forty.

13.5.10
If New Orleans's levee system had been built to withstand a hurricane of category 3 or higher, then it would not have been breached during Hurricane Katrina in 2005.

14

Behavioral Reasoning

THE PRACTICAL SYLLOGISM

In this chapter and the next, we examine practical reasoning. This is the kind of reasoning we engage in when we make decisions or choices about what to do, how to feel, or what values to embrace, including moral ones.

The ancient Greek philosopher Aristotle called this kind of reasoning *practical syllogism*. As you have seen, a syllogism is a form of deductive reasoning having two premises. In a *practical* syllogism, the first premise (the major premise) is a rule that prescribes or rates (evaluates) something. The second premise (the minor premise) is a statement of particular fact that is itself often the conclusion of an inductive inference. In line with these two premises, the conclusion in turn prescribes or rates something in particular.

Here is one of Aristotle's own examples:

> *Major premise rule:* If anything is sweet, then it should be tasted.
> *Minor premise report:* This is sweet.
> *Behavioral conclusion*: This should be tasted.

As you can see, the above argument takes the form of a (valid) *hypothetical syllogism* in which the minor premise affirms the antecedent (see chapter 3). The major premise is a practical rule. It prescribes an action if its antecedent is satisfied. It says that *if* anything is sweet, then it *should* be tasted. Here, the function of the word "should" is to *prescribe* tasting the sweet thing. In this book we will refer to a term that performs this logical function of prescribing action as a *prescriptive term* or (for short) a *prescriptive*. Practical syllogisms often (although not always) include a prescriptive, which can signal the conclusion of behavioral reasoning. A number of terms in natural language can function as prescriptive terms.[1] Table 14.1 lists some popular ones.

---

1. Note that these terms may also be used nonprescriptively: for example, "He should be home by now."

Table 14.1

Prescriptive Term	Example
should	You *should* taste this.
ought	You *ought* to taste this.
must	You *must* taste this.
right/wrong	It is *right* to taste this.
moral obligation	You have a *moral obligation* to taste this.
duty	You have a *duty* to taste this.

These conclusion indicators can signal *behavioral conclusions*—that is, conclusions that prescribe an action. Prescriptives may also occur in conjunction with generic conclusion indicators as in, for example, "Therefore, you should taste this." Inasmuch as prescriptives also occur in the consequent of the major premise, they can also provide a cue to finding the major premise. However, as discussed below, in ordinary language arguments, the major premise rule of practical syllogisms may not be explicitly stated by the author, in which case you will have to formulate it for yourself.

The minor premise of a practical syllogism *files a report* under a rule. For example, it says that such and such *is* one of the sweet things referred to in the major premise rule. Notice how the conclusion—that this should be tasted—then prescribes what you should *do*. The prescribed action in the rule (as well as its prescriptive) is inherited by the conclusion and applied to the particular thing referred to in the minor premise.

Once you deduce this conclusion, notice how, if nothing prevents you and you don't change your mind, you will, in fact, go ahead and actually taste this sweet thing. This close logical connection between the premises of the practical syllogism and the action prescribed by the conclusion led Aristotle to claim that the conclusion itself was an action.[2]

Accordingly, where *r* represents a particular fact claim and *a* represents a prescribed action, the form or structure of an action-prescribing practical syllogism can be schematized as follows:

Major premise rule: If r, then a.
Minor premise report: r.
Behavioral conclusion: a.

For example, Aristotle's sample syllogism replaces the variables r and a in the above argument form with the following substitutions:

r = this is sweet.
a = this should be tasted.

Thus, by plugging these values into the above argument form, we get the following practical syllogism:

---

2. However, Aristotle's claim that an action can be *deduced* from a set of statements is controversial and shall not be maintained in the treatment of practical reasoning in this book.

Major premise rule: If this is sweet, then this should be tasted.[3]
Minor premise report: This is sweet.
Behavioral conclusion: This should be tasted.

BEHAVIORAL REASONING

In this book we will refer to *action-prescribing* practical syllogisms having the above-described structure as *behavioral reasoning*.[4] Many of the arguments advanced in the course of ordinary life, including moral arguments, take this form. When people make decisions about what to do, the basic argument behind their reasoning also typically takes this form. You can find and formulate each part of behavioral reasoning by proceeding in the following order and by asking the following questions at each stage:

1. *Find the conclusion.* What is the action being prescribed by the person advancing the argument in question?
2. *Find the minor premise report.* What is the particular fact claim *r* given to try to justify doing *a*?
3. *Find the major premise rule.* What rule do you get when you plug the values found for a and r (in steps 1 and 2) into the formula "If r, then a"?

Notice how, by identifying the conclusion first (constructing your argument from the ground up, so to speak), you can systematically construct the basic argument.

A BASIC EXAMPLE:
BILL O'REILLY'S RUDENESS ARGUMENT

For example, look at the following argument given by popular Fox News show host Bill O'Reilly:

Yeah, I'm obnoxious. Yeah, I cut people off. Yeah, I'm rude. You know why? Because you're busy.

---

3. Notice that the scope of this major premise rule is restricted to *this* sweet thing. However, as a rule it is *generalizable*. That is, for any other sweet thing that is *exactly* like this sweet thing, the rule of tasting it would also apply. It would be inconsistent to say that *this* sweet thing should be tasted but that *another* sweet thing that is *exactly like* it shouldn't be tasted. Indeed, in such a case there would need to be something relevantly different about this other sweet thing that would account for the differential treatment. For example, maybe the other sweet thing is poisonous, or maybe it is more fattening. But in *the absence of any such relevantly different property*, we would have to say that any other sweet thing should also be tasted.

4. In chapter 16 we will examine practical syllogisms where the conclusion is a *rating or evaluation* rather than an explicit prescription of action. As you will see, this related type of practical syllogism is involved in emotions and for this reason will be called *emotional reasoning*.

Finding O'Reilly's Behavioral Conclusion

In this argument, O'Reilly is attempting to justify being obnoxious, cutting people off, and being rude to his guests. Clearly, this is the set of actions he is prescribing:

> *Behavioral conclusion:* I should be obnoxious and rude to my guests and cut them off.

Notice that the prescriptive "should" has been included in the conclusion in order to present its prescriptive force. When you set up arguments found in ordinary language, such editorial tweaking is permissible. The language you use to cast the argument should reflect as closely as possible the original. However, as long as your editing leaves the meaning of the argument—its premises and conclusion— intact, this is acceptable.

Finding O'Reilly's Minor Premise Report

Next, the "and why?" functions as a premise indicator that signals his minor premise report. This is the *reason* he is giving for his behavioral conclusion. This is that "you [the viewers] are busy." Thus, O'Reilly's argument, so far, looks like this:

> *Minor premise report:* The viewers are busy.
> *Behavioral conclusion:* I should be obnoxious and rude to my guests and cut them off.

Finding O'Reilly's Major Premise Rule

Since the major premise is the one that fits the "If r, then a" formula, we can find this premise by plugging in the aforementioned values for r and a:

> a = I should be obnoxious and rude to my guests and cut them off.
> r = the viewers are busy.

When these values are inserted into the major premise formula, we get this:

> *Major premise rule:* If the viewers are busy, I should be obnoxious and rude to my guests and cut them off.

Notice that O'Reilly does not express this premise; instead, it is assumed. As discussed earlier (see chapter 3), logicians refer to such arguments as enthymemes, or enthymematic arguments. This is an argument that has a missing part, either one or more premises or a conclusion. In fact, arguments in ordinary language are often enthymematic. In the case of practical syllogisms, the major premise is commonly not expressed by the person making the argument. We must therefore fill it in so that we are in a position to examine *all* premises of the argument. Indeed, as you will see, it is often the premises that are not explicitly stated that contain fallacies.

Accordingly, O'Reilly's behavioral reasoning, fully articulated, is as follows:

Major premise rule: If the viewers are busy, I should be obnoxious and rude to my guests and cut them off.
Minor premise report: The viewers are busy.
Behavioral conclusion: I should be obnoxious and rude to my guests and cut them off.

Now we are in a better position to examine the premises of O'Reilly's reasoning to see if they hold water, and, indeed, there are reasons to question both premises. First, the major premise rule is questionable because there can also be polite ways to treat guests who may be taking up "too much" airtime. Indeed, many TV and radio show hosts have found it possible to diplomatically thank a guest for his or time and thus move on.

Second, O'Reilly's rule shows a general intolerance for individuals with whom he may not see eye to eye. While he, as the host, is entitled to exercise some control over his show, this does not mean that his judgment that a given guest is wrong-headed or is wasting time should trump the right of the guest to his or her views or to be treated respectfully. Some moral philosophers, notably the eighteenth-century philosopher Immanuel Kant, have made *respect for persons* the cornerstone of their moral theory. One does not, in Kant's view, respect guests as persons by being obnoxious to them, cutting them off, or acting rudely in order to save time for the "busy viewers."

Third, O'Reilly does not know how busy his viewers really are, which accordingly makes his minor premise speculative. Indeed, many viewers may watch his show as a form of entertainment and not necessarily perceive themselves to be taking time from their busy schedules to gain valuable information.

Exercise Set 14.1

For each of the following arguments, find the (1) conclusion, (2) minor premise report, and (3) major premise rule. Then, briefly discuss the soundness of the argument.

14.1.1
"Do not allow yourselves to be deceived: Great Minds are Skeptical." —Friedrich Nietzsche

14.1.2
In America, there is supposed to be a separation between church and state. That's why the state shouldn't prevent gay people from marrying based on religion.

14.1.3
"It is a good thing to proceed in order and to establish propositions. This is the way to gain ground and to progress with certainty." —Gottfried Leibniz

14.1.4
Mercy killing can be preferable to letting a suffering patient die insofar as it can accomplish the ultimate goal, the death of the patient, in a manner that is quicker and less painful.

14.1.5
Since lawyers are officers of the court as well as their clients' advocates, they should not allow their clients to take the stand and lie under oath.

(continued)

14.1.6
"To me the worst thing seems to be for a school principally to work with methods of fear, force and artificial authority. Such treatment destroys the sound sentiments, the sincerity, and the self-confidence of the pupil. It produces the submissive subject." —Albert Einstein

14.1.7
"We must plan for freedom and not only for security, if for no other reason than that only freedom can make security secure." —Karl Popper

14.1.8
"By all means marry. If you get a good wife, you'll be happy. If you get a bad one, you'll become a philosopher . . . and that is a good thing for any man." —Plato

REASONING CONTAINING A SUBARGUMENT: ADOLPH EICHMANN'S REFUSAL TO TAKE RESPONSIBILITY FOR HIS NAZI WAR CRIMES

Now consider the following argument:

> I was one of the many horses pulling the wagon and couldn't escape left or right because of the will of the driver.

These were among the last words penned by Adolph Eichmann while he awaited execution for Nazi war crimes. This "architect of the Holocaust" and lieutenant colonel of the Nazi Schutzstaffel, or SS, was responsible for devising the plans for systematically transporting hundreds of thousands of Jewish people to concentration camps, sending them to die in gas chambers.

Step 1: Finding Eichmann's Conclusion

Notice that Eichmann portrays himself as a helpless victim. He wants you to think he shouldn't be held responsible for the Holocaust. This is really the practical conclusion he wants *you* to infer from his premises, even though his argument is enthymematic and he does not himself explicitly state this conclusion.

Step 2: Finding Eichmann's Minor Premise Rule

So what are his premises? Eichmann speaks in metaphor, but his meaning is clear: he was one of many German soldiers ("one of the many horses pulling the wagon") who had no other choice ("couldn't escape left or right") but to assist in the mass genocide. Thus, Eichmann's conclusion and minor premise, without the metaphor, are as follows:

> *Minor premise rule:* I, like all other German soldiers, had no other choice but to cooperate in the genocide.
> *Behavioral conclusion:* I should not be held responsible for the genocide.

Step 3: Finding Eichmann's Major Premise Rule

Now, it's easy to find the major premise rule, which fits the "If r, then a" formula. Given the above minor premise report (r) and behavioral conclusion (a), the argument is as follows:

> *Major premise rule:* If I, like all other German soldiers, had no other choice but to cooperate in the genocide, then I should not be held responsible for the genocide.
> *Minor premise rule:* I, like all other German soldiers, had no other choice but to cooperate in the genocide.
> *Behavioral conclusion:* I should not be held responsible for the genocide.

Here the major premise rule appears to be reasonable. Indeed, if Eichmann really had no other choice, then it would not seem to make sense to hold him responsible for criminal actions.

However, there is also another level to Eichmann's argument, namely, his attempt to defend the above minor premise report that he had no other choice. Here, Eichmann's defense is "because of the will of the driver": that is, because his fuehrer, Adolf Hitler, ordered it. So here is Eichmann's defense:

> *Minor premise:* Hitler ordered me to cooperate in the genocide.
> *Conclusion:* I, like all other German soldiers, had no other choice but to cooperate in the genocide.

Notice that this argument is not strictly a behavioral syllogism because its conclusion is not an action. Instead, the conclusion is actually the minor premise report of the prior practical syllogism. This second syllogism is accordingly used to support a premise in the prior argument. Let us call such a supportive argument a *subargument*, which we can define as an argument used to support a premise of another argument.

Notice that this subargument is incomplete and requires a major premise in order for the conclusion to follow deductively, that is, necessarily, from the premises.[5] So, here is the argument with this missing major premise added:

> *Major premise:* If Hitler ordered me to cooperate in the genocide, then I, like all other German soldiers, had no other choice.
> *Minor premise:* Hitler ordered me to participate in the genocide.
> *Conclusion:* I, like all other German soldiers, had no other choice but to participate in the genocide.

You can now see that Eichmann's attempt to exempt himself from responsibility for his actions rests on the (major) premise that if Hitler ordered these actions, then he had no other choice but to cooperate. However, this premise is both false and dangerous.

There is a difference between having no other choice and having one that you do not prefer. French existentialist philosopher Jean-Paul Sartre made this

---

5. See also the discussion of enthymemes in chapter 3.

distinction abundantly clear. Sartre, who himself fought against the Nazis in the French underground, eloquently expressed the point:

> If I am mobilized in a war, this war is my war; it is in my image and I deserve it. I deserve it first because I could always get out of it by suicide or by desertion; these ultimate possibles are those which must always be present for us when there is a question of envisaging a situation. For lack of getting out of it, I have chosen it. This can be due to inertia, to cowardice in the face of public opinion, or because I prefer certain other values to the value of the refusal to join the war (the good opinion of my relatives, the honor of my family, etc.). Anyway you look at it, it is a matter of a choice.[6]

Surely Eichmann could have refused to send masses of people to their death and instead accepted the consequences for this refusal, even if it meant his own execution. It would appear that Eichmann preferred to help Hitler (and, indeed, to carry out his job skillfully) than to accept the consequences of refusing. Thus, from Sartre's perspective, Eichmann's premise is false. Instead of accepting his freedom and responsibility, Sartre would say, he lived in "bad faith"—that is, he lied to himself and to the world about the choices he, in fact, made.

Insofar as choices are deliberate, they involve reasoning. The reasoning that Eichmann used to come to his decision to follow Hitler's orders might well have taken the form of a disjunctive syllogism whose major premise was a set of alternative possibilities joined by an "or."[7] For example, it might have looked something like the following:

> I can (1) commit suicide, or (2) desert, or (3) refuse, or (4) follow orders.
> Rule out possibilities 1–3.
> Therefore, follow orders.

Insofar as Eichmann chose one option over another and deliberately helped Hitler instead of opting out, Eichmann made a choice. As such, his minor premise, which says he had—and therefore made—*no* choice, is false.

This does not mean that had Eichmann been willing to fess up and take responsibility, his past actions would have proved any less reprehensible. Nevertheless, a preliminary step toward meaningful change for the future is accepting responsibility for past mistakes, rather than hiding them behind a veil of metaphor and false premises. The German people had to come to such acceptance of responsibility after Hitler was finally defeated. If it had been left to individuals who reasoned like Eichmann—reasoning he persisted in even up to the day he was hanged—Germany might never have begun the arduous task of rebuilding its democracy and making constructive amends.

A nation's willingness to subject its own reasoning to rational inspection is a mark of an open society. The refusal to do so is a mark of dogmatism and thus a closed society. In the next section of this chapter, we will undertake an analysis of a more extended practical argument that led the United States to undertake a war in Iraq.

---

6. Jean-Paul Sartre, *Being and Nothingness* (New York: Simon & Schuster, 1968), 708.
7. Disjunctive syllogisms were discussed in chapter 4.

Exercise Set 14.2

For each of the following arguments, construct the conclusion, minor premise, and major premise of the main argument and then construct any subargument that is made to justify a premise of the main argument.

14.2.1
Telling half truths is wrong because it involves deceiving others. It involves deceiving others because it leaves out details needed for others to make a rational choice.

14.2.2
A person who is HIV positive and sleeps with another person who is unaware of this person's HIV-positive status can and should be charged with a felony. Such an act constitutes a willful endangerment of the life of another person. This is because HIV is a life-threatening disease.

14.2.3
"Homosexuality is abnormal and hence undesirable—not because it is immoral or sinful, or because it weakens society or hampers evolutionary development, but for a purely mechanical reason. It is a misuse of bodily parts." —Michael Levin

14.2.4
"We are each of us the experiencing subject of a life, a conscious creature having an individual welfare that has importance to us whatever our usefulness to others. As the same is true of those animals that concern us (the ones that are eaten and trapped, for example), they too must be viewed as the experiencing subjects of a life, with inherent value of their own. . . . When it comes to the case for animal rights, then, what we need to know is whether the animals that, in our culture, are routinely eaten, hunted and used in our laboratories, for example, are like us in being subjects of a life. And we do know this." —Tom Regan

14.2.5
"Pornography is morally objectionable, not because it leads people to show disrespect for women, but because pornography itself exemplifies and recommends behavior that violates the moral principle to respect persons. The content of pornography is what one objects to. It treats women as mere sex objects 'to be exploited and manipulated' and degrades the role and status of women." —Ann Gary

14.2.6
"Learned institutions ought to be favorite objects with every free people. They throw that light over the public mind which is the best security against crafty and dangerous encroachments on the public." —James Madison

ANALYZING EXTENDED ARGUMENTS: THE CASE OF WEAPONS OF MASS DESTRUCTION IN IRAQ

The following is excerpted from a speech delivered by President George W. Bush on October 7, 2002, before he took the United States to war in Iraq:

Tonight I want to take a few minutes to discuss a grave threat to peace. . . . The threat comes from Iraq.

We know that the [Saddam Hussein] regime has produced thousands of tons of chemical agents, including mustard gas, sarin nerve gas, VX nerve gas. . . . Saddam

Hussein also . . . has ordered chemical attacks on Iran, and on more than forty villages in his own country. These actions killed or injured at least 20,000 people. . . . And surveillance photos reveal that the regime is rebuilding facilities that it had used to produce chemical and biological weapons. . . .

Iraq possesses ballistic missiles with a likely range of hundreds of miles. . . . We've also discovered through intelligence that Iraq has a growing fleet of manned and unmanned aerial vehicles that could be used to disperse chemical or biological weapons across broad areas. . . .

And that is the source of our urgent concern about Saddam Hussein's links to international terrorist groups. Over the years, Iraq has provided safe haven to terrorists such as Abu Nidal. . . . We know that Iraq and al-Qaeda have had high-level contacts that go back a decade. . . . We've learned that Iraq has trained al-Qaeda members in bomb-making and poisons and deadly gases. And we know that after September the 11th, Saddam Hussein's regime gleefully celebrated the terrorist attacks on America. Iraq could decide on any given day to provide a biological or chemical weapon to a terrorist group or individual terrorists. . . .

The evidence indicates that Iraq is reconstituting its nuclear weapons program. Saddam Hussein has held numerous meetings with Iraqi nuclear scientists. . . . Satellite photographs reveal that Iraq is rebuilding facilities at sites that have been part of its nuclear program in the past. Iraq has attempted to purchase high-strength aluminum tubes and other equipment needed for gas centrifuges, which are used to enrich uranium for nuclear weapons. . . .

Knowing these realities, America must not ignore the threat gathering against us. Facing clear evidence of peril, we cannot wait for the final proof—the smoking gun—that could come in the form of a mushroom cloud. . . . Saddam Hussein must disarm himself—or, for the sake of peace, we will lead a coalition to disarm him.

Let's take a careful look at President Bush's reasoning.

Step 1: Find the Conclusion

Clearly, Bush's main argument is behavioral. This is because his main objective is to justify taking action. In setting out this behavioral argument, the first step is, as you have seen, to identify the conclusion, which is the *action* he is attempting to justify. This behavioral conclusion is asserted in the last line of the above excerpt from Bush's speech—namely that we must lead a coalition to disarm him if he doesn't disarm himself. In other words, we must take military action.

Step 2: Find the Minor Premise Report

The second step is to identify the minor premise report—that is, the fact claim Bush is using to try to justify taking military action against Iraq if Hussein fails to disarm. Notice that Bush states this premise at the start when he points to the threat posed by Iraq. And his contention that this threat (to the U.S. homeland) is imminent becomes abundantly clear in the concluding paragraph, which says, "We cannot wait for the final proof—the smoking gun—that could come in the form of a mushroom cloud."

Accordingly, we can frame the conclusion and minor premise of Bush's behavioral reasoning as follows:

Minor premise report: Iraq (under Hussein) poses an imminent security threat to the United States.
Behavioral conclusion: Either Hussein disarms, or we must lead a coalition to disarm Iraq.

Step 3: Formulate the Major Premise Rule

Since the major premise rule links the minor premise report to the behavioral conclusion, we are now in a position to add this rule to Bush's argument:

Major premise rule: If Iraq (under Hussein) poses an imminent security threat to the United States, then either Hussein disarms, or we must lead a coalition to disarm Iraq.
Minor premise report: Iraq (under Hussein) poses an imminent security threat to the United States.
Behavioral conclusion: Either Hussein disarms, or we must lead a coalition to disarm Iraq.

Notice that taking military action against Iraq as prescribed in the conclusion of Bush's argument is *conditional* (it depends on whether Hussein chooses to disarm himself); therefore, the major premise rule also must include this condition. This condition added to the major premise makes it sound quite reasonable. Of course, a nation should defend itself against an imminent attack if the aggressor refuses to back down! The rule here seems quite reasonable (at least if you are not a pacifist).

But what about the minor premise report that Iraq poses an imminent security threat to the United States? Does Bush present adequate evidence to support it? This last question is incredibly important because the justification for invading a sovereign nation, risking mass devastation of its infrastructure at the cost of billions of American dollars and thousands of human lives (both American and Iraqi), depended on it.

Identifying Subarguments

Notice that Bush constructs a *subargument* to support his minor premise report. Recall that a subargument is used to support a premise of another argument. Not infrequently, subarguments that support minor premises of practical syllogisms are inductive. As you have seen (chapters 9–13), an inductive argument is one in which the conclusion is more or less probable in relation to the premises.

For example, to support his minor premise that Iraq poses an imminent threat to U.S. security, Bush maintains that Iraq has chemical and biological weapons, is reconstituting its nuclear weapons program, has ballistic missiles, and has means for deploying its chemical and biological weapons. Bush also suggests that Hussein may give these weapons to terrorists to use against the United States and reminds us of Hussein's past history of using weapons of mass destruction (WMD). More exactly, here is his argument:

Premises:

1. Iraq possesses WMD and is presently developing nuclear weapons.
2. It could decide on any given day to provide a biological or chemical weapon to a terrorist group or individual terrorists.
3. It already has a history of using WMD to kill thousands of people.

Conclusion: Iraq poses an imminent security threat to the United States.

Notice that the conclusion of the above subargument makes a *prediction* about Hussein's becoming complicit in a terrorist attack on the United States in the near future.[8] Since this conclusion follows from its premises with a degree of probability, this argument is clearly inductive. Thus, even if this argument's premises are true, its conclusion can still be false.[9] Unfortunately, premises 1 and 2 of Bush's argument themselves rest substantially on unjustified fact claims.

Consider premise 2 above, which is itself a conclusion from an inductive argument. Here is the subargument Bush gives to support this premise:

Premises:

1. Iraq and al-Qaeda have had high-level contacts that go back a decade.
2. Saddam Hussein has trained al-Qaeda members to make bombs and poisonous gases.
3. Over the years, Iraq has provided safe haven to terrorists such as Abu Nidal.
4. Saddam Hussein celebrated the September 11 terrorist attacks.

Conclusion: Iraq could decide, on any given day, to provide a biological or chemical weapon to a terrorist group or individual terrorists.

However, the September 11 Commission, set up by Congress in 2002 to investigate the circumstances surrounding the September 11, 2001, attacks, found that there was never a "collaborative relationship" between Hussein and al-Qaeda, thereby disconfirming premises 3 and 4 and, as such, "challenging one of the Bush administration's main justifications for the war in Iraq."[10]

Now, consider premise 1, in particular its claim that Iraq was developing nuclear weapons. Here is Bush's (inductive) subargument for this premise:

Premises:

1. Hussein has held numerous meetings with Iraqi nuclear scientists.

---

8. See chapter 10 for a discussion of predictive inductive inferences.

9. One possible line of criticism of this argument is to say that the argument *magnifies risks* (see chapter 10). Thus, the fact that Saddam Hussein used chemical weapons against his own people and against the Iranians more than two decades ago does not mean that Iraq is *now* an "imminent security threat" to the United States. However, as discussed below, the main problem with the argument lies not with the degree of probability by which the conclusion follows from the premises but instead with the premises themselves.

10. Walter Pincus and Dana Milbank, "Al Qaeda-Hussein Link Is Dismissed," *Washington Post,* June 17, 2004. Retrieved on February 1, 2008, from www.washingtonpost.com/wp-dyn/articles/A47812 -2004Jun16.html.

2. Satellite photographs reveal that Iraq is rebuilding facilities at sites that have been part of its nuclear program in the past.

3. Iraq has attempted to purchase high-strength aluminum tubes and other equipment needed for gas centrifuges, which are used to enrich uranium for nuclear weapons.

Conclusion: Iraq is developing nuclear weapons.

If the fact claims made in the above premises, taken together, are true, then they do indeed lend *some* measure of probability to the conclusion that Iraq is developing nuclear weapons. However, this hypothesis was never carefully investigated prior to the U.S. invasion of Iraq. In fact, premises 1 and 2 never were supportable and turned out to be false. As for premise 3, in 2004, the Iraq Survey Group, a multinational force organized by the Pentagon and the CIA to search for WMD in Iraq, found that Iraq's interest in aluminum tubes appeared to be for allowable production of 81 mm rockets rather than nuclear centrifuges.[11] Moreover, in 2002, prior to the U.S. invasion of Iraq, when Ambassador Joseph Wilson went to Niger in Africa to investigate whether Hussein had attempted to purchase "uranium yellowcake" in order to build nuclear weapons, he found no evidence to support this fact claim. Wilson concluded that "some of the intelligence related to Iraq's nuclear weapons program was twisted to exaggerate the Iraqi threat."[12]

Nor did the Iraq Survey Group find any other WMD of the kind the president had mentioned (chemical and biological weapons, for example). Hussein had not produced such weapons after 1991, and contrary to Bush's claims, he did not have stockpiles of them when the war began. Apparently, economic sanctions taken against Hussein had worked, and any chemical and biological weapons that remained had obsolesced and lost their potency. While this didn't mean Hussein did not have ambitions of rebuilding his WMD program, he clearly did not pose an *imminent* threat to the security of the United States that justified a preemptive attack.

As such, the reasoning that took us to war with Iraq was flawed: the subarguments used to support the alleged threat that Iraq posed to U.S. security contained unjustified premises. These premises included that Saddam Hussein had WMD, a nuclear weapons program, and connections with al-Qaeda. All of these premises were speculative and later proven to be false. Had the Bush administration examined its own premises and insisted on adequate evidence for them, it would have seen the weakness of its arguments. Thus, it was not poor intelligence that was responsible for the Bush administration's decision to go to war in Iraq. It was poor logic!

Unfortunately, most Americans believed these premises to be warranted. Why?

---

11. "Weapons of Mass Destruction (WMD): Iraq Survey Group Final Report," GlobalSecurity.org. Retrieved on February 1, 2008, from www.globalsecurity.org/wmd/library/report/2004/isg-final-report/isg-final-report_vol2_nuclear-05.htm.

12. Joseph C. Wilson, "What I Didn't Find in Africa," *New York Times*, July 6, 2003. Retrieved on February 1, 2008, from www.nytimes.com/2003/07/06/opinion/06WILS.html?ex=1372824000&en=6c6aeb1ce960dec0&ei=5007.

Mass Media, Blind Conformity, and the
Climate of Fear in Post-9/11 America

After the September 11, 2001, attacks, the facts about Iraq's alleged WMD program were not reliably presented to the American public. One main reason for this was the failure of the American mainstream corporate media to do its job of keeping citizens informed.

For example, consider the behavioral reasoning of former CBS news anchor Dan Rather when he appeared on the *Late Show with David Letterman* six days after the September 11, 2001, attacks. Rather stated,

> George Bush is the president. He makes the decisions, and . . . wherever he wants me to line up, just tell me where. And he'll make the call.[13]

In Rather's argument, the conclusion is the *action* prescribed, namely, "lining up." In this context, this seems to mean doing whatever Bush says. The minor premise, which supplies the *reason* that is intended to justify performing this act, is that "Bush is the president." The major premise then connects this minor premise with the conclusion:

> *Major premise rule:* If Bush is the president, then I should do whatever he tells me to do.
> *Minor premise report:* Bush is the president.
> *Behavioral conclusion*: I should do whatever Bush tells me to do.

Notice how the major premise in the above argument prescribes blindly *jumping on the bandwagon* to follow a leader.[14] Rather gives no other basis for following the president than that the president is in fact the leader ("He makes the decisions").[15] However, the traditional role of the American press has been to make sure that governmental power and authority are not abused. It is supposed to act as a "fourth estate"—that is, a fourth branch of government that reinforces our system of checks and balances. When reporters blindly follow a leader without asking questions, they actually shirk their professional responsibilities.

In fact, not only reporters but average citizens in a democracy also have a responsibility to ask questions rather than blindly follow their leaders. This is the core meaning of *critical* thinking. To act otherwise can have dangerous consequences. Consider the following words:

> Why of course the people don't want war. But, after all, it is the leaders of the country who determine the policy and it is always a simple matter to drag the people along, whether it is a democracy, or a fascist dictatorship, or a parliament, or a communist dictatorship. Voice or no voice, the people can always be brought to the bidding of

---

13. "Rather's Retirement and Liberal Bias," Fairness and Accuracy in Reporting (FAIR), March 2, 2005. Retrieved online on December 12, 2008, from www.fair.org/index.php?page=2460.
14. This fallacy of blind conformity will be discussed further in chapter 19.
15. More exactly, Rather justifies his rule by this further (pure hypothetical) syllogism:

If Bush is the one who makes the decisions, then I should do whatever he tells me to do.
If Bush is the president, then he is the one who makes the decisions.
Therefore, if Bush is the president, then I should do whatever he tells me to do.

the leaders. That is easy. All you have to do is tell them they are being attacked, and denounce the peacemakers for lack of patriotism and exposing the country to danger. It works the same in any country.[16]

It is chilling to learn that these are the words of Hermann Goering, Adolf Hitler's *Reichsmarschall*. Dan Rather's practical syllogism illustrates Goering's point. Its major premise—"If Bush is the president, then I should do whatever he tells me to do"—might just as well have substituted the name "Hitler" for "Bush." In fact, eight months after the 9/11 tragedy, in a BBC television interview, Rather himself admitted that he and other journalists had been intimidated about "asking the toughest of the tough questions" for fear of being branded unpatriotic.[17] In the aftermath of 9/11, the threat of terrorism was freshly ingrained in the minds of Americans. During this unstable time in U.S. history, fear and intimidation about being called "unpatriotic" for questioning government authority was substituted for sound reason, just as Goering had predicted.

RED ALERT! THINK FOR YOURSELF!

As discussed earlier (see chapter 11), even a renowned newspaper such as the *New York Times*, whose popular slogan is "All the News That's Fit to Print," fell down on the job and, in the end, admitted to shallow reporting in its coverage of the WMD issue prior to the U.S. invasion of Iraq. In retrospect, the editor wrote,

> But we do fault ourselves for failing to deconstruct the W.M.D. issue with the kind of thoroughness we directed at the question of a link between Iraq and Al Qaeda, or even tax cuts in time of war. We did not listen carefully to the people who disagreed with us. Our certainty flowed from the fact that such an overwhelming majority of government officials, past and present, top intelligence officials and other experts were sure that the weapons were there. We had a groupthink of our own.[18]

Though not exactly as apologetic as it could have been and not something the paper was willing to print on its front page, the *Times*'s own *inductive* argument for mistakenly concluding that there were WMD in Iraq was clear:

Premise: The majority of government officials, top intelligence officers, and other experts are sure that there are WMD in Iraq.
Conclusion: There are WMD in Iraq.

The *Times* drew this conclusion from its uncritical acceptance of the testimony of the very government officials it was, as a trusted member of the fourth estate, charged with investigating. Instead of following up on the disconfirming (probability-lowering) testimony of others who disagreed with these officials, it ignored this testimony.

---

16. G. M. Gilbert, *Nuremberg Diary* (New York: Farrar, Straus and Company, 1947), 278–79.

17. N. Solomon, "Media War and the Rigors of Self-Censorship," in *Censored 2003*, ed. Peter Phillips (New York: Seven Stories Press, 2003), 241–42.

18. "A Pause for Hindsight," *New York Times*, July 16, 2004. Retrieved on November 28, 2004, from www.commondreams.org/views04/0716-15.htm.

This conclusion, based on the fallacious *parroting* of biased testimony, was, as already discussed, shown to have been false.[19] Unfortunately, as you have seen, it was used to support the minor premise of one of the gravest behavioral syllogisms in American history. This "groupthink" in lieu of careful investigative reporting contributed to the false premise that Iraq posed an imminent threat to the security of the United States and therefore to the conclusion that we should launch a preemptive strike. Here was a behavioral syllogism that helped to fuel a bloody war in which thousands of lives, both Iraqi and American, were lost. So the need to examine the premises of one's behavioral reasoning before acting on its conclusion cannot be stressed enough.

Asking questions instead of blindly relying on the beliefs of others is the core of what it means to be a critical thinker, and, as you can see, it can make the difference between life and death. Whether in personal or in professional life, be the issue of national importance or private concern, the ability to examine the premises that ultimately ground one's conduct is of inestimable value.

Exercise Set 14.3

14.3.1

The following is an excerpt from a televised interview with former president Richard Nixon conducted by David Frost and aired on May 19, 1977. Construct Nixon's main argument.[1] That is, provide the conclusion, minor premise, and major premise of his practical syllogism. Then, discuss the veracity of its premises.

Frost: The wave of dissent, occasionally violent, which followed in the wake of the Cambodian incursion, prompted President Nixon to demand better intelligence about the people who were opposing him. To this end, the Deputy White House Counsel, Tom Huston, arranged a series of meetings with representatives of the CIA, the FBI, and other police and intelligence agencies. These meetings produced a plan, the Huston Plan, which advocated the systematic use of wiretappings, burglaries, or so-called black bag jobs, mail openings and infiltration against antiwar groups and others. Some of these activities, as Huston emphasized to Nixon, were clearly illegal. Nevertheless, the president approved the plan.

Frost: So what in a sense, you're saying is that there are certain situations, and the Huston Plan or that part of it was one of them, where the president can decide that it's in the best interest of the nation or something, and do something illegal. . . .

Nixon: Exactly. Exactly. If the president, for example, approves something because of the national security, or in this case because of a threat to internal peace and order of significant magnitude, then the president's decision in that instance is one that enables those who carry it out, to carry it out without violating a law. Otherwise they're in an impossible position.

Frost: But when you said . . . "If the president orders it, that makes it legal," as it were: Is the president in that sense—is there anything in the Constitution or the Bill of Rights that suggests the president is that far of a sovereign, that far above the law?

---

1. "Nixon's Views on Presidential Power: Excerpts from an Interview with David Frost," Landmark Cases.org. Retrieved online on April 10, 2009, from www.landmarkcases.org/nixon/nixonview.html.

---

19. The fallacy of parroting was discussed in chapter 11.

Nixon: No, there isn't. There's nothing specific that the Constitution contemplates in that respect. I haven't read every word, every jot and every title, but I do know this: That it has been, however, argued that as far as a president is concerned, that in war time, a president does have certain extraordinary powers which would make acts that would otherwise be unlawful, lawful if undertaken for the purpose of preserving the nation and the Constitution, which is essential for the rights we're all talking about.

14.3.2

The following is an excerpt from President George W. Bush's 2006 State of the Union address presented on January 31, 2006. Construct Bush's main argument. That is, provide the conclusion, minor premise, and major premise of his practical syllogism. Compare Bush's reasoning with Nixon's. Consider whether Bush's reasoning was any more or less convincing in 2006 than Nixon's was in 1977.

Bush: It is said that prior to the attacks of September the 11th, our government failed to connect the dots of the conspiracy. We now know that two of the hijackers in the United States placed telephone calls to al Qaeda operatives overseas. But we did not know about their plans until it was too late. So to prevent another attack—based on authority given to me by the Constitution and by statute—I have authorized a terrorist surveillance program to aggressively pursue the international communications of suspected al Qaeda operatives and affiliates to and from America. Previous Presidents have used the same constitutional authority I have, and federal courts have approved the use of that authority. Appropriate members of Congress have been kept informed. The terrorist surveillance program has helped prevent terrorist attacks. It remains essential to the security of America. If there are people inside our country who are talking with al Qaeda, we want to know about it, because we will not sit back and wait to be hit again.

14.3.3

In the following excerpt from *The Prince*, written in 1513 after the overthrow of the Republic of Florence threw him into exile, Niccolo Machiavelli gives direction to state leaders. Construct Machiavelli's main argument and discuss the veracity of its premises especially as they relate to the contemporary state.

The Prince ought to have no other aim or thought, nor select anything else for his study, than war and its rules and discipline; for this is the sole art that belongs to him who rules, and it is of such force that it not only upholds those who are born princes, but it often enables men to rise from a private station to that rank. And, on the contrary, it is seen that when princes have thought more of ease than of arms they have lost their states. And the first cause of your losing it is to neglect this art; and what enables you to acquire a state is to be master of the art.

14.3.4

The following is excerpted from "The Report of the South Dakota Task Force to Study Abortion," which was the basis of the South Dakota Human Life and Protection Act that became law in South Dakota on March 6, 2006, and was subsequently defeated on November 7, 2006, in a public referendum. The act illegalized abortion except to save the life of a pregnant woman, but even then it encouraged physicians to exercise "reasonable medical efforts" both to save the life of the pregnant woman and to continue her pregnancy. Construct the main argument as well as any subarguments, and discuss the veracity of the premises:

DNA fingerprinting and the refinement of it by polymerase chain reaction (PCR) techniques developed in the mid-1990s have proven that each human being is totally unique immediately at fertilization. . . . A human being at an embryonic age and that human being at an adult age are naturally the same, the biological differences are due only to the differences in maturity. Changes in methylation of cytosine demonstrate that the human being is fully programmed for human growth and development for his or her entire life at the one cell age. . . . It is now clear that the mother's unborn child is a whole human being throughout gestation and that she has an existing relationship with her child. . . .

(continued)

The fact that the unborn child is a whole separate unique living human being is not without significance for our culture and our state. The right to live does not derive from government. If it is truly, as we know it to be, an intrinsic natural right, it is enjoyed by every single human being, no matter how poor or wealthy, strong or weak, age of maturity, or state of dependence. We find that the unborn child possesses intrinsic rights that are in perfect harmony with and equal to the intrinsic rights of that child's mother. As for the sovereign state of South Dakota, we recognize that the State has both the right and the unqualified duty to protect every human being and their personal intrinsic rights, including the pregnant mother's natural intrinsic right to her relationship with her child, and the child's intrinsic right to life. These cherished rights are compatible and harmonious, regardless of the unfortunate circumstances that sadly invoke thoughts that she may not be able to avail herself of her great rights. It is the law, as it represents the collective interests of the individuals for whom the law exists, that must protect life.

14.3.5

The following excerpt is taken from the "Immorality of Embryonic Stem Cell Research" by Fr. Juan Carlos Iscara, a professor of church history and theology at Saint Thomas Aquinas Seminary.[2] It represents the view of the Roman Catholic Church on embryonic stem cell research. Such research involves the use and destruction of human embryos in order to derive lines of stem cells that may in turn hold promise for curing a host of diseases, including diabetes, Alzheimer's, Parkinson's, spinal cord injuries, and heart disease. According to Iscara, upon conception a new human individual is formed. He further maintains that at this point, the being thus formed fits St. Thomas Aquinas's definition of a person as a "distinct being, subsisting in an intellectual nature." That is, he contends it is a separate, subsistent life with the capacity for developing reason.

Construct Iscara's main argument, and examine its premises. Compare his reasoning with that of the South Dakota Task Force:

> Once we have accepted the notion that the human embryo is a human person, all ethical puzzlement should vanish like an unhealthy fog under the sun. Concrete, negative precepts—as the Fifth Commandment's prohibition to kill an innocent—oblige and are to be observed semper et pro semper, that is, always and without exceptions. The voluntary destruction of an innocent human being is murder, equally forbidden by divine and natural law, and usually by the civil laws in agreement with those fundamental laws. The "harvesting" of embryonic stem cells requires the destruction of the embryo—then, it is murder. No objective, even though noble in itself, such as the foreseeable advantage to science, to other human beings or to society, can in any way justify experimentation on living human embryos or fetuses, whether viable or not, either inside or outside the mother's womb. "A good end does not make right an action which in itself is wrong." The debate is over.

14.3.6

The following excerpt is taken from John Stuart Mill's "Speech in Favor of the Death Penalty."[3] Mill is one of the founders of the theory of ethics known as "utilitarianism," which, as mentioned in chapter 1, assesses the morality or rightness of actions according to their ability to produce the best possible consequences. For Mill, this translated into the ability of an action to produce the greatest balance of pleasure over pain than any alternative action. You should keep this view in mind as you read and analyze Mill's argument in favor of capital punishment.

Construct Mill's main argument as well as any subarguments, and consider whether his reasoning is sound:

---

2. Fr. Juan Carlos Iscara, "Immorality of Embryonic Stem Cell Research," Society of Saint Pius X. Retrieved online on August 10, 2008, from www.sspx.org/against_the_sound_bites/immorality_embryonic_stem_cell_research.htm.

3. John Stuart Mill, "Speech in Favor of the Death Penalty," Ethics Update, University of San Diego. Retrieved online on April 10, 2009, from http://ethics.sandiego.edu/Books/Mill/Punishment/index.html.

When there has been brought home to any one, by conclusive evidence, the greatest crime known to the law; and when the attendant circumstances suggest no palliation of the guilt, no hope that the culprit may even yet not be unworthy to live among mankind, nothing to make it probable that the crime was an exception to his general character rather than a consequence of it, then I confess it appears to me that to deprive the criminal of the life of which he has proved himself to be unworthy—solemnly to blot him out from the fellowship of mankind and from the catalogue of the living—is the most appropriate as it is certainly the most impressive, mode in which society can attach to so great a crime the penal consequences which for the security of life it is indispensable to annex to it. I defend this penalty, when confined to atrocious cases, on the very ground on which it is commonly attacked—on that of humanity to the criminal; as beyond comparison the least cruel mode in which it is possible adequately to deter from the crime. If, in our horror of inflicting death, we endeavour to devise some punishment for the living criminal which shall act on the human mind with a deterrent force at all comparable to that of death, we are driven to inflictions less severe indeed in appearance, and therefore less efficacious, but far more cruel in reality. Few, I think, would venture to propose, as a punishment for aggravated murder, less than imprisonment with hard labor for life; that is the fate to which a murderer would be consigned by the mercy which shrinks from putting him to death. But has it been sufficiently considered what sort of a mercy this is, and what kind of life it leaves to him? If, indeed, the punishment is not really inflicted—if it becomes the sham which a few years ago such punishments were rapidly becoming—then, indeed, its adoption would be almost tantamount to giving up the attempt to repress murder altogether. But if it really is what it professes to be, and if it is realized in all its rigour by the popular imagination, as it very probably would not be, but as it must be if it is to be efficacious, it will be so shocking that when the memory of the crime is no longer fresh, there will be almost insuperable difficulty in executing it. What comparison can there really be, in point of severity, between consigning a man to the short pang of a rapid death, and immuring him in a living tomb, there to linger out what may be a long life in the hardest and most monotonous toil, without any of its alleviations or rewards—debarred from all pleasant sights and sounds, and cut off from all earthly hope, except a slight mitigation of bodily restraint, or a small improvement of diet?

15

✦

Refutation in
Practical Reasoning

In *sound* reasoning, the conclusion you infer must follow from the premises. If the reason is inductive, this means that its conclusion must follow with a degree of probability that makes it reasonable to believe (and act on) the conclusion. If the reasoning is deductive, the conclusion must necessarily follow from the premises. That is, the argument must be formally valid—have a valid form—and therefore avoid formal fallacies such as those discussed earlier in this book. However, sound reasoning requires more than just that the conclusion follow from the premises. *The premises themselves must also be rational or justified.* As you have already seen, the conclusions of valid deductive arguments can turn out false unless the premises are also true.

The importance of having rational premises in doing practical reasoning cannot be overstated. Recall how former CBS journalist Dan Rather and even the esteemed *New York Times* betrayed the public trust by blindly accepting whatever government officials told them and how President George W. Bush led us to war in Iraq based on unjustified and false premises (see chapter 13). Whether someone is making a decision that could affect thousands of people—as in the case of Rather, the *New York Times*, and the president of the United States—or one's own personal welfare, avoiding unjustified or false premises in practical reasoning can be of inestimable value.

Accordingly, it is useful to have at one's disposal some methods for showing a premise to be false or unjustified. Such methods may be called *methods of refutation*, and there are several kinds: (1) deductive falsification, (2) showing that there is insufficient inductive evidence, (3) reductio ad absurdum, and (4) showing a double standard. In what follows we will examine each of these methods of refutation.

DEDUCTIVE FALSIFICATION

In some cases *a premise can deductively be shown to be false based on evidence that contradicts the premise*. For example, DNA testing has been used successfully to refute the premises of legal reasoning that have sent at least 130 innocent people to prison, including twelve who spent time on death row.

One such individual was Ray Crones, who spent ten years in prison, three on death row, for the murder of a Phoenix cocktail waitress. Falsely branded the "snaggletooth killer" on the basis of bogus forensic evidence that attempted to match his teeth to the teeth marks on the neck of the victim, he was later exonerated by DNA analysis of the saliva left on the victim's tank top.

If Crones was the snaggletooth killer, then he was guilty of a capital crime. This was the gist of the practical rule applied in his case. But the crux of the legal reasoning that led the jury to conclude that Crones was, in fact, the snaggletooth killer can be cast as the following valid hypothetical syllogism:[1]

> *Major premise:* If Crones's teeth caused the wound on the victim's neck, then he killed the victim.
> *Minor premise:* Crones's teeth caused the wound on the victim's neck.
> *Conclusion:* Crones killed the victim.

Despite the fact that there was further evidence to disprove the above minor premise, Crones was not exculpated until DNA testing turned up a match between the DNA in the saliva and another person who was already serving time in an Arizona prison for child molestation. The syllogism that falsified this premise was accordingly this one:

> *Major premise:* If Crones's teeth caused the teeth marks on the victim's neck, then the saliva on the areas of the victim's tank top where Crones bit through it would match Crones's DNA.
> *Minor premise:* The DNA on the tank top did not match Crones's DNA.
> *Conclusion:* Crones's teeth did not cause the teeth marks on the victim's neck.

As you can see, the syllogism is valid, a case of denying the consequent. Accordingly, given the truth of the premises, the conclusion necessarily follows and therefore serves to refute and falsify the minor premise in the original syllogism.[2]

Exercise Set 15.1

Construct reasoning that might be used to falsify each of the following claims. Then, discuss whether the argument you have formulated is sound. In some cases, you may find it useful to surf the Internet to gather evidence for the minor premise of your argument.

---

1. "Man Convicted on Erroneous Bite Mark Identification Evidence Finally Free; Served 10 Years for Crime He Didn't Commit," Forensic-Evidence.com. Retrieved online on April 9, 2009, from forensic-evidence.com/site/ID/bitemark_ID.html.

2. This is how a hypothesis gets "tested." If the DNA had matched Crones's teeth, the evidence would have "converged upon" (supported) and increased the probability that Crone committed the murder. But the evidence instead diverged from and, in fact, deductively falsified this hypothesis. See the discussion of testing hypotheses in chapter 12.

15.1.1
Inhaling second-hand cigarette smoke poses no health risks to people.

15.1.2
All congressmen are heterosexual.

15.1.3
Blacks tend to be less intelligent than whites.

15.1.4
The earth is only about six thousand years old.

15.1.5
God is all-powerful, all-good, and all-knowing.

15.1.6
Anna Nicole Smith committed suicide.

INSUFFICIENT INDUCTIVE EVIDENCE

Showing that a premise is false must be distinguished from establishing that there is insufficient evidence to justify believing it. In the former case, one has reason to disbelieve the premise (believe that it is false); in the latter case, one has reason to withhold belief (neither believe nor disbelieve it). For example, as we have seen in chapter 12, in our justice system a defendant must be proven "guilty beyond a reasonable doubt." So, if the preponderance of inductive evidence is not sufficient to establish guilt beyond a reasonable doubt, then the defendant may be acquitted. For example, it is not uncommon for the state not to pursue prosecution of a defendant in drug and contraband cases where possession cannot be established.

In medical contexts, a set of symptoms can sometimes be consistent with a number of different diagnoses so that the belief that one of these diagnoses is correct becomes irrational. And, occasionally, even when further testing is pursued to rule out some of these alternatives, it is still not possible to make a determinant diagnosis. For example, morbid obesity can present an obstacle for using ultrasound and radiography to make diagnoses, and in some cases, no diagnosis at all can be assigned to a set of symptoms.[3]

In chapters 9–13, we examined different kinds of fallacies that discredit fact claims. These included *inductive* fallacies such as hasty generalizing, which involves inferring a universal or quasi-universal statement (a statement about all or most) on an insufficient sampling of group members. For example, I would have insufficient evidence for my claim if I tried to infer that all or most priests were homosexual pedophiles based on a relatively small sampling of priests known to have molested male children.

There are also some statements that seem *impossible* to verify. For example, according to philosopher Karl Popper, some psychological premises, such as the

---

3. "Obesity an Increasing Obstacle to Medical Diagnosis," Radiological Society of North America, July 25, 2006. Retrieved online on April 18, 2009, from www2.rsna.org/pr/target.cfm?ID=284.

Freudian one that young females suffer from an unconscious state of penis envy, do not seem to be subject to either verification or falsification.

Since the major premises of practical syllogisms *prescribe* rather than report things, these premises are not inferred by induction as are their minor premises. This is a linguistic point about the difference between statements in the imperative mood (commands) and those in the indicative mood (descriptions). Unlike indicatives, imperatives are neither true nor false. For example, the traffic sign that says "yield" is neither true nor false. While you cannot verify this command, you can, indeed, verify whether in fact someone has yielded. Nevertheless, as you will see, some commonplace rules prescribe unrealistic feats—for example, always having the approval of others. Since it is highly improbable that you will always get the approval of everyone, a rule that required this would not be realistic. As the philosopher Immanuel Kant pointed out, "ought" implies "can." Hence it makes no sense to prescribe something that is not even feasible.

Exercise Set 15.2

Discuss why the evidence given for each of the following inferences is not sufficient:

15.2.1
Evidence: Bob has had a cough for six months.
Therefore, Bob has lung cancer.

15.2.2
Evidence: Blondes are often portrayed as dumb in the media.
Therefore, blondes tend to be dumb.

15.2.3
Evidence: The car started stalling out after I took it for an oil change at the Quickie Lube.
Therefore, they must have done something to harm the engine when they changed the oil.

15.2.4
Evidence: Tylenol works on me when I have body aches and pains.
Therefore, it should work equally well on my dog.

15.2.5
Evidence: The dog that viciously attacked that little girl was a pit bull. I have heard similar stories about how pit bulls have turned on their masters.
Therefore, pit bulls tend to be vicious.

15.2.6
Evidence: The elevator has been working for the past fifty years, and it has always been safe.
Therefore, I'm sure it's safe to use.

Exercise Set 15.3

Respond to the following questions and provide reasons for your response:

15.3.1
Is there sufficient evidence for the statement "There's life in other galaxies besides ours"?

REDUCTIO AD ABSURDUM

A useful way to refute a premise, including a major premise, is to show that it leads to absurdity. This method of reductio ad absurdum ("reduction to the absurd") was a favorite of the ancient Greek philosopher Socrates, who often used it to expose the holes in the ideas of others. Although Socrates himself left no writings, he appears as the central character in a number of dialogs written by his student, Plato. In one famous dialog called "The Euthyphro," Socrates queries a young man named Euthyphro about the nature of piety (holiness). Euthyphro is charging his own father with impiety for allegedly having neglected to death a serf who in a drunken rage had slain a domestic servant. As the account goes, Euthyphro's father had placed the perpetrator in a pit without food and water and had intended to leave him there until he received instruction from the interpreters of the gods about what to do with him. However, in the interim, the prisoner died. Intent on seeing justice done, Euthyphro states,

> Piety is doing as I am doing; that is to say, prosecuting anyone who is guilty of murder, sacrilege, or of any similar crime—whether he be your father or mother, or whoever he may be—that makes no difference; and not to prosecute them is impiety. And please to consider, Socrates, what a notable proof I will give you of the truth of my words, a proof which I have already given to others:—of the principle, I mean, that the impious, whoever he may be, ought not to go unpunished.

Here we have Euthyphro's basic practical syllogism:

> *Major premise:* If a person is guilty of impiety, then he ought to be punished for it.
> *Minor premise:* My father is guilty of impiety (by virtue of having neglected the serf to death).
> *Conclusion:* My father ought to be punished for his impiety.

Clearly, Euthyphro's argument trades on an understanding of impiety, so Socrates asks him for his definition. "Piety," responds Euthyphro, "is that which is dear to the gods, and impiety is that which is not dear to them." Socrates then confirms with Euthyphro that gods resemble people in having different opinions about what is good and evil, just and unjust, honorable and dishonorable. Given this understanding, Socrates proceeds to draw out the consequences of Euthyphro's view:

> Socrates: Then the same things are hated by the gods and loved by the gods, and are both hateful and dear to them?

Euthyphro: True.

Socrates: And upon this view the same things, Euthyphro, will be pious and also impious?

Euthyphro: So I should suppose.

Socrates: Then, my friend, I remark with surprise that you have not answered the question which I asked. For I certainly did not ask you to tell me what action is both pious and impious: but now it would seem that what is loved by the gods is also hated by them. And therefore, Euthyphro, in thus chastising your father you may very likely be doing what is agreeable to Zeus but disagreeable to Cronos or Uranus, and what is acceptable to Hephaestus but unacceptable to Here, and there may be other gods who have similar differences of opinion.

With this final stroke of logic, Socrates draws out the blatant contradiction in making piety depend on what is agreeable to the gods and, therefore, in basing his judgment about his father's guilt on the basis of this inconsistent standard.

Exercise Set 15.4

Reduce each of the following statements to the absurd:

Freedom means doing whatever you want whenever you want.

If you do something bad, then you are bad.

If the president says something, then it must be true.

A person should never, under any circumstances, tell a lie.

All parents must sacrifice their happiness for the sake of their children's happiness.

We must be prepared to sacrifice our civil liberties in order to defend our democracy against the terrorists.

DOUBLE STANDARDS

Another way to refute a premise is to show that it is based on a double standard. Consider, for example, the following argument advanced by well-known radio celebrity and host Rush Limbaugh on his show on October 5, 1995:

There's nothing good about drug use. We know it. It destroys individuals. It destroys families. Drug use destroys societies. . . . And so if people are violating the law by doing drugs, they ought to be accused and they ought to be convicted and they ought to be sent up. What this says to me is that too many whites are getting away with drug use. . . . The answer to this disparity is not to start letting people out of jail because we're not putting others in jail who are breaking the law. The answer is to go out and find the ones who are getting away with it, convict them and send them up the river, too.

Limbaugh's main practical syllogism can be boiled down to the following:

Major premise: If people are violating the law by doing drugs, they ought to be accused, and they ought to be convicted, and they ought to be sent up.
Minor premise: There are many white people who are getting away with using drugs.
Conclusion: These white people who are getting away with using drugs ought to be accused, and they ought to be convicted, and they ought to be sent up.

This argument does not acknowledge the view that drug addiction is a disease that requires treatment rather than punishment. Instead, the major premise unconditionally treats *all* illegal drug users as criminals and insists that they be prosecuted. Thus, there was some irony in learning in October 2003 that Rush Limbaugh, a white man, was himself addicted to illegally obtained painkillers. By his own principle, we would expect Limbaugh to accept his own conviction and incarceration. However, Limbaugh, who illegally acquired thousands of dosages of OxyContin and other painkillers over a several-year period from several different doctors, pleaded "not guilty" to "doctor shopping," a third-degree felony punishable by up to five years in prison. Limbaugh did his best to keep himself out of prison, including undertaking a legal battle to protect the privacy of his medical records, a battle that he, with the assistance of his high-priced attorney, took all the way to the Florida Supreme Court. According to his attorney, Roy Black, when the threat of being imprisoned had passed, Limbaugh felt "a great burden lifted from his shoulders."

As Limbaugh himself perceived, many poor nonwhites do not have the money to support the kind of legal defense he himself received. Had his own rule been consistently applied, he would have gone to prison like those less well off than he. It is often easy for people to impose harsh restrictions on others if the same restrictions are not likely to be imposed on themselves. If Limbaugh was willing to accept the principle espoused in his major premise, he also needed to see it applied in his own case. If he was unwilling to do so, then he was not entitled to claim its legitimacy in the case of others, especially those who could not afford the price of a skilled attorney like Roy Black.

To be consistent, Limbaugh either had to give up his principle or admit that he himself should spend time in jail. Given his aggressive legal battle to exempt himself from prison, it is reasonable to conclude that he was unwilling to accept the logical implications of his own principle and therefore was not justified in claiming to accept this principle in the first place.

Limbaugh explained that he became addicted to painkillers as a result of a lower-back problem. We can certainly understand how this could happen and can empathize with him. Nevertheless, this does not logically exempt him from his own principle as he espoused it. Indeed, all individuals with drug addictions can offer some explanation for the genesis of their addictions. Limbaugh's refusal to be "sent up the river" along with all other transgressors underscores his hypocrisy. It is not merely his failure to practice what he preached that was disingenuous. Out of weakness of will, people can act against their own best judgment and violate principles to which they truly subscribe. This is what makes us all fallible, imperfect, and human. However, admitting our fallibility is one thing; denying that there is any double standard, covering it up with rationalizations and excuses, or otherwise refusing to fess up is quite another.

Exercise Set 15.5

Discuss whether there is a double standard in each of the following. If you think there is a double standard, how, in your view, should it be resolved?

15.5.1
Many politicians condone sending other parents' children off to war but refuse to send their own children.

15.5.2
Eighteen-year-olds can serve their nation in the military, but they are not permitted to drink.

15.5.3
Despite the Equal Pay Act and more recent legislation prohibiting employment discrimination, men get paid more than women for the same work. In 2005, women's earnings were on average 77 percent of men's, and black women received even less, 71.7 percent of men's earnings.

15.5.4
America has a thriving nuclear weapons program, while it has repeatedly sought to prevent what it calls "rogue states" from developing nuclear weapons of their own.

15.5.5
Many U.S. states have fetal homicide laws according to which a person who kills a fetus in the course of killing its mother is guilty of a double homicide. Yet these states also permit abortion in the first and second trimesters.

15.5.6
Oregon's Death with Dignity Act permits assisted suicide. Yet (active) euthanasia is illegal in Oregon.

Exercise Set 15.6

Give at least three other examples of double standards, and discuss how you think they should be resolved.

INFORMAL FALLACIES IN PRACTICAL REASONING

In chapters 2–8, we studied deductive reasoning and examined a class of fallacy known as *formal fallacies*—for example, the fallacies of denying the antecedent, affirming a disjunct, and undistributed middle term. These fallacies, we have seen, are mistakes in reasoning that render the argument formally invalid as the conclusion fails to follow *necessarily* from the premises. Then, in chapters 9–13, we looked at inductive reasoning and examined *inductive fallacies*—for example, hasty generalization, magnifying risks, the fallacy of unsupported hypothesis, and the post hoc fallacy. These fallacies, we have seen, are mistakes in reasoning that fail to make the conclusion of the argument *probable* in relation to the premises.

However, there is still a further class of fallacy whose members are often referred to as *informal fallacies*. These fallacies are not related to the form of the argument as in the case of deductive fallacies. Nor do they concern the probabilistic relationship of premises to conclusion as in the case of inductive fallacies. Rather, these fallacies represent a class consisting of *irrational assumptions and misuses of language contained in the premises of arguments*. The characteristic mark of these assumptions and linguistic errors is that they have a *long, proven track record of frustrating personal and interpersonal happiness*. That is, they tend to have dangerous and self-destructive consequences. Logicians and some psychologists have accordingly identified these fallacies, named them, and shown others how to find and dispose of them in their practical reasoning.

A number of these informal fallacies arise as suppressed (unstated) major premise rules in practical reasoning. For example, recall Dan Rather's argument discussed in chapter 14:

> *Major premise rule:* If Bush is the president, then I should do whatever he tells me to do.
> *Minor premise report:* Bush is the president.
> *Behavioral conclusion:* I should do whatever Bush tells me to do.

In this argument, the major premise rule represents an instance of a type of "bandwagon" thinking known as *authoritarianism*.[4] Those who are led by this assumption in their practical reasoning engage in apelike acceptance of authorities such as state and media representatives. This assumption is clearly the opposite of freethinking, and it is a major obstacle to an open society.

Other informal fallacies concern abuses of language—for example, using *emotive terms* like "idiot" and "moron," instead of fact claims, to manipulate, intimidate, and coerce others. We will examine informal fallacies in part II of this book.

---

4. This fallacy will be examined in chapter 19.

16

Emotional Reasoning

EMOTIONAL REASONING

According to Aristotle, actions are not the only sort of conclusions that can be deduced from practical syllogisms. He also believed that people can in some sense infer their *emotions* from the premises of a practical syllogism. For example, he said that "anger and sexual appetites and some other such passions" are "under the influence (in a sense) of a rule and an opinion [a report]."

The idea that our emotions arise from reasoning about the events in our lives and not from the events themselves was also later expressed by the Greek Stoic philosopher Epictetus:

> It is not the things themselves that disturb men but their judgments about these things. For example, death is nothing dreadful, or else Socrates too would have thought so, but the judgment that death is dreadful, *this* is the dreadful thing. When, therefore, we are hindered, or disturbed, or grieved, let us never blame anyone but ourselves, that means, our own judgments.

Since so much of everyday reasoning is emotional, understanding how such reasoning works can be edifying. However, to reach such an understanding, one needs to know what an emotion is in the first place.

WHAT'S IN AN EMOTION?

Philosophers have disagreed about what an emotion is. Some have identified emotions with certain visceral changes that occur in your body. For example, according to William James, an emotion "is nothing but the feeling of a bodily state and it has a purely bodily cause." For example, he states, "What kind of an emotion of fear would be left if the feeling neither of quickened hear-beats nor of shallow breathing, neither of trembling lips nor of weakened limbs, neither of goose-flesh nor of visceral stirrings, were present, it is quite impossible for me to think." At the other extreme, some have defined emotions as value judgments. For example, according to Robert Solomon, an emotion just *is* "an evaluative (or a normative) judgment." For example, according to Solomon, "I cannot be angry if I do not believe that someone has wronged or offended me. . . . My anger is that set of judgments." On the other hand, some philosophers have defined emotions purely in terms of behavior. For example, in his classic work *The Concept of Mind*, philosopher Gilbert Ryle held that anger amounts to a tendency to display certain forms of behavior associated with being angry, such as yelling, scowling, clenching of fists, and so forth.

While philosophers have found reason to reject all of these definitions, each nevertheless captures an important element of an emotion. In fact, current-day cognitive behavioral psychologies, notably rational-emotive behavior therapy, have maintained that emotions are an amalgamation of changes in cognition (beliefs, especially evaluative ones), physiology, and behavior. As psychologist Albert Ellis suggests, "What we call an emotion mainly seems to include (1) a certain kind of forceful thinking—a kind strongly slanted or biased by previous perceptions or experiences; (2) intense bodily responses, such as feelings of pleasure or nausea; and (3) tendencies toward positive or negative actions in regard to the events that seem to cause the strong thinking and its emotional concomitants."

According to one school of philosophy known as phenomenology, all states of consciousness, including emotions, refer to something outside themselves, such as a person, an event, a problem, or a thing. According to Edmund Husserl, a leading representative of this school of thought, "The essence of consciousness, in which I live as my own self, is the so-called intentionality. Consciousness is always conscious of something." For example, when one is angry, one is angry *about* something, such as someone deliberately cutting you off on the highway, being lied to by your significant other, being passed over for a raise, getting a grade that is lower than you think you deserve, and so on. Your anger has an *intention*, which means that it is directed toward or focused on something.

Strictly speaking, the intentional object of an emotion is a statement of particular fact. For example, your anger refers to the fact that *this person has deliberately cut you off on the highway*. Notice also that the intentional object need not be a true statement. So you can be angry about a person's deliberately cutting you off on the highway even if it is really false that the person did it deliberately. Similarly, one can be depressed about having a serious illness even though the diagnosis was based on a false positive. In such cases the emotion can be said to rest on a false *minor* premise. As we will see, this is because the intentional object of an emotion is the statement of particular fact from which the emotion is inferred.

An emotion also involves a *rating* or *evaluation* of a particular aspect of its intentional object. For example, anger about a person having deliberately cut you off on the highway would include a strong negative rating of either the person's action ("What a horrible thing he's done") or a strong negative rating of the *person* him- or herself who performed the action ("that no-good, rotten . . . ").

In fact, the cognitive ("thinking") dimension of an emotion (E) can be defined in terms of the emotion's intentional object (O) plus its rating (R). We then get the following formula for defining an emotion:

Table 16.1

Emotion	Intentional Object	Rating
Anger	An action	You strongly, negatively rate the action itself or the person who did it.
Guilt	A moral principle, which you perceive yourself to have violated	You strongly condemn the violation or yourself for the violation.
Shame	An action or state of yours	You perceive others to be strongly, negatively morally judging you, your action, or state. You perceive this judgment to be extremely undesirable and as a reason for you also to strongly, negatively morally judge yourself, your action or state.
Depression	An event or state of affairs	You strongly, negatively rate this event or state of affairs, and on the basis of this rating you bleakly perceive your own existence.
Grief	The loss of someone (a person or animal) you cherish	You bleakly perceive your own existence on the basis of the loss.
Anxiety	A future event or possible future event having certain forecasted consequences	You perceive these forecasted consequences to be so bad that you must ruminate over them.
Jealousy	A person or state of a person who has something that you want but don't have	You rate negatively this person's having that which you lack.
Pity	A person (or animal) who is suffering in some particular way	You strongly negatively rate this suffering and think that something should be done to stop it if possible.

$$E = (O + R)$$

Table 16.1 lists definitions of some emotions that proceed in terms of this formula.

Exercise Set 16.1

Define the following emotions in terms of their intentional objects and rating elements. Note that the first two of these emotions have negative ratings, while the last two have affirmative ratings.

Emotion	Intentional Object	Rating
Embarrassment		
Disappointment		
Romantic love		
Gratitude		
Empathy (Hint: compare pity)		

HOW TO IDENTIFY AN EMOTION AND FIND ITS PREMISES

Suppose your philosophy instructor has asked you to do a class presentation tomorrow on Plato's theory of forms. You are now tossing and turning in bed, thinking about giving the presentation tomorrow, and you keep thinking what a fool you'll make of yourself if you mess up and your classmates all laugh at you.

What emotion are you experiencing?

You can easily identify it by the $E = (O + R)$ formula. The object of this emotion is clearly the event of making the presentation tomorrow that has certain forecasted consequences—namely messing up and having your classmates laugh at you. You rate these consequences as so bad (they will make you a fool) that you must keep yourself up thinking about them. So here is an emotion about a *future* event to which you ascribe possible consequences you think are so bad that you must keep ruminating over them. Clearly, this meets the definition of *anxiety* provided in table 16.1.

> Anxiety:
> *Intentional object* = tomorrow, in delivering my presentation on Plato's theory of forms, I might mess up.
> *Rating* = I will make a fool out of myself.

Once you are able to define the intentional object and the rating of an emotion, you can then easily find the premises from which the conclusion of your emotional reasoning is being deduced. This is because the report expressed in the minor premise of the practical syllogism equates to the statement of the intentional object. The rule expressed in the major premise then equates to the conditional (if-then) statement connecting the intentional object to the rating:

> *Rule (in major premise):* If O, then R.
> *Report (in minor premise):* O.

Applying these formulae to the present example, one can easily construct the premises from which the conclusion of the emotional reasoning is deduced:

> *Rule:* If I mess up and everyone laughs at me (O), I will make a fool out of myself (R).[1]
> *Report:* Tomorrow, in delivering my presentation on Plato's theory of forms, I might mess up, and everyone will laugh at me (O).
> *Conclusion:* I might make a fool out of myself tomorrow (R).

Notice the form of the above syllogism:

> If O, then R.
> O.
> Therefore, R.

---

1. Strictly speaking, this major premise rule is probabilistic: "If I might mess up and everyone laughs at me (O), then I might make a fool out of myself." Since predictions about the future are always probabilistic, this quality of not knowing whether one will *definitely* experience a set of negatively perceived consequences is an inherent condition of anxiety.

This is the standard form of a practical syllogism that people use to sustain their emotions. For example, as long as you keep deducing the possibility of making a fool out yourself, you will continue to experience anxiety over your upcoming presentation.

This does not mean that such cognitive changes are all there is to an emotion. As stated earlier in this chapter, there are also behavioral changes that make up elements of an emotion. For example, in the present case, you might decide to be absent tomorrow in order to avoid the possibility of messing up and being laughed at.[2] There are also physiological changes that typically occur during emotional states. For example, during your state of anxiety, your heart rate, respiration, and endocrine activity can increase, thereby contributing to keeping you tossing and turning in your bed instead of falling asleep.

Exercise Set 16.2

Identify the emotion in each of the following cases. Identify the intentional object and rating elements. Then, construct the emotional reasoning.

16.2.1
That no-good, rotten SOB, Alex, took my car without my permission and drove it into a tree. I hope he rots in hell for this!

16.2.2
My life is meaningless now that she's dead. I just can't stand to live like this.

16.2.3
She's got two beautiful children and a husband who loves her, and look at me. I'm not even married.

16.2.4
It's almost midnight, and he hasn't come home from work. He probably got into an accident, or got mugged and is lying in an alley somewhere, or maybe he's even dead.

(continued)

2. Such behavioral changes are themselves conclusions deduced from further behavioral syllogisms. These syllogisms have as their major premise a behavioral rule linking a rating (R) to a behavioral change (B). Such a rule has the form, If R then B. The minor premise is then the rating (R) deduced from the prior syllogism. Accordingly, the behavioral change is a deduction from a practical syllogism having the following form:

If R, then B.
R.
Therefore, B.

In the present example, my conclusion to not show up for class would be deduced from the following syllogism:

Behavioral rule: If I might make a fool out of myself (R), then I should avoid coming to class (B).
Rating (the conclusion of the prior syllogism): I might make a fool out of myself.
Conclusion: I should avoid coming to class (B).

In this case, unless I change my mind or something prevents me from avoiding the class, I *will* avoid it.

16.2.5
My wife left me. I lost my job. And now I find out that I was abandoned by my mother when I was an infant and that the woman I have called mother all my life is really my aunt. Not even my own mother wanted me. I must be the world's biggest loser.

16.2.6
At the meeting today, everybody loved my new advertising campaign. Everything was going so great! Then, I had to go and trip over my shoelace, crash into the president, and knock his hair piece off. You should have seen the look on his face!

16.2.7
I was really expecting to be the next department chair. I thought that I was a shoe-in, but Joe Bigelo got the job instead. Oh well, that's too bad, but certainly not the worst thing in the world.

REFUTING IRRATIONAL PREMISES IN EMOTIONAL REASONING

Much of the emotional stress people experience is deduced from irrational premises. In other words, people often disturb themselves unnecessarily. The advantage of being able to identify an emotion and the premises of one's emotional reasoning is that one is then in a position to determine whether these premises are rational.

There are also certain commonplace informal fallacies (irrational assumptions) that undergird many destructive emotions. By having a catalog of these fallacies at one's disposal, it is possible to check the premises of emotional reasoning for them in order to avoid many of the unnecessary stresses of practical living. Let us call these irrational assumptions that lead to unnecessary stress *fallacies of emotion*. Fallacies of this kind will be examined in detail in chapters 17 and 18. For now it is important to note that, like other informal fallacies that can occur in the premises of practical reasoning, they can be refuted using methods such as those described in chapter 15.

Consider, for example the major premise rule in the above example:

If I mess up and everyone laughs at me (O), I will make a fool out of myself (R)

Notice that this premise negatively rates *the person* as a fool instead of rating the act of messing up. But this is irrational. Even if you do something foolish, that doesn't make *you* a fool. Indeed, if doing something foolish made people fools, then all of us would be fools, for who among us has not ever acted foolishly? Here, then, is the reductio ad absurdum of this premise. The fallacy inherent in it, known as *self-damnation*, self-defeatingly confuses the berating of one's act with the berating of one's entire self.

Exercise Set 16.3

Provide a refutation for each of the following emotional rules. If necessary, review the methods of refutation discussed in chapter 15 before completing these exercises.

16.3.1
If something goes wrong in your life, then your whole life is without value.

16.3.2
If something does not go your way, then the world is not the way it must be, and you cannot and must not ever accept such a flawed universe.

16.3.3
If you have a problem, then you must continue to disturb yourself over it and never let yourself be happy until the problem is completely resolved.

16.3.4
If I find something difficult or challenging, then it must be beyond my capacity to tolerate, and I cannot and must not ever hope to succeed at it.

16.3.5
If I feel upset, then someone or something else made me upset, and I cannot and should not try to change the way I feel.

16.3.6
If someone I consider my friend betrays me, then this must be absolutely the worst thing that could possibly happen to me.

16.3.7
If someone appears to have some desirable feature, then this person or thing must be absolutely and totally terrific, perfect, and the best of its kind in the entire universe.

COGNITIVE DISSONANCE

Realizing that one is deducing a conclusion from a fallacious premise does not automatically assure that one will stop deducing the conclusion from it. Frequently, people in this situation still continue to make the unsound inference even though they appreciate on an intellectual level that this is irrational. However, they may still not appreciate it on an *emotional* level. This state of conflict is commonly known as *cognitive dissonance*. When one is in a state of cognitive dissonance, one is still disposed to act and feel in ways supported by the faulty premise(s). For example, even if you realize that you are being irrational in forecasting yourself as a fool, you may still continue to experience anxiety over making your presentation in the morning. This is because you may still be physiologically and behaviorally disposed to feel anxious.

While cognitive dissonance is typically experienced as an uncomfortable tension between rational and irrational thinking, it can also be a healthy sign that one is beginning to deal rationally with one's faulty practical reasoning. The realization of such a tension means that one perceives a fallacy. In the absence of this realization, it is not likely constructive change will occur. However, like an itch that one desires to scratch, one may take the course of least resistance, which may be to sustain the self-defeating emotion by continuing the fallacious line of reasoning.

In this state of cognitive dissonance, rational constraint is necessary to offset the irrational tendency. This constraint consists of two components: (1) finding an *antidote* to the fallacious emotional reasoning that gives rational direction, and (2) exercising *willpower* to apply the antidote.

Exercise Set 16.4

Discuss at least two examples of states of cognitive dissonance that you are presently experiencing or have experienced in the past. Be specific about the irrational rule underlying the cognitive dissonance.

FINDING AN ANTIDOTE TO A FALLACIOUS PREMISE IN EMOTIONAL REASONING

The refutation of a faulty premise in emotional reasoning is an important step toward correcting it. The refutation points out a hole in the reasoning that needs to be repaired. As when trying to fix a leaky pipe, unless you can see exactly where the plumbing is leaking, it is not likely you will be able to repair the hole. Constructing a refutation of a fallacious premise is thus a preliminary to constructing an antidote to it. An *antidote* to a fallacious premise can be usefully thought of as a prescription for overcoming the fallacy.

Philosophical theories and ideas can be helpful in constructing such counterprescriptions to irrational thinking. Indeed, since philosophy itself aims at providing a rational understanding of the world, it is not unreasonable to expect that it can provide a storehouse of such corrective wisdom. For example, consider ancient Roman Stoic philosopher Epictetus's comments about trying to control things that aren't in one's control. According to Epictetus, this is the main source of human anxiety.

> Some things are under our control, while others are not under our control. Under our control are conception, choice, desire, aversion, and in a word, everything that is our own doing; not under our control are our body, our property, reputation, office and, in a word, everything that is not our own doing. . . . Remember, therefore, that if what is naturally slavish you think to be free, and what is not your own to be your own, you will be hampered, will grieve, will be in turmoil, and will blame both gods and men; while if you think only what is your own, to be your own, and what is not your own to be, as it really is, not your own, then no one will ever be able to exert compulsion upon you, no one will hinder you, you will blame no one, will find fault with no one, will do absolutely nothing against your will, you will have no personal enemies, no one will harm you, for neither is there any harm that can touch you.

Stoics believed that as events in the external world just happen, it is vain to attempt to control them. Still, people are capable of controlling how they *think* about these events. "It is not the things themselves that disturb men," Epictetus writes, "but their judgments about these things." For example, he admonishes,

> When I see anyone anxious, I say, what does this man want? Unless he wanted something or other not in his own power, how could he still be anxious? A musician, for

instance, feels no anxiety while he is singing by himself; but when he appears upon the stage he does, even if his voice be ever so good, or he plays ever so well. For what he wishes is not only to sing well, but likewise to gain applause. But this is not in his own power.

Following Epictetus, psychologist Albert Ellis further distinguishes between a *preference* and a *demand*. While Epictetus speaks in terms of "wishing" for things that are not yours to control,[3] Ellis maintains that it is the *demand* for such control, rather than a mere preference for it, that leads to emotional disturbance. Thus, if I simply *preferred* that my classmates not laugh at me if I happened to mess up but didn't demand it (that is, I didn't say that they *must* not laugh at me), I would not seriously disturb myself over the possibility of their laughing at me. On the other hand, if I *demand* that my classmates not laugh at me, then I will create undue anxiety for myself about the possibility of messing up. Indeed, my major premise, "If I mess up and everyone laughs at me, I will make a fool out of myself," makes my self-worth dependent on whether or not my classmates approve of me. However, others' response to me is not anything of my "own doing"; it is instead of *someone else's* doing. It is accordingly not something that one can rationally demand.

Looking at it from Epictetus's perspective, the main problem people face when they confront anxiety is how to deal with things that are out of their power to control. According to Epictetus (and Ellis), *you shouldn't demand what you can't control.* In giving up this demand, I would release myself from *having* to perform without messing up. And in giving oneself permission to mess up, one would give up the perceived basis for degrading oneself.

Accordingly, one can use Epictetus's wisdom to construct an antidote for overcoming anxiety about messing up. Here is a rational formulation of such an antidote:

> If my classmates' laughing at me is not something I can control, then I shouldn't demand that they not laugh at me.

Notice that this antidote can now serve as a *replacement* for the prior, fallacious major premise ("If I mess up and everyone laughs at me, I will make a fool out of myself") in a new, rational, practical syllogism:

> *Major premise:* If my classmates' laughing at me is not something I can control, then I shouldn't demand that they not laugh at me.
> *Minor premise:* My classmates' laughing at me is not something I can control.
> *Conclusion:* I shouldn't demand that my classmates not laugh at me.

We will refer to such a syllogism as *antidotal reasoning* because it provides a rational fix for the irrational syllogism that leads to self-defeating anxiety.

In preoccupying and disturbing myself with how others might view me if I make a mistake, I demand control over what is not in my power to control. On the other hand, in accepting the above antidotal reasoning, I can free myself to

---

3. Epictetus does also himself speak elsewhere in terms of "demands": for example, he states, "*Demand* not that events should happen as you wish; but wish them to happen as they do happen, and you will go on well" (my italics).

concentrate on doing well on my presentation (which is something I *can* control), instead of preoccupying and disturbing myself with how others are going to view me. Epictetus's point is to try one's best at things under one's own control (things that are of my own doing) without also getting bogged down with what others might think and without placing fruitless demands to perform on oneself.

Notice that the antidotal reasoning has the same hypothetical form as the original emotional reasoning it was intended to replace:

If O, then R.
O.
Therefore, R.

By replacing O (object) with "My classmates' laughing at me is not something I can control" and R (rating) with "I shouldn't demand that my classmates not laugh at me," we get the antidotal reasoning.

Antidotal reasoning can accordingly be thought of as a prescription for an alternative, more rational emotion. What emotion would you thus have if you accepted this antidotal reasoning instead of the fallacious reasoning it is intended to correct? Epictetus would say peace or tranquility—that is, a state free of demandingness. He writes,

> If you would improve, lay aside such reasonings as prevent tranquility. It is better to die with hunger, exempt from grief and fear, than to live in affluence with perturbation. It is better your servant should be bad than you unhappy. Is a little oil spilt? A little wine stolen? Say to yourself, "This is the purchase paid for peace, for tranquility, and nothing is to be had for nothing." When you call your servant, consider it possible he may not come at your call; or if he doth, that he may not do what you would have him do. He is not of such importance that it should be in his power to disturb you.[4]

Some Guidelines for Constructing Antidotes and Antidotal Reasoning

In line with the above discussion, here are four important guidelines for constructing antidotes and antidotal reasoning:

1. *The antidote (major premise rule) fits the "If O, then R" formula.* For example, "If my classmates' laughing at me is not something I can control, I shouldn't demand that my classmates not laugh at me" fits this hypothetical formula. The antecedent is descriptive (it reports something), while the consequent prescribes something (it rates something).
2. *R prescribes a corrective to the fallacy being addressed.* For example, "I shouldn't demand that my classmates not laugh at me" corrects the self-damnation fallacy in "I will make a fool out of myself."
3. *R is rational and constructive.* It is not enough that R avoids the fallacy it is intended to correct. It must also prescribe something rational. For example, "I should threaten to harm my classmates" appeals to force to try to fix a fallacy

4. "Epictetus: Encheiridion," Public Bookshelf. Retrieved online on March 25, 2009, from www.publicbookshelf.com/public_html/Outline_of_Great_Books_Volume_I/epictetus_bea.html.

and generally leads to other problems, such as a dysfunctional relationship based on fear.[5]

4. *The minor premise (O) is supported by the facts.* For example, it is unrealistic to expect to control your classmates' response as you can your own.

Notice that these standards do not tell us what antidotes to construct in overcoming a given fallacy. Instead, they provide general, logical parameters within which you can bring to bear a wide range of antidotal wisdom. The formulation of antidotes and antidotal reasoning is thus a creative process. In the area of social reform, this process is perhaps the one we most often associate with creative genius.

For example, Martin Luther King Jr.'s antidote to violence was nonviolence and agape (love). Henry David Thoreau fought against slavery and war with civil disobedience. Jesus gave us the golden rule. Elizabeth Stanton stood against sexist and misogynistic social and political practices by leading one of the first comprehensive women's rights movements in America. John Stuart Mill heralded the principle of harm to others as the limit to government inference in the private affairs of citizens. These and many others whom we admire for their profound insights were not driven by blind hatred, envy, desire for revenge, or other self-destructive emotions but wielded creative antidotes and antidotal reasoning identified with love, tranquility, empathy, respect, and other such constructive emotions.

The Method of Consequent Replacement for Finding Antidotes

One method of constructing an antidote to a fallacious rule that fits the "If O, then R" form consists of the following three steps: (1) drop the consequent of the rule that commits the fallacy, (2) replace the consequent with one that repairs the fallacy, and (3) make suitable adjustments to the antecedent, if necessary, in light of the new consequent. For example, consider again the fallacious rule "If I mess up and everyone laughs at me, I will make a fool out of myself." The method of consequent replacement with respect to this rule is illustrated in table 16.2.

Table 16.2

Step 1: Drop consequent that commits fallacy
If I mess up and everyone laughs at me, then _____

Step 2: Replace with consequent that repairs fallacy
If I mess up and everyone laughs at me, *then I shouldn't demand that my classmates not laugh at me.*

Step 3: Make suitable adjustments to antecedent
If my *classmates' laughing at me is not something I can control*, then I shouldn't demand that they not laugh at me.

---

5. The dysfunctional nature of the appeal to force is discussed in chapter 20.

> **Exercise Set 16.5**
>
> For each of the emotional rules given in Exercise Set 16.3, construct an antidote using the method of consequent replacement that satisfies the above guidelines. Remember, the process of formulating an antidote to a fallacious major premise rule is a creative one.

EXERCISING WILLPOWER

As important as finding an antidote to a faulty premise is to rationally overcoming cognitive dissonance, it is still usually not enough. This is because it is one thing to know what one should do and quite another to do it. When a person is in an intense, irrational, emotional state, it is not an easy matter to calm down with rational self-talk. Thus, Aristotle asked, "How can a man fail in self-restraint when believing correctly that what he does is wrong?" He answered that it was due to weakness of the will. That is, in an intense emotional state, driven by faulty reasoning, the path of least resistance is generally to resolve cognitive dissonance in favor of the faulty reasoning and therefore to keep it up.

According to Aristotle, a self-restrained person in contrast to an unrestrained person is able to resolve cognitive dissonance rationally because he has cultivated *willpower*. The word "cultivation" is crucial here since, according to Aristotle, such rational self-control is not an innate biological capacity that arises full-blown at birth. As he made clear, it is a product of practice and effort. A useful analogy here is to a muscle. Like a muscle, willpower can be increased by putting it into practice.

Anyone who has attempted to resist the allure of a sumptuous but fattening dessert has experienced the flexing of his willpower muscle. If you manage to constrain yourself from taking a second helping of your favorite dessert, you have had a perception of your willpower doing its job. Similarly, in a state of cognitive dissonance, willpower is that internal muscle that helps you resist and overcome an irrational emotion and take a rational antidote instead.

A bodybuilder would not start by bench-pressing a few hundred pounds. Instead she would start with lighter weights, working up to the heavy ones. Similarly, willpower can best be cultivated by starting "light" and working up to the heavier lifts. For example, if you have an anger-management problem, you will probably find it easier to control your temper if you have a disagreement with a coworker over a relatively minor work-related issue than if you discover that your lover has been having an affair with your best friend. Still, people are quite capable of strengthening their willpower muscles by tackling events like the first one and working up to much more difficult situations. As Aristotle emphasized, such constraint arises as a result of habits cultivated through practice. That is, the more practice you get in successfully controlling yourself, the more habituated you will become to doing so.

In the present example in which you are experiencing anxiety about making a class presentation, you will need to exert willpower in order to overcome an ir-

Table 16.3

Faulty Premise	Refutation	Antidote/s	Exercise Willpower
If I mess up and everyone laughs at me, I will make a fool out of myself.	If this premise were true then we'd all be fools.	If my classmates' laughing at me is not something I can control, then I shouldn't demand that they not laugh at me.	I stop demanding that I get the approval of my classmates, turn over, get comfortable, and go to sleep.

rational tendency to make yourself anxious. Here, it is not enough to refute the fallacious premise of your emotional reasoning and find an antidote to it. You must also *stop* yourself from continuing the irrational line of reasoning and *replace* it with rational, antidotal reasoning. This is where willpower comes in. Accordingly, you can say to yourself,

> This stuff about making a fool out of myself is absurd. If messing up at something made a person a fool, then everyone would be a fool, which is absurd. As Epictetus would tell me, I shouldn't demand what isn't mine to control. Let the others think of me whatever they will, and whatever happens, happens. That's okay with me.

Accordingly, as table 16.3 illustrates, by (1) refuting the faulty premise, (2) constructing an antidote to it, and (3) exercising willpower in concert with that antidote, you can get into a comfortable position, shut your eyes, and go to sleep.

It is also possible to *practice* exercising one's willpower over an irrational emotion by engaging in *shame-attacking* exercises. For example, suppose you are embarrassed to eat in a restaurant by yourself. You can identify your emotional reasoning, including the fallacious premise from which you deduce your negative rating (for example, "If people think I'm some kind of misfit with whom no one cares to dine, then that's a terrible thing that must never happen to me"). You can then refute this premise ("If this is so 'terrible,' then what am I going to say about choking to death in the restaurant!"). Then, you can construct a suitable antidote ("If people are so irrational as to berate me without even knowing me, then I should rather enjoy my meal than dignify their bad logic"). Then, you can flex your willpower muscle by going to the restaurant armed with your rational antidote.

LOGIC-BASED STRESS MANAGEMENT

In this chapter you have seen that you can follow a logical sequence of steps to overcome an irrational emotion. Emotions like actions can be based on unsound practical syllogisms. By exposing the fallacy in this reasoning, refuting it, finding an antidote, and exercising willpower to implement the antidote, one can head off self-defeating emotions. Table 16.4 summarizes the steps in this *logic-based* method for dealing with emotional stress in life circumstances.

Table 16.4

STEP 1. *Identify emotion*

Emotion (E) = Intentional Object (O) + Rating (R)
E.g., Anxiety:
O = future event or possible future event having certain forecasted consequences (e.g., in delivering my presentation I might mess up and everyone will laugh at me)
R = forecasted consequences perceived to be so bad that you must ruminate over them (e.g., I might make a fool out of myself)

STEP 2. *Construct emotional reasoning*

Major Premise/Rule: If O then R
Minor Premise/Report: O
Conclusion: R
E.g.,
Rule: If I mess up and everyone laughs at me (O), I will make a fool out of myself (R)
Report: Tomorrow, in delivering my presentation on Plato's theory of forms, I might mess up and everyone will laugh at me (O)
Conclusion: I might make a fool out of myself tomorrow (R)

STEP 3. *Refute fallacious premise/s*

Modes of refutation:
• Deductively falsify premise
• Show there's insufficient inductive evidence
• Show an absurd consequence
• Show a double standard
E.g., "If messing up made fools of us then we'd all be fools."

STEP 4. *Find antidote/s to fallacious premise/s*

(A) Apply method of consequent replacement:
    • Drop fallacious consequent
    • Replace consequent with rational one that avoids fallacy
    • Make suitable adjustments to antecedent
    E.g., change "If I mess up and everyone laughs at me, then I will make a fool of myself" to "If my classmates' laughing at me is not something I can control, then I shouldn't demand that they not laugh at me."
(B) Construct antidotal reasoning:
    E.g.,
    Major Premise: If my classmates' laughing at me is not something I can control, then I shouldn't demand that they not laugh at me.
    Minor Premise: My classmates' laughing at me is not something I can control.
    Conclusion: I shouldn't demand that my classmates not laugh at me.

STEP 5. *Exercise willpower to implement conclusion of antidotal reasoning*

E.g., I stop telling myself that my classmates must not laugh at me.

Exercise Set 16.6

16.6.1
Flex your willpower muscle.
Stop yourself in the midst of doing something you are inclined to do but know is wrong (for example, eating the entire bag of potato chips, getting into a shouting match, or speeding to get to an appointment). Discuss your faulty thinking, your cognitive dissonance, and what you said to yourself in order to get yourself to stop the wrongful behavior.

16.6.2
Try a shame-attacking exercise.
Pick out a situation in which you know you would feel embarrassed (for example, walking a banana on a string down a crowded city street,[1] eating alone in a restaurant, or whatever else you want—so long as it's legal and moral!) Then, push yourself to do it while practicing your cognitive skills—finding the irrational premise, refuting it, and finding a suitable antidote. Discuss your experience, your cognitive dissonance, and what you said to yourself before and while you performed the act in question. If your effort was aborted, then discuss what you think went wrong, and try this exercise again until you complete it.

---

1. This example is due to Albert Ellis.

II

INFORMAL FALLACIES

17

Inferences from "Must," "Awful," and "Can't"

In part I of this book, we examined behavioral and emotional reasoning. In part II, we will examine the types of informal fallacies that infect the premises of these kinds of practical reasoning. This chapter examines some key fallacies often found in the premises of emotional reasoning, which lead to avoidable and counterproductive emotional stress in everyday life.

THE LINGUISTIC THEORY OF EMOTIONS

The language we use to interpret and assess reality can have a profound influence on how we respond emotionally to a situation. For example, calling something "awful," "horrible," or "terrible" can provide the rating needed for negative, self-destructive emotions like anger, depression, anxiety, fear, and guilt. Telling yourself that you "can't stand" a person or thing can lead to low frustration tolerance and loss of self-control toward the given person or thing. Making damning ratings, such as calling oneself "worthless" or "good for nothing," can drive deep, dark depression leading to dangerous, self-destructive behaviors, including suicide.

As you will see, *fallacies of emotion always involve the use (or misuse) of certain types of language in the premises (especially in the major premise rule) of one's emotional reasoning, which tend to promote destructive and self-defeating emotional responses.* The study of fallacies of emotion is thus largely the study of the patterns of language that people use to disturb themselves and the ways in which they can avoid or overcome such self-defeating linguistic activities.

DEMANDING PERFECTION

In chapter 16, we discussed briefly the importance of distinguishing between having and expressing preferences and desires and the use of the words "must," "ought," and "should" to make demands. According to psychologist Albert Ellis, in turning our preferences and desires into "Jehovian musts and commands," human beings are self-responsible for creating much of their own emotional stress. Ellis writes,

> Once people creatively transmute their Jehovian musts and commands, they usually actively bring about inappropriate and self-defeating feelings, such as panic, depression, rage, self-pity, and global inadequacy. Their dogmatic shoulds and musts also frequently lead to behavioral disorders, such as neurotic avoidance, withdrawal, procrastination, compulsion, and addiction.

By "transmuting musts and commands," Ellis is speaking of the *inference* that people make from their desires and preferences to musts, oughts, and shoulds. The inference in question is as follows:

I want (prefer) x.
Therefore, x must (ought, should) be.

For example, let x = getting As on all my exams. In this case, I then conclude that I must get As on all my exams.

As you can see, this inference is enthymematic and is missing its major premise rule. To complete the syllogism, let us add this rule. Where x is replaced with the aforementioned substitution, we arrive at the following practical syllogism:

Major premise rule: If I want (prefer) that I get As on all my exams, then I must (ought, should) get As on all my exams.
Minor premise report: I want (prefer) that I get As on all my exams.
Conclusion: I must (ought, should) get As on all my exams.

As you can see, the above syllogism is formally valid, but the major premise rule added to make it valid commits the *fallacy of demanding perfection*, or the fallacy of demanding that reality conform to one's desires, preferences, hopes, or wishes. This is a fallacy because the world is not a perfect place; therefore, it is unrealistic to require that we *always* get what we want. In demanding, commanding, and requiring reality to match up with our desires or preferences, we therefore set ourselves up for failure and for a considerable amount of stress along the way. Thus, the student who demands As on all exams places a considerable amount of unnecessary stress on herself.

This does not mean that one should not aim high, even for the stars. The fallacy is not in shooting for the stars; it is in *demanding* that one reach them. There is also a difference between disappointment and depression. Not getting what one wants can be disappointing, but it is only when these desires are catapulted into absolutistic demands that the basis for depression is set.

The Contradictoriness of Absolutistic Musts

Popular conclusions drawn from demanding perfection include the following:

- I must always have the approval of others, especially those special to me.
- I must never make a mistake or fail to perform perfectly.
- Things must always go my way.

- I must always be treated fairly.
- Nothing bad must happen to me or to my significant others.
- I must always be able to control everything or at least what is important to me.
- I must succeed at whatever I try or at least at whatever is important to me.
- I must never lose anything of substantial value to me.
- My body must not have any noticeable imperfections or flaws.
- I must have absolute certainty about something before acting on it.
- You must want whatever I want.

All of the above demands are absolutistic, that is, unconditional, and they invariably lead to irreconcilable contradictions. Since reality inevitably falls short of such demands, the world constrained by these musts engenders a contradiction: what must be, is not. As long as one holds on to these demands, resolution of this contradiction is impossible, and one lives perennially in a state of emotional disequilibrium. For example, the material world gives us probability but not absolute (100 percent) certainty; one's body is material, by its nature imperfect, and subject to aging; good fortune is by definition a function of variables beyond one's control, and it invariably runs out. It is therefore not surprising that those who *demand* absolute certainty, perfect bodies, and perpetual good luck will run into a contradiction.

Of course, it makes sense to prefer the approval of others, success, fairness, good fortune, control, and physical attractiveness. Indeed, most humans do want these things. But preferences or desires do not *have* to be true; demands do. As Ellis surmises,

> Once [people] vigorously stay with their preferences and find that these are (or soon may be) thwarted, people then have appropriate or self-helping feelings of concern, sadness, disappointment, and frustration, which motivate them to strive for more of what they want and less of what they don't want. They rarely feel and behave neurotically when they stay with these appropriate feelings.[1]

Thus, Ellis's general antidote for avoiding self-defeating emotions and experiencing the more constructive feelings is to stick to expressing one's preferences rather than inferring musts (oughts, shoulds) from them.

Exercise Set 17.1

17.1.1
Most people demand perfection in at least some way or another. Give at least one example of a demand for perfection of your own. If you are unable or not prepared to give an example of your own, then give an example of the demand for perfection of another person with whom you are acquainted, such as a friend, relative, or classmate. In the latter case, you are advised to use a fictitious name for this person and to eliminate any identifying features

(continued)

---

1. Albert Ellis, "Philosophical Principles of RET," *International Journal of Applied Philosophy* 5, no. 2 (Fall 1990): 35-41.

from your example, unless you have the express permission of this person to mention his or her name in this capacity.

17.1.2
How has the stated demand for perfection affected your personal life or that of the person making this demand? In particular, has it increased the level of stress? If so, in what way(s)?

Absolutistic Musts versus Rational Musts

Ellis's antidote notwithstanding, not all inferences from desires and preferences to musts, oughts, and shoulds are irrational. Sticking *just* to preferences, refusing to ever infer *any* musts, can lead to complacency and stagnation. Thus, you might say, "Sure, I want the world to be fair, but face it, the world just isn't. Therefore, I should be prepared to tolerate injustice."

But how willing should we be to tolerate injustice? When the despot or tyrant takes our civil rights away, should we console ourselves with the distinction between preferences and demands?

Notice that standing our ground does not mean that we should be willing to make substantial sacrifices for *every* cause. Indeed, some injustices are worth standing against firmly, but still others may not be worth the effort. Here, then, is a reasonable distinction between rational and irrational musts, oughts, and shoulds.

The musts that Ellis tells us to avoid are absolutistic and dogmatic. They tell us that we must (ought, should) never, under any circumstances, tolerate injustice and that we must always be able to control things, gain the approval of others, attain success, have good fortune, and so on.

On the other hand, rational musts are provisional and contingent. For example, consider the moral command that we must not lie. This command makes sense if we understand it provisionally; that is, if other things are equal, we must not lie. But in some cases, other things may not be equal; that is, there may be some extenuating or overriding circumstance present. It may be, for example, that the lie is motivated to avoid substantial harm to a third party. Thus, in such a case, it will not do to say, "You lied to me, and you must never lie." This is absolutistic thinking, the kind that leads to *needless* emotional stress.

Means-End Antidotes to Demanding Perfection

Some rational musts state *means-end relationships*. For example, "If you want to be healthy, you must exercise several times a week." This hypothetical statement gives practical advice about how to satisfy a preference or desire. It asserts that there is a causal relationship between what is desired (health) and exercise, and it accordingly prescribes the latter as a means of achieving the former. This sort of must (ought, should) can support sound inferences from desires to musts.[2]

---

2. For example, the following is a sound argument:

If I want to be healthy, I should exercise several times a week.
I want to be healthy.
Therefore, I should exercise several times a week.

The means-end form can be useful in formulating constructive antidotes to demanding perfection. The standard form of such antidotes is "If you want . . . then you must (should, ought) . . . " Here are some examples of constructive means-end antidotes for overcoming demanding perfection:

- If you want to achieve your goal, then you must not wait to be certain before acting on it.
- If you want to learn things, then you must be prepared to make mistakes.
- If you want to improve the fitness of your body, then you should stop demanding perfection about small cosmetic issues and work on important things like diet, exercise, and stress reduction.

Each of the above prescriptions provides a rational antidote to demanding perfection and supports rational inferences from wants to musts or shoulds. Each provides a practical means to satisfying a desired end. For example, the first of these points to the impossibility of attaining one's goal (whatever it may be) if one waits to be certain before taking steps to attain it. Indeed, if one waits to be absolutely certain, then one will *never* act because one can never be absolutely certain about matters of fact. Similarly, the demand that one always be successful overlooks the importance of failure in the pursuit of success. Lest one make mistakes, one is not likely to accumulate the knowledge to eventually succeed. Thus, the second of the above antidotes is a useful means-end antidote to demanding success. Likewise, the demand for a perfect body cannot be made here on earth where there are no "heavenly bodies." Thus, if one truly cares about one's body, then one will be good to it. One can be good to one's body by properly nourishing it, giving it the exercise it requires for good cardiovascular health and muscle tone, and concentrating on avoiding needless stress—which includes making irrational demands about one's body.

This does not mean that reasonable people cannot disagree about when a must, ought, or should is rational. Thus, we can disagree about what constitutes an extenuating circumstance to telling a lie or about what kinds of exercise can be healthful. Nevertheless, rational debate comes to a halt when one insists on absolutistic commands and demands. These are the musts that leave no room for debate and invariably run up against irreconcilable contradictions.

Exercise Set 17.2

Formulate at least one means-end antidote to the example(s) of demanding perfection you provided in Exercise Set 17.1. First, state the absolutistic, dogmatic must you are addressing. Then, use the standard hypothetical form "If you want . . . then you must (should, ought) . . . " to formulate a means-end antidote to it. Discuss why you think this antidote could be useful in helping to overcome this particular demand for perfection.

The Egocentric Fallacy

One type of demanding perfection involves demanding that others share one's same desires, preferences, beliefs, or values or that reality itself conform to one's desires, preferences, beliefs, or values. Since this kind of demanding perfection is ego-centered, it can aptly be called the egocentric fallacy.[3] Any inference of the following type would commit this fallacy:

> I want (desire, prefer, believe, or value) x.
> Therefore, you too must want (desire, prefer, believe, or value) x.

For example, because I like action thrillers, I infer that my significant other must also like them. Because I am a committed Christian, I think that others must be committed Christians and share my religious fervor. Because I am against abortion, I think that everyone else must be against it as well.

Doxastic Demands

Another version of the egocentric fallacy takes the form of a *doxastic demand*—that is, a demand that reality itself conform to what one believes. In this manner, this fallacy turns the ancient view of true belief on its head. According to Aristotle, "To say of what is that it is not, or of what is not that it is, is false, while to say of what is that it is, or of what is not that it is not, is true."[4] Thus, according to this ancient view of truth, for any statement p, if my belief that p is true, then it is a fact that p, and if my belief that p is false, then it is not a fact that p.[5]

In contrast, in the case of a doxastic demand, it is not facts that make one's beliefs true; conversely, it is one's *belief* that makes something a fact. For example, if I believe that gay marriage is morally wrong, then that is how it must be. Or if I believe that the theory of evolution is false, then it must, in fact, be false.

As such, people who make doxastic demands tend to be intolerant and dogmatic. If I think that *my* belief sets the standard of reality, then I will automatically reject the beliefs of anyone who disagrees with me; accordingly, I will discount any evidence that conflicts with my belief inasmuch as it is my belief that determines what constitutes evidence in the first place. Indeed, insofar as one commits this fallacy, one will have difficulty forging functional (mutually satisfying) interpersonal relationships with others, especially if these other people happen to be freethinkers.

Not surprisingly, doxastic demands have been at the root of great iniquity. For example, Nazis and white supremacists never had a rational argument for the superiority of the white race. Instead, they had a groundless ideological belief, based on which they sought the destruction of Jews, blacks, gypsies, and other so-called nonwhites. In the sixteenth century, the Roman Catholic Church wanted it to be true that the sun and all the other planets revolved around the earth, thereby giving humankind a privileged place in the universe, thus squaring with the church's religious teachings. So, it turned these teachings into a dogmatic demand for conformity and persecuted the scientists of the day who questioned this "conventional wisdom."

---

3. More colloquially, it has also been called the "world revolves around me" fallacy. See Elliot D. Cohen, *The New Rational Therapy* (New York: Rowman & Littlefield, 2007).
4. Aristotle, *Metaphysics*, in *The Basic Works of Aristotle*, trans. W. D. Ross, bk. 4, chap. 7, 749.
5. This view of "true" is commonly referred to as the "correspondence theory of truth."

This does not mean that people who make doxastic demands necessarily make them about everything they believe. For example, a person may demand conformity to her religious beliefs without demanding conformity to her views on other matters (for example, art or politics), so long as they don't conflict with her views on religion. However, insofar as one makes doxastic demands, one is likely to experience considerable emotional stress in coping with realities that do not conform to what one believes and in dealing with others who do not share these beliefs.

Exercise Set 17.3

17.3.1
As you have just seen, doxastic demands (demanding that reality conform to one's beliefs) have led to destructive, self-defeating behavioral consequences. Provide at least three other examples of this fallacy that have had such consequences.

17.3.2
Provide at least one means-end antidote to the following egocentric inference: "I believe in God; therefore, you too should believe in God."

17.3.3
Philosopher David Hume had the following to say about beauty:

> Beauty is no quality in things themselves: It exists merely in the mind which contemplates them; and each mind perceives a different beauty. One person may even perceive deformity, where another is sensible of beauty; and every individual ought to acquiesce in his own sentiment, without pretending to regulate those of others. To seek the real beauty, or real deformity, is as fruitless an enquiry, as to pretend to ascertain the real sweet or real bitter.

Is there a difference between Hume's view of beauty and someone who commits the egocentric fallacy? Do you agree with Hume's subjectivist approach to judgments about beauty, or do you think that there are at least some independent standards for assessing beauty? Defend your responses.

AWFULIZING

As mentioned earlier, we can use words such as "awful," "horrible," and "terrible" to seriously disturb ourselves. These terms, however, have different senses, not all of which are seriously self-disturbing.

In one sense of "awful" (and synonyms like "horrible" and "terrible"), we might say, "It's awful that it rained all weekend, and we couldn't go to the beach." In this context, the word "awful" is being used to convey disappointment or relatively mild frustration. In this sense, the use of the word "awful" can be rational and does not usually lead to dangerous or self-destructive behavior and emotions.

In a second sense, we might use the word "awful" to appraise a situation or event as not merely an inconvenience (as in the first sense) but rather one that is extremely bad. In this sense of "awful," we judge a thing to be *bad enough* to have crossed a threshold beyond which something can appropriately be called awful.

This would include such things as genocide, natural disasters, torture, murder, and rape. While most people would agree that these things cross this awfulness threshold, there may still be disagreement about where exactly the marker should be located on a scale of increasingly bad things. For example, most of us would agree that the molestation and murder of a child is worse than losing one's fortune; however, there may still be disagreement about whether the loss of one's fortune crosses the awfulness threshold. In this sense, the use of the word "awful" can also be rational, and, within reason, there is considerable room for disagreement about where exactly to locate the awfulness threshold.

Notice that this second sense is a *relative* sense. That is, in this sense, things are called awful relative to their position on a scale of bad things. In contrast, there is yet a third, nonrelative sense according to which "awful" means "absolutely bad"—that is, the worst thing possible. In this sense, the loss of a beloved is not merely awful relative to other things such as the loss of one's money, but it is so bad that there is nothing that is or can be worse. This sense has been applied to such things as getting fired from one's job, being divorced by one's spouse, failing an exam or a course, asking someone out on a date and being refused, and losing in a competitive sport. However, none of these things have arguably crossed the threshold to warrant being called awful in the second relative sense, let alone awful in an absolutistic sense.

In fact, *nothing* is really awful in this third absolutistic sense because no matter how bad something may be, something worse can always be conceived. For example, being tortured to death slowly is a relatively awful thing, but being tortured to death even more slowly is worse.[6] Two holocausts can be worse than one, three worse than two, and so on. Well, what about the earth being destroyed so that all life forms on it cease to exist? But it would be even worse if the destruction was long and protracted and living creatures suffered a brutal death, and it would be even worse than that if the brutality were even more protracted or the pain even more intense, and so on.

The point is that a progressive scale of bad things does not terminate with the absolutely worst thing conceivable but rather presents an infinite progression without end. Thus, there is no single thing that is the (absolutely) worst thing possible because there is always something even worse that one can conceive.[7] It is therefore a fallacy to rate something as awful in the sense of being the worst thing possible. Albert Ellis has colorfully referred to this fallacy as awfulizing.

Awfulizing is accordingly the fallacy of reasoning from bad to worst. That is, the fallacy is in drawing the following inference:

---

6. This example is due to Albert Ellis.

7. At the other end of the spectrum, the same argument can be made for the claim that there is something "terrific" meaning *the very best possible*: for example, the best possible parents, the best possible guitarist, the best friend, and so forth. These fictions can be used to set the stage for irrational emotions. For example, losing the best boyfriend or girlfriend possible would mean that you would never find anyone as good as this person again. And this could set the stage for depression. However, the absolute best is as fictional as the absolute worst. They simply do not exist—at least not within the confines of space and time here on earth. This fallacy of ascribing absolute goodness to a thing is sometimes called terrificizing. See Elliot D. Cohen, *Caution: Faulty Thinking Can Be Harmful to Your Happiness* (Fort Pierce, Fla.: Trace-Wilco, 1994).

It is bad (or very bad) that p.
Therefore, it is (absolutely) awful that p.

This inference moves from the assessment of something as relatively bad, that is, bad to a certain degree relative to other things that are bad, to the assessment of its being absolutely bad—that is, awful in the sense of being the worst thing possible.

As you can see, the above inference is enthymematic, and its validity depends on a major premise rule that links the given premise to the given conclusion. With this missing premise in place, the valid inference is as follows:

Major premise rule: If it is bad (or very bad) that p, then it is (absolutely) awful that p.
Minor premise report: It is bad (or very bad) that p.
Conclusion: It is (absolutely) awful that p.

The fallacy is accordingly in the major premise that validates the inference. Even if something is *very bad* (relatively speaking), this does not mean that it is *absolutely* bad. This is the fallacy of awfulizing. For example, let p = my spouse divorced me. The fallacious inference would then be as follows:

Major premise rule: If it is very bad that my spouse divorced me, then it is awful that my spouse divorced me.
Minor premise report: It is very bad that my spouse divorced me.[8]
Conclusion: It is (absolutely) awful that my spouse divorced me.

Here the person making the inference rates the badness of the divorce as absolutely bad—that is, as the worst thing possible. As such, there can be no good to come of the divorce, for otherwise it would not be the worst thing possible. This absolutistic rating forecloses any positive options left for the future. Thus, there will now be a lonely dissolute existence with no chances of ever finding anyone else. As you can see, the absoluteness of the badness rating in the major premise rule leads to a depressive emotional state. If the person in question wants to be happy, then this inference defeats this goal by prescribing a bleak outlook for the future. In this way, awfulizing can be destructive of human happiness.

This is not to discount the gravity of some loses. For example, there is no consolation in telling a person who has just learned of the death of a loved one to look on the bright side, for in the early stages of grieving, there simply is no perception of the bright side. The rating of the loss is accordingly absolutistic. To one in this unfortunate situation, it is absolutely awful, the worst possible thing that could have happened, and one is inclined to look askance at those who say otherwise.

This is indeed part of the grieving process. Grief starts with fallacious reasoning—awfulizing, demanding perfection, and other fallacies—but grief is not *worked through* until these fallacies are exposed and refuted and rational antidotes are found. This is, in fact, what it means to work through one's grief.

---

8. Strictly speaking, this report is itself a rating deduced from a prior inference:

If my spouse divorced me, then it is very bad that my spouse divorced me.
My spouse divorced me.
Therefore, it is very bad that my spouse divorced me.

The refutation of awfulizing is straightforward. There is simply no evidence to support the existence of anything that is absolutely bad. To the contrary, there are increasing degrees of badness in the universe, and they can increase ad infinitum, but the idea of a *totally* catastrophic, terrible, horrible, and awful thing is a fiction for which there is no evidence.[9]

Here are three suggested antidotes to awfulizing:

- If it is bad (or very bad) that p, then instead of using words like "terrible," "horrible," and "awful" to rate the badness of p, you should use words like "bad," "very bad," "unfortunate," and "tough break."
- If it is bad (or very bad) that p, then you should put p into perspective by seeing it *in relation to* other things that might have been even worse than p.
- If it is bad (or very bad) that p, then use the experience of p to learn and thus to grow wiser and stronger.

The first of these antidotes essentially tells us not to infer the absolutistic badness of something because we think it is bad but rather to keep our discourse at the level of relative badness. Thus, instead of using absolutistic language, we should use language that is consistent with this relativity, such as "bad" and even "very bad." In this way, we can avoid and block the irrational inference to absolutistic badness.

The second suggested antidote tells us to put our present bad situation into perspective by comparing it with something that seems to us much worse. As Epictetus has suggested,

> Keep before your eyes day by day death and exile, and everything that seems terrible but most of all death; and then you will never have any abject thought, nor will you yearn for anything beyond measure.[10]

For example, the person who has just gone through an unwanted divorce can think of this unfortunate event in relation to other, more tragic events, such as one's own death, which would have been worse. Thus, this person can say, "Well, at least I still have my life and maybe eventually, when I'm ready, I can start to date. In the meantime, I can still enjoy a good meal, enjoy the company of my friends, advance my career, make contributions to the lives of others through charitable work, and much more that I wouldn't be able to do if I didn't have my life."

The third antidote tells us to turn a bad experience into something positive. This antidote has its roots in the theory of suffering espoused by Friedrich Nietzsche. "Profound suffering," said Nietzsche, "makes noble" and "separates the sufferer from the uninitiated." According to Nietzsche, by virtue of a person's suffering,

---

9. Elliot D. Cohen, *What Would Aristotle Do? Self-Control through the Power of Reason* (Amherst, N.Y.: Prometheus Books, 2003), ch. 10.

10. Epictetus, *Encheiridion*, in *From Plato to Derrida*, ed. Forrest E. Baird and Walter Kaufmann, fourth ed. (Upper Saddle River, N.J.: Prentice Hall, 2003), 261.

he *knows more* than the cleverest and wisest could possibly know, and that he knows his way and has once been "at home" in many distant, terrifying worlds of which "*you know nothing.*"[11]

For example, some of us who have struggled with health issues or physical handicaps have learned to appreciate good health and the facility that goes with it. In fact, there have been many famous, disabled persons in the course of history who have achieved greatness either because of their handicap or despite it. The ancient Greek poet Homer was blind. Danish philosopher Søren Kierkegaard suffered from epilepsy, as did Joan of Arc, the patron saint of France. Helen Keller, prolific author and advocate for the disabled, was both deaf and blind. Actor Michael J. Fox was diagnosed with Parkinson's disease in the late 1990s and became an advocate for stem cell research. In Nietzsche's view, the suffering of these individuals was ennobling and separated them from "the uninitiated."

As these examples suggest, in their suffering, people can find the courage to pursue new meanings and purposes to their lives. "Man," said Nietzsche, "as the animal that is most courageous, most accustomed to suffering, does not negate suffering as such: *he wants* it, even seeks it out, provided one shows him some *meaning* in it, some *wherefore* of suffering."[12] The idea here is that bad situations are largely what people make of them. One person can see his misfortune as a challenge to overcome, while another can wallow in self-pity, become alcoholic, and self-destruct. For Nietzsche, what becomes of us in adversity is not carved in stone but largely depends on what we ourselves choose to make of the situation.

Exercise Set 17.4

Provide at least three examples of people (yourself, someone you know, or a historical figure) whose handicaps have had a positive influence on their own lives or the lives of others.

Exercise Set 17.5

Most of the following passages contain explicit use of the word "awful" or related terms. Discuss the senses in which these terms are used. Do any of these passages commit the awfulizing fallacy?

(continued)

---

11. Friedrich Nietzsche, "What Is Noble?" sec. 270 of *Beyond Good and Evil*, trans. Helen Zimmern, in *The Philosophy of Nietzsche* (New York: Random House, 1954), 596.
12. Friedrich Nietzsche, "Ascetic Ideals," essay 3, sec. 28 of *The Genealogy of Morals*, trans. Horace B. Samuel, in *The Philosophy of Nietzsche*, 792.

17.5.1
"I couldn't watch *Moulin Rouge*; it was awful." —A response to the question, "What is the worst movie you have ever seen?" from Askville, a website operated by Amazon.com[1]

17.5.2
"It was awful. It was the most unreal thing. The building just went down, almost in slow motion, and an entire cloud just spread over lower Manhattan" —Eyewitness account of the collapse of one of the Twin Towers on September 11, 2001[2]

17.5.3
"She would never know freedom in love, but would remain forever a guilty wife, with the menace of detection hanging over her at every instant; deceiving her husband for the sake of a shameful connection with a man living apart and away from her, whose life she could never share. She knew that this was how it would be, and at the same time it was so awful that she could not even conceive what it would end in. And she cried without restraint, as children cry when they are punished." —From Leo Tolstoy's *Anna Karenina*, ch. 6

17.5.4
"I lost all my hair. My face was so awful I hid for a long time. If I had been alone I probably would have killed myself but my mother was there every day taking care of me, even though she was sick herself. I stayed alive for her." —Survivor of Hiroshima[3]

17.5.5
"I lost everything. I lost both of my parents. Lost both my godparents. My aunt is having serious issues right now and I'm such a ****** that I can't help her. I began dating this guy, love of my life, lost him too. Lost my research position. Lost my good health. Lost my money. Now I lost my job and found out I'm not getting paid for my last project (my boss, unbeknownst to me, has a history of not paying his employees and is being sued by 21 of them currently . . . did NOT know that before I started working for him). I'm laying here in bed, completely numb. I'll probably start crying again soon. I literally have NOTHING, and I've never felt worse. I always believed there was a silver lining to every cloud, and every time something bad happened to me, something good would follow. Well, I can prove that's a ******* myth." —Anonymous post[4]

17.5.6
"You said this was your most challenging film, but you've done these huge, blockbuster epics. Why was this one so difficult?"
Roland Emmerich: "But not outdoors! I mean, this was just a stupid thing to do. I was really regretting it, trust me. And it's just a . . . just terrible. I always had luck with the weather but not this one. It was just awful, awful, awful." —Interview with writer/director Roland Emmerich regarding the inclement weather conditions (rain, snow, and fog) he encountered on location in the filming of the movie *10,000 BC*[5]

1. Anonymous blogger, Askville. Retrieved online on April 10, 2009, from http://askville.amazon.com/watch-moulin-rouge-awful/DiscussionPost.do?requestId=18136539&commentId=18139820&commentNumber=6&pageNumber=1.
2. Suzanne Herel, "'It Was Awful—the Building Just Went': New Yorkers Describe Seeing Worst Happen," *San Francisco Chronicle*, September 11, 2001. Retrieved online on April 2, 2009, from www.esubjects.com/curric/general/english_two/unit_two/pdf/ItWasAwful_HardNews.pdf.
3. David McNeill, "My Face Was So Awful I Hid. I Would Have Killed Myself Had It Not Been for My Mother," *Independent*, July 31, 2005. Retrieved online on April 10, 2009, from www.independent.co.uk/news/world/asia/my-face-was-so-awful-i-hid-i-would-have-killed-myself-had-it-not-been-for-my-mother-500869.html.
4. "I Cannot Begin to Describe What I'm Going through Right Now," Help.com. Retrieved online on April 10, 2009, from http://help.com/post/177163-i-cannot-begin-to-describe-what-i.
5. Rebecca Murray, "Roland Emmerich Interview—10,000 BC Movie at Wonder Con," About.com. Retrieved online on December 4, 2008, at http://video.about.com/movies/Roland-Emmerich-Interview.htm.

Exercise Set 17.6

Yahoo! Answers asked, "What is the worse thing(s) in the world?" and received the below responses.[1] However, voters could not agree on a best answer. For each of the answers provided, top it by thinking of something worse. Why do you think the voters couldn't agree on a best answer?

17.6.1
Answerer 1: "Persons or a 'people' who think they can do no wrong and get away with it. It happens all over the world."

17.6.2
Answerer 2: "The worse thing in the world is that you don't know what it is."

17.6.3
Answerer 3: "Difficult to judge between Zionism and cursers of companions."

17.6.4
Answerer 4: "WAR."

17.6.5
Answerer 5: "Unbelief/lack of a position/apathy."

17.6.6
Answerer 6: "Child Abuse. Period. There are a lot of bad things, but abusing a helpless little child ~~ it's just rotten."

17.6.7
Answerer 7: "The ego, perhaps."

17.6.8
Answerer 8: "Prejudice, ignorance, war, murder, and abuse of any kind."

17.6.9
Answer 9: "The worst thing in this world, personally, I think is ignorance and narrow mind-edness."

17.6.10
Answerer 10: "Foolish questions. Definitely."

17.6.11
Answerer 11: "Ignorance"

17.6.12
Answerer 12: "Few Teenagers were engaged in a serious debate on what was the worst thing in the World? The sum up was a long list of painful deaths: Eaten by a crocodile, Run over by a road roller, Boiled in oil, Burned in Fuel, Die under locomotive engine . . . ! The list was long and gruesome. They asked this issue to their pastor. He answered them simply. 'THE WORST WAY TO DIE IS CHRIST LESS.'"

---

1. "What Is the Worse Thing(s) in the World?" Yahoo! Answers. Retrieved online on April 11, 2009, from http://answers.yahoo.com/question/index?qid=20081119003020AAZISe5.

CAN'TSTIPATION

Another word with important implications for how we think, feel, and act is the four-letter word "can't." With this word, we have the power to seal our own fate. As just mentioned, we have the ability to interpret situations of adversity in ways that can add new meanings and purposes to our lives. However, in saying "I can't," we can foreclose our potential for dealing constructively with difficult situations.

Can'tstipation involves obstructing one's own creative potential, amid difficult or challenging situations, by holding on to and refusing to "excrete" (get rid of) the word "can't." Where the variable x is an activity or action, the inference involved in commission of this fallacy is as follows:

> I find x to be difficult or challenging.
> Therefore, I can't do x.

With the validating major premise rule in place, this inference is as follows:

> *Major premise rule:* If I find x to be difficult or challenging, then I can't do x.
> *Minor premise rule:* I find x to be difficult or challenging.
> *Conclusion:* I can't do x.

For example, let x = passing organic chemistry. Then, the conclusion would be, "I can't pass organic chemistry."

Notice that in saying that one can't do x, one relieves oneself of the responsibility of even *trying* to do x; for, given that the point of trying to do x is to do x, it is futile to attempt to do what one simply can't do. This means that the *can't* in this inference is implicitly evaluative: It implies that one shouldn't even try to do x. Accordingly, in the commission of *can'tstipation*, there is a further implicit level of inference that piggybacks on the first:

> *Major premise rule:* If I find x to be difficult or challenging, then I can't do x.
> *Minor premise rule:* I find x to be difficult or challenging.
> *Conclusion:* I can't do x.
> *Secondary major premise rule:* If I can't do x, then I shouldn't try to do x.
> *Conclusion:* I shouldn't try to do x.

Thus, the self-defeating nature of *can'tstipation* lies in the fact that it prescribes not even trying to do things one regards as difficult or challenging. This is self-defeating because one will not accomplish anything difficult or challenging due to one's own failure to even try. And, indeed, most things worth accomplishing are difficult or challenging.

There are at least two broad kinds of *can'tstipation*: emotional and volitional.[13] Let us examine each in its turn.

---

13. A third type of *can'tstipation* can also be distinguished—namely behavioral *can'tstipation*. This form involves *refusal to expend willpower to address behavioral problems*—that is, to change self-defeating or destructive behavior when it is difficult or challenging to do so. See Cohen, *The New Rational Therapy.* However, since this form of *can'tstipation* always appears to involve volitional *can'tstipation*, that is, weakness of willpower in making the desirable behavioral changes, it is not discussed separately in this book.

Emotional *Can'tstipation*

This form of *can'tstipation* involves the refusal to try to control one's emotions. It is typically based on the assumption that emotions are outside human control. Instead, it is thought that emotions always have external causes and that we are therefore passive recipients of our emotions. The chain of reasoning involved in this form of *can'tstipation* appears to be as follows:

1. If I am feeling upset, then someone or something *caused* me to feel upset.
2. If someone or something caused me to feel upset, then I cannot help feeling upset.
3. If I cannot help feeling upset, then I shouldn't try to change the way I feel.
4. Therefore, if I am feeling upset, I shouldn't try to change the way I feel.

While premises 2 and 3 seem reasonable, premise 1 raises both theoretical and practical problems. This premise places emotions outside our own control and blames them on external causes.

The thesis expressed in premise 1 is reflected in the language we often use to describe the genesis of our emotions. For example, the following are popular ways we have of blaming our emotions on external causes:

- You really piss me off.
- That aggravates me.
- You depress me.
- It makes me feel like dying.
- She's driving me crazy.
- He makes me feel guilty.
- I have a bad temper because I'm Latin.

Notice that in making these statements, one, in effect, gives oneself permission to continue to be emotionally upset instead of attempting to deal rationally with one's emotions. As long as you assume that you can't control your emotions because they are caused by external conditions outside your control, you will cease to do anything about changing them.

This does not address the deep metaphysical question that philosophers have debated from antiquity—namely, the gnawing question of whether human beings can freely choose how to behave or there are really always underlying causes that completely determine human responses. This is an important philosophical question. However, whether or not human beings have such "free will" in a metaphysical sense is not relevant to the practical question of whether we can change our emotions by changing the way we speak and think about them. Thus, even if our emotions are, in the end, completely determined by causal factors, this does not mean that the way we conceptualize them is not a causal factor in changing them.

In fact, cognitive-behavior psychology, especially Rational Emotive Behavior Therapy (REBT), has been quite successful in helping millions of people overcome problems of depression, anger, guilt, and anxiety by helping them to change the way they think. One important aspect of such therapy is taking responsibility for one's emotions instead of blaming them on other people or on external circumstances. For example, instead of saying, "You are upsetting me" or "You are pissing me off," one can speak in responsibility-bearing language and say, "I am upsetting myself," "I am driving myself crazy," "I am aggravating myself," "I am pissing myself off," and so forth. Speaking in the latter way makes constructive change realistic. Otherwise, no such change is likely.

The word "can't" itself hides one's responsibility by disclaiming one's ability to deal with one's own emotions. From an existential viewpoint, this is to live an inauthentic existence: that is, to hide behind false pretenses or excuses. About such excuse making, the French existentialist Jean-Paul Sartre had this to say:

> The existentialist does not believe in the power of passion. He will never agree that a sweeping passion is a ravaging torrent which fatally leads a man to certain acts and is therefore an excuse. He thinks that man is responsible for his passion.

If we are responsible for our passions, then we should not rationally say "can't." We should rather change "can't" to "won't" to bring our language in line with our responsibility. Thus, instead of saying, "I can't help feeling depressed," we should rather say, "I won't (or I don't choose to) address my depression."

Addressing one's emotions typically involves working on them not just cognitively but also behaviorally. Thus, REBT combines both cognitive and behavioral techniques. For example, an REBT therapist or life coach might instruct a person who has intense anxiety about dating to push herself to go out on a date. By getting rid of the "can't," as in "I can't help my anxiety," and replacing it with "I won't," the anxious individual takes an important step toward overcoming the anxiety. For now, she has no excuses to fall back on but the lack of her own choosing.

Exercise Set 17.7

In each of the below passages taken from Internet posts, the speaker denies having control over an emotion. Find the language that expresses this lack of emotional control. Then, change this language to language that accepts responsibility for the emotion in question. Does this linguistic change help to empower the speaker to take emotional control? What sort of behavioral changes might the speaker also make to improve his or her situation?

17.7.1
"We used to have a great sex life with each other and although this became a problem before we got married I thought it was just a phase or that we could get thru it. I've given up trying to initiate sex because he just 'rejects' me every time. It doesn't matter what I do, what I wear, what I try. He just has no desire to be with me. I can't help feeling depressed and bad about myself and find myself thinking that there is something wrong with me. He says he wants to want to have sex with me but the desire is just not strong enough for him that he actually wants to do something about it. I am pretty much his first partner other than his 'first' but that was not a great experience for him."[1]

---

1. Anonymous post, Sexual Health Forums, HisandHerHealth.com. Retrieved online on April 11, 2009, from www.hisandherhealth.com/cgi-bin/ubb_newshe/ultimatebb.cgi?ubb=get_topic;f=1;t=003317;p=0.

17.7.2

"My parents are really poor and don't give me any pocket money. We're in loads of debt but I can't help feeling angry that all my friends can afford new clothes whenever they like and I can't. They are starting to make fun of me because of it" (age fifteen).[2]

17.7.3

"I have been with my girlfriend for almost 4 years, and lately she has been telling me what to do (more like tell me what not to do). Like she can spend a whole day, when I barely see her all week, going out with her friend and I will sit at home, but if I want to go out she says I can't because she is bored and she wants to do something. There is no give and take, and it drives me absolutely crazy. I have tried talking to her and she says that I blow her off all the time, when I really don't. What do I do?"[3]

17.7.4

"Jealousy is harming my relationship with my boyfriend. We've been together for three years and he's given me no reason to doubt him but I keep remembering he cheated on his wife with me. My jealousy gets out of control when he mentions other women. He's told me he is fed up with it but I can't help myself. A previous boyfriend cheated on me and I have a broken family because my dad had an affair, so trust is an issue. I'm scared he might be tempted if I don't keep a careful eye on him or I might miss the signs if he does have an affair."[4]

17.7.5

"I don't seem to be able to control my temper. I get very irritated and sometimes see red and then it all comes spilling out. I am ashamed to say that I often shout and say horrible things when I am really angry. I don't mean them and I feel awful afterwards. Bottling it up makes me feel worse because I then find myself sulking. I have a high-stress job and think that might have something to do with it, but it's no excuse. Please help—I feel I am not a very nice person."[5]

---

2. Anonymous post, "Questions You Have Asked," Mike's Medical Choices. Retrieved online on April 11, 2009, from www.mikesmedicalchoices.co.uk/family.htm.

3. Anonymous post, "I Love My Girlfriend, but She Pisses Me Off . . . ?" Yahoo! Answers. Retrieved online on April 11, 2009, from http://answers.yahoo.com/question/index?qid=20070825215549AAGjIRC.

4. Anonymous post, "I Can't Control My Jealous Rages," Dear Miriam, Mirror.co.uk. Retrieved online on April 17, 2009, from http://blogs.mirror.co.uk/dear-miriam/2008/09/i-cant-control-my-jealous-rage.html.

5. Anonymous post, "How to Be Happy: I Can't Control My Temper," *Independent*. Retrieved online on April 11, 2009, from www.independent.co.uk/life-style/health-and-wellbeing/healthy-living/how-to-be-happy-i-cant-control-my-temper-448114.html.

Volitional *Can't*stipation

Volitional can't*stipation*, sometimes referred to as low frustration tolerance, involves the refusal to expend the willpower to address difficult or challenging issues. Instead, one gives up easily when confronted with low levels of frustration.

Albert Ellis has ascribed the name "I-can't-stand-it-itis" to this fallacy because those who commit it often use the phrase "I can't stand it" or equivalent language to stifle their creative capacity. Thus, the inference involved in this form of *can't*stipation is as follows:

Major premise rule: If I find x difficult or challenging, then *I can't stand x.*
Minor premise report: I find x difficult or challenging.
Conclusion: Therefore, *I can't stand x.*

For example, here are some conclusions that might be deduced in committing this fallacy:

- I can't stand not getting what I want right away.
- I can't stand waiting until I can afford to buy that new Mustang.
- I can't stand studying for exams.
- I can't stand waiting for someone who's late.
- I can't stand my math professor.
- I can't stand being lied to.
- I can't stand rejection.
- I can't stand it when others disagree with me.
- I can't stand spending Sundays with my in-laws.
- I can't stand getting behind a slow car.
- I can't stand making mistakes.

All of the above do not merely express low frustration tolerance but tend to promote it. That is, in telling oneself these things, one gives oneself permission not to tolerate frustration and thus to give in to it. A basic antidote to low frustration tolerance is to cultivate willpower. Aristoteles Santas has defined willpower as

> (a) the power or ability to refrain from doing something (either before you do it, or while in the midst of doing it) even though you are strongly inclined to do it; or (b) the power or ability to continue doing something even though we are strongly inclined not to.[14]

For example, the person who "can't stand" to wait to get what he wants exercises willpower when he pushes himself to continue to persist in waiting, even though he is strongly inclined not to. And the person who can't stand to study for exams exercises willpower when she refrains from quitting studying, even though she is strongly inclined to do so.

In many respects we live in a culture that supports immediate gratification and accordingly promotes low frustration tolerance in getting what we want. Thus, the value of fast food is not in its quality but rather in its rapidity of delivery. Dial-up computer connections have been replaced with broadband and wireless connections not because these more advanced technologies deliver higher-end information but largely because the same information can be accessed more quickly. Television sets that do not have remotes for quicker access to alternative stations are now obsolete. Movies can now be downloaded from the Internet, making a trip to Blockbuster an unnecessary waste of time. Airplanes are more popular than trains for traveling long distances, and if we had the facility to decompose ourselves and rematerialize elsewhere in a nanosecond, air travel would probably become obsolete too. Virtual reality is beginning to replace real-time experiences, and now many of us sit in front of a monitor instead of relating to others in the flesh.

It seems probable that this trend toward immediate gratification will continue, and therewith our tolerance for frustration will continue to decline. As most whose

---

14. Aristoteles Santas, "Willpower," *International Journal of Applied Philosophy* 42 (Fall 1988): 9–16.

TV remotes have failed or who have had to wait for a slow Internet connection can attest, technological advances have decreased our tolerance for waiting to get what we want and accordingly softened our willpower "muscle." The importance of exercising this muscle may therefore be greater now than ever before.

As discussed in chapter 16, there are ways in which we can increase our ability to tolerate things we find difficult or challenging. We can do this by actually *doing* the things for which we have limited tolerance. This might include doing *shame-attacking exercises*. For example, if you think you can't stand rejection, then you can place yourself in a situation in which you are rejected (disapproved of) and thereby prove to yourself that you *can* indeed stand to be rejected. As mentioned in chapter 16, you could try doing something you would be embarrassed to do, such as pulling a banana on a string down a crowded street. Or if you are embarrassed to speak up in class, you can force yourself to do so, notwithstanding your strong inclination against it.

As also discussed in chapter 16, building willpower is a gradual process. So, you can build up to the things that, for you, take the greatest amount of willpower. For example, someone who has a phobia of elevators and "can't stand" to ride them by herself might try riding an elevator with a companion before going solo, or stepping into and out of one at first, then riding a few floors, and then riding several more floors.

That volitional *can't*stipation is irrational is easy to show. Its refutation can be put in terms of its self-defeating consequences: If we never tried to overcome difficult or challenging things and instead told ourselves that we couldn't stand them, then we would have few positive accomplishments to our credit. Indeed, most of the things we are proud of have come as a result of exercising our willpower in accomplishing difficult or challenging tasks.

In its literal sense, "can't stand" implies the impossibility of standing. This accordingly confounds the distinction between something's being a challenge to stand and impossible to stand. That which is difficult for a person to accomplish is still not necessarily impossible for the person to accomplish. Thus, we speak honestly when we change the "can't stand" to "difficult to stand" in cases where there is not a literal impossibility of our being able to stand something. For example, one cannot stand being struck by a Mack truck. However, one can literally stand to go through a divorce.

In some cases, what one claims not to be able to stand is actually something that one simple dislikes. For example, "I can't stand to wait in line." However, in telling oneself that one can't stand something that one merely dislikes, one gives oneself permission not even to try to stand it. One constructive antidote in such cases can be to change the "I can't stand" to "I won't stand" or "I choose not to stand" the thing in question, thereby taking responsibility for the decision not to stand it.

Exercise Set 17.8

In each of the following passages taken from Internet blogs, the speaker uses the term "I can't stand" to support low frustration tolerance. (1) Replace the "can't" with more realistic

(continued)

responsibility-bearing language. (2) Formulate an antidote that the speaker might use to respond rationally to his or her situation. (3) Discuss steps the speaker might take to strengthen his or her willpower to act in line with the proposed antidote.

17.8.1
"I'm a severe road rager, I can't stand slow drivers, stupid drivers and I can't do the speed limit, really bad habit but I can't help it!"[1]

17.8.2
"I can't stand my mother-in-law. She is nosey, lazy, and greedy. SHE LIVES WITH US. My husband says he feels bad to make her leave. We've asked her to give us more time alone. She doesn't. She has no plans to leave anytime soon. What do I do?"[2]

17.8.3
"I can't stand it when people lie, and say that they did it to protect me. I don't need protecting; I can handle the truth. I can take a lot more than people might think, and lying to me just makes me more angry."[3]

17.8.4
"I think I am the most jealous boyfriend alive. I flip out when I see my girl talking to any guy I do not know. We've been going out for a while now—about three years—and it has always been like this. She met someone a couple of weeks ago in her class and they have been doing homework together, studying and so on, and I can't stand it. I have total faith in my girlfriend, but it's just that I can't trust the guy that she's hanging out with. I'm not worried about her leaving me for another guy, but I can't stand it when she spends time with him and not with me. I can't stand it when she tells me that it's nothing and I know that it is nothing. So can you help me out here? I want to know what can help me with my jealousy before I start beating every guy she looks at other than me."[4]

17.8.5
"I can't stand when my husband criticizes me. He does it with love—to grow, and usually what he says is right. He's not rude, doesn't yell or personally attack, but I still don't like being criticized. I don't want to grow anymore, I don't care that it's good for me. I wish he would stop. Thanks for the vent."[5]

---

1. Anonymous post, "Driving," Ozzu Webmaster Forum. Retrieved online on April 11, 2009, from www.ozzu.com/general-discussion/driving-t26622.html.

2. Anonymous post, "In-laws," Answerbag.com. Retrieved online on April 11, 2009, from www.answerbag.com/q_view/405866.

3. Anonymous post, "I Can't Stand It When People Lie," Post Secret Community. Retrieved online on April 11, 2009, from www.postsecretcommunity.com/chat/viewtopic.php?t=173010&highlight=&sid=20a6e39af25513be4a6b8673e6344a43.

4. Student post, "The Jealous Boyfriend Syndrome," *The Daily*, February 25, 2003. Retrieved online on April 11, 2009, from http://dailyuw.com/2003/2/25/jealous-boyfriend-syndrome.

5. Anonymous post, "I Can't Stand When My Husband Criticizes Me," Peer Trainer. Retrieved online on April 11, 2009, from www.peertrainer.com/LoungeCommunityThread.aspx?ForumID=1&ThreadID=104594.

Exercise Set 17.9

The below is from an anonymous post by a high school student.[1] Read it, and answer the questions that follow.

---

1. Anonymous post, Forums, Teenhelp.org. Retrieved online on January 10, 2009, from http://forums.teenhelp.org/showthread.php?t=94231.

I have a problem. I am scared to do my homework. Why should I be scared to do my homework? I am practically a straight A student (I got screwed and got one B last year, and I can't seem to get over it). My problem is that I am a perfectionist, to the point where I absolutely have to do it right or I can't do it. I am scared to write my English essays because of all the mistakes I make. I think "I should" do them perfectly, and in the past some of my essays got A+'s and the teacher read them out loud to the class. I'm scared to do my Physics problems, and I am not even sure if I am supposed to do them or not. . . . . I can't stand to make mistakes, and I am seriously scared to read bad comments on my writing. It causes such strong emotional pain that it is sometimes physical pain.

17.9.1
What emotion is this student experiencing?

17.9.2
What fallacies is this student committing? (Hint: There is more than one.)

17.9.3
Using the E = (O + R) formula discussed in chapter 16, formulate this student's emotional reasoning, refute his or her irrational premise(s), and provide an antidote for each irrational premise. (Hint: there is going to be a practical syllogism for each fallacy you find.)

18

Damning Thoughts and Dutiful Worrying

In chapter 17, we saw how the language we use can affect the way we feel. In particular we looked at self-defeating and destructive uses of the words "must," "awful," and "can't" and their equivalents. In this chapter we look at damning language as well as the use of moral language to self-defeatingly and destructively upset oneself. More specifically, we examine the fallacies of (1) damnation, and (2) dutiful worrying.

SELF-DAMNATION AND DAMNATION OF OTHERS

Self-damnation involves total devaluation of oneself, whereas *damnation of others* involves total devaluation of another person or persons, based on some perceived defect in oneself or the other person(s). With their respective major premise rules in place, the respective inferences drawn in each of these forms of damnation are as follows:

1. Self-damnation:

   Major premise rule: If I have a defect or set of defects F, then I'm totally worthless.
   Minor premise report: I have F.
   Conclusion: I'm totally worthless.[1]

---

1. Sometimes, when pressed, a person who draws this inference will admit that she is not totally worthless but will still contend that she is virtually (for the most part) worthless. This quasiuniversal claim assumes that a person consists of parts such that when most of them are valueless, the person is mostly valueless. This assumes that the whole is equal to the sum of its parts; however, it makes sense to suppose that the whole is distinct from the sum of the parts. For example, water consists of two parts hydrogen and one part oxygen, but water has properties that make it distinct from the sum of the parts. For example, water is wet, but this is not equally true of hydrogen or oxygen. Similarly, persons are the bearers of rights, obligations, and responsibilities, but this is not equally true of actions, feelings, or other aspects of persons.

2. Damnation of others:

> *Major premise rule:* If a person S has a defect or set of defects F, then S is totally worthless.
> *Minor premise report:* S has F.
> *Conclusion:* S is totally worthless.

For example, in the case of self-damnation, let F = having made a mistake on the job. In the case of damnation of others, let F = having committed adultery, and S = your spouse.

Each of the above major premise rules makes the faulty assumption that what's true of the part is necessarily true of the whole.[2] For example, the fact that your spouse has been unfaithful does not mean that he or she is a totally worthless person. If this were true, then the statement "S did something bad, but S is not a bad person" would be self-contradictory, which it is not. As imperfect beings, all of us do bad things at some point in our lives. If this inference were sound, then all human beings would be bad. Similarly, the mere fact that one has made a mistake at work does not make one worthless; otherwise, we all would be worthless.

Exercise Set 18.1

Each of the following contains one or more instances of the fallacy of damnation. For each instance, (1) indicate whether the fallacy committed is self-damnation or damnation of others, (2) formulate the emotional reasoning (major premise rule, minor premise report, and conclusion), (3) dispute any fallacious premises, and (4) provide an antidote.

18.1.1
"When I look at myself in the mirror I want to throw up. I hate the way I look. I hate my personality. I hate who I am. I'm not blaming anyone. I only blame myself. I am afraid God will punish me for thinking this way so I hide it from everyone. But it's true. I really hate myself. I am so pathetically ugly I don't know how anyone can look at me. I avoid mirrors whenever I can. If anyone looks at me my face turns red from embarrassment. I can't look anyone in the eyes. I am miserable and alone because I know nobody can ever love me. I am unlovable. I am nothing. I am worthless. I am garbage."[1]

18.1.2
"I am so damn angry cuz of my husband wanting to see his Narcissistic EVIL family of origin after all the abusive evil crap they've said and done to BOTH of us. But he wants to go see them, cuz he loooooooves them and wants to know he still cares. You asshole, how could you love, let alone care about those evil abusers called your Mother and your Sister, Father, Brother Inlaw's and Sister in law. . . . Until you cut them out of your life, I can't have peace and joy with you, or trust you for that matter. Anyone who would care for those pieces of crap you call parents and siblings and spouses, is sick in the head."[2]

---

1. Posted by "Garbage," "I Am Worthless," CyberPsych, April 2007. Retrieved online on April 6, 2009, from http://cyberpsych.org/cgi-bin/penpals.pl?read=16322.
2. Anonymous post, "Husband 149," Angry.net. Retrieved online on April 6, 2009, from www.angry.net/people/h/husbands2.htm.

---

2. This assumption is often referred to as the fallacy of composition. In these terms, damnation can be said to be a type of fallacy of composition. This general fallacy will be discussed in chapter 21.

Approval Damnation

One common type of self-damnation is *approval damnation*. This type involves basing one's self-worth on whether or not one gets the approval of others. The inference made here, including the assumed major premise rule, is as follows:

Major premise rule: If I don't have the approval of person(s) S, then I'm totally worthless.
Minor premise report: I don't have the approval of S.
Conclusion: I am totally worthless.

For example, S might be a significant other, one's peers, one's employer, or one's friends. This inference generates intense anxiety because if one makes one's value rest on the approval of others, then one keeps oneself in a constant state of anxiety as to whether one will be a worthy person or a worthless one. As we saw in chapter 16, the Stoic philosopher Epictetus admonishes us not to try to govern things outside our power to control, such as what others think of us. As a result of attempting to do so, we fail to focus on what is, indeed, in our power to control, such as our own deeds, and thereby increase the odds of failing at what we attempt to accomplish. Thus, approval damnation is self-defeating because one is less apt to get the approval of others by seeking it. Recall Epictetus's musician, who concentrates on the audience rather than on his singing, thereby increasing his level of anxiety and his chances of messing up (chapter 16).

There is a physiological explanation for this also. In a state of anxiety, our blood goes to our gross muscles and away from our brain, thereby preparing us for "fight or flight" but making it harder to think. In the performance of activities that involve fine motor coordination, such as executing a difficult musical passage with a musical instrument (say on a classical guitar), this can impair one's ability to perform well.

Consider also the commonplace example of test anxiety, where one's mind seems to "go blank." This can be a result of the intense emotional stress one undergoes as a result of making one's self-worth a function of whether one gets the approval of others.

Exercise Set 18.2

Provide at least one example of approval damnation. This example can be from your own thinking or that of another person whom you know. (If you choose a person other than yourself, be sure to adequately disguise the identity of this person.)

Exercise Set 18.3

In the following case, actress Marilyn Monroe engaged in approval damnation. What emotion was she experiencing? Formulate her emotional reasoning, dispute any of its fallacious premises, and construct a rational antidote to it.

(continued)

I'm a failure as a woman. My men expect so much of me, because of the image they've made of me and that I've made of myself, as a sex symbol. Men expect bells to ring and whistles to whistle, but my anatomy is the same as any other woman's. I can't live up to it.[1]

1. "Marilyn Monroe: Biography," TV.com. Retrieved online on April 6, 2009, from www.tv.com/marilyn-monroe/person/109708/biography.html.

Achievement Damnation

Another common form of self-damnation is *achievement damnation*, which involves making one's self-worth a function of one's achievements. The inference here, including the assumed major premise rule, is as follows:

Major premise rule: If I fail at x, then I am myself a failure.
Minor premise report: I failed at x.
Conclusion: I am myself a failure.

For example, let x = athletic activity, such as playing baseball. Not uncommonly, athletes make their self-worth a function of their athletic performance. As long as they are doing well, they are worthy, but as soon as they fail, they are worthless has-beens. This creates a roller coaster ride where one day one is up and the next down. Indeed, even when one is riding high, there is still the impending anxiety lurking in the background of the possibility of future failure and the plunge into worthlessness.

Notice, too, how achievement damnation can piggyback on approval damnation. That is, one may make one's self-worth hinge on one's achievements as a means to attaining the approval of others. This "inference chain" is then as follows:

1. If I don't have the approval of others, then I'm a failure.
2. If I fail at x, then I won't get the approval of others.
3. Therefore, if I fail at x, then I'm a failure.
4. I failed at x.
5. Therefore, I'm a failure.

From chapter 3, you should recognize the inference from premises 1 and 2 to the conclusion in 3 as a *valid pure hypothetical syllogism*. See how the conclusion in 3 then becomes the major premise rule for the second-tier inference from 3 and 4 to the conclusion in 5.[3] Notice that this latter inference from 3 and 4 to 5 is none other than the inference involved in achievement damnation and that the major

3. Note that the standard form of emotional reasoning as derived from the E = (O + R) formula applies to this secondary tier but not to the primary tier. This is because the standard form of emotional reasoning (if O, then R; O; therefore, R) is a *mixed* hypothetical syllogism (affirming the antecedent), whereas the primary tier, from which the secondary tier is deduced, consists of a *pure* hypothetical syllogism.

premise rule of this inference in 3 is itself a deduction from the major premise rule of approval damnation in 1. In this way, achievement damnation can piggyback on approval damnation.

Accordingly, if one's achievement damnation depends on approval damnation, one can give up the former by giving up the latter. Thus, if one is able to overcome one's tendency to make one's self-worth depend on the approval of others, one may no longer damn oneself for failing to achieve. Such a logic-based manner of finding one's premises and disputing them can in this way be a potent tool for helping oneself as well as others overcome self-defeating and irrational emotional reasoning.[4]

Exercise Set 18.4

Provide at least one example of achievement damnation. This example can be from your own thinking or that of another person whom you know. (If you choose a person other than yourself, be sure to adequately disguise the identity of this person.)

Exercise Set 18.5

18.5.1
In an interview, *Sex and the City* star Sarah Jessica Parker disclosed the following:

> I'm always nervous before a job! I always think I'm going to be fired. I always think I can't do it. I always think I'm going to disappoint somebody, myself included.[1]

Is Parker committing achievement damnation? Is she committing approval damnation? Is her pre-stage anxiety avoidable? If so, how? If not, why not?

18.5.2
Former Seton Hall University basketball player *Danny Hurley* once disclosed the following:

> I had it in my head that anything short of being an NBA player, I'm a failure. . . . When I wasn't performing like an NBA player, I started getting depressed.[2]

Formulate Hurley's emotional reasoning. If there are any fallacious premises, dispute them and provide an antidote.

---

1. Ethan Aames, "Interview: Sarah Jessica Parker on 'Failure to Launch,'" Cinema Confidential, March 8, 2006. Retrieved online on December 6, 2008, at www.cinecon.com/news.php?id=0603081.
2. Associated Press, "Sports People: Hall's Hurley Explains," *New York Times*, January 18, 1994.

Damnation of Self and Others: Distinguishing between Deed and Doer

In the cases of self-damnation and the damnation of others, an important antidote to overcoming these fallacies is the realization that *there is a difference between deed*

---

4. See, for example, Elliot D. Cohen, "Philosophical Counseling: Some Roles of Critical Thinking," *Essays in Philosophical Counseling*, ed. Ran Lahav (Lanham, Md.: University Press of America, 1995).

and doer. A person can do something stupid, dumb, foolish, or idiotic, but that does not necessarily make the person herself stupid, dumb, foolish, or idiotic. There is a logical gap here that cannot be assumed away.

In fact, while words like "stupid," "dumb," and "idiotic" can meaningfully be applied to actions, they are ill suited for application to persons. As applied to actions, such terms signify acts that should not be repeated. As applied to persons, such terms serve to devalue the entire person and tend to subsume every aspect of a human being under the one devaluating label. The fool, the idiot, or the dumb person is thus perceived to be nowise competent, and every word or deed of this person is to be discounted or viewed with incredulity.[5]

Applying words like "good" and "bad" to a person raises similar problems. It is of course possible to argue that when a person does enough evil things, he can *himself* be globally rated as a *morally* bad or evil person. In this view, there is a threshold of viciousness such that when it is reached, one earns the right to call the person in question a bad person. For example, one can argue that Adolf Hitler was a "monster," just as Albert Schweitzer was a morally good person. The latter had a reverence for all life, while the former set up death camps. Notwithstanding any positive aspects of Hitler's character (he was a vegetarian and liked dogs), we could say, on the moral threshold view, that the moral gravity of his misdeeds went well beyond any reasonable threshold for qualifying one as a morally bad person.

Nevertheless, global moral ratings of persons are not very useful. The purpose of moral evaluation is constructive. We may want to know about a person's moral character if we are interested in employing, befriending, avoiding, defending against, teaching, or otherwise relating interpersonally with the person. However, damning persons (oneself or others) rather than rating their actions is not generally very helpful for these purposes. Thus, informing another that a certain person is no good is typically too general to be of much use. In contrast, informing another that this person has a history of lying, performing violent crimes, and breaking promises is likely to be more useful. For example, our criminal justice system does not punish people for being bad persons. The system punishes offenders for having intentionally committed certain definable, unlawful acts, which must be proven by introducing evidence in a court of law.

Therapeutically, the application of damning terms to persons is self-defeating. For example, if a person is depressed, has low self-esteem, or suffers from extreme guilt, then applying damning ratings reinforces the negative emotion and is therefore self-defeating. Thus, telling a person with low self-esteem that she is stupid serves to support the negative self-rating, and telling the guilty person that he is a bad person keeps the person focused on his own irremediable badness rather than on deciding to make moral amends for the future. Better then to criticize the deed rather than the doer.

The philosopher Immanuel Kant provides a further, related philosophical rationale for avoiding damnation of self and others. According to Kant, we should "so act

---

5. This is also why the American Psychiatric Association speaks of persons with certain defined mental illness and does not use its classifications to designate persons. For example, people can have schizophrenia or paranoid personality disorder; however, this does not make them "schizophrenics" or "paranoids." Such global psychiatric labels are dehumanizing and degrading. See the American Psychiatric Association's *Diagnostic and Statistical Manual of Mental Disorders*, fourth ed.

as to treat humanity, whether in your own person or in that of any other, in every case as an end in itself, never as means only." By an "end in itself," Kant intends to say a *person*, and by a "means only," he intends to say an *object or thing*. Thus, Kant is telling us to treat oneself and others as persons rather than as objects.

For Kant, the value of an object is conditional—that is, it has value only insofar as it can be used for some extrinsic purpose. For example, a pen has value insofar as one can use it for writing. As soon as the pen's ink is used up, it is no longer of value, and one can dispose of it. In contrast, for Kant, a person has unconditional worth—that is, its value does not depend on its usefulness for some purpose outside itself—thus it is, as he says, an "end in itself."

Applying Kant's distinction, we confuse objects with persons when we call persons worthless, especially when we do so because we think they have failed to fulfill a certain desired end or purpose. This does not mean that a person cannot be criticized for performing worthless acts, but it does mean that the person herself still continues to be an end in itself, a being whose value is unconditional and does not depend on its usefulness.

For Kant, the worth of human beings as distinct from objects lies in the fact that they, *as persons*, are *rational beings*. As rational beings, persons are *autonomous* agents; that is, they are self-determining beings capable of making up their own minds and acting according to their judgments. This sets them apart from objects, which are determined and moved by external causes.

Kant holds that as rational, self-determining agents, humans are bearers of a *right of self-determination*. This means that we cannot manipulate and use people without their consent as though they were mere objects, for such treatment would violate their right of self-determination, which stems from their rational nature. Damning oneself or others is a form of such disrespect for the rational autonomy of persons. This is because in damning persons, one denies their nature as rational, self-determining beings by relegating them to the status of nonpersons or mere objects.

Such disrespect is not uncommon in our society. People may be called derogatory names that deny their worth and dignity as persons before they are seriously harmed and even killed. According to psychologist Albert Bandura,

> Self-sanctions against cruel conduct can be disengaged or blunted by divesting people of human qualities. Once dehumanized, they are no longer viewed as persons with feelings, hopes, and concerns but as subhuman objects. They are portrayed as mindless "savages," "gooks," "satanic fiends," and the like. Subhumans are regarded as insensitive to maltreatment and capable of being influenced only by harsh methods. If dispossessing antagonists of humanness does not blunt self-reproof, it can be eliminated by attributing bestial qualities to them. It is easier to brutalize victims, for example, when they are referred to as "worms"[6]

Bandura argues that such dehumanizing epithets permit terrorists to engage in mass killing without experiencing guilt. It is also this damnation of others that permits an abusive husband to beat his wife mercilessly. If he declares that she is

---

6. Albert Bandura, "Mechanisms of Moral Disengagement in Terrorism," in *Origins of Terrorism: Psychologies, Ideologies, Theologies, States of Mind*, ed. W. Reich (Cambridge: Cambridge University Press, 1990), 161–91. Quote taken from page 13 of pdf version retrieved online on September 8, 2008, from www.des.emory.edu/mfp/Bandura1990MoralDis.pdf.

"filth" and "slime," then he can, at least for the moment, feel vindicated in beating her to a pulp.

Likewise, on the battlefield, "the enemy" is not perceived as a person like oneself but is instead first tagged as less than human before being killed. Thus, in Iraq, enemy combatants can be disposed of through "clearing operations." The "enemy" is "wasted," while civilians are only "collateral damage." The lamentable truth about war—be it just or unjust—is that it is damningly dehumanizing.

Exercise Set 18.6

Below is a post of an anonymous blogger. Read it carefully, and respond to the questions that follow.

I'm a failure. Yup I failed my exams and I want to die right now. My teacher just confronted me about it and he said there's no other way to fix it. It's really hard for me. You know its okay for me if this is my first time but its not. I'm already so far behind. I'm supposed to graduate this year but because of my back subjects I was behind and yes I already accepted the fact that I won't graduate this year. Yes I'm okay with it but I blew it. I blew my last chance. I wanna cry right now but I can't. I don't want my family to see me cry. No amount of encouragement will lift me up right now, nothing. I want to kill myself but I know its wrong and I don't want to take the easy way out. I'm so ashamed of myself right now. I feel so dumb and stupid. It was my own fault anyway. I didn't study hard enough. I'm so lazy. I can't blame anybody else but myself. I don't care what everybody thinks but this time I do and I failed. I failed my self.[1]

18.6.1
What emotion(s) is this student experiencing?

18.6.2
Formulate the student's emotional reasoning. (Hint: the student's emotional reasoning consists of two practical syllogisms that piggyback on each other, as illustrated earlier in this chapter (section on achievement damnation).)

18.6.3
What fallacy or fallacies is the student committing?

18.6.4
Provide a disputation for any fallacy you have found in the student's emotional reasoning.

18.6.5
What antidote(s) would you prescribe to help the student overcome this fallacy or set of fallacies?

---

1. "I'm a Failure," Soulcast, March 21, 2007. Retrieved online on December 6, 2008, from www.soulcast.com/post/show/55464/I'm-a-failure...

GLOBAL DAMNATION

Global damnation involves total devaluation of the world based on some perceived defect. The inference in this type of damnation, including the assumed major premise rule, is as follows:

Major premise rule: If the world has a defect or set of defects F, then the world is totally bad.

Minor premise report: The world has F.
Conclusion: The world is totally bad.

For example, let F = there being terrorists. The fact that there are terrorists who have devoted themselves to taking innocent civilian lives to achieve their political ends, no matter how misguided or malicious these ends might be, does not mean that the world as a whole is a bad place. In fact, it has been argued that the existence of evil provides an occasion for greater goods to be actualized. As the seventeenth-century philosopher Gottfried Leibniz relates, "The general of an army will prefer a great victory with a slight wound to a state of affairs without a wound and without a victory."

In this regard, we should be reminded that the demand of some politicians to "win the war on terror," even at the cost of hundreds of thousands of lives, both military and civilian, is perfectionistic. The phrase "win the war on terror" implies a moment in time when all terrorists are defeated and the world is rid of them at last. But, like "winning the war on drugs," it is unrealistic to expect this ever to happen. Nor need it ever happen for the world to be a good place to live.

An Antidote to Global Damnation: Seeing the Larger Picture

Leibniz's message is clear: one shouldn't lose sight of the larger picture for the sake of some bad aspect of the whole. Of course, this may be easier said than done in cases of substantial loss, such as the death of a significant other. Such serious losses often become the intentional objects of depression, and understandably so. Nevertheless, working through such a depression often involves seeing that the bleakness shrouding one's existence is a function of a kind of tunnel vision that rivets attention on the loss, blocking perception of it as part of a larger whole that is not necessarily bad and may in fact have much to offer. So the widower can find companionship or even a new lover, discover new talents in himself never before tapped, travel the world, expand his knowledge horizons, forge new and interesting relationships, devote himself to a worthy cause, and so on.

These are things that in the darkness of depression are not considered or taken seriously because the mind is riveted squarely and almost exclusively on the loss, which swallows up and taints the whole. The fallacy inherent in this bleak outlook on life is not revealed until the inference "This loss is bad; therefore, my whole existence is bad" is shown to rest on the faulty assumption that what's true of the part is not necessarily true of the whole and that there are also other parts of the whole that converge to make a tolerable, even a very good whole, notwithstanding the serious loss.

Exercise Set 18.7

For each of the following worldviews, indicate whether it commits the fallacy of global damnation. If so, provide a disputation and an antidote. If not, is it a rational worldview, or is it not rational for some other reason?

(continued)

18.7.1
"The world is a bad place with some pockets of goodness here and there."[1]

18.7.2
"The world we live in is the worst place to live. It runs off of evil and corruption."[2]

18.7.3
The world is neither good nor bad, even though there are some good things as well as some bad things in it.

18.7.4
"It's the people who are bad that makes it all seem bad. But then you have kindhearted people who make it feel like a safe happy place. I guess it all depends on the humans. There's some that are evil and cold, and then some that are kind and caring. I would say, that myself, is mostly friendly but I know some humans that are truly cruel. Like I said, it all depends on the humans and how they react, and who you are around."[3]

18.7.5
"GOD IS A MYTH, evolution is fact, and just because you are stupid and think that there is a god, you believe in god because it makes you feel safe and secure. The truth is the world sucks."[4]

---

1. Anonymous post, "Roadkill Diaries," Small Dead Animals. Retrieved online on April 11, 2009, from www.smalldeadanimals.com/archives/002913.html.
2. Anonymous post, "The World Sucks," Big Think. Retrieved online on April 11, 2009, from www.bigthink.com/outlook-the-future/6063.
3. Anonymous post, "Do You Believe the World Is a Kind Place or Bad Place?" Yahoo! Answers. Retrieved online on April 11, 2009, from http://answers.yahoo.com/question/index?qid=20081104114512AAxBNyD.
4. Anonymous post, Antispore. Retrieved online on January 11, 2009, from http://antispore.com/2008/09/11/understand-my-beliefs-please.

DUTIFUL WORRYING

It would be a great oversimplification to say that worry can and should always be avoided, for some measure of anxiety may indeed be inevitable in the course of meeting some of the challenges of living. For example, even the ancient philosopher Democritus acknowledged the degree of worry that is inevitably part of succeeding at being a parent. Said Democritus, "Raising children is an uncertain thing; success is reached only after a life of battle and worry."[7] Still, worry can be chronic, excessive, and counterproductive.

One self-defeating kind of worry can appropriately be called the *fallacy of dutiful worrying*. This type of worry involves prescribing a moral duty to ruminate and disturb oneself over a problem one perceives to be serious until one is certain (or almost certain) that a solution to this problem has been found. The inference involved in this irrational type of worry is accordingly,

---

7. "Worry Quotes," Said What? Quotations. Retrieved online on April 9, 2009, from www.saidwhat.co.uk/topicquote/worry.

I believe that x is a serious problem.
Therefore, I must continue to ruminate and disturb myself about x until it is definitely solved.

Notice that the "must" in this inference is a *moral* one: that is, one that prescribes a moral duty to disturb oneself. It is not simply saying that, as a matter of fact, one is psychologically compelled to ruminate and disturb oneself over the problem. It is instead saying that one is *morally required* to do so. Thus, the major premise rule assumed in this inference is a moral rule:

> *Major premise rule*: If I believe that x is a serious problem, then I must (I am morally required to) continue to ruminate and disturb myself about x until it is definitely solved.
> *Minor premise report*: I believe that x is a serious problem.
> *Conclusion:* I must continue to ruminate and disturb myself about x until it is definitely solved.

For example, let x = child performing poorly in school. Thus, a parent tells herself that she has a moral duty to continue to ruminate and disturb herself about her child's poor performance until it is certain (or virtually certain) that the problem is solved. This would include forgoing any pleasurable activities because, according to this fallacious line of thinking, to enjoy oneself when one's child is having problems in school would violate a parental duty to worry about it. Consequently, the parent will keep herself suspended in a heightened state of distress until the problem goes away or she finds another problem about which to worry.

Further, if x is a duty for a given person, then it is also a duty for any other person who is relevantly situated. This is sometimes called the "universalizability" of moral judgments.[8] This means that if a given moral rating (good, bad, dutiful, right, or wrong) applies to one case, it would be inconsistent to deny that it applies to any other relevantly similar case. Thus, if a mother has a duty to ruminate and worry about her child's class performance by virtue of being a parent of the child, then the father, by virtue of being a parent, also has the same duty. Thus, the mother will enlist the father in dutiful worrying and will perceive any attempt by the father to escape this fate as a moral failing on his part. In this way, the fallacy of dutiful worrying tends to spread to other members of a family or other close affiliations and to create a stressful environment for all involved.

Moreover, dutiful worrying is typically not restricted to any single kind of problem and tends to become chronic and a central activity. As such, no sooner does one problem go away than the dutiful worrier finds another to take its place. Accordingly, this fallacy tends to propagate a steady stream of stress for all concerned.

Because dutiful worrying typically includes a demand for certainty, and because certainty is not something that, strictly speaking, is even possible in solving everyday problems, it is often very hard for dutiful worriers to content themselves

---

8. R. M. Hare, *Freedom and Reason* (London: Oxford University Press, 1963), 7–29.

that a problem is finally resolved. Often, the rumination revolves around whether a possible solution really is the correct one. For example, the parent might persist in worrying even after she has hired a tutor to improve her child's class performance. Indeed, it is still possible that the tutor will be unsuccessful in helping the child to improve his grades. Accordingly, the fallacy tends to be a rather thorny and persistent one.

Exercise Set 18.8

Each of the following appears to be an example of dutiful worrying. (1) Identify the speaker's emotion, (2) formulate his or her emotional reasoning, (3) dispute the major premise rule, and (4) provide an antidote to this rule.

18.8.1
"I have a 2yr old and a 6mth old and just worry all the time. We had a scare with the baby and he ended up in hospital last month and since then I'm worse. I'm always worrying about something happening to my husband or one of the kids. Even worry about that I'm going to drop the baby or about my toddler falling over. Was considering not going on holiday as I was worried about the journey and although it was all fine I was worrying the whole time. I know I need to chill a bit and my husband who knows some of this does tell me to try and relax but it's not something I can just switch off."[1]

18.8.2
"I always have a terrible dilemma that the last song I wrote is going to be the last song ever and it gets worse every time. . . . It always resolves itself, but I feel like I must worry about it. If I don't worry about it, it's not going to resolve itself." —Andy Partridge[2]

18.8.3
"I can't stop worrying and I haven't been able to do anything peacefully or concentrate on anything for the past 2 weeks! First of all, I'm worried about my grades. I usually get all A's or maybe a B, but this quarter I'm doing really badly for some reason. I have A's in every subject, but in science I have a 76. I have been working really hard on my science fair lab report . . . so I can raise my grade, but I'm worried that it won't go up and my parents will be mad. Along with that, I have a 64 in PE. This is because a while back, I missed a week and a half of school because I was sick and missed running the mile we do in the quarter worth 20 points. . . . And now I can't stop worrying about my grades. Not only this, but a long time ago, my cousin gave me a software CD to borrow. It didn't work so I didn't use it, but I kept it on my desk. I don't know what happened to it, but I can't seem to find it anywhere. And to make matters worse, he asked me if he could have it back because he needs a program on it. And I lost it! So I'm worried about this too!"[3]

18.8.4
"My husband is not one bit phased about infertility and going through IVF and yet I worry and get stressed about it all the time! Every time I mention it he is just like, don't worry about it and everything is going 2 be fine! Is it because he is not the cause and I am and if it was

1. Anonymous post, Coffee House Beta, Netmums. Retrieved online on April 11, 2009, from www.netmums.com/coffeehouse/advice-support-523/advice-support-40/pnd-depression-support-55/211950-how-do-i-stop-panicking-s.o-much.html
2. Cited in Bruce Pollock, "The X-Factor," *Guitar Magazine* (January 1986). Retrieved online on April 11, 2009, from http://website.lineone.net/~ssleightholm/articles/xfactor.htm.
3. Anonymous post, "I Can't Stop Worrying! Help!?" Yahoo! Answers. Retrieved online on April 11, 2009, from http://answers.yahoo.com/question/index?qid=20071216173030AA7LT4O.

the other way around and he was would he be more worried because I would still worry if it was him! How can he be so calm?"[4]

18.8.5

"I have significant health anxiety. . . . I finally get closure on a given illness and another pops up right away. My husband never worries about his health, and can't understand why I do so much. Not only do I worry about mine, but his and my son's as well."[5]

18.8.6

"I obsess about even the smallest things in life, so you can imagine how I am with the biggest. I go over things and over things in my mind. Dissecting them, rethinking them, focusing on every last detail. I worry. I play things over and over in my mind. And I find it really hard to let things go, especially when I feel they could have been avoided, if only I'd been more on top of things.

Last night I woke up in the middle of the night sobbing. . . . I hate infertility. . . . Up until now, this was my biggest fear. I want closure. I want to be able to walk away knowing I did everything I could. That's why I put myself in a position to have no regrets. I ate all the right foods, got all the right bodywork, asked all the right questions, came to the best clinic and lab in the country. . . . I listened to all those nagging voices in my head. Except one. And that is what woke me up with uncontrollable sobbing, regret, and a feeling that it's my fault for ignoring the voice in my head that told me we were triggering too early. . . . That I should have at least called and told them my concerns. And now it is too late. Half my eggs were immature, and I can't help feeling that if I had of listened to my gut feeling, I could somehow have changed the outcome and got us almost double the chances. But what I'm even more afraid of, is that if this cycle fails . . . I will always be asking 'what if?' And that is a fate worse than anyone should ever have to bear. Because I'm afraid that that question will torture me forever. I know I need to stop. I need to focus on the good. But right now, I'm just so afraid. And can't stop asking: What if?"[6]

---

4. A Confused Kendra, "Why So Calm????" Infertility Support Group, *Daily Strength*, May 3, 2008. Retrieved online on December 10, 2008, from http://dailystrength.org/c/Infertility/advice/3230301-why-so-calm.

5. Anonymous post, Anxiety Zone.com. Retrieved online on April 11, 2009, from www.anxietyzone.com/index.

6. Anonymous post, "Worry, Guilt, and the Burden of 'What if?'" Wayward Stork, November 15, 2008. Retrieved online on April 11, 2009, from http://waywardstork.blogspot.com/2008/11/worry-guilt-and-burden-of-what-if.html. php?topic=6684.0;wap2.

An Antidote to Dutiful Worrying:
Accepting your Freedom to Choose in the Face of Uncertainty

What then can a dutiful worrier do to stop committing the fallacy of dutiful worrying? French existentialist philosopher Jean-Paul Sartre has offered one constructive antidote. According to Sartre, we must always choose, notwithstanding the ambiguity and uncertainty of the future. If we waited to be sure about what to do about the problems of everyday living, we would never act. Moreover, according to Sartre, there are no hard-and-fast standards that can save us from the inevitability of having to choose in the face of uncertainty.

To illustrate, Sartre tells the story of one of his students who came to see him during the Nazi occupation of France. This young man was struggling with a choice between joining the Free French forces to avenge the death of his brother, who was killed by the Nazis, and staying at home to care for his mother. He knew that his mother depended on him and would be devastated if he left her and, even worse, was killed in trying to defeat the Nazis. But if he stayed at home to care for her, then he would miss the opportunity to avenge the death of his brother and to help defeat the Nazis. On the one hand, he could probably help his mother but would forfeit the possibility of having an impact on the lives of many other people. On the other hand, he was uncertain about how much good he could do if he enlisted. He could, for example, get stuck at a desk job and would therefore sacrifice his mother's welfare in vain.

Sartre's advice to the young man cut through the precariousness of the situation. "You're free," he said, "to choose, that is, invent." If the student waited to be certain about what to do, he would be making his decision by not deciding. If he waited for an omen or some sign about what to do, he would in the end be the one who had to interpret it as a sign or omen. Unavoidably, the student simply had to decide. The point of telling the student that he was "free" and that he should "invent" was to admonish him that the answer to his problem resided in his own creative power to decide and not in some external power that would tell him what to do or make the decision for him.

This does not mean that there are no rational bases for choosing. For example, the student would have defeated his purposes by committing suicide. Nor does it mean that every decision is as hard as the one confronting this student.[9] In any case, one must still choose in order to rationally address a problem, and one cannot demand certainty before making that choice.

Dutiful worriers choose to upset themselves over a perceived problem rather than to make a reasonable choice in the face of uncertainty or ambiguity. Thus, the mother distressed over her child's poor performance in class chooses to worry rather than to brave a choice (for example, deciding to get the child a tutor) and then following through on it. Instead, she demands certainty, shrinks from making a choice, and keeps herself suspended in distress.

Accordingly, Sartre's antidote to dutiful worrying is this: when faced with a problem one thinks is serious, one must be prepared to make a choice, despite the uncertainty or ambiguity of the outcome. In so choosing, one acknowledges one's freedom in creating or "inventing" a solution to the problem. In failing to choose, one hides this freedom behind a pseudo-duty to upset oneself.

Exercise Set 18.9

Find at least three other antidotes to dutiful worrying. Note that the Internet can be a rich source of philosophical insights into coping with worry. You may therefore find it useful to Google worry quotes.

Exercise Set 18.10

Below, a blogger globally damns the world (says it "sucks"), enumerates the many problems he or she perceives to exist in the world, and then suggests that we shirk a "duty to be socially involved" if we do not worry about these issues.

9. One criticism of Sartre is that not all choices are as ambiguous as his example suggests.

My life doesn't particularly suck—well, kind of, but—but the world does. Poverty. War. Global warming. Peak Oil and the energy crisis. Bowling alone, and the disintegration of community. Sexism. Homophobia. Racism. Sundown towns [racially segregated areas]. Prison. The Drug Wars. . . . The past eight years in the U.S. "Education." Information overload. Healthcare in the US. Misunderstanding of mental illness, and discrimination against the mentally ill. The brokenness of democracy, representative or otherwise. Corruption. Terrible city planning in the past 30 years. . . .

It's pretty normal for these things to be a little depressing. But what about when they get really depressing? What about when you're suicidally depressed (probably not primarily due to the above-mentioned ills), and all these issues are just weighing you down? What do you do? Stop reading the news, stop following all of it? Put yourself in a cocoon and lead your own little life and don't worry about the bigger picture? Try to forget, as much as possible, that there's anything out there to worry about? But then, are you somehow deserting a duty to be socially involved? (After all, millions of people in the US doing just that are often given a big share of blame, perhaps deservedly, for the pitiful condition of politics here.) Are you putting yourself at risk of being personally harmed for not following these issues? What if something happens where then it really would make sense for you to move to Canada, if you really thought about it? (In my case, it'd be Spain or the Netherlands, but same diff.) I'm afraid to stop reading about all this stuff, and afraid to keep reading.[1]

18.10.1
Do the presumed social ills that the speaker enumerates mean that the "world sucks"?

18.10.2
Is there a difference between a "duty to be socially involved" and a duty to worry about social problems?

18.10.3
Do you think the speaker is correct that many people avoid concerning themselves with social ills in order to keep from becoming depressed about them?

18.10.4
How can we be healthily "socially involved" (that is, take an active interest in what's wrong in society) without making ourselves depressed over social problems?

18.10.5
In chapter 4, we looked at dilemma thinking. Here the speaker appears to be suggesting that there is a dilemma regarding being socially involved. Formulate the speaker's dilemma argument. Is this dilemma a true dilemma or a false one? (You may wish to review the structure of dilemma arguments and the methods for showing a dilemma argument to be false.)

---

1. Anonymous post, "The World Sucks," Metablog, July 3, 2008. Retrieved online on April 11, 2009, from http://pdf23ds.net/2008/03/07/the-world-sucks.

FALLACY SYNDROMES

Fallacies may occur in patterns, or *syndromes*. That is, one fallacy may be used to support a further fallacy. These syndromes frequently occur in emotional reasoning and are often responsible for destructive emotions. Two such fallacy syndromes are discussed here: (1) magnifying risks/awfulizing/*can'tstipation* and (2) demanding perfection/global damnation.

Magnifying Risks/Awfulizing/*Can't*stipation

In this syndrome, one first predicts that some event will (probably) happen based on the mere fact that it can happen—that is, that it is possible for it to happen.

This inference commits the fallacy of magnifying risks.[10] Then, based on this faulty prediction, one infers that it will be awful. This is the fallacy of awfulizing. Finally, based on the awfulness of the event, one infers that one will be unable to stand it. This last fallacy is (volitional) *can't*stipation.

When these inferences are fully formulated, the chain of inferences in this syndrome looks as follows:

1. *Magnifying risks*: If it is possible that x will happen, then x will happen.[11]
2. It is possible that x will happen.
3. Therefore, x will happen.
4. *Awfulizing*: If x happens then it (x's happening) will be awful.
5. It will be awful.
6. Can't*stipation:* If it is awful, I won't be able to stand it.
7. Therefore, I won't be able to stand x.

For example, let x = graduating college and ending up flipping burgers for the rest of my life. Given this substitution instance, the conclusion is that I won't be able to stand graduating college and ending up flipping burgers for the rest of my life.

As you can see, this syndrome creates *anxiety*. As we saw in chapter 16, anxiety involves the prediction of consequences rated as so bad that one perceives the need to ruminate over them. This matches the cognitive landscape generated by the above chain of inferences. Thus, one who paints his future in terms of a lifetime of burger flipping and perceives this as awful, therefore intolerable, will ruminate over this prediction and accordingly experience intense anxiety.

One can begin to work through such anxiety by identifying and disputing the fallacious premises contained in its chain of emotional reasoning. For example, the inference from premises 1 and 2 to the conclusion 3 is not sound because premise 1 turns the mere possibility of something's happening into an actuality. But what evidence do I have for inferring an actual lifelong career in burger flipping from the mere possibility? Indeed, if this inference were accepted, then one might as well infer that one will graduate college and end up being the richest person in the world since this is also possible.

But even if one did in fact end up graduating college and having a lifelong career of burger flipping, this still would not be absolutely awful—that is, the worst thing in the world. For example, it would be worse to spend one's life in a prison camp being slowly and brutally tortured to death.

As for the inference from premises 5 and 6 to the final conclusion 7—that I won't be able to stand it—the "won't be able to stand it" should really read, "I don't want it to happen." But, of course, there are many things we do not want, but that doesn't mean we can't stand them.

In this way, one can exhibit the chain of emotional reasoning that may be generating one's anxiety and then proceed to dispute its irrational premises.

---

10. As discussed in chapter 10, this version of magnifying risks has sometimes been called Finagle's or Murphy's Law. It is irrational because predictions must be based on empirical evidence drawn from our experience of past uniformities and not merely from the fact that something can happen.

11. A weaker, probabilistic version of this fallacy is also possible: if it is possible that x will happen, then x will probably happen. See chapter 10.

Exercise Set 18.11

In the below quote, actor Dennis Haysbert expresses his thoughts about accepting the leading role as Nelson Mandela in the 2007 film *The Color of Freedom*. Read the quote, and answer the questions that follow.

> Boy, if I do this [play the role of Nelson Mandela in a movie about Mandela], what if I fail? What if I don't do it justice? If I mess this up, people are going to laugh. And what if [Mandela] gets pissed off?' I couldn't stand to disappoint one of the people I regard as one of the top five human beings ever to grace this planet.[1]

18.11.1
What emotion is Haysbert experiencing?

18.11.2
Construct Haysbert's emotional reasoning. (Hint: the argument involves three chained practical syllogisms such as the chain of syllogisms illustrated in this section. However, in the present case, the argument is enthymematic, and awfulizing is assumed but not stated. You will therefore need to add the syllogism that contains awfulizing.)

18.11.3
Refute each of the major premise rules in each of the three syllogisms exposed in 18.11.2.

18.11.4
Provide an antidote to each of the major premise rules refuted in 18.11.3.

---

1. "Dennis Haysbert: The '24' Actor Lands the Role of His Life Playing Nelson Mandela," *The Independent*, May 9, 2007. Retrieved online on December 10, 2008, at www.independent.co.uk/news/people/profiles/dennis-haysbert-the-24-actor-lands-the-role-of-his-life-playing-nelson-mandela-448082.html.

Demanding Perfection/Global Damnation

Another popular syndrome involves demanding perfection and then, seeing that the world does not meet one's demand, damning the world as a whole. The chain of inferences involved in this syndrome is as follows:

1. *Demanding perfection:* If the world is not the way I want it to be, then it is not the way it must be.
2. The world is not the way I want it to be.
3. Therefore, the world is not the way it must be.
4. *Global damnation:* If the world is not the way it must be, then the world is a bad place.
5. Therefore, the world is a bad place.

For example, consider the following condemnation of the world lodged by one blogger:

dkc's Big Huge Political Essay about
Why the World Sucks on a Big Unstoppable Way

Well, I think the title says it all. I don't think the world will be a nice, peaceful place. A place where everyone smiles, giggles and laughs. Where people help each other out. Where people care. Ever. There are too much stupid, ignorant people who care more about themselves than other human beings. It's a shame, but it's true. People care more about what they wear, or with who they are, while they should be worried about wars, a-socializing and the unhealthy look of beauty.[12]

As you can see, DKC is here damning the whole world based on the perfectionistic demand that everyone smile, giggle, and laugh and that people care. Clearly DKC wants the world to match his or her idealistic demand and, because it doesn't, thinks the world "sucks on a big unstoppable way."

Obviously, people like DKC, who lament that the world is not made to perfection (at least according to what they think perfection would entail), themselves have a difficult time smiling, giggling, and laughing. Instead, this jaundiced perspective tends to color the events in their lives, and they accordingly tend to be depressed and unhappy.

So what antidotes are there for overcoming the demanding perfection/global damnation syndrome? Here is what another blogger who has suffered from this self-destructive syndrome has to say:

> Can someone explain why being jaded and cynical is necessary to survive in the adult world? I admit, I'm one of the many. . . . I wanted so much to be liked by everyone and when I sensed someone didn't like me, I went on the attack. Protecting myself. But, no more. Today it feels wrong and inhuman.
>
> Inside I'm a softy. I'm sensitive, emotional and idealistic. It seems to me that there's no reason to try and hide that. There's no one I really need to impress, no one I have to win over. I need to just treat others as I want to be treated, with dignity and respect and kindness. It's not that hard if you make it your focus. . . .
>
> As of today, this moment, I will start to practice this philosophy. I will greet each day with love and respect and decency in my heart and I will let those with whom I come in contact know this. I may not always make the grade, but with practice and persistance, I will succeed. And, hopefully, I will make a difference.[13]

Here, this blogger (let's call him or her Sam) confesses a tendency to turn the desire to be "liked by everybody" into a self-defeating, perfectionistic demand and to go "on the attack" when the world does not fully conform to this desire. But Sam is insightful enough to realize the problematic nature of this reasoning and has hit upon a creative "philosophy" for overcoming it. Sam realizes that he does not *need* to impress or win over others. Instead, his antidote, as he expresses it, is to "treat others as I want to be treated, with dignity and respect and kindness."[14] This is a reversal of the bleak, counterproductive syndrome that leads to depression and unhappiness.

---

12. DKC (anonymous blogger), Windows Live. Retrieved on April 9, 2009, from kiimya.spaces.live.com/blog/cns!FB9538F71AB6AAD4!3036.entry.

13. Anonymous blogger, Wordpress.com. Retrieved on August 10, 2008, from myeverchanging-moods.wordpress.com/2008/03/20/more-on-why-the-world-sucks.

14. Sam's philosophy resembles that of Immanuel Kant, who, as we have seen, says that we should treat others as well as ourselves as "persons," or "ends in themselves." Kant also says that we should "act so that the maxims of our actions could be turned into a universal law of nature." That is, as Sam puts it, we should "treat others as I would want to be treated." See Kant, *Groundwork of the Metaphysics of Morals*, trans. H. J. Paton (New York: HarperCollins, 1964).

In addition, not uncommonly, people who have a tendency to demand perfection and attempt to overcome this tendency will demand that they not ever demand perfection. However, Sam realizes that he is not likely to always "make the grade" and that he will need to practice and persist in order to succeed. Thus, he appears to be aware of the self-defeating character of demanding perfection *about* demanding perfection.

Exercise Set 18.12

In the following, taken from an Internet blog, the speaker expresses a bleak global outlook characteristic of depression. Read it, and respond to the questions that follow.

I HATE LIFE!!! & I HATE PEOPLE!!! (depression)
    I think, it's because I hate both life/and, people in general . . . and, that's why I'm Socially Phobic. Of course, I must also add I hate myself, as well. . . . In fact, I confess, I most probably hate me much more than I hate anything/or, anybody else.
    So, what does all of this boil down to, I wonder, Depression?! Because, that would mean, then, I've been suffering from Depression for an awful long long time . . . extending way back into the very youngest childhood that I can remember?!
    It's like not a day goes by when I can honestly say I loved living . . . as no day is ever, truly, perfect.
    And, there's not a single person on earth who I can honestly say I love to perfection . . . because, quite truly, we've all got faults!.
    Perfection, maybe, that's the root of my problem. . . . I'm disgusted with myself/others/and, life in general . . . because, absolutely nothing is ever PERFECT!
    Instead, everything, blooms—but, then, never remains constant. . . . Instead, it all just merely waxes, and, wanes! With nothing ever staying exactly the same.[1]

18.12.1
What fallacy or syndrome does the speaker appear to exhibit?

18.12.2
Formulate the speaker's emotional reasoning. (Hint: this will consist of a chain of two practical syllogisms as illustrated in the present section.)

18.12.3
Refute each of the two major premise rules in the speaker's emotional reasoning as formulated in 18.12.2.

18.12.4
Provide an antidote for each of the major premise rules that you refuted in 18.12.3

18.12.5
What behavioral changes might the speaker make to back up the antidotes you provided in 18.12.4?

18.12.6
The speaker says, "I must also add I hate myself, as well. . . . In fact, I confess, I most probably hate me much more than I hate anything/or, anybody else." Why might he or she hate him- or herself more than anything or anybody else?

(continued)

---

1. Anonymous post, blogger, "I Hate Life!!! & I Hate People!!! (Depression)," Mombu. Retrieved online on December 10, 2008, from www.mombu.com/medicine/medicine/t-i-hate-life-i-hate-people-depression-1533445 .html.

> 18.12.7
> The speaker states that "everything, blooms—but, then, never remains constant. Instead, it all just merely waxes, and, wanes! With nothing ever staying exactly the same." Why do you think the speaker finds change, apparently as it is manifested in the physical world, to be so unsettling? In your estimation, how pervasive in the human population is this aversion to change?[2] Do you think this aversion to change (and desire for permanence in our imperfect world) is a common factor in human depression?
>
> ――――――――――
>
> 2. See, for example, Plato's response to this question in his "Allegory of the Cave" in *Republic*, ch. 7.

LEARNING TO SPEAK THE RATIONAL EMOTIVE LANGUAGE

Will Sam's philosophy (as discussed in the last section of this book) work? Much depends on one's willpower to reframe the world in new ways and to persevere. It is easy to allow a long-standing habit of demanding and damning to direct one's emotional reasoning, and it is much harder to push oneself in the opposite direction of greeting each day "with love and respect and decency in [one's] heart." Harder yes, but usually still possible. Some of us may have to work harder than others, but all of us will invariably have to work at it. So what is the nature of this work?

As you have seen, we have embraced the *linguistic theory of emotions*. This theory holds that our emotions are largely a function of the language we use to frame the world. Thus, perfectionistic language, such as "I *need* everybody to like me," turns one's desires into unrealistic, unattainable, self-defeating demands. Damning language, such as the world or the people in it "suck," frames negativistic ideation that tends to lead to self-destructive emotions like anger and depression. Telling oneself that one *can't* help the way one feels grants one permission to continue to fly out of emotional control. Calling something (totally) "awful," "horrible," or "terrible" creates intense anxiety. Combining such linguistic behavior into syndromes, such as the two discussed in this chapter, fortifies these self-destructive emotional responses and undermines one's potential for adaptive emotional responses.

On the other hand, adopting philosophies that characterize human beings affirmatively as "persons" or "ends in themselves" (loci of "intrinsic worth and value") who have "dignity," "deserve respect," and should be treated "with kindness" can be instrumental in helping us to reframe more positively and optimistically how we think and, consequently, how we feel about others and, in turn, about the world itself.

So the kind of work we are talking about is primarily linguistic in nature. This means that we have to exert our willpower to speak a different language, one that avoids the vocabulary of fallacies of emotions and their syndromes. Veritably, human beings can become fluent in alternative languages, so it stands to reason that at least most of us can become fluent in the discourse of rational emoting. If you know the language rules of both languages, you can catch yourself speaking the old, self-destructive language and immediately correct it to the new language. Thus, you can catch yourself about to call *someone* "stupid" and immediately correct your grammar to say, "That was a stupid *act*." Or you can catch yourself telling yourself, *"He's* really pissing me off," and correct your grammar to reflect your responsibility, as in *"I'm* really *making myself* angry." Or you can drop the "can't" and change it to "I won't," or you can change "I must" to "I want" or "awful" to "unfortunate," but not "the worst thing in the world." And eventually you can become fluent in this new language; that is, you can learn to think in terms of it without having to go through the intermediate steps of translating.

19

+

Bandwagon Arguments

In the previous two chapters, we examined fallacies in emotional reasoning that promote self-destructive emotions. For the remainder of the book, we will focus on fallacies in practical reasoning that tend to impede successful interpersonal relations.

One common type of fallacy that fits the latter description involves blind obedience to what others say or do. Some of the greatest atrocities in history have been committed at the hands of people who mindlessly conform. From blind adherence to authority and outdated traditions to unquestioning subservience to the tyranny of popular opinion, citizens' unreflective and irrational following of others has been a chief hindrance to a free and open society. The present chapter examines some of these destructive types of conformity.

THE BANDWAGON

The term *bandwagon argument* or the phrase "jumping on the bandwagon" is often used to refer to a cluster of related social fallacies.[1] These fallacies arise when one fails to do one's own thinking but instead takes as one's primary reason for acting in a certain manner the mere fact that others are so acting, have so acted, or are telling one to so act. Here, the fallacy is not in deciding to do what others are doing or have done or in doing what one is told to do; instead, it is in the lack of any independent, rational thinking.

Where x represents a particular act or a type of action, and S represents a single individual (an authority), a group (for example, a peer group or cultural group),

---

1. The term *bandwagon* literally refers to a highly decorated wagon used to transport a band that plays music during a parade. These wagons came into common use in the early twentieth century in political campaigns to attract attention to candidates for political office who rode in them. The phrase "jumping on the bandwagon" was used as a derogatory term to criticize people who followed these candidates without knowing their views.

or a nameless, faceless "everybody" or "they," all bandwagon arguments are constructed along the following lines:

Major premise rule: If S does/tells me to do x, then I should do x.
Minor premise report: S does/tells me to do x.
Conclusion: I should do x.

For example, where S = all my friends and x = smoking crack, an instance of a bandwagon argument would be as follows:

If all my friends are smoking crack, then I should too.
All my friends are smoking crack.
Therefore, I should smoke crack too.

Here, there is consensus without rational inspection, mere imitation in order to "fit in" rather than forethought about the dangers of smoking crack. This is the kind of behavioral reasoning that motivates youth to join gangs and to perform antisocial, destructive acts that these individuals, by themselves, would not otherwise perform. This is also the behavioral reasoning behind what is commonly referred to as "peer pressure."

Of course, if one were to ask for a justification for why one should do what one's friends are doing, including performing self-destructive actions like taking dangerous drugs, one might hear something like this: "If I don't do what they're doing, I won't look cool or be one of the guys." Here, there is a desire to blend in and not to look odd. Psychologist Eric Fromm has eloquently expressed this thrust toward jumping on the bandwagon:

I ought to do what everybody does, hence, I must conform, not be different, not "stick out"; I must be ready and willing to change according to the changes in the pattern; I must not ask whether I am right or wrong, but whether I am adjusted, whether I am not "peculiar," not different. The only thing which is permanent in me is just this readiness for change. Nobody has power over me, except the herd of which I am a part, yet to which I am subjected.[2]

This is the kind of thinking that motivates people to dress in uniform ways, undergo unnecessary plastic surgery, get Botox injections, hide their sexual identities, vote in unison down party lines instead of voting their consciences, support unjust wars, embrace mainstream social values, change or hide their cultural and religious identities, and do sundry other things to try to "fit in."

Thus, one might seek security by attempting to fit in with what "everybody" is doing—for example, cheating on an exam. According to this faulty way of thinking, if everybody is cheating, then I am insulated from moral responsibility if I also cheat. Psychologist Albert Bandura has referred to this phenomenon as *moral disengagement.*

According to Bandura, we can "disengage," or turn off, the moral standards by which we regulate our own conduct by reinterpreting detrimental conduct

---

2. Erich Fromm, *The Sane Society* (New York: Henry Holt & Co, 1990), 153–54.

as nevertheless serving moral purposes, thereby "displacing" or "diffusing" our personal responsibility for it, disregarding or misrepresenting its harmful consequences, or blaming and dehumanizing the victim.[3] The bandwagon argument can serve as a mechanism of moral disengagement by helping to diffuse one's responsibility among or absorb it into the "everyone." Bandura writes,

> Where everyone is responsible no one is really responsible. . . . Any harm done by a group can always be ascribed, in large part, to the behavior of other members. People, therefore, act more harshly when responsibility is obfuscated by a collective instrumentality than when they hold themselves personally accountable for what they do.[4]

However, the argument "Everyone is doing x; therefore, I am not blameworthy for doing x" is not a sound one. Moral responsibility can be *equally* ascribed to each member of a group. Thus, given a rule against cheating on exams, it makes no difference how many other students cheat. If I cheat, then I too violate the rule against cheating, and I too am subject to whatever moral sanction (for example, receiving an F in the class) is attached to the rule. Thus, bandwagon arguments do not truly diffuse moral responsibility.[5]

Nevertheless, while the number of people who support an action or policy, for example, an anti–gay marriage policy,[6] does not make it morally acceptable, popular opinion can be a major stumbling block for the cultivation of individuality, free expression, and freethinking. John Stuart Mill astutely perceived that the opinions held by the masses could be even more oppressive than some forms of political despotism, penetrating deeply into the details of life and "enslaving the soul" itself.

According to Mill, protection against the tyranny of government was not enough. There needed also to be protection against

> the tyranny of the prevailing opinion and feeling; against the tendency of society to impose, by other means than civil penalties, its own ideas and practices as rules of conduct on those who dissent from them.[7]

For example, despite the fact that in America there is currently no law against being an atheist, a homosexual, an unwed mother, or a forty-year-old virgin, there is still a significant social stigma attached to being any of these things.

---

3. Albert Bandura, "Mechanisms of Moral Disengagement in Terrorism," in *Origins of Terrorism: Psychologies, Ideologies, Theologies, States of Mind*, ed. W. Reich (Cambridge: Cambridge University Press, 1990), 161–91. Quote take from p. 2 of pdf version retrieved online on September 8, 2008, from www.des.emory.edu/mfp/Bandura1990MoralDis.pdf.

4. Bandura, "Mechanisms of Moral Disengagement in Terrorism," 11.

5. Not discussed here is the more controversial, philosophical issue of whether there can be such a thing as *collective moral responsibility* in which the group itself, and not just the individuals comprising it, is morally responsible for a collective, untoward action. For a discussion of this question, see "Collective Responsibility," *Stanford Encyclopedia of Philosophy*. Retrieved online on September 8, 2008, from plato.stanford.edu/entries/collective-responsibility.

6. See this chapter, section on traditionalism.

7. John Stuart Mill, *On Liberty*, Penn State Electronic Classic Series, 7. Retrieved online on September 5, 2008, from www2.hn.psu.edu/faculty/jmanis/jsmill/liberty.pdf.

As an antidote to this tyranny of the masses, Mill encouraged what he called "experiments of living." Accordingly, Mill held that there

> should be different experiments of living; that free scope should be given to varieties of character, short of injury to others; and that the worth of different modes of life should be proved practically, when any one thinks fit to try them. It is desirable, in short, that in things which do not primarily concern others, individuality should assert itself.[8]

Notice that Mill was not prescribing anything that harmed others, nor was he suggesting things that he thought might be self-destructive. Rather, he was encouraging us to try new, innovative ways of living with an eye toward discovering practically useful ones.

For Mill, in his day, such experiments in living would have definitely included the liberation of women, whom he believed males had subjugated and deprived of higher education, equal opportunity in the workplace, and the right to vote.[9] Indeed, without attempts to challenge mainstream practices, women might never have even attained the vote. But how many other "experiments of living" are we now overlooking? Society stagnates unless we are prepared to push the envelope in challenging the status quo.

Exercise Set 19.1

19.1.1
List at least three historically significant challenges to the status quo that have resulted in important social change.

19.1.2
List at least three ways you think we might now challenge the status quo in order to make innovative and valuable improvements to our society. This is what you call "thinking outside the box." Don't be afraid to think outside the box!

19.1.3
Your local McDonald's may have a sign that reads "Over 99 Billion Served." Is that a good reason to patronize McDonald's? What questions might it be reasonable to ask before purchasing a Big Mac?

Authoritarianism

Another type of bandwagon argument is *authoritarianism*: that is, blind obedience to another person or persons in a position of authority. "Authority" here refers to a position of knowledge or power. Recall journalist Dan Rather's argument discussed in chapter 14: "George Bush is the president. He makes the decisions,

---

8. Mill, *On Liberty*, 66.
9. In fact, in 1869, Mill published a powerful essay entitled "The Subjection of Women," in which he argued against such subjection. See John Stuart Mill, "The Subjection of Women," Penn State Electronic Classic Series. Retrieved online on September 5, 2008, from www2.hn.psu.edu/faculty/jmanis/jsmill/sub_wom.pdf.

and . . . wherever he wants me to line up, just tell me where. And he'll make the call." As a representative of the fourth estate, it was Rather's job to question governmental authority and not simply to "line up" wherever he was told.

But it is not journalists alone who have such a responsibility. A serious affront to the existence of an open society is blind obedience by the governed to the governor. In a democratic and free nation, elected government officials are presumed to be accountable to the people and to govern with the informed consent of the governed. Indeed, keeping informed about the activities of government is an important antidote against the fallacy of authoritarianism, for one commits this fallacy when one consents to an authority without adequate evidence on which to base one's consent. This is not to disavow the importance of authority as though the only choices were between lawless contempt for authority on the one hand and blind conformity to it on the other.

Still, the history of oppressive regimes is a testament to the tendency of many to place unwarranted trust in an authority and then to absolve themselves of responsibility for the atrocities committed at the hands of the authority. As Bandura discusses, this tendency is "gruesomely revealed" in the socially sanctioned mass executions conducted by Nazi prison commandants and their staff, who disavowed any personal responsibility for their inhumanity. These individuals morally disengaged from their inhumane conduct by displacing their moral responsibility for it onto the authority who ordered the atrocious acts (namely Adolf Hitler).[10] This displacement of personal responsibility permitted them to engage in acts that their standards of conduct would otherwise have condemned.

But in the process of denying their responsibility, these individuals lost their personal freedom and autonomy. As Fromm points out, in oppressive systems such as fascism, Nazism, and Stalinism, an individual can purchase security and refuge from moral responsibility only at the expense of giving up his personal decision-making power, projecting it instead onto the leader, the state, or the "fatherland," to whom he must then submit and whom he must worship. Such an individual, Fromm said, "escapes from freedom into a new idolatry. All the achievements of individuality and reason, from the late Middle Ages to the nineteenth century are sacrificed on the altars of the new idols."[11] This passivity and loss of autonomy is a very high price to pay to escape moral responsibility.

Exercise Set 19.2

Give at least three examples of authoritarianism. These cases can be from the annals of history, or they can involve personal encounters, including your own experiences in submitting to an authority or the experiences of others whom you have known. For each example, describe how submission to the authority in question involved displacement of personal responsibility and loss of personal freedom and decision-making power.

---

10. See, for example, chapter 14 of this book for a look at the reasoning behind Adolph Eichmann's refusal to take responsibility for his Nazi war crimes.

11. Fromm, *The Sane Society*, 237.

Informed Consent as an Antidote to Authoritarianism: Paternalism in Health Care

The transfer of responsibility to authorities and the consequent loss of decision-making power are often a product of *social institutions whose rules require total or near-total deference to authority*. Totalitarian governments like Nazi Germany provide instructive examples of such total passivity and deference to authority; however, there are also many other examples of this, even within democratic societies.

In general, the potential for committing the fallacy of authoritarianism increases when power is institutionalized in a way that treats the subject of an authority as a passive recipient of the authority. The "paternalistic" model of medical practice affords an instructive example of such institutionalized passivity. According to this view, "the doctor knows best"; therefore, a patient should not question his judgment. For centuries, it was a given that when a physician prescribed a medication or a therapy, the patient was expected to comply—no questions asked.

According to the 1847 American Medical Association (AMA) code of ethics,

> The obedience of a patient to the prescriptions of his physician should be prompt and implicit. He should never permit his own crude opinions as to their fitness, to influence his attention to them. A failure in one particular may render an otherwise judicious treatment dangerous, and even fatal.[12]

As such, patients were taught to believe that their opinions did not count because they were "crude." They were accordingly divested of any medical decision-making authority, which was instead placed in the hands of the physician, whom the patient was expected, as a matter of course, to obey. Here, however, is what the AMA now says:

> Informed consent is more than simply getting a patient to sign a written consent form. It is a process of communication between a patient and physician that results in the patient's authorization or agreement to undergo a specific medical intervention. . . . [The] patient should have an opportunity to ask questions to elicit a better understanding of the treatment or procedure, so that he or she can make an informed decision to proceed or to refuse a particular course of medical intervention.[13]

According to the AMA, in this process of communication, the physician should disclose and discuss with the patient his or her diagnosis, the proposed treatment, its risks and benefits, available alternative treatments and their risks and benefits, and the risks and benefits of not undergoing a treatment.[14] This is what informed consent means in this context, and if the patient is not provided with such informed consent, he or she is not prepared to make an autonomous medical decision.

---

12. American Medical Association Code of Ethics, Article 2, "Obligations of Patients to Their Physicians," 1847.
13. AMA, "Informed Consent." Retrieved online on March 25, 2009, from www.ama-assn.org/ama/pub/category/4608.html.
14. AMA, "Informed Consent."

The patient thus commits the fallacy of authoritarianism in this context by taking the physician's advice without giving *informed consent* as defined. Unfortunately, while medical practice has changed its institutional stripes to include respect for patient autonomy, some physicians in practice would still prefer their patients to obey blindly rather than ask questions and use critical thinking in making personal health-care decisions. Freethinkers are not likely to be well received by such physicians and are best advised to seek medical treatment elsewhere.

In today's practice of medicine, it is also part of the standard of informed consent that patients get a second medical opinion from an independent physician before undertaking serious medical treatment. This second, independent medical opinion is typically provided by a specialist: that is, an authority who has special knowledge in the area of medicine under consideration. For example, coronary bypass surgery would call for a second (and maybe even a third) opinion from a cardiologist who specializes in performing this type of surgery. In fact, physicians often encourage their patients to get a second opinion; however, this is not universally true, and patients may therefore need to take the initiative to seek out a second opinion on their own.

Exercise Set 19.3

Provide at least two examples of cases in which a physician acted paternalistically toward a patient by failing to obtain the patient's informed consent prior to treating the patient. In each of these cases, what might the patient have done differently to better protect him- or herself against such medical authoritarianism? These cases may be gleaned from personal experiences or case studies, such as medical malpractice cases involving failure to obtain informed consent. You can find such case examples on the Internet or in other appropriate ethical and legal resources, such as medical ethics casebooks and medical case law books.

Misuse of Authority

Authority can also be misapplied. That is, someone who is an authority in one area may be mistakenly assumed to be an authority in another area. For example, some people attempt to satisfy their medical needs by consulting a veterinarian. However, while there is overlap in knowledge of veterinary medicine and human medicine, there are also significant differences. Thus, medications that may work for certain purposes on animals are not suitable for human beings, and vice versa.

In some cases, the confusion of authority may in fact be legally and socially sanctioned. For example, physicians today are legally permitted to prescribe medications for anxiety, depression, attention deficit hyperactivity disorder (ADHD), and other psychological problems. The assumption here is that these problems have physiological causes and can therefore be medically addressed. However, physicians, such as general practitioners and internists, do not ordinarily receive training in psychology as part of their medical training and therefore may not have adequate knowledge to determine whether, for example, a child has ADHD and is a proper candidate for drug therapy or is having an adjustment problem related to a recent family crisis.

The misuse of authority is endemic to the advertising world. Print ads and TV commercials abound in which celebrities endorse products that have little or nothing to do with the celebrity's area of expertise. From movie stars to politicians, celebrities or well-known figures appear in advertisements when they are no more qualified to speak about the efficacy of the products being sold than anyone else. Yet manufacturers pay these individuals large amounts of money just to lend their celebrity to these products.

For example, a 2002 ad employed Dorothy Hamill, a renowned former champion figure skater, to advertise the Merck product Vioxx, a nonsteroidal, anti-inflammatory arthritis and pain-relief medication.[15] Subsequently, Vioxx was voluntarily withdrawn from the shelves in 2002 by Merck after a study showed that long-term use of the drug increased the risk of a heart attack or stroke. As a figure skater, Hamill would have had no more expertise about this product than any other user or potential user of the product. Yet Merck was counting on her celebrity as a figure skater to help increase drug sales.

Another classic example is Senator Bob Dole's 1999 infomercial for Pfizer, the maker of Viagra, a popular drug for erectile dysfunction.[16] In this ad, Dole admonished, "It may take a little courage to ask your doctor about erectile dysfunction but everything worthwhile usually does." While Dole suffered from erectile dysfunction as a result of having had surgery for prostate cancer, he was no more qualified to speak about this drug than any other person with erectile dysfunction. His political expertise had nothing whatsoever to do with expertise about erectile dysfunction or the use of Viagra to treat it. Nevertheless, Pfizer used Dole's reputation and expertise as a statesman to sell the product.

Exercise Set 19.4

Provide at least two examples of advertisements or commercials that commit the fallacy of misuse of authority. You may find such ads on the Internet or in mass media such as pop culture magazines.

The Fallacy of Traditionalism

A related form of bandwagon argument that has presented a major stumbling block to creativity and advancement—scientifically, philosophically, morally, and spiritually—is blind adherence to past practices. Mistakes made in the past are indeed likely to repeat themselves if they are made in the name of tradition. The *fallacy of traditionalism* refers to adherence to tradition (religious or secular) for tradition's sake, even at the expense of abridging fundamental human rights.

---

15. Vioxx Ad. Retrieved online on April 9, 2009, from www.frankwbaker.com/dorothy.jpg.
16. Dole Ad. Retrieved online on April 9, 2009, from www.frankwbaker.com/dole.jpg.

Traditions are indeed a fact of social existence, and they can and do serve the useful function of fostering camaraderie and unity among groups of people. Thus, a holiday feast of turkey on Thanksgiving can remind us of our shared American heritage and unite us in giving thanks for our hard-earned constitutional rights as enshrined in the Bill of Rights. But tradition can also be a thorn in the side of a free nation when it becomes exclusionary and divisive. This happens when traditions are forced upon others even at the expense of causing them great unhappiness for no greater reason than that the traditions in question are traditions. Thus, in our nation, women were once deprived of the right to vote, attain a decent education, and work outside the home—all because of the long-standing tradition prescribing that "a woman's place is in the home."

Those who cling to traditions for their own sake typically claim the right, and even the duty, to use the arm of the law to enforce them. This idea of legal enforcement of tradition for its own sake received its classical formulation in 1959 when the British jurist Lord Patrick Devlin wrote his famous polemic against the legalization of homosexuality in England. Devlin wrote,

> The institution of marriage . . . bridges the division, if there is one, between politics and morals. Marriage is part of the structure of our society and it is part of the basis of a moral code which condemns fornication and adultery.[17]

According to Devlin, a society is not something that is held together physically but is instead a "community of ideas" that is held together by a shared morality. Since heterosexual marriage is part of that community of ideas, if these "invisible bonds of shared morality" were relaxed too much, people would drift apart, and the society would be destroyed. "The bond is part of the price of society," said Devlin, "and mankind, which needs society, must pay the price." For this reason—to preserve this essential glue that holds society together—a society has the right to use the arm of the law to preserve its existence. Thus,

> if society has a right to make a judgment and has it on the basis that a recognized morality is as essential to society as say, a recognized government, the society may use the law to preserve morality in the same way that it uses it to safeguard anything else that is essential to its existence.[18]

This sociopolitical ideology rests on no more than the fallacious appeal to, and enforcement of, tradition for tradition's sake. As Oxford jurisprudence professor H. L. A. Hart maintained in his notable response to Devlin, there is no credible argument that society would be destroyed if gay people were permitted to marry. While society might *change* by becoming more tolerant of gay rights, it would surely not also abandon truly essential components of the moral code such as proscriptions against murder, rape, theft, and other felonious crimes.[19] So deflated, the substance of Devlin's argument was no more than the fluff of the fallacious appeal to tradition.

---

17. Lord Patrick Devlin, "Morals and the Criminal Law," in *Morality and the Law*, ed. Richard A. Wasserstrom (Belmont, Calif.: Wadsworth, 1971), 33.

18. Devlin, "Morals and the Criminal Law," 34.

19. H. L. A. Hart, "Immorality and Treason," in Wasserstrom, *Morality and the Law*, 49–54.

According to Lord Devlin, if the average person places something beyond his limits of tolerance and finds it so abhorrent that he has "intolerance, indignation, and disgust" for it, then society has a legal right to eradicate it.[20] Thus, according to Devlin, we need not have any *rational* basis whatsoever for restricting the liberty of others or rejecting a new social program or idea; we need only aver that we are not accustomed to it (it is not part of a standing tradition) and the average person is intensely disgusted by it. This could include anything from gay marriage to socialized medicine.

For example, Devlin's use of intense, unreflective emotion as a legal criterion has more recently been applied to gay marriage by right-wing syndicated talk show radio host Michael Savage, who stated,

> They [liberal judges] make homosexual wedding the law of the land, when 90% of the American people find it repugnant! And sickening! And disgusting! And don't wanna accept it! And don't wanna live in a degenerate nation![21]

While Savage's statistic about how many Americans are opposed to gay marriage appears to be groundless, this may be beside the point. The idea of using such irrational emotions to determine the law of the land is antithetical to a free and open society, which, as we have seen, is based on *rational* consensus. In the next chapter, we will examine some major varieties of emotional appeals used to manipulate and sway the rational judgment of others.

Exercise Set 19.5

Each of the following describes a traditional practice. For each, indicate whether or not the adherents to the practice are committing the fallacy of traditionalism. Defend your response.

19.5.1
"The elevation of the women's power scenarios at the expense of the role of the male in a great number of television offerings is becoming more and more obvious. . . . The husband-father has always been the representative for God in the home, but it is crystal clear that those who present this role as one of no power, authority and importance are advocating un-Christian and unworthy life credos. . . . The educational aspects of such programs are very powerful, especially on young minds." —John M. Stevens[1]

19.5.2
"The tradition has always been that when a U.S. president is overseas, partisan politics stops at the water's edge." —Rahm Emanuel (said in response to a speech presented by President George W. Bush in May 2008 to the Israeli parliament in which Bush implicitly criticized

1. John M. Stevens, cited in Austin Kline, "Depiction of Men on TV un-Christian," Austin's Atheism Blog, About.com, January 19, 1994. Retrieved online on December 22, 2008, from http://atheism.about.com/b/2004/01/19/depiction-of-men-on-tv-un-christian.htm

---

20. Devlin, "Morals and the Criminal Law," 40.
21. Eric Boehlert and Jamison Foser, "Savage: Same Sex Marriage: 'Repugnant,' 'Sickening,' 'Disgusting.'" Media Matters, May 27, 2004. Retrieved online on September 6, 2008, from mediamatters.org/items/200405260005.

then senator Barack Obama for claiming that he would negotiate with nations such as Iran and Syria)[2]

19.5.3

"Based on findings from traditional Jewish sources, our Torah scholars have determined that matrimonial descent has always been the sole family factor for Jewish identity since the Giving of the Torah." (This means that one is considered to be Jewish by birth if and only if one's mother is Jewish.)[3]

19.5.4

"For most young girls who start daydreaming about the day they get married, they picture themselves in a white wedding dress that billows around them as they take that walk down the aisle to stand beside their handsome groom. For most women, the tradition of being married in a white bridal gown is simply the only option considered and seems to be a tradition that stretches way back into history."[4]

19.5.5

"For the three Meike siblings Don, Peter and Barb, ranching has always been the only way of life. They have carried on the tradition their grandfather started in the early 1900s. 'Our parents taught us many important lessons,' Barb said. 'The first of these being that ranching is a hard business.' 'Dad used to say that "it's not doing what you like, it's learning to like what you do,"' Barb said. The three Meikes know those are words to live by."[5]

19.5.6

"Consuelo Gurany wasn't born yet, the Mexican Revolution was taking place and World War I was about to start when her family began the tradition of *las posadas*—enacting Mary and Joseph's walk through Bethlehem seeking shelter. . . . On Sunday, Gurany, 80, who suffers from arthritis and has trouble getting around, showed delicate Nativity scenes with more than 100 pieces and spoke of keeping the tradition alive among her family members. As the oldest family member, she organizes the *posadas*, leads in prayer, cooks tamales and leads the processions which will begin Tuesday and continue through Christmas Eve. . . . It takes Gurany several days and help from several family members to set up two Nativity scenes inside her home and two in her front yard. Gurany said she continues the tradition because of her faith."[6]

19.5.7

"In *Warrior Marks*, Alice Walker asks the women in a village why they allow their daughters to be mutilated. The answer always comes back: 'It's tradition.' What does this tradition mean to the women in this culture? Circumcision defines who is in the cultural group. In societies where most women are circumcised, those who are not are seen as outsiders or otherwise socially unacceptable. Uncircumcised women are seen as unmarriageable, and many societies have no place for unmarried women. Belonging to part of a group is desirable

(continued)

2. Sheryl Gay Stolberg, Elisabeth Bumiller, and Brian Knowlton, "Bush Speech in Israel Seen as Attack on Obama," *International Herald Tribune*, May 15, 2008. Retrieved online on December 22, 2008, from www.iht.com/articles/2008/05/15/america/prexy.php.

3. "Jewish Identity," Jewish America, March 11, 1998. Retrieved on December 22, 2008, from www.jewishamerica.com/ja/content/askjewish/AskUs6.cfm.

4. Mike Selvon, "There Is Great Tradition behind the White Wedding Dress," Enzine Articles. Retrieved online on December 22, 2008, from http://ezinearticles.com/?There-Is-Great-Tradition-Behind-The-White-Wedding-Dress&id=1201417.

5. Katie Hulet, "Raising a Tradition: The Meike Siblings East of Kaycee Reveal the Secrets of Success behind a Long-Time Ranching Family," WyomingStockDog.com, December 1, 2006. Retrieved online on April 6, 2009, from http://wyomingstockdog.com/article.php?story=20061201085626520.

6. Stephanie Sanchez, "Posada Has Been Family's Tradition Since 1913," *El Paso Times*, December 15, 2008. Retrieved online on December 16, 2009, from www.elpasotimes.com/ci_11233940?source=most_emailed.

for most humans; we depend on our association with others, such as our family and friends. It is difficult to break with tradition, as it often causes us to become outcasts from our chosen groups. Breaking with the tradition . . . in these societies is not a simple choice for women, so many continue to follow tradition even when the pain dictates otherwise."[7]

---

7. "Female Genital Mutilation (FGM)," Third World Women's Health. Retrieved on December 22, 2008, from http://haneydaw.myweb.uga.edu/twwh/fgm.html#who. Female circumcision involves the removal of all or part of the external female genitalia, including the clitoris. It is practiced in some countries in Africa, Asia, and the Middle East and among some immigrant populations in Australia and the United States.

20

✢

Emotional Appeals

Emotional appeals are fallacies that use nonrational tactics such as threats, intimidation, and the appeal to blind pity instead of rational argument to manipulate the thoughts, deeds, and emotions of others. This chapter examines three major types of emotional appeals: (1) appeal to force, (2) well poisoning, and (3) misuse of pity.

APPEAL TO FORCE

An appeal to force always involves making a conditional threat. The form of such a threat is a conditional statement. The consequent of this conditional statement stipulates a coercive measure to be imposed by a first party on a second party: that is, something that the first party believes the second party would find seriously undesirable and would therefore not want. The antecedent of the conditional statement, in turn, specifies a condition under which the first party will impose the coercive measure on the second party. For example, a judge makes a conditional threat when he says to a defendant, "If you don't sit down, I will hold you in contempt of court."

In ordinary language contexts, the consequent is sometimes unstated. For example, "You better not betray me" might in a given context be shorthand for "If you betray me, then I'll do physical harm to you." The coercive measure may also be psychological in nature, as in a threat to withdraw affection if the second party fails to cooperate in some way with the first party.

There is a fundamental difference between threatening another person and presenting a rational argument. Threatening someone is manipulative, whereas reasoning with someone is not. The second party who responds to a threat made by the first party does so out of fear of the consequences of not complying with the first party. The second party is thus forced or coerced into compliance, whereas a party who acts as a result of rational argument does so autonomously—that is, freely.

The appeal to force is not necessarily a fallacy. For example, a first party who threatens to use force on a second party as a last resort, after having first exhausted all rational arguments, need not have committed a fallacy. Thus, a nation might threaten to apply economic sanctions to another nation if it continues not to comply with a nuclear nonproliferation treaty. The fallacy of appeal to force arises when the first party lacks a good reason for threatening the second party. This is the case when appeals to reason have not first been adequately exhausted. For example, a parent commits this fallacy when, without first attempting to use rational argument, he straightaway threatens to take the car keys away from his teenage son if the child does not improve his grades.

In some cases, a threat itself may be unreasonable, as in cases of extortion and blackmail. In such instances, there may simply be no good reason for the second party to comply with the first party. For example, a scammer lacks a good reason for a potential victim to willfully hand over his money in exchange for a bogus product or service.

Appeals to Force in Interpersonal Relations

Interpersonal relationships based on the appeal to force tend to be dysfunctional. This means that they tend to create more dissatisfaction than satisfaction. This is because such a relationship is based on an imbalance of power in which one party to the relationship dominates and manipulates the other.

On the other hand, functional relationships tend to be based on respect for individual autonomy. Thus, functional spousal relationships involve a partnership between two individuals who mutually respect each other's right of self-determination. In such a relationship, the parties accept responsibility for their malfeasances and attempt to make changes because they desire to satisfy their partners and to maintain a relationship based on trust, solidarity, and mutual respect. This is diametrically opposed to a relationship based on the appeal to force, which involves forced cooperation. Forced cooperation, however, tends to breed fear, resentment, hostility, and distrust between the parties.

For example, here is testimony from a person who was involved in such a forced relationship:

> I was . . . in love with him, [but] soon my love turned to fear and I stayed because he threatened me and my family. . . . I won't get into all the details but I ended up scared, alone, confused etc. He cheated on me, hit me, lied to me, threatened me and ruined anything that was important to me. But for some reason the thing that bothered me the most was how unfair and unreasonable he was. I was raised to be fair and reasonable and I couldn't understand that he wasn't. I thought if I loved him enough and explained things to him I could change him.[1]

According to this woman, the appeal to force in the form of threats to self and family led her to stay in a dysfunctional relationship. Still, despite having been beaten and cheated on, she found the loss of rationality in the relationship most

1. Anonymous blogger, "Very Worried and Confused," Experience Project. Retrieved online on April 9, 2009, from www.experienceproject.com/stories/Am-A-Victim-Of-Domestic-Violence/120737.

disconcerting. It is precisely this void of rationality that makes appeals to force so destructive of human happiness. This woman sought a loving relationship based on mutual respect for rational self-determination, not a forced relationship.

As most social workers will attest, such dysfunctional relationships between parents also bleed over to the nuclear family in general and affect the functionality of relationships with children, in turn spawning further generations of the same dysfunctionality. Thus, the children of such abusive families oftentimes grow up to become themselves the perpetrators of spousal abuse or the victims of it.[2]

The best general antidote to the appeal to force is to seek out and foster relationships based on reason rather than groundless threats. It is sometimes possible to find early signs of a budding dysfunctional relationship based on threats. For example, a boyfriend who threatens to break up with his girlfriend if she won't sleep with him provides a glimpse of what such a relationship might turn into if it is allowed to continue along the same trajectory of appeals to force. Once this fallacy becomes an entrenched habit of relating, the relationship qualifies as dysfunctional.

Appeals to Force in International Relations

According to Plato, governments can also be dysfunctional. For Plato, just as reason should guide the individual soul, so too should it guide the state.[3] Unfortunately, as Plato perceived, there are dictatorial regimes that rule not by reason but instead by irrational appeals to force. In such cases, fear rather than reason provides the foundation of obligations to obey laws and government policies. This is the basis of a closed society whose leaders would prefer to have citizens who respond robotically to their demands rather than to have freethinkers as citizens. This is the opposite of a democratic society, which openly seeks the creative input of the governed.

International relations follow suit. A nation can attempt to set itself up as a world dictator that rules by force of military threat. It can, however, also lead by the democratic example it sets for other nations to follow.

In recent years, there has been considerable emphasis in American politics on establishing and maintaining the United States as the preeminent world power. In fact, a blueprint for such a "new order" was drafted in February 1992 at the end of the George H. W. Bush administration, when Defense Department staffers Paul Wolfowitz, I. Lewis Libby, and Zalmay Khalizad, acting under then Secretary of Defense Dick Cheney, drafted the Defense Planning Guidance. This document, now known as the "Wolfowitz Doctrine," advocated massive increases in defense spending for the purposes of strategic proliferation and buildup of military defenses to establish the United States as the world's sole superpower. Advocating preemptive attacks with nuclear, chemical, or biological weapons, it proclaimed that "the U.S. must show the leadership necessary to establish and protect a new order that holds the promise of convincing potential competitors that they need

---

2. "Domestic Violence and Children," Better Health Channel. Retrieved online on April 9, 2009, from www.betterhealth.vic.gov.au/bhcv2/bhcarticles.nsf/pages/Domestic_violence_and_children.

3. Plato, *The Republic*, trans. Benjamin Jowett. Project Guttenberg. Retrieved online on April 9, 2009, from www.gutenberg.org/files/1497/1497-h/1497-h.htm.

not aspire to a greater role or pursue a more aggressive posture to protect their legitimate interests."[4]

In 2007, a politically influential research institute known as the Project for the New American Century (PNAC) was founded by William Kristol and Robert Kagan for the purposes of advancing the basic tenets of the Wolfowitz Doctrine.[5] This organization claimed that in order to fulfill its role as global leader, the United States had to fight and decisively win multiple large-scale wars as well as conduct "constabulatory" (military-policing) missions throughout the world. At the same time, it emphasized the buildup and modernization of its weapons of mass destruction, including biological weapons. According to PNAC, "Advanced forms of biological warfare that can 'target' specific genotypes may transform biological warfare from the realm of terror to a politically useful tool." This means biological weapons that have the capacity to wipe out specific races of people, a form of genocidal warfare![6]

According to PNAC's "Statement of Principles,"

> The history of the 20th century should have taught us that it is important to shape circumstances before crises emerge, and to meet threats before they become dire. The history of this century should have taught us to embrace the cause of American leadership.[7]

This idea of "meeting threats before they become dire" in turn set the stage for what became known as the "Bush Doctrine," enunciated by President George W. Bush in 2002 and used as a basis for the U.S. invasion of Iraq in March 2003. According to this doctrine of "preemptive war," the United States has the right to attack a foreign nation that in its estimation poses a potential threat to its security, even if this nation poses no immediate threat and no attack by it is imminent.[8] This doctrine represents a departure from prior international law, in particular the Charter of the United Nations, which prohibits the use of international force that is not in self-defense after an armed attack or undertaken with the approval of the United Nations.[9] According to chapter 1, article 2.4 of the U.N. Charter, "All Members shall refrain in their international relations from the threat or use of force against the territorial integrity or political independence of any state, or in any other manner inconsistent with the Purposes of the United Nations."[10]

---

4. Patrick E. Tyler, "U.S. Strategy Plan Calls for Insuring No Rivals Develop a One-Superpower World," *New York Times*, March 8, 1992. Retrieved online on March 25, 2009, from work.colum .edu/~amiller/wolfowitz1992.htm.

5. See "About PNAC," Project for the New American Century. Retrieved online on April 9, 2009, from www.newamericancentury.org.

6. Project for the New American Century, "Rebuilding America's Defenses: Strategy, Forces and Resources for a New Century," The New American Century, September 2000. Retrieved online on March 25, 2009, from www.newamericancentury.org/RebuildingAmericasDefenses.pdf.

7. Project for the New American Century, "Statement of Principles." Retrieved online on March 25, 2009, from www.newamericancentury.org/statementofprinciples.htm.

8. "The Bush Doctrine and the U.S. Military," Encarta. Retrieved online on March 25, 2009, from www.peace.ca/bushdoctrine.htm.

9. Charter of the United Nations, chapter 7, especially arts., 39, 41, 42, and 51. Retrieved online on March 25, 2009, from www.un.org/aboutun/charter.

10. Charter of the United Nations. Retrieved online on March 25, 2009, from www.un.org/aboutun/charter.

Some have questioned the idea of "preemptive war" on the grounds that it enables a nation to act precipitously and thus to short-circuit the prospects for a diplomatic solution to an international dispute. A nation claiming the right to invade another nation, even if it poses no imminent threat, might be more likely to seek a military solution to its disagreement than to patiently attempt a diplomatic one.[11]

On the other hand, the United States could seek to avoid military encounters instead of establishing a policy of engaging in multiple large-scale wars and military-policing missions throughout the world. It could denounce invasion of sovereign nations unless these nations do indeed pose an imminent threat to its homeland, in concert with established international law. Instead of building up its own stable of weapons of mass destruction, while it threatens other nations that attempt to do the same, it could instead spearhead a worldwide program of consistent de-escalation of weapons of mass destruction. And instead of warming up to the idea of using genocidal warfare as a "politically useful tool," it could consistently condemn the use of such weapons, no matter who uses them.

Insofar as the appeal to force leads to dysfunctional relations, whether on the individual, national, or international level, it is sound reasoning to avoid this fallacy. As mentioned, the best general antidote to this fallacy is the appeal to reason. This does not mean that making or carrying out threats is *never* justified; instead, it means that such manner of relating should be saved for a last resort when all rational means have been exhausted. It may be no less of a fallacy to base national and international policy on the appeal to force than it is to base a personal relationship, such as a marriage, on it.

Exercise Set 20.1

In what follows, anonymous blogger Dr. Forbush makes the claim that politics is generally driven by fear and then lists some of the fears he claims tend to define political party affiliation (Democrat or Republican). Read Dr. Forbush's comments and answer the questions that follow.

In general I think that it is safe to assert that politics is driven by fear. In support of this assertion I would draw your attention to the great success of negative advertising when compared to positive advertising. In general people are afraid that their leaders will take advantage of the power that we entrust them with.

Since we all know that there are many things to be afraid of I would suggest that people align themselves with people of similar fears. Here are a few fears, and I would suggest that after reading each fear it will become apparent which political party embraces that fear in order to create that critical mass needed to secure that 51% needed to govern.

   1. Fear that a foreign power will invade the USA.
   2. Fear that employers will take advantage of their employees.
   3. Fear that minorities are being mistreated.
   4. Fear that the government will take away private property rights.

(continued)

---

11. Richard Falk, "The New Bush Doctrine," *Nation*, June 27, 2002. Retrieved online on March 25, 2009, from www.thenation.com/doc/20020715/falk.

5. Fear that American culture will be destroyed by the invasion of foreign culture.
6. Fear that we are slowly destroying our planet with pollution and other destruction.
7. Fear that minorities will take over and force the WASPs into subjugation.
8. Fear that religious zealots will write religious doctrine into public law.
9. Fear that criminals will destroy social order.
10. Fear that the Government will take away our basic rights.

Obviously there are more fears professed by each political group. Some people might suggest that they are fearful of all of these things while others will suggest that they are fearful of very few of these things. However, each and every one of us can take these fears and order them from top worry to least worry. And, in doing so, looking at your top 5 of these will point your political arrow in the direction of your preferred political party.[1]

20.1.1
Which of the above-listed fears do you think are most closely aligned with the Republican Party? Which are most closely aligned with the Democratic Party?

20.1.2
Do your best to list your own "top five" fears out of those listed above. Does your selection point you in the direction of your own party affiliation or leaning?

20.1.3
Do you agree with Dr. Forbush that politics is based on fear? Defend your response.

20.1.4
In your estimation, did the Bush administration use fear as a basis for manipulating Americans into getting policies passed through Congress with the support of the American people? If so, what policies in particular were based on such manipulation of fear?

20.1.5
Such issues as gay marriage and stem cell research have been heavily debated by the American people. In your estimation, is this debate driven by fear?

20.1.6
We can safely assume that at least some fears are rational. What is the difference between a rational and an irrational fear? What can we, as Americans, do to avoid basing our political views on irrational fears?

---

1. Dr. Forbush. Retrieved online on December 22, 2008, from http://drforbush.tblog.com.

WELL POISONING

As discussed in chapter 4, on September 20, 2001, when the dust from the September 11, 2001, attacks had not yet settled, President George W. Bush said, "Either you are with us, or you are with the terrorists." Although he was addressing leaders of nations, his message also resonated with American citizens and even journalists. For example, as columnist Gregory Dennis stated,

> I could not help but think his threat was directed, not only at foreign leaders, but at me as well. Is it true that if I disagreed with his actions, I would be no better than the terrorists themselves; that I would be, dare I say . . . "un-American?"[12]

---

12. Gregory D. Dennis, "Silencing Dissent," *The Tech*, October 12, 2001. Retrieved online on March 25, 2009, from www-tech.mit.edu/V121/N50/col50gregd.50c.html.

The message that Dennis received was, you are "un-American," "unpatriotic," and maybe even a "terrorist" or a "traitor" if you don't stand with President George W. Bush. Despite the black-or-white fallacy inherent in this statement, it was still effective in intimidating others, including some in the media, into agreeing with the president's Iraq War policy.

The mechanism driving such manipulation is known as *well poisoning* or *poisoning the well*. This involves the attempt to cast something in a negative light in order to intimidate or frighten others into disclaiming or dissociating themselves from it. Such emotional appeals often use negatively charged emotive language for this purpose.

After having lived through the tragedy of the September 11, 2001, attacks, very few Americans would have contentedly accepted the label of "terrorist." The Bush administration knew this, and such intimidation provided a powerful device for manufacturing consent to a war that, as we have seen in chapter 14, was sold to the American public based on shoddy evidence.

In March 2003, taking their cue from President Bush's "with us or with the terrorists" logic, Republican representatives Bob Ney of Ohio and Walter Jones of North Carolina put up a sign at the register of the House cafeteria that stated, "Update: Now Serving in All House Office Buildings, 'Freedom Fries.'" They did this after France refused to support the U.S. invasion of Iraq. Many Americans followed the lead, denouncing and mocking the French for their "beret-wearing, wine-drinking, cheese-eating, Jerry Lewis–loving, literature-deconstructing, surrendering-to-the-Germans ways." As mentioned in chapter 4, the *New York Post* also called France and Germany "the axis of weasels" and ran a front-page photo that grafted giant weasel heads onto the French and German ambassadors to the United Nations.[13]

According to a Gallup poll taken in March 2003, the majority of Americans disliked the French, which represented a reversal of the static trend in the past decade for Americans to think favorably of the French.[14] While most Americans were at least able to see through the silliness of destroying French wine and renaming French fries "freedom fries" and French toast "freedom toast," this reversal in attitude speaks volumes about the dangerous susceptibility of many people to being manipulated and intimidated into changing their minds.

Political campaigns are notorious for playing on this human vulnerability to get votes. One very popular example of this is the so-called 3:00 a.m. ad put out by the Hillary Clinton campaign during its 2008 bid for the Democratic nomination for president of the United States. This video ad portrayed a child safely asleep in bed in the darkness and quiet of 3:00 a.m. The ad contained the following lines:

> It's 3 a.m., and your children are safe and asleep.
> But there's a phone in the White House, and it's ringing.
> Something's happening in the world.
> Your vote will decide who answers that call.

---

13. International Correspondents, CNN Transcripts, February 14, 2003. Retrieved online on February 14, 2009, from transcripts.cnn.com/TRANSCRIPTS/0302/14/i_c.01.html.

14. "France's Image Deteriorates after Media Criticism," Agendasetting.com. Retrieved online on April 9, 2009, from www.agendasetting.com/research/case_studies/eng3.pdf.

> Whether it's someone who already knows the world's leaders, knows the military—someone tested and ready to lead in a dangerous world.
>
> It's 3 a.m., and your children are safe and asleep.
>
> Who do you want answering the phone?

Clearly, the objective of this ad was to poison the well against the other front runner for the Democratic nomination (Barack Obama) by frightening voters into imagining someone answering the call who lacked the extensive political experience Clinton claimed to have.

Notice the use of emotively active phrases, such as "dangerous world," as well as the ad's attempt to raise in the minds of parents what is likely to be their greatest fear—namely that of something bad happening to their children. Thus, the ad plays both on voters' guilt and their fear. It aims at manipulating the fear that something might happen to their children if they don't vote for Hillary Clinton, and it plays on their propensity to experience guilt by suggesting that they would be jeopardizing the lives of their children if they didn't vote for her.

As discussed in chapter 16, we have considerable control over our emotional responses to situations. This is because these emotions are based on reasoning, and we have considerable control over how we reason. Indeed, if we accepted that Clinton was the most competent candidate to make decisions that could impact the lives of our children, then we would likely feel emotional guilt if we voted for someone other than Clinton. However, we have the power to scrutinize this premise and to demand evidence. Clearly, Clinton obtained much of the experience that she was speaking of in her capacity as first lady when her husband, William Jefferson Clinton, was president. But we should ask ourselves if most of this experience was even relevant to answering 3:00 a.m. phone calls. If it was, then we might expect to see more former first ladies throwing their hats into the ring. In fact, at the time of the campaign, Hillary Clinton had been a senator for about seven and a half years, while her opponent, Barack Obama, had been a senator for about four and a half years. This was a net difference in years of senatorial experience of three years in favor of Clinton. Did that alone make her more "tested and ready to lead in a dangerous world"? The answer to this question is not as clear as Clinton's ad would have led us to believe.

Exercise Set 20.2

Following are two commentaries. The first contains excerpts from a July 27, 2007, blog by conservative media pundit Michelle Malkin in which she criticizes Charles Schumer, Democratic senator from New York, for his regrets for having voted in favor of Bush's Supreme Court justice selections, John Roberts and John Alito.[1] The second is an excerpt from a "Special Comment" airing on December 6, 2007, on MSNBC's *Countdown with Keith Olbermann*. In this commentary, liberal pundit Keith Olbermann criticizes President George W. Bush for his claim not to have known about a recent national intelligence estimate in

1. Michelle Malkin, "Chuckie Schumer Admits: He's an Idiot . . . More: 'There Is No Doubt That We Were Hoodwinked,'" MichelleMalkin.com, July 27, 2007. Retrieved online on December 23, 2008, from http://michellemalkin.com/2007/07/27/chuckie-schumer-admits-hes-an-idiot.

which it was disclosed that Iran had discontinued its nuclear weapons program in 2005.[2] Read Malkin's and Olbermann's critiques, and respond to the questions that follow.

> "Chuckie Schumer Admits: He's an Idiot . . . More: 'There Is No Doubt That We Were Hoodwinked'"
>
> Sen. Charles Schumer plays the "dupe" card. Yes, you can question his competency now. He admits it—he's an idiot: . . .
>
> "Were we duped?" he asked.
>
> "Were we too easily impressed by the charm of nominee Roberts and the erudition of nominee Alito?" Schumer asked. "Did we mistakenly vote our hopes when our fears were more than justified by the ultraconservative records of these two men?"
>
> "Yes," he said
>
> As penance for the Democrats' self-admitted stupidity, Schumer is now threatening to snuff any new confirmations of Bush high court nominees. . . . Just a reminder that Chuck Schumer was the ringleader of the appalling circus that the Alito hearings devolved into last year. The made-for-TV antics and bloviating prompted none other than Robert Byrd to take to the floor to condemn the proceedings. . . . And now Schumer has the gumballs to bleat that the Dems were "duped" and "hoodwinked"? —Michelle Malkin

> "Special Comment"
>
> Finally, as promised, a "Special Comment" about the President's cataclysmic deceptions about Iran. There are few choices more terrifying than the one Mr. Bush has left us with tonight. We have either a President who is too dishonest to restrain himself from invoking World War III about Iran at least six weeks after he had to have known that the analogy would be fantastic, irresponsible hyperbole, or we have a President too transcendently stupid not to have asked, at what now appears to have been a series of opportunities to do so, whether the fairy tales he either created or was fed, were still even remotely plausible. The pathological presidential liar, or an idiot-in-chief. It is the nightmare scenario of political science fiction: A critical juncture in our history and, contained in either answer, a President manifestly unfit to serve, and behind him in the vice presidency, an unapologetic warmonger who has long been seeing a world visible only to himself. —Keith Olbermann

20.2.1
Identify all emotive language in the Malkin passage.

20.2.2
Identify all emotive language in the Olbermann passage.

20.2.3
In your estimation, should media pundits resort to well poisoning of the sort contained in these two passages? (Keep in mind that media pundits are presumed to be editorializing in contrast to reporting hard news.)

20.2.4
It seems safe to say that many, if not most, media pundits use strong emotive language. Nevertheless, there can still be a difference between competent media pundits and those who are not. What is the difference? Is Malkin competent? Is Olbermann competent? (You should feel free to Google further work of these two media personalities in answering these questions.)

20.2.5
What can consumers of news do to guard against being taken in by media pundits who use well poisoning to sell their views?

---

2. Brad Wilmouth, "Olbermann Calls Bush 'Pathological Liar or Idiot-in-Chief," NewsBusters, December 7, 2007. Retrieved online on December 23, 2008, from http://newsbusters.org/blogs/brad-wilmouth/2007/12/07/olbermann-calls-bush-pathological-liar-or-idiot-chief.

Exercise Set 20.3

20.3.1
On the Internet, find at least one further example of a political ad or speech advanced by a politician (as opposed to a journalist or media pundit) that uses well poisoning in its effort to score votes over a political opponent. Identify any emotive language used to poison the well. In your estimation, what measures can citizens of a democratic nation take in order to avoid being taken in by such political well poisoning?

20.3.2
The use of well poisoning by advertisers to frighten or intimidate consumers into purchasing their clients' products is commonplace in today's marketing environment. For example, in one advertisement for Rexona antiperspirant, a blind man drops a bag of garbage in front of a sexy woman in a green dress who has not (presumably) used Rexona. (Message: use Rexona or smell like a garbage dump!)[1] Find at least one advertisement that uses fear in such a way to sell a product.

---

1. Rexona ad, You Tube. Retrieved on December 22, 2008, from www.youtube.com/watch?v=RdGyrEZHUBQ.

MISUSE OF PITY

The sympathy or pity we feel for our fellow human beings moves us to help others in their times of need. It moves us to transcend narrow self-interest for the sake of helping to alleviate the pain and suffering in the world. According to philosopher David Hume, it is the emotion that undergirds all of the other moral sentiments, such as beneficence, humanity, friendship, gratitude, natural affection, and public spirit.[15]

Unfortunately, pity can also be misused. The *fallacy of misuse of pity* arises when one reaches a conclusion on the basis of pity instead of taking into account relevant facts or evidence or when one person tries to get another person to reach such a conclusion.

This fallacy often involves self-serving manipulation: (1) a first party presents himself (or another person or group of persons whom he represents) in a manner that is intended (by the first party) to arouse pity in a second party (for example, the first party cries), (2) the first party intends this arousal of pity in the second party to be a reason for the second party to do something x that the first party desires (for example, buying her something), and (3) the second party discounts relevant facts or evidence in doing x (buying something he can't afford).

While all three of the stated elements are commonly present, the fallacy of misuse of pity can also occur when just the third element is present, as when the first party does not intend to arouse pity in the second party, but the second party nevertheless acts out of pity for the first party, even though there is good reason

---

15. David Hume, *An Enquiry Concerning the Principles of Morals*, sec. 2, pt. 1. Retrieved online on April 9, 2009, from www.gutenberg.org/dirs/etext03/nqpmr10.txt.

not to do so. For example, one picks up a homeless hitchhiker (or a stray animal) out of pity without due consideration for the possible danger posed to oneself or other passengers.

The fallacy might also be committed when only the first two stated elements are present, as when the first party attempts to get the second party to act out of pity without due regard to relevant facts or evidence. For example, a bogus charitable organization displays pictures of emaciated children in order to get others to send money, even though no evidence is provided that the money will truly go to helping starving children.

A commonplace example of this fallacy is that of a defense attorney in a murder trial who appeals to the jury to feel pity for his client, who was raised in an abusive household. Indeed, we may feel sorry for those who have been victimized by others; however, this pity is irrelevant to the question of whether the defendant committed murder. As we have seen in discussing the O. J. Simpson case (chapter 12), our criminal justice system requires that a defendant be proven to have committed the crime "beyond a reasonable doubt." The question is thus whether the evidence does exactly this. Feeling pity for the defendant does not create such a reasonable doubt and cannot substitute for evidence.

Pity has been successfully misused by bogus charities to collect money for anything from hurricane relief to starving children in Africa. One common practice of scammers is to send e-mail messages out en masse that appeal to pity for purposes of getting recipients to send money or gaining access to bank accounts or credit card information. Unfortunately, enough people fall for these scams to make them a lucrative industry.

For example, the following e-mail message was posted to an Internet site that keeps track of such scams:

My Dear Beloved One,

My name is Mrs. Keith Patrick, widow to late Mr. James Patrick, former owner of PETROLEUM AND GAS company, here in Kuwait. I am 68 years old, suffering from long time cancer of the breast. From all indications my condition is really deteriorating and it's quite obvious that I won't live more than 2 months according to my doctors. This is because the cancer stage has gotten to a very bad stage, I don't want your pity but I need your trust.

My late husband died early last year from heart attack, and during the period of our marriage, we couldn't produce any child. My late husband was very wealthy and after his death, I inherited all his business and wealth. The doctor has advised me that I will not live for more than 2 months, so I have now decided to spread all my wealth, to contribute mainly to the development of charity in Africa, America, Asia and Europe. Am sorry if you are embarrassed by my mail. I found your e-mail address in the web directory, and i have decided to contact you, but if for any reason you find this mail offensive, you can ignore it and please accept my apology.

Before my late husband died he was a major oil tycoon, in Kuwait and deposited the sum of 5 million dollars (Five million dollars) in a company/Bank in Europe some years ago, thats all i have left now, i need you to collect this funds and distribute it yourself to charity homes and the needy. So that when i die my soul can rest in peace. The funds will entirely be in your hands and management. I hope God gives you the wisdom to touch very many lives, that is my main concern. 20% of this money will be for your time and effort, while 80% goes to charity homes and the needy. Please reply back to me on this email; mrs_keithpatrick@yahoo.com[16]

   Best Regards.

   Mrs. Keith Patrick.

Notice that this message states, "I don't want your pity but I need your trust." Paradoxically, by making this disclaimer, the scammer hopes to increase the chances that the recipient of the message will act out of pity. This is because a person who is dying of terminal cancer and not looking for pity from others will seem more honorable, therefore *more worthy of pity*, than a person who does in fact want the pity of others. Similarly, the apologetic demeanor of the message ("If for any reason you find this mail offensive, you can ignore it and please accept my apology") and the scammer's claim to be mainly concerned to "touch very many lives" are intended to give the request an air of sincerity and honor—again making it more likely that the e-mail recipient will act out of pity for her.

   Obviously, in order to "collect" the $5 million, one would have to provide one's bank account information; however, this is not mentioned at this juncture. Had Mrs. Patrick requested this information during this initial contact, she would have appeared too eager and exposed her true intentions. So, poor dying Mrs. Patrick has left such a mundane concern to be raised by her potential prey.

Rational Pity as an Antidote to the Misuse of Pity

This does not mean that because of the existence of such scams, we should turn off our pity and numb ourselves to the suffering and pain of the less fortunate. Indeed, as Hume surmised, such a world would be missing a chief ingredient of morality: the care of people for people.

   Still, our pity should be informed by the relevant evidence. The Mrs. Patricks of the world prey on those whose pity is blind: that is, not tempered or constrained by rational inspection of the evidence. What evidence do we have that Mrs. Patrick is really who she says she is? How do we know that such an unknown entity won't simply abscond with our money or our identities? Unless one has reasonable answers to such questions of evidence, it is folly to be motivated by pity.

   Charitable giving makes us *human* beings, but the sad faces of children on an ad may only be the bait of scam artists. Even when charities are legitimate, we may still not know what percentage of our gift goes to helping the ones in need, rather than to paying for administrative costs. Other things being equal, a charity that apportions a greater percentage of gifts received to helping the ones in need is the preferred charity. Asking the relevant questions can in this regard make the difference between helping others and wasting our time and money.

   The Internet and computer technologies have indeed opened new ways to the misuse of pity to scam human beings out of their savings, their personal property, and even their identities. However, such exploitation of human emotion requires that people place blind trust in others. When people ask questions and

---

16. Scam e-mails, 419 Baiter.com. Retrieved February 14, 2009, from www.419baiter.com/_scam_emails/419_emails_16017.html.

make decisions based on evidence and sound reasoning, they are less likely to be exploited.

Exercise Set 20.4

Find at least one example of a plea for help from a person, group of persons, or organization that you think is a misuse of pity. Then find at least one example that you believe avoids this fallacy. (You may find the Internet a useful source of such examples. Your examples may also be drawn from personal experiences.) Explain the differences between the cases that make one a fallacy and the other not.

Exercise Set 20.5

In 1995 Susan Smith, a twenty-three-year-old South Carolinian, was convicted of murdering her three-year-old and fourteen-month-old sons by rolling her car into a lake while the two children were asleep in the back seat. Smith had a troubled background.[1] Her father had committed suicide when she was six. Her stepfather sexually molested her when she was sixteen. Her ex-husband had cheated on her. She had attempted suicide at least twice in her life, once at the age of thirteen and again shortly after her high school graduation in 1989. Smith was sentenced to life in prison for her crimes rather than given the death penalty. Was it a fallacious misuse of pity to take these background conditions into account in sentencing her?

---

1. Bill Hewitt, "Tears of Hate & Pity," *People*, March 13, 1995. Retrieved online on December 23, 2008, from www.people.com/people/archive/article/0,,20105269,00.html.

Exercise Set 20.6

In the following, an anonymous blogger discusses a dysfunctional (abusive) relationship she is in. She contends that she stays (and "feels stuck") in this relationship because she feels sorry for her significant other. Read what she says, and respond to the questions that follow.

> I feel stuck. I got into a relationship a year ago and I now wish I had never met him. He can be a great guy and I think someday he will grow up, but right now he's still extremely inmature. He was raised in an extremely abusive family and he's continuing the trend of abuse. . . . Today I was yelling at him to get out of my way and he grabbed me by the back of the neck and held his hand over my mouth. He always carries a pocket knife. He took it out and held it to my throat. . . . We're not even together as boyfriend and girlfriend. But I still go to his apartment to talk to him because he gets lonely and I'm too weak to just say goodbye. Not because I love him, but because I feel sorry for him. When I think of him sitting in his apartment alone, I just think about how scared and lonely he must of been when he was a little boy. We were walking around Walmart today after all of this happened and I started crying. I kept looking around at all of the people wondering if they felt safe with the person they were with. If they had ever been choked or had a knife held to their throat. I kept wondering what I did to deserve getting hurt like this. I can't talk to anyone about what happens behind our closed doors. I feel like it's turned into our dirty little secret and for some reason I want to protect him.[1]

(continued)

---

1. Anonymous post, Abuse, Face the Issue Forums. Retrieved online on April 11, 2009, from www .facetheissue.com/community/archive/index.php?t-276.html.

20.6.1
Is the pity this woman is experiencing rational?

20.6.2
Based on what she says above, construct the emotional reasoning that appears to be sustaining the woman's pity. (Suggestion: review the definition of pity provided in chapter 16.)

20.6.3
Refute any irrational premises in the emotional reasoning constructed in 20.6.2.

20.6.4
Provide a rational antidote to any irrational premises refuted in 20.6.3.

20.6.5
The woman states, "I'm too weak to just say goodbye." This suggests that she lacks sufficient willpower to end her relationship. What might she do to increase her willpower?

20.6.6
Victims of domestic violence are often in greater danger of being harmed by the perpetrator when they attempt to leave the abusive relationship. What measures might this woman take to protect herself if she decides to leave the relationship?

RESPECT FOR RATIONAL SELF-DETERMINATION

As we have seen, all emotional appeals, whether in the form of appeals to force, well poisoning, or the misuse of pity, attempt to short-circuit rational thinking in order to affect the way other human beings respond. On a national level, in the last decade, there has been a shift away from a U.S. national defense policy based on the use of force as a last resort toward one of threats backed by an aggressive policy of preemptive war. At the same time, there has also been bountiful use of intimidation of citizens as well as the media through the use of well-poisoning language, such as "unpatriotic," "un-American," "terrorist," and "liberal media."

On the familial level, we have seen how relationships based on threats, the use of force, and even pity can be seriously dysfunctional. We have seen how such emotional appeals can lead to dysfunctional relationships on a global scale. And we have seen how a moralizing emotion like pity can be used against people of goodwill.

But all such emotional appeals can harm our families, friendships, and national and global ties only if we allow them to do so by surrendering our commitment to rational argument. Philosopher Immanuel Kant's moral theory prescribes that all human beings treat each other as "ends in themselves," that is, as rational, self-determining persons, rather than as mere things or objects to be manipulated and used as "mere means." Against Kant's appeal to reason, emotional appeals demean humanity by treating people as though they were objects. They degrade the human ability to engage in a rational discussion and to come to mutually agreeable conclusions based on the facts.

Such manipulative tactics degrade not only those targeted for such manipulation but also those who employ these devices, because in substituting coercion and chicanery for rational argument, one assumes that this is the only way one can achieve one's desired goals. This in turn means that those who use these manipulative tactics are themselves incapable of relating to others as rational persons and of commanding the respect accorded to rational persons. Such tactics therefore degrade all of us insofar as we are all human beings.

pg. 347-358: Ending point

- personal attacks
  [* ad hominem]
- Multiplying wrongs
- appeal to ignorance

21

Irrelevant Appeals

Irrelevant appeals are appeals to considerations that do not provide evidence or support for the conclusion under consideration. Chapter 20 examined emotional appeals, which are a kind of irrelevant appeal. This is because threats, intimidation, and the manipulation of pity do not provide evidence or support for a conclusion. For example, a jury's pity for a defendant accused of murder does not support a verdict of not guilty.

In this chapter we look at several more commonplace types of irrelevant appeal. In particular, we examine (1) personal attacks, (2) multiplying wrongs, (3) the appeal to ignorance, (4) circular reasoning, (5) sweeping generalizations, (6) the fallacy of composition, and (7) the fallacy of division.

PERSONAL ATTACKS

Personal attacks[1] involve attempting to disprove a statement by discrediting the person who made it or about whom it has been made. Personal attacks can take the form of name calling or claiming that the person in question is a hypocrite, has a questionable past, or has some other perceived character flaw or imperfection. The fallacy is committed when this attack on the person is irrelevant to the truth of the statement in question.

Abusive Personal Attacks

The name-calling version, often referred to as an *abusive personal attack*, involves the use of pejorative ascriptions to the person—for example, "idiot," "moron," "crazy," "asshole," and "bastard."[2] However, calling someone names like these

---

1. Also called, in Latin, *argumentum ad hominem*, meaning literally "argument against the man."
2. See also damnation of others, chapter 18.

does not count as evidence against a statement made by the person in question or about whom the statement has been made. For example, consider the following statement about Senator John Kerry, which was made during his 2004 campaign for the U.S. presidency:

> I said a couple of weeks back that John Kerry was too strange to be President, and a week or two earlier that he was too stuck-up to be President. Since I'm on an alliterative roll, let me add that he's too stupid to be President. What sort of idiot would make the centrepiece of his presidential campaign four months of proud service in a war he's best known for opposing?[3]

Here, Kerry is said to be too "strange," "stuck-up," and "stupid" to be president, and he is also called an "idiot" because his campaign stressed his military service record in the Vietnam War, even though he later opposed this war. Notice that calling Kerry all these names provides no evidence refuting his qualifications for the presidency or demonstrating that his campaign was in any way misguided. These terms are factually vacuous. Yet the author is attempting to pass these appellations off as evidence.

Tu Quoque (You Don't Practice What You Preach)

A further type of personal attack is sometimes called the *tu quoque* ("you also"). This fallacy tries to disprove a statement by showing that the person who made it is a hypocrite—that is, that he doesn't practice what he preaches. However, even a person who does not practice what he preaches can preach the truth.

For example, an alcoholic parent who warns his children about the dangers of drugs and alcohol can still speak the truth. Thus, it is a fallacious personal attack to argue that the parent doesn't practice what he preaches; therefore, his warning should not be heeded. The fact that such a parent does not provide a good role model is not evidence against the veracity of his advice. In fact, paradoxically, such a parent might have strong evidence for the dangers of drugs and alcohol as gleaned from his own addiction problem. Moreover, in some cases, such a person can provide a good role model of what *not* to do.

Consider the following attack on former vice president Al Gore, who is well-known for his admonitions about global warming:

> Graciously, Gore tells consumers how to change their lives to curb their carbon-gobbling ways. . . . But if Al Gore is the world's role model for ecology, the planet is doomed. For someone who says the sky is falling, he does very little. . . . Public records reveal that . . . he and his wife Tipper live in two properties: a 10,000-square-foot, 20-room, eight-bathroom home in Nashville, and a 4,000-square-foot home in Arlington, Va. . . . But according to public records, there is no evidence that Gore has signed up to use green energy in either of his large residences. . . . The issue here is not simply Gore's hypocrisy; it's a question of credibility. If he genuinely believes the apocalyptic

---

3. Mark Steyn, "Kerry: Strange, Stuck-up . . . and Stupid," Telegraph.com.uk, August 23, 2004. Retrieved online on March 25, 2009, from www.telegraph.co.uk/opinion/main.jhtml?xml=/opinion/2004/08/24/do2402.xml.

vision he has put forth and calls for radical changes in the way other people live, why hasn't he made any radical change in his life?[4]

Notice that the author contends that the issue is not just one of Gore's (alleged) hypocrisy but "a question of credibility." However, two distinct questions must not be confused: (1) does Gore practice what he preaches? and (2) are Gore's claims true?

In 2006 Gore starred in a popular documentary titled *An Inconvenient Truth*, which attempts to lay out carefully the scientific evidence for global warming and the planetary dangers it poses if humans are not proactive in averting them. Unfortunately, in launching a personal attack on Gore, the author does not address any of the evidence Gore presents in his film. Yet this is exactly what the author would have had to do in order to address the credibility of Gore's claims about global warming. Although pointing to Gore's failure to practice what he preaches (assuming he doesn't practice what he preaches) may speak to whether or not he is a good role model for his views, it has no bearing on the veracity of his views about global warming, which is a matter of evidence.

If the author simply intended to point out that Gore was not a consistent representative of his own views, then that would have been a relatively benign point, given the significance of the issue of global warming. Unfortunately, by confusing the issue of practicing what one preaches with the issue of credibility, he has invited his readers to draw a conclusion about the potential planetary crisis posed by global warming. Given the tremendous stakes involved in drawing such a conclusion, especially if Gore happens to be right about the evidence, this is not a relatively benign matter.

Prejudicial Attacks

Some personal attacks attempt to destroy a person's credibility in a particular area by pointing to a personal trait that is unrelated to competence in that area but may carry a social stigma or is associated with prejudice. For example, in September 2008, an openly gay Air America radio host, Rachel Maddow, got her own political talk show on MSNBC. Complaining about what he perceived to be MSNBC's "left-wing agenda," media analyst Tim Graham stated the following about Maddow when he was interviewed on Fox News:

> Not only is the damage already done, the damage continues. Not only are they keeping these people on for an hour a night, they're adding this lesbian Air America radio host, Rachel Maddow, on every night. So, I mean, they're really entrenching and solidifying a left-wing agenda on this network. Not just pulling something back.[5]

Notice that Graham referred to Maddow as "this lesbian Air America radio host," as if her sexual preference were evidence of her lack of competence in anchoring

---

4. Peter Schweizer, "Gore Isn't Quite as Green as He's Led the World to Believe," *USA Today*, December 7, 2006. Retrieved online on April 9, 2009, from www.usatoday.com/news/opinion/editorials/2006-08-09-gore-green_x.htm.

5. Fox News interview with Tim Graham of Media Analysis MRC, September 10, 2008. Retrieved online on March 25, 2009, from www.pensitoreview.com/2008/09/10/fox-news-d-team-sneers-lesbian-maddow.

a political talk show. Indeed, the fact that Maddow was a lesbian was plainly irrelevant to such competence. Nor was it relevant to whether she was "left-wing" since gay people can be conservative, centrist, or liberal, just like anyone else. More to the point, the attack appeared to have been aimed at a still commonplace prejudice against gays in an effort to get viewers to look askance at Maddow's credibility.

Genetic Attacks

An attack on a person need not be a fallacious personal attack if it can be shown to be relevant to disproving the statement in question. For example, arguing that a politician is not a viable candidate for public office due to a history of graft and corruption is not a personal attack inasmuch as this personal history is relevant to the candidate's ability to execute the duties of the office in question.

However, in some cases, an attack on the personal history or genesis of a person is irrelevant. For example, this would be the case if one were to discount parenting advice because the person giving it had a troubled past or came from a divorced household. In such cases, one can be said to commit the fallacy of *genetic personal attack*. This is when one tries to discredit what another person says by launching an irrelevant attack on his or her genesis or personal history.

Unfortunately, it seems that genetic personal attacks have sometimes been at the root of unfair legal practices. For example, U.S. rape laws prior to the 1970s allowed that the former unchastity of the prosecutrix could be used to impeach her complaint. This effectively created a legal double standard for women and men in rape cases. A prosecutrix had to remain chaste in order to receive a fair legal defense, while the sex life of a male defendant was not considered relevant.

Further, a woman could have been consenting in prior sexual encounters but not in the case under litigation. Just because a woman may have agreed to have sex with *some* individuals does not mean that she has agreed to have sex with *everyone*. Thus, beginning in the 1970s and continuing through the early 1980s, most U.S. states enacted so-called rape shield laws. These laws afforded rape complainants some legal protection against exploitation of their prior sexual relations with third parties as a way of trying to establish consent to sex with the defendant.

Nevertheless, these laws still allow for some problematic exceptions, such as permitting prior sexual relations with the defendant to count as admissible evidence. Since many rapes occur between prior sexual partners, such as spouses, ex-spouses, and boy- and girlfriends, allowing the prior sexual history of the defendant to count as admissible evidence can effectively pierce the protective barrier offered by a rape shield.

Thus, there are still questions as to whether current legal safeguards are sufficient to protect the victims of rape against further victimization by the court system itself. In the end, this may well depend on the discretionary application of the laws by judges and juries so that those who are victims of rape are not further victimized by fallacious personal attacks.

Conflicts of Interest

A commonplace way of dismissing the claim of another is to try to show that the claimant has a conflict of interest. In this context, to have a conflict of interest means to have a personal interest that has the potential to affect one's independence of judgment. For example, one might try to show that the findings of a drug study financed by a pharmaceutical company with a financial stake in its outcome are not credible due to a conflict of interest.

However, a conflict of interest does not necessarily disqualify a judgment but instead may underscore the need to look carefully at the evidence that supports it. This is why, for example, the *Journal of the American Medical Association* (*JAMA*) requires authors of studies to sign detailed financial-disclosure statements and includes any pertinent details with the publication of the research findings. According to *JAMA*, "Editors . . . have an obligation to present pertinent information related to the financial aspects of the articles they publish so readers can interpret the findings in light of this information."[6]

Nevertheless, according to *JAMA*, while conflicts of interest may "represent the potential for biased judgment," they are still "not an indicator of the likelihood or certainty that such judgments or compromises will occur."[7] Thus, the dismissal of findings due to a real or apparent conflict of interest without first examining the evidence upon which these findings are based is unjustified. While the potential biases of researchers are indeed serious concerns, it is the evidence and the inferences drawn from it that need to be inspected in order to determine the soundness of the findings.

In professional and business contexts, however, conflicts of interest can be relevant to assessing the credibility of one's judgment, as when a corporate or governing body is voting on an issue for which a member has a conflict of interest that could prejudice the vote. In such cases, arguing that the member's vote should not count may not be a fallacious personal attack. For example, in 2003 the Bush administration awarded a no-bid contract to Halliburton to do reconstruction work in Iraq. Because then Vice President Dick Cheney had been a former CEO of this giant corporation, one senator later called for a congressional investigation into whether the vice president had a role in awarding the no-bid contract.[8] In this context, where taxpayer dollars are being used to fund a private company, public accountability and the avoidance of even the appearance of a conflict of interest are arguably a serious concern and not a fallacious personal attack.

---

6. Catherine D. DeAngelis, MD, MPH; Phil B. Fontanarosa, MD; and Annette Flanagin, RN, MA, "Reporting Financial Conflicts of Interest and Relationships between Investigators and Research Sponsors," *JAMA* 286 (2001): 89–91. Retrieved online on January 3, 2009, from jama.ama-assn.org/cgi/content/full/286/1/89.

7. DeAngelis, Fontanarosa, and Flanagin, "Reporting Financial Conflicts of Interest."

8. Robert Yoon, "Democrats Want Cheney-Halliburton Probe," CNN.com, June 1, 2004. Retrieved online on April 18, 2009, from www.cnn.com/2004/ALLPOLITICS/06/01/cheney.halliburton/index.html.

MULTIPLYING WRONGS

It is quite common to find people attempting to defend objectionable conduct by claiming that it was done in retaliation for something wrong done to them. This type of irrelevant appeal has been used to try to justify anything from name-calling to murder. The fact is, by doing something wrong to another person who did something wrong to you, one does not rectify the first wrong but instead simply adds an additional wrong to the prior one. The old adage "Two wrongs don't make a right" is fundamentally sound. When you add one wrong (W) to a second wrong, you get two wrongs, not one right (R). That is, $(1W + 1W) = 2W$, but not $(1W + 1W) = 1R$.

Notice that the correctness of the first of these two equations assumes that W in each of its occurrences stands for the same value. Typically, W refers to a *moral* wrong.[9] Thus, if one person does something morally wrong to another person (say, lying), who in turn responds by doing something morally wrong to the first person (say, breaching a confidence), then we have two moral transgressions and not the coalescence of two wrongs into a single state of moral rightness (justice).

This *fallacy of multiplying wrongs* is quite prevalent in intimate relationships. In such contexts, "getting back" or "getting even" often means doing something one perceives to be even worse. For example, Jack might cheat on Jane, and then Jane might retaliate by cheating with Jack's best friend. Unfortunately, this mode of relating tends to exacerbate relationship problems rather than resolve them.

---

9. "Moral" is used here as distinct from "legal," although morally wrong acts that figure in this equation can also be illegal, such as when a motorist intentionally runs another car off the road as a way of "getting back" at the other driver.

In one famous example, a woman, suspecting her husband of having an affair, went to a Houston hotel, confronted her husband, got into a screaming match with the other woman, and then, with her teenage daughter in the passenger seat, proceeded to run her husband over, leaving the car parked on top of her dead husband's body.[10] The woman was now looking at a prison sentence for murder, and her child no longer had either parent there to raise her. Both spouses were also dentists whose practices were ended in that one moment of "getting even."

It is sometimes said that "revenge is sweet," but realistically speaking, it tends to be self-defeating, as was true in the above case. However, this does not mean that retribution, as such, is a fallacy. For example, there is no fallacy committed when a person is found guilty of a crime by a court of law and made to pay, say, by serving time in a state or federal prison.

In such cases of justified retribution, the logic is not one of visiting one wrong upon another. Instead, the logic is one of a justified and rational response to wrongful conduct. Thus, it is not wrong to put the jealous wife who murdered her husband in prison for her criminal conduct. However, it is patently wrong for the wife to have murdered her husband in the first place.

The Case of Capital Punishment

Some have argued that capital punishment commits the fallacy of multiplying wrongs. By this perspective, the legal practice of putting someone to death who has been found guilty of murder is not morally justifiable and is therefore (morally) wrong. The reasons for this conclusion vary and include the following: capital punishment is cruel and inhumane, it discriminates against minorities and those who cannot afford private counsel, it costs too much money to execute someone, it does not serve as a deterrent to murder and may even encourage additional violence, and it invariably leads to the execution of the innocent.[11]

On the other hand, others see the practice of capital punishment as morally acceptable and therefore do not believe that it commits the fallacy of multiplying wrongs. For example, some of these proponents believe that capital punishment does indeed deter murder or at least prevents a murderer from committing further murders. Others believe that it constitutes a just desert for someone guilty of murder. Still others argue that it costs less than keeping someone in prison for life.[12]

Accordingly, there is no settled view on whether capital punishment provides an example of multiplying wrongs. Much depends on the force of the arguments on either side. Given the definition of multiplying wrongs as doing something wrong to rectify a wrong, if capital punishment could reasonably be shown to be morally wrong, then it would, by definition, be a version of this fallacy. However, given that there is, presently, rational debate on whether capital punishment is (morally) wrong, it is questionable that it commits this fallacy.

---

10. "Jealous wife ran over cheating husband three times," The Sydney Morning Herald.com, August 6, 2002. Retrieved online on April 9, 2009, from www.smh.com.au/articles/2002/08/06/1028157922214.html.

11. Jeffrey Olen, Julie Van Camp, and Vincent Barry, *Applying Ethics: A Text with Readings* (Belmont, Calif.: Wadsworth, 2007).

12. Olen, Van Camp, and Barry, *Applying Ethics*.

Notice that the *legal* status of capital punishment is irrelevant to whether or not it commits this fallacy. States that permit capital punishment do consider the executioner's act justifiable homicide and therefore not (legally) murder. However, this still does not make it *morally* justified killing. This is because, notwithstanding its legal status, it can still be morally wrong. Only by assuming that what is legal must also be moral can the lawfulness of capital punishment automatically make it moral. However, this assumption is not necessarily true. For example, the Jim Crow laws legalized racially separate public facilities (such as restrooms and drinking fountains), but that didn't make the treatment blacks received under such laws moral.

Acting in Self-defense

Multiplying wrongs must also be distinguished from acting in self-defense. A person who defends herself against a second person engaged in wrongful conduct toward her need not have done anything wrong in defending herself. Therefore, she need not have committed this fallacy.

For example, the law permits a police officer in the line of duty to use deadly force on another person who is threatening his or her life or the lives of others. Similarly, a private person, group of people, city, state, or nation can defend itself against an assailant and not commit this fallacy.

However, cases of morally *unjustified* use of retaliatory force do commit this fallacy. For example, al-Qaeda could not rationally hope to rectify any perceived injustice committed by the West by flying planes into the World Trade Center and Pentagon, taking the lives of nearly three thousand people. Terrorist attacks like this do not rectify wrongs; instead, they make things worse.

Rational Dialog as an Antidote

A constructive antidote to multiplying wrongs is engagement in rational dialog between disputants. From the "tit for tat" of interpersonal relations to mass genocide committed in Rwanda, Darfur, and Bosnia, history has repeatedly shown that attempts at rectifying a perceived wrong by committing a further moral transgression tend to inflame hostilities and add more misery and suffering to the world.

In contrast, open, rational dialog permits grievances to be voiced, possible solutions explored, and mutually agreeable settlements reached. All too often, whether in the context of interpersonal relations or international ones, wrongs are heaped upon wrongs in an effort to attain justice. In the end, the antagonists must come to the peace table anyway and engage in rational dialog. Unfortunately, by then valuable assets, including human lives, have been needlessly wasted.

Exercise Set 21.3

In the following passage from "Timothy McVeigh Must Not Die: An Eye for an Eye Leaves the Whole World Blind," Mario Giardiello maintains that capital punishment is always wrong because it is always wrong to kill.[1] Giardiello refuses to admit any legitimate exceptions to killing, including capital punishment in the case of Timothy McVeigh, who was sentenced to death and executed on June 11, 2001, for bombing a federal building in Oklahoma City on April 19, 1995, killing 168 people. Is Giardiello's argument a sound one? Provide a rational defense of your response.

> Simply put: I am against killing of any kind because it is never right to kill. Let God be the judge of these poor souls and let us be more concerned with being better role models for our children. As a teacher I believe instituting the death penalty teaches our children that sometimes it is okay to kill. I disagree. I think it is always wrong and we should send out a consistent message to our children: it is always wrong to kill. Killing people can never be good for our children. Not even for the "unapologetic and unflinching in the face of death" Timothy J. McVeigh. For the sake of the nineteen children killed in the blast let's teach all others that it is never okay to kill not even for the government. Beating a child for hitting is giving our children mixed messages. So is showing them that some people in some situations deserve to be murdered. Let's be consistent in teaching our children.

---

1. Mario Giardiello, "Timothy McVeigh Must Not Die: An Eye for an Eye Leaves the Whole World Blind," PoliticalUSA.com, March 15, 2001. Retrieved online on January 3, 2009, from www.politicalusa.com/columnists/giardiello_mario/mario_019.htm.

APPEAL TO IGNORANCE

A lack of evidence cannot itself ordinarily be counted as evidence. The *fallacy of appeal to ignorance* is committed when one attempts to prove a conclusion true because there is insufficient evidence to prove it false or to prove it false because there is insufficient evidence to prove it true. This fallacy is often committed in the context of highly debated issues. For example, an atheist (disbeliever in God's existence) might argue that God does not exist because there is insufficient evidence to prove that God does exist. On the other hand, a theist (believer in God's existence) might argue that God does exist because there is insufficient evidence to prove that God does not exist.

The fallacy sometimes arises in moral disagreements. Just because one has shown that a moral argument has a questionable premise, it does not follow that the conclusion of the argument is false. For example, consider the argument from personhood, a very popular antiabortion stance:

Major premise: All acts of killing innocent persons are wrong.
Minor premise: All abortions are the killing of an innocent person.
Conclusion: All abortions are wrong.

A popular line of attack against this argument is to attempt to show that the minor premise is questionable because it is not clear how to define a person, and in any case, it is unlikely that at an early embryonic stage, any reasonable definition of personhood (say, one in terms of the capacity to think, socially interact, or live outside the uterus) will be satisfied. Further, with respect to the major premise, it has been argued that not all acts of killing innocent persons are wrong. For example, in so-called lifeboat cases, one innocent person may need to die in order that the others may live. Thus, in the case of locked twins (where one twin is breech and locked at the chin with the other), one twin will need to be decapitated in order for the other to be delivered. Otherwise both twins will die.

There are also, of course, the more usual lines of attack on the major premise as a universal statement. What if the mother's life is in danger unless the fetus is aborted? Or what if the pregnancy is due to rape or incest? Does this still mean that it's wrong to abort the fetus if, as the minor premise says, it is an innocent person?

So what do these criticisms prove? If they are successful, they show only that the argument from personhood, in its present form, fails to prove true the conclusion that all abortion is wrong. But neither does this failure prove false the conclusion that all abortion is wrong. This conclusion might still be true because it might still be possible to find another argument that proves it to be so. Unless we can provide a convincing argument to show that there are no such arguments, we must rest our case with having shown only that this particular argument has not succeeded in proving the conclusion true.

The Appeal to Ignorance and WMD in Iraq

Prior to invading Iraq, the Bush administration argued that the leader of Iraq, Saddam Hussein, had not cooperated with the weapons inspectors who were looking for weapons of mass destruction (WMD) in Iraq. It is arguable that at least part of the reason for the Bush administration's suspecting that there were WMD in Iraq was its belief that Hussein had not provided sufficient evidence that there were no such weapons in Iraq. If this is the case, then it may have been at least partly a fallacious appeal to ignorance that took us to war in Iraq.

Here is what President George W. Bush said in his State of the Union address on January 28, 2003, before taking the United States to war in Iraq on March 20, 2003:

> The United Nations concluded in 1999 that Saddam Hussein had biological weapons sufficient to produce over 25,000 liters of anthrax. . . . *He's given no evidence that he has destroyed it.* The United Nations concluded that Saddam Hussein had materials sufficient to produce more than 38,000 liters of botulinum toxin. . . . *He's given no evidence that he has destroyed it.* Our intelligence officials estimate that Saddam Hussein had the materials to produce as much as 500 tons of sarin, mustard and VX nerve agent. . . . *He has given no evidence that he has destroyed them.* U.S. intelligence indicates that Saddam Hussein had upwards of 30,000 munitions capable of delivering chemical agents. . . . *He's given no evidence that he has destroyed them.* From three Iraqi defectors we know that Iraq, in the late 1990s, had several mobile biological weapons labs. . . . *He's given no evidence that he has destroyed them.*[13]

From the obvious repetition of the statement "He's given no evidence that he has destroyed them," it is clear that Bush based his conclusion that Hussein still had WMD on a lack of evidence rather than on evidence. Thus, his argument appears to have been that

---

13. George W. Bush, State of the Union, January 28, 2003. Italics added. Retrieved online on September 27, 2008, from www.whitehouse.gov/news/releases/2003/01/20030128-19.html.

Saddam Hussein has given no evidence that he destroyed his WMD.
Therefore, Saddam Hussein did not destroy his WMD.

This argument is clearly a fallacious appeal to ignorance. As mentioned in chapter 14, it turned out that Saddam Hussein did not have stockpiles of WMD when the war began, and whatever few of them remained were so old that they had obsolesced.

In some cases, however, it may not be a fallacy to use the lack of evidence as being itself evidence. For example, after the U.S. invasion of Iraq, the more the United States and its allies searched Iraq for WMD, the more evident it became that there simply were no such dangerous weapons. So, ironically, the lack of evidence for the existence of WMD actually became evidence that there really were no such weapons after all. Why? Because if there were such weapons, we would have found them![14]

Here is an argument that supports the conclusion that there are no WMD in Iraq:

We have no evidence to prove that there are WMD in Iraq.
We would have found evidence for WMD in Iraq had there been such weapons in Iraq.
Therefore, there are no WMD in Iraq.

Without the second premise, the above argument would commit the fallacy of appeal to ignorance. However, with this premise added, this argument appears to be sound. Thus, in cases such as this one, in which we are justified in believing that our lack of evidence is due to the fact that there really is no such evidence, we do not commit a fallacious appeal to ignorance by using such lack of evidence as evidence.

Asking for Evidence as an Antidote to the Fallacious Appeal to Ignorance

As a general antidote against committing the fallacy of appeal to ignorance, it is important to ask where the evidence is for a conclusion before embracing it. When you hear phrases like "It has not been proven," "There is no evidence," and "There is no reason to believe," then ordinarily we would expect the *withholding* of belief. For example, if there is no evidence (or at least not sufficient evidence) to believe that God exists, then agnosticism (neither affirming nor denying the statement that God exists) is appropriate.

In other words, the lack of evidence means that we must proceed with an open mind, keeping open the possibility of future evidence that may either confirm or disconfirm the conclusion in question. This open-mindedness·in the face of insufficient evidence is what we would expect from a critical and free thinker. Basing one's conclusions on the appeal to ignorance is not.

---

14. The only other possibility was that prior to or during the invasion, Saddam destroyed these weapons or else hid them elsewhere in the world. This claim, however, is itself questionable and lacks supportive evidence.

Exercise Set 21.4

Each of the following arguments addresses the absence of evidence for something. Discuss the rationality of each, and indicate whether a fallacious appeal to ignorance has been committed.

21.4.1

"I read a statistic somewhere that said that there are 100 billion stars in the Milky Way, and another 100 billion galaxies out there. Why would earth be the only planet with water, oxygen, and nutrient rich ground out there? That's just what's required for life as we know it. Who's to say there aren't other life forms out there that can use other resources to survive." —Blogger[1]

21.4.2

"Sometimes atheists assert that there is no proof that God exists. The only problem is that an atheist cannot logically make that claim. In order to state that there is no proof for God's existence, the atheist would have to know all alleged proofs that exist in order to then state that there is no proof for God's existence. But, since he cannot know all things, he cannot logically state there is no proof for God's existence. At best, an atheist can only state that of all the alleged proofs he has seen thus far, none have worked. He could even say that he believes there are no proofs for God's existence. But then, this means that there is the possibility that there is a proof or proofs out there and that he simply has not yet encountered one."[2]

21.4.3

"Is there anyway for you to prove that I am conscious at all? Since you can't see what I'm seeing and feel what I'm feeling, how do you know I am experiencing the same things that you are? Right now, science cannot prove that the color green looks the same to you as it does to me. What's even weirder is that you can't prove scientifically that anyone else is conscious in the same way you are. In other words, you cannot prove that others around you are having the same first person subjective experience you are. . . . So if you can't be sure anyone but you is actually conscious, how can you be sure of anything? Wouldn't it then be possible that everything in the world was imaginary like a dream? I'm not saying this is the likely answer, I'm just asking, given what we don't know about the universe and ourselves, isn't it possible?" —Steve Olson[3]

21.4.4

"There is no such thing as ghosts! In order for me to believe in ghosts and hauntings I would have to believe in a miriad of other supernatural things like souls, the after life. etc. I have seen no real proof of ghosts just a bunch of frauds running around with weird equipment trying to be the Ghostbusters!" —Blogger[4]

---

1. Aconstas1, "Re: The Disclosure Project," VodaHost, March 21, 2007. Retrieved on January 3, 2009, from www.vodahost.com/vodatalk/reviews-share-your-thoughts/9417-disclosure-project.html.

2. Christian Apologetics and Research Ministry, "There Is No Proof That God Exists," carm.org. Retrieved online on January 3, 2009, from www.carm.org/atheism/noproof.htm.

3. Steven Olson, "Do You Know What Is Real?" SteveOlson.com. Retrieved online on April 7, 2009, from www.steve-olson.com/do-you-know-what-is-real.

4. Phreekshow, "There Is No Such Thing As Ghosts!" Blurtit, October 27, 2007. Retrieved online on January 3, 2009, from www.blurtit.com/forandagainst/There_Is_NO_Such_Thing_As_Ghosts.

CIRCULAR REASONING

Circular reasoning involves attempting to infer a conclusion from a set of premises that contains the very conclusion being inferred. The problem with such an argument is not that it is invalid; it isn't. Indeed, the argument form, "p, therefore p," is valid. The problem with any argument of this form is that it is empty and useless.

Logically Equivalent Circularity

Consider, for example, this argument given by President George W. Bush in Philadelphia on December 12, 2005:

> It's a myth to think that I'm not aware that there's opinions that don't agree with mine, because I'm fully aware of that.[15]

The phrase "It's a myth to think that" is a longer way of saying "It is false that," and the phrase "I'm not aware that" means "It's false that I'm aware that." Thus, more formally stated, Bush's argument looks like this:

> I am fully aware that there are opinions that don't agree with mine.
>   Therefore, it is false that it is false that I'm aware that there are opinions that don't agree with mine.

Accordingly, the form of this argument is as follows:

> p.
> Therefore, not (not-p).

Notice, however, that p is logically equivalent to not (not-p).[16] Hence, Bush's argument is valid but entirely vacuous, a case of deriving p from p.

Extended Circularity

Of course, the circularity of circular reasoning may loom wider. Consider the following dialog:

> Matt: I need to buy a car.
>
> Barb: Why do you need a car?
>
> Matt: I need it to get to work.
>
> Barb: Why do you need to get to work?
>
> Matt: So that I can make money.
>
> Barb: Why do you need to make money?
>
> Matt: So that I can buy a car.

Here, Matt ultimately argues that he needs a car because he needs to buy the very same car that he needs. Clearly, unless Matt can provide an independent reason

---

15. George W. Bush, Philadelphia, PA, December 12, 2005. Retrieved online on April 9, 2009, from politicalhumor.about.com/library/blbushisms2005.htm.

16. This follows from the rule of double negation. For example, the statements "It is raining" and "It is not the case that it is not raining" are logically equivalent. See chapter 5.

for needing a car (that is, one that doesn't assume the very same need he is trying to justify), he fails to justify his purported need for a car.

Circularity That Conceals Important Issues

Circular arguments can not only fail to provide rational justifications for one's conclusions but also serve to conceal substantive issues behind a veil of empty truisms. For example, consider the following argument presented by one blogger:

> You shouldn't be praised for doing the right thing, you should do it because it's the right thing to do.[17]

The phrase "right thing to do" means the same thing as "what you should do." Thus, "You should do the right thing because it's the right thing to do" means "You should do what you should do because it's what you should do." Of course, this is true, but it's also lame.

The same blogger goes on to give this example:

> I've seen it over and over. My friend made it through rehab and they said you are a hero for doing this.

Here, the blogger uses "going through rehab" as an example of "the right thing to do" and complains that his friend should have gone through rehab because it was the right thing to do (what he should have done), and others shouldn't have praised him for it.

Notice that if going through rehab was the right thing for his friend to have done, then there must have been something about rehab *in virtue of which* it was the right thing to do—for example, that it could help his friend kick a dangerous addiction. Thus, without circularity, the blogger might have instead said that his friend should have gone through rehab because it could have helped him to kick a dangerous addiction, and others shouldn't have extended praise for this.

But why not extend praise? Shouldn't people be encouraged to seek rehab, thereby taking responsibility for their addiction problems, and supported for doing so? After all, isn't this a central component of support groups like Alcoholics Anonymous? Unfortunately, regardless of the answers to these questions, by getting entangled in a web of synonymy relationships between moral terms, the blogger never gets past empty truisms to address such substantive questions. In this manner, circular reasoning can conceal important issues, and one can waste a considerable amount of time spinning one's wheels.

Exercise Set 21.5

Provide at least one example of a logically equivalent circular argument, an extended circular argument, and a circular argument that conceals an important issue. You may gather these examples from Internet sources, other media sources, or personal experiences.

---

17. Anonymous blogger, Help.com. Retrieved online on April 9, 2009, from help.com/post/176484 -help-wanted-heroes-wanted-t.

SWEEPING GENERALIZATION

Sweeping generalization is the opposite of hasty generalization.[18] While the latter infers universal statements from particular statements, sweeping generalization infers particular statements from universal statements. The fallacy arises when one attempts to apply a rule to a particular case to which it does not properly apply.

To use an example from philosopher H. L. A. Hart, suppose there is a municipal rule that says, "No vehicles are allowed in the park."[19] Clearly, the rule would include automobiles and motorcycles, but what about skateboards? Insofar as the purpose of the rule is to prevent dangers to picnickers and others who are using the park, it would be arguable that skateboards should also be considered vehicles. But what about an old World War II tank that might be placed on display? Would this also constitute a "vehicle" for purposes of the municipal rule?

If the word "vehicle" is taken literally, then we also have to exclude the tank from the park, just like automobiles and motorcycles. On the other hand, this would not appear to follow the spirit of the rule, which presumably is to keep park goers safe. In this case, insisting that the tank be kept from the park would commit the fallacy of sweeping generalization. This is because the municipal rule in question was not intended to apply in such a case.

Compare the U.S. Justice Department's attempt to apply a federal drug-trafficking law to an Oregon state law that allowed physician-assisted suicide. In 1994, the state of Oregon passed the Oregon Death with Dignity Act (ODDA) by public referendum (the state passed it again in 1997 by public referendum after it had been challenged and tied up in the courts). This act permitted a physician to assist in the suicide of a competent, terminally ill patient by allowing the physician to prescribe a lethal dosage of a drug upon both written and oral request by the patient.

However, in 2001, then Attorney General John Ashcroft issued a directive (the so-called Ashcroft Directive), which sought to illegalize the ODDA by declaring it in violation of the Controlled Substance Act (CSA) of 1970. The latter act was intended to combat drug abuse by defining the parameters of legitimate and illegitimate distribution and dispensation of controlled substances such as heroin, cocaine, and opium.

However, the Ninth Circuit Court invalidated the Ashcroft Directive, arguing that it was unlawful and unenforceable because it violated the plain language of the CSA, contravened Congress's express legislative intent, and overstepped the bounds of the attorney general's statutory authority.[20]

As the court surmised, the "express legislative intent" (or "spirit") of the CSA was to stop drug traffickers from promoting drug abuse, not to punish physicians for helping terminally ill patients seek "death with dignity." Therefore, any

---

18. See chapter 9.

19. H. L. A. Hart, *The Concept of Law* (London: Oxford University Press, 1961), 124.

20. United States Court of Appeals for the Ninth Circuit, *State of Oregon v. John Ashcroft, Attorney General,* May 7, 2003, Findlaw.com. Retrieved online on April 9, 2009, from files.findlaw.com/docviewer/viewer_news.html#http://news.findlaw.com/hdocs/docs/deathwithdignityact/orash52604opn.pdf.

attempt to apply this law to physician-assisted suicide was a misuse of the law. It was a fallacy of sweeping generalization.

In 2006, in *Gonzales v. Oregon*, the Supreme Court followed the Ninth Circuit's reasoning and affirmed that the CSA did not apply to the case of physician-assisted suicide.[21] Thus, the Supreme Court did not address whether a citizen had a constitutional right to die; nor did it say that Congress could not enact laws barring states from allowing doctors to help patients end their lives. The decision was simply a declaration that the CSA could not *rationally* be applied to the case of physician-assisted suicide. This underscores that there are meaningful limits to what can be subsumed under a legal rule.

Legal rules also admit of exceptions: that is, cases where there are extenuating circumstances that militate against applying the rule. For example, ordinarily a health-care provider would be required to obtain the informed consent of a patient or her legal guardian before providing treatment. However, in emergency situations where the administration of treatment is necessary in order to save the life of the patient, the health-care provider may lawfully administer the necessary treatment without the explicit consent of the patient. In such cases, consent is taken to be implied, even though the patient has not actually consented. Under these conditions, it is a sweeping generalization to insist on the explicit consent of the patient at the expense of letting her die.

Like legal rules, the *moral* rules that we apply in the contexts of everyday life also admit of relevant exceptions. Thus, while we would ordinarily expect a person to obey the rule of keeping promises, cases may arise in which competing moral considerations conflict with the keeping of a promise. For example, what if keeping a promise would lead to the infliction of serious bodily injury or death to a third party? In such a case, it is impossible to at once satisfy both rules—promise keeping and not harming others. Accordingly, one such rule will have to be allowed to take precedence over the other.

This means that everyday moral rules such as keeping one's promises, telling the truth, not stealing, and not harming others cannot *all* be taken to be absolute—that is, as being without exception. This is because such rules, as just illustrated, can conflict with each other in practical situations. This, in turn, means that any set of potentially conflicting moral rules must always include some exceptions. To claim otherwise is to extend the application of such rules beyond their logical limits and therefore to commit the fallacy of sweeping generalization.[22]

This potential for conflict must also be accommodated in any system of codified ethical rules such as those of professional ethics. For example, Rule 1.6 of the American Bar Association's *Model Rules of Professional Conduct* requires that a law-

---

21. *Supreme Court of the United States, Gonzales, Attorney General, et al. v. Oregon et al.*, Cornell University Law School. Retrieved online on April 9, 2009, from www.law.cornell.edu/supct/html/04-623. ZS.html.

22. Some ethical theories, such as that of Immanuel Kant, avoid conflict by appealing to only *one* absolute rule ("the categorical imperative") as the standard of morality. In this way, Kant avoids having to make exceptions to rules. However, as critics of Kant point out, this is to purchase consistency and avoid conflict at the expense of an inflexible view of morality. For example, for Kant, deceitful promising is *always* wrong, even if it is undertaken to save many lives. See, for example, Thomas E. Hill Jr., *Dignity and Practical Reason in Kant's Moral Theory* (Ithaca, N.Y.: Cornel University Press, 1992), especially ch. 10.

yer not disclose information related to representation of a client. However, it also permits disclosure of such confidential client information "to prevent reasonably certain death or substantial bodily harm."[23] Hence, a lawyer who insisted that she *must* keep her client's confidence, even in the face of "reasonably certain death or substantial bodily harm," would extend the requirement to keep clients' confidences beyond what the American Bar Association intended and would therefore commit the fallacy of sweeping generalization.

Exercise Set 21.6

Provide at least one example of a sweeping generalization. This example may be found on the Internet or in other media sources.

THE FALLACY OF COMPOSITION

The *fallacy of composition* is committed when one infers that a whole thing has a certain property because some or all of its parts have it. For example, because each part of a machine is simple, we cannot infer that the machine *as a whole* is also simple. Quite obviously, the conclusion does not follow since a very complex machine could have numerous simple parts. In general, we cannot therefore assume that what is true of the part is necessarily true of the whole. By reasoning from this assumption, one commits the fallacy of composition.

A prevalent example of this fallacy is one sometimes used to charge media companies with being liberal. This argument proceeds as follows:

Reporters tend to be liberal.
Therefore, the media companies in which reporters are employed tend to be liberal.

Clearly, the major premise of this argument is a version of the fallacy of composition—that what's true of the part must be true of the whole:

(Major premise) If reporters tend to be liberal, then the media companies in which they are employed must be liberal.
Reporters tend to be liberal.
Therefore, the media companies in which reporters are employed are liberal.

While it may be true that many journalists are socially liberal (for example, pro-choice and anti–death penalty), this does not mean that the companies in which they are employed, such as the major television and cable networks and the major newspapers, are also socially liberal. Actually, as will be discussed in chapter 22, these giant corporations tend to be driven more by concern for increasing their bottom lines than by promoting a liberal social agenda. Consequently, it does not

---

23. American Bar Association, *Model Rules of Professional Conduct* (2008). Rule 1.6. Retrieved online on October 2, 2008, from www.abanet.org/cpr/mrpc/rule_1_6.html.

much matter what the views are of the individual journalists working for these large news corporations. What ultimately gets aired will depend on the editorial policies of the corporation, which are in turn largely a function of what is profitable. Unfortunately, the frequent talk about "the liberal media" fails to distinguish between what is true of individual journalists and what is true of the news corporations that employ them.

The fallacy of composition, as just illustrated, needs to be distinguished from hasty generalization. In the latter, one infers a universally quantified statement from a particular statement. A universally quantified statement says something about each and every member of a class of things. For example, the fact that some men cheat on their spouses does not mean that each and every man cheats on his spouse. This would be a hasty generalization.

In contrast, in committing the fallacy of composition, one infers a statement about a whole from a statement about its parts. However, a statement about a whole is not the same thing as a universally quantified statement. For example, in saying that the membership of Weight Watchers is expanding, we do not mean that *each and every member* of Weight Watchers is expanding.

In chapter 18, we discussed damnation. This fallacy is a form of fallacy of composition. For example, because there are bad things in the world, it does not follow that the world as a whole is bad. In fact, having bad things in the world might make the world even better. For example, danger is bad; however, without danger, we could not have courage, and arguably a world where there is courage is better than a world where there is not. More generally, a world without evil would be a world without virtue, since virtue consists in overcoming some evil or other. Yet a world with virtue is arguably a better world than one without it.

It is also a fallacy of composition to infer that a property that applies to some aspect of a person must also apply to the person *as such*. Epictetus makes this point clear:

> The following statements constitute a *non sequitur*: "I am richer than you are, therefore I am superior to you"; or, "I am more eloquent than you are, therefore I am superior to you." But the following conclusions are better: "I am richer than you are, therefore my property is superior to yours"; or, "I am more eloquent than you are, therefore my elocution is superior to yours." But *you* are neither property nor elocution.[24]

Thus, what is true of some part of a person (the superiority of one's wealth or elocution) is not necessarily true of *the person* (the superiority of the person).

A further, related version of the fallacy of composition consists of attributing to someone a disposition to think, feel, or act in a certain way because he or she has thought, acted, or felt in that way before on limited occasions. For example, a person is not benevolent for having performed a singular kind act; nor is a person pessimistic for having thought pessimistically about some specific thing; nor is a person negative for having been negative on a given occasion.

Thus, it is a fallacy of composition to argue,

---

24. Epictetus, *Encheiridion*, in *Philosophic Classics: From Plato to Derrida*, ed. Forrest E. Baird and Walter Kaufmann, third ed. (Upper Saddle River, N.J.: Prentice Hall, 2007), 266.

You acted in a virtuous way (told the truth, or showed courage, or kept your promise, etc.).
Therefore, *you* are virtuous (truthful, courageous, trustworthy, etc.).

Indeed, this inference is a fallacy because to have a particular virtue means to have a settled *disposition* to perform in the said virtuous way.

Dispositional properties such as virtues and temperament are arguably formed as a result of practice. As Aristotle stated,

> By doing the acts that we do in our transactions with other men, we become just or unjust, and by doing the acts that we do in the presence of danger, and being habituated to feel fear or confidence, we become brave or cowardly. The same is true of appetites and feelings of anger; some men become temperate and good-tempered, others self-indulgent and irascible, by behaving in one way or the other in the appropriate circumstances.[25]

Accordingly, one cannot correctly be called brave for having acted bravely on a limited set of occasions, for the settled habit or disposition of bravery is not thereby established.

Just how often one must behave in a given virtuous manner before one can correctly be said to acquire the virtue (courage, truthfulness, friendliness, justness, or the like) cannot be precisely quantified. However, this does not mean that there are no clear cases of one who is virtuous in a given way and one who is not. Thus, a chronic liar can readily be distinguished from a truthful person, even though there are questionable cases in between.

As discussed in chapter 18, it is generally not constructive to apply negative global ratings such as "evil" and "no good" to persons. The same can also be said of *affirmative* global ratings such as "good" and "virtuous." This is because, like negative global ratings, affirmative global ratings fail to provide adequate action guides for forging interpersonal relations. Thus, in befriending or hiring a person, we may be interested in knowing whether he or she can be trusted to keep confidences. In such practical contexts, sticking to the specific virtuous behavioral, emotional, or cognitive dispositions is accordingly more to the point than speaking in terms of global ratings.

Exercise Set 21.7

Determine which (if any) of the following contains a fallacy of composition.

21.7.1
Plato was a philosopher and a teacher. Therefore, all philosophers are teachers.

(continued)

---

25. Aristotle, *Nicomachean Ethics*, in *The Basic Works of Aristotle*, ed. Richard McKeon (New York: Random House, 1941), bk. 2, ch. 1, 953.

21.7.2

"Have the carpenter . . . and the tanner certain functions or activities, and has man none? Is he born without a function? Or as eye, hand, foot, and in general each of the parts evidently has a function, may one lay it down that man similarly has a function apart from all these? What then can this be?" —Aristotle[1]

21.7.3

The Beatles were a great rock band because John Lennon was a great musician and song-writer.

21.7.4

Humans are better than all other animals because they are more intelligent.

21.7.5

"Earlier this month, as part of a regular check up, I had an echo cardiogram. The results showed that my heart is pumping oxygen back into my veins at the rate of 71%. That may not sound impressive; however, the doctor then told me the normal range is 60–65%. I am happy to include this statistic in my testimonial. I am happy to be a 65 year old female in such good shape."[2]

21.7.6

The economy is improving because the stock market is improving.

21.7.7

Everything in the world has a cause. Therefore, the world itself must have a cause—and this cause we call God.

---

1. Aristotle, *Nicomachean Ethics*, bk. 1, ch. 7.
2. Anonymous training client, Scott Fitness.com. Retrieved online on January 4, 2009, from www.scottfitness.com/trainers/trainers-jeff-fisk.php.

THE FALLACY OF DIVISION

The *fallacy of division* is the converse of the fallacy of composition. Whereas division assumes that what is true of the part must also be true of the whole, composition assumes that what is true of the whole must also be true of the part. That is, composition infers that a part has a given property because the whole has it. For example, the fact that water is wet does not mean that hydrogen and oxygen are also wet. Because a human being is a person, it does not follow that the parts of a person (arms, legs, and so forth) are also persons.

We have just seen that from the fact that the reporters of a media company may be socially liberal, one cannot infer that the media company itself is socially liberal. This inference is not improved by reversing its direction. Thus, from the fact that a media company is bottom-line oriented, one cannot infer that the reporters who work for the company are themselves also bottom-line oriented.[26] Nor can one infer that these reporters agree with the policies that the company itself holds. In fact, most reporters are vigilant in covering the news, and many do so out of a

---

26. "Reporters" here must be distinguished from high-paid anchors of major news corporations such as Chris Matthews of MSNBC or Bill O'Reilly of Fox, who may be as bottom-line oriented as the companies they work for. Nevertheless, it is still a fallacy of division to assume that such journalists are so oriented simply because the companies they work for are this way.

sense of professional responsibility. Many even risk their lives on the ground in war zones and in other dangerous circumstances. Hence, it is a fallacy of division to assume that if reporters work for large media corporations that are bottom-line oriented, they cannot be dedicated journalists. Unfortunately, criticisms of reporters lodged by some left-leaning media critics are misplaced when they are aimed at reporters rather than at the companies that employ them.

Consider, for example, the following critique of journalistic institutions:

> Judith Miller, the mousy Bush Administration propaganda mouthpiece forced to retire from The New York Times last week, is hardly an anomaly. American journalism is contaminated by widespread institutional corruption. . . . The sad fact is that Miller and [Jason] Blair, rather than rare exceptions, reflect the endemic vices of elitism, unaccountability and star worship that afflict our journalistic institutions beginning with top management.[27]

Here, this critic points to Judith Miller and Jason Blair, two defamed *New York Times* reporters and claims that they are not rare exceptions among but paradigmatic of reporters. Yet this critic gives no reason for accepting this conclusion beyond pointing to two reporters who were (allegedly) corrupt. But it is a hasty generalization to argue that because Blair and Miller are corrupt, all (or most) reporters are corrupt. And it is a fallacy of division to argue that because journalistic institutions are corrupt, all (or most) reporters who work for them are corrupt.

Notice that the critic fails to distinguish between levels of operation within a journalistic institution. Thus, he claims that the corruption he says exists in journalistic institutions starts with top management and goes down to the level of field reporters. The confusion, however, appears to be the critic's failure to distinguish between what may be true of one level of operation and what may be true of another. For example, Rupert Murdoch, the CEO of News Corporation, parent of Fox News, may, and indeed does, have different interests and concerns than a reporter who is risking his or her life on the ground in Iraq. Therefore, corruption at the corporate managerial level does not imply corruption at the level of field reporter. It is only by committing the fallacy of division that such an inference can be sustained.

This does not mean that a journalist who willingly works for a corrupt media organization does not bear responsibility for supporting a corrupt institution. Nor does it mean that there are no corrupt reporters who sell their journalistic souls to such media institutions. However, it is another matter to say that because a reporter works for an institution that is "afflicted with elitism, unaccountability and star worship," this reporter must also be afflicted with the same qualities.

Division may also in some cases be partly behind misplaced violence and hatred toward others. For example, terrorists who have proclaimed the United States "the Great Satan" have targeted U.S. citizens under the assumption that what's true of a nation is true of its people. A similar confusion may arise when an American president declares a cluster of nations to be "the axis of evil" and then proceeds to invade one of those nations. When a soldier opens fire, it may then not be so clear to him whether he is aiming at an "axis of evil" or a human being.

---

27. Ted Rall, "How the Media Can Restore Credibility," uExpress.com, November 15, 2005. Retrieved online on March 25, 2009, from www.uexpress.com/tedrall/index.html?uc_full_date=20051115a.

Exercise 21.8

Determine which (if any) of the following contains a fallacy of division.

21.8.1
All humans are mortal. Socrates is human. Therefore, Socrates is mortal.

21.8.2
The membership of Weight Watchers is expanding. John is a member of Weight Watchers. Therefore John is expanding.

21.8.3
Led Zeppelin's most celebrated composition was "Stairway to Heaven." Therefore, it was the most celebrated composition of the band's lead guitarist, Jimmy Page.

21.8.4
Jesus was crucified for the sins of humankind and died. Therefore Jesus was crucified and died for your sins.

21.8.5
Illinois politics are notoriously corrupt. President Barack Obama was an Illinois senator before he was elected president, so you know what that makes him.

Exercise Set 21.9

Each of the following contains at least one of the fallacious irrelevant appeals discussed in this chapter. Find at least one fallacy in each, and explain and defend your selection.

21.9.1
"He's an idiot because he's an idiot, not because he's a NY'er."[1]

21.9.2
The First Amendment of the U.S. Constitution says that Congress shall make no law abridging freedom of speech. Therefore, defamation laws (laws against slander and libel) are unconstitutional.

21.9.3
I think, therefore I exist. —Rene Descartes (Hint: compare "I walk; therefore, I exist")

21.9.4
You should eat healthy foods because it's good for you.

21.9.5
"When You're Smiling, the Whole World Smiles with You" (song title)

21.9.6
God exists because the Bible says so, and the Bible is, after all, the word of God.

---

1. Anonymous post, City-Data.com. Retrieved online on April 11, 2009, from www.city-data.com/forum/atlanta/257435-whats-up-atlanta-2.html.

21.9.7

"So if you say something that is untrue to me and in the right circumstances, I will call you a liar. I have no regret having called him [George W. Bush] a liar, because he lied." —Senator Harry Reid[2]

21.9.8

Harvard University was ranked number one among national universities for 2009 by *U.S. News and World Report*. Therefore, Harvard's philosophy department must be the top philosophy department in the nation.

21.9.9

"['Barack Obama'] sounds to me like a Middle Eastern type of name and whether or not he's born here in the United States, he doesn't seem like, to me, somebody who is trustworthy. . . . You can't trust anybody these days, so who's to say he's not a terrorist and we just don't realize it yet?"[3]

21.9.10

"Well I asked what you personally believe, not what can be proven. Beliefs are never based on facts or proof, they're based on what you feel in your heart. And for argument's sake, nobody can prove there isn't a life after death either. So why believe there isn't just based on a lack of proof? You could easily believe there is because of a lack of proof otherwise." —Blogger[4]

21.9.11

"The catholic church is corrupt, it's leaders are corrupt, it's priests are child molesters and worse..the whole organization is misogynistic and homophobic and should be banned by any civilized country." —Blogger[5]

21.9.12

Get Revenge on People Who Have Done You Wrong!

We stand ready to help you get revenge and let these individuals know exactly what you think of them—your identity is never divulged . . . NEVER! People send beautiful flower arrangements to loved ones to let them know how special they are. Well, we have a great idea . . . how about sending DEAD flower arrangements to someone to let them know how unspecial they are. Read what one of our customers has to say about our service:

Testimonial: "Just wanted to thank you guys for providing such great service. I wish I could have seen my ex's face when he got that box of dead roses! You guys really made my day. I'm glad I got even with that jerk. More people need to know about this service, so I'm telling my girlfriends because I'm pretty sure they know some jerks too. Most guys are anyway."[6]

21.9.13

"My dad asked me if I smoked up today and gave me a lecture about it. I wanted to laugh in his face. I mean, who does he think he's fooling, acting all protective and concerned? Just

(continued)

2. "Video: Reid Defends Iraq, 'liar' statements," ThinkProgress.org. Retrieved online on January 2, 2009, from http://thinkprogress.org/2007/04/23/video-reid-defends-iraq-liar-statements.

3. John Lynch, "Who Says He's Not a Patriot," Stranger Fruit, June 26, 2008. Retrieved online on April 11, 2009, from http://scienceblogs.com/strangerfruit/2008/06/whos_to_say_hes_not_a_terroris.php.

4. katsmeow1213(2737), "Life after Death," Mylot.com. Retrieved online on January 2, 2009, from www.mylot.com/w/discussions/1798072.aspx.

5. FrankKZ, "Buzzboard Notes," Buzzdash. Retrieved online on January 2, 2009, from www.buzzdash.com/polls/how-relevant-do-you-think-the-pope-is-to-the-worlds-non-catholics-101822.

6. Anonymous post, The Payback.com. Retrieved online on January 2, 2009, from www.thepayback.com. This website helps people to "get even" with others.

last month, I watched him light up after dinner. And then there's that smell that comes from his bedroom door on Sunday afternoons; like I don't know what that is! Anyway, how can he come in here and tell me NOT to do something that I know he does?"[7]

21.9.14
"HIV" antigens are defined as such not on the basis of being shown to belong to HIV, but on the basis that they react with antibodies in Aids patients. Aids patients are then diagnosed as being infected with HIV on the basis that they have antibodies which react with those same antigens.[8]

21.9.15
"I believe in everything until it's disproved. So I believe in fairies, the myths, dragons. It all exists, even if it's in your mind. Who's to say that dreams and nightmares aren't as real as the here and now?" —John Lennon

---

7. "Family Guide," Substance Abuse and Mental Health Services Administration. Retrieved online on January 3, 2009, from www.family.samhsa.gov/set/practicepreach.aspx.
8. Neville Hidgkinson, "The Circular Reasoning Scandal of HIV Testing," The Business, May 21/22, 2006. Retrieved online on January 2, 2009, from http://aidsinfobbs.org/redribbon.htm.

22

✛

Sophistical Arguments

A sophistical argument is a fallacious argument intentionally fashioned to try to deceive or mislead someone.[1] This chapter examines four types of fallacies that often occur in sophistical arguments: (1) fallacies of ambiguity, (2) lifting out of context, (3) news slanting, and (4) the straw man fallacy.

FALLACIES OF AMBIGUITY

An ambiguous word, phrase, or statement is one that has two or more different meanings. A *fallacy of ambiguity* arises when a conclusion is reached as a result of confusing these distinct meanings.

This fallacy may be committed unintentionally, as when one faultily constructs a sentence. Statements whose meanings are ambiguous due to faulty linguistic construction are called *amphibolies*. For example, consider the following statement by President George W. Bush: "One of my concerns is that the health care not be as good as it can possibly be."[2] It is doubtful that Bush meant to say that it was one of his goals to provide inferior health care. However, the negation placed inside this statement did indeed lend to this interpretation.

Still, ambiguity can also be tactically used as an *intentional* mode of deception. Consider the infamous message that President William Jefferson Clinton presented to the American people on January 26, 1998, regarding his alleged sexual relations with a White House intern, Monica Lewinsky:

> But I want to say one thing to the American people. I want you to listen to me. I'm gonna say this again. I did not have sexual relations with that woman, Miss

---

1. The term *sophistical* derives from the Sophists, a group of Greek philosophers in the fifth century BC who appear to have skillfully used fallacious reasoning to manipulate truth.
2. George W. Bush, on military benefits, Tipp City, Ohio, April 19, 2007.

Lewinsky. I never told anybody to lie, not a single time—never. These allegations are false.[3]

What Clinton did not say, however, was that by "sexual relations" he meant "sexual intercourse." Given this definition, Clinton could "truthfully" state that he "did not have sexual relations with that woman" and that "these allegations are false." This is because he never did, in fact, have sexual *intercourse* with Monica Lewinsky. What Clinton did not mention was that Lewinsky had performed oral sex on him.

Clinton's case involved an equivocation on the phrase "sexual relations." As discussed in chapter 8, an *equivocation* involves using a term in two different senses in order to reach a conclusion. In this case, Clinton used the phrase "sexual relations" *ambiguously,* apparently to confuse the American people about his relation with Monica Lewinsky. He used this term ambiguously because he failed to clarify the sense in which he intended it. Here is the inference he hoped the American people would make:

> President Clinton said he wanted us to listen to him that he did not have *sexual relations* with Miss Lewinsky and that this allegation is false.
> Therefore, President Clinton did not have *sexual relations* with Miss Lewinsky.

Unfortunately, the sense of the phrase "sexual relations" that Clinton had in mind in the premise (that he did not have sexual intercourse) was not the broader sense (which included not having oral sex) that he intended the American people to understand in the conclusion.

Exercise Set 22.1

Identify the ambiguity (the distinct senses of words, phrases, or statements that are or might be confused) in each of the following:

22.1.1
"Wal-mart . . . do they like make walls there?" —Paris Hilton

22.1.2
"Natural gas is hemispheric. I like to call it hemispheric in nature because it is a product that we can find in our neighborhoods." —George W. Bush

22.1.3
I hope he gets everything he deserves (said of one's enemy).

22.1.4
"All men are created equal." —Declaration of Independence

22.1.5
John Franklin has recently completed a PhD degree in philosophy with a specialization in medical ethics. He has gotten a job as a professor and clinical ethicist in a teaching hospital.

---

3. "Deposition in the Jones Sexual Harassment Lawsuit," Washington Post.com. Retrieved on line on April 9, 2009, from www.washingtonpost.org/wp-srv/politics/special/clinton/stories/what clintonsaid.htm.

As part of his job, he conducts ethics consults with patients who are having ethics problems. When he introduces himself to these patients, he states, "Hi, my name is Dr. Franklin."

22.1.6
"You say that you have a dog."
"Yes, a villain of a one," said Ctesippus.
"And he has puppies?"
"Yes, and they are very like himself."
"And the dog is the father of them?"
"Yes," he said, "I certainly saw him and the mother of the puppies come together."
"And is he not yours?"
"To be sure he is."
"Then he is a father, and he is yours; ergo, he is your father, and the puppies are your brothers."[1]

22.1.7
"Heard from a New Zealand interviewer . . . re global warming:
'It's very important for New Zealanders to try to help, even if it doesn't make a difference.'"[2]

22.1.8
"The only proof capable of being given that an object is visible, is that people actually see it. The only proof that a sound is audible, is that people hear it; and so of the other sources of our experience. In like manner, I apprehend, the sole evidence it is possible to produce that anything is desirable, is that people actually desire it." —John Stuart Mill[3]

22.1.9
Everybody has some sort of philosophy of life. So, everybody is a philosopher.

22.1.10
"Amnesty means that you've got to pay a price for having been here illegally, and this bill does that." —George W. Bush on the immigration reform bill[4]

---

1. Plato, *Euthydemus*, trans. Benjamin Jowett. Retrieved online on January 6, 2009, from http://classics.mit.edu/Plato/euthydemus.html.
2. "Fallacies: Logical Trick of the Week: Sophistry," Maggie's Farm, May 18, 2008. Retrieved online on January 7, 2009, from http://maggiesfarm.anotherdotcom.com/archives/8484-Fallacies-Logical-Trick-of-the-Week-Sophistry.html.
3. John Stuart Mill, *Utilitarianism*, ch. 4. Retrieved online on April 11, 2009, from http://ebooks.adelaide.edu.au/m/mill/john_stuart/m645u/chapter4.html.
4. George W. Bush, speech presented on June 26, 2007, Washington, D.C. Retrieved online on April 11, 2009, from www.wnd.com/news/article.asp?ARTICLE_ID=56378.

LYING VERSUS TELLING A HALF-TRUTH

President Clinton eventually apologized for misleading the nation about his sexual relations with Monica Lewinsky. On August 17, 1999, he said, "I misled people, including even my wife. I deeply regret that," and on December 11, 1999, he said, "I never should have misled the country, the Congress, my friends and my family."[4] So he apologized for *misleading* people but not for lying.

---

4. AllPolitics, "Clinton's Evolving Apology for the Lewinsky Affair," CNN.com, February 12, 1999. Retrieved online on April 9, 2009, from www.cnn.com/ALLPOLITICS/stories/1999/02/12/apology.

Lying involves saying something one believes to be false with the intent of deceiving another. However, one can also mislead by providing some information while leaving out other information that is necessary to gaining an accurate understanding of the situation. This is commonly referred to as *telling a half-truth.* Here is what telling a half-truth and lying have in common: both involve the intent to deceive.

President Clinton told a half-truth when he denied having sexual relations with Monica Lewinsky because he failed to mention that he was taking the phrase "sexual relations" to mean "sexual intercourse." Apparently, he did this knowing that such an omission would mislead the public about the nature of his relationship with Monica Lewinsky. So, strictly speaking, Clinton did not lie. He told a half-truth.

Arguably, lying tends to be morally objectionable in that it involves deliberate deception. In deliberately deceiving another, one manipulates that other like an object and breaches a fundamental trust that serves to promote successful personal and interpersonal relations.

Since telling a half-truth also involves deliberate deception, it is therefore arguable that half-truths also tend to be morally objectionable for the same reasons. Whether saying something false, or lying, rather than simply leaving out pertinent information, or telling a half-truth, makes the moral transgression worse may, however, be a matter of debate.

Exercise Set 22.2

In your estimation is lying morally worse than telling a half-truth? Would President Clinton's moral transgression have been worse had he lied (said something false) rather than simply failed to be forthcoming about his definition of "sexual relations"? Defend your responses.

LIFTING OUT OF CONTEXT

Another means of deception is taking remarks made by others out of the context in which the remarks were made. This is because words, sentences, and larger expanses of language derive their meaning from the larger contexts in which they are imbedded. For example, "You need a tune-up" can mean one thing when your automotive mechanic says it and quite another when your massage therapist says it.

A popular motive for lifting remarks out of context is to defend one's own position against another's or to attack another's in the course of defending one's own. Children often do this sort of thing. For example, little brother might complain to mother that big brother hit him, while omitting to mention that the alleged hitting occurred in the course of fending off an attack by little brother. But this is not just child's play. Politicians commonly resort to this tactic in trying to gain an advantage over their opponents.

For example, during the 2008 presidential campaigns, on four occasions, Democratic vice presidential nominee Senator Joe Biden accused Republican presidential nominee John McCain of having voted twenty times against funding alternative energy. However, when FactCheck.org analyzed the Obama-Biden campaign's list of votes, they found the number was actually eleven. In the other nine instances on the campaign's list, McCain voted against *mandatory use* of alternative energy, or in favor of allowing exemptions from these mandates. Yet Biden's saying twenty times rather than eleven made McCain's claim to have favored developing alternative energies sound that much more inconsistent.[5]

Not only can written or spoken language be lifted out of context; so, too, can photographs and videotapes. For example, the ability of network news to present reality photographically also gives it the power to manipulate reality to create the public image it desires. An instructive example of this is its ability to shape the image of the president.

Historically, in some cases, this image has been positive. For example, President Ronald Reagan was often filmed in dignified postures, such as riding tall on a horse. In contrast, the media portrayed President Gerald Ford as clumsy. When Ford stumbled, the media was often there to photograph it. "Every time I stumbled," complained Ford, "or bumped my head or fell in the snow, reporters zeroed in on that to the exclusion of almost everything else. The news coverage was harmful. . . . [This] helped create the impression of me as a stumbler. And that wasn't funny."[6]

Photographic lifting out of context is also evident in the coverage of politically charged events by different news organizations. For example, on September 30, 2000, the *New York Times* published a photograph of an Israeli police officer holding up a club as he stood over a young man who was battered and bleeding. The caption identified the young man as a Palestinian and clearly gave the impression that the Israeli soldier had beaten him. However, as it turned out, the young man was really a Jewish American student who was studying abroad in Israel, and the Israeli officer had actually come to the aid of the young man after he and two friends were pulled from a taxi by a group of Palestinians and beaten and stabbed.[7] The *Times* ended up having to print a correction.[8]

Notice that the unfolding of this event involved a seamless progression of motions through time and space that led to the three victims being pulled from their taxi by a group of Palestinians, which led to their being beaten and stabbed by the group, which led to the Israeli officer coming to the aid of one of the victims, which led to. . . . Hence, zeroing in on just one segment of this motion as it unfolded through time and space, lifting it out of the context of its surrounding sequence of motions, presented a misleading and incriminating half-truth.

---

5. "FactChecking Biden-Palin Debate: The candidates were not 100 percent accurate to say the least," FactCheck.org, October 13, 2008. Retrieved online on April 9, 2009, from www.factcheck.org/elections-2008/factchecking_biden-palin_debate.html.

6. Gerald Ford quoted in Fred Smoller, "Network News Coverage of the Presidency: Implications for Democracy," in *Philosophical Issues in Journalism*, ed. Elliot D. Cohen (New York: Oxford University Press, 1994), 148.

7. In fact, riots that were part of the intifada had just broken out that day.

8. "The Photo That Started It All," Honest Reporting, October 20, 2000. Retrieved online on April 9, 2009, from www.honestreporting.com/articles/reports/The_Photo_that_Started_it_All.asp.

In a similar manner, lifting words out of context can be a pernicious way of distorting the message a person is trying to communicate. One striking example of this is a campaign ad run by the John McCain campaign during McCain's 2008 bid for president. The campaign published a video ad on the Internet mockingly portraying McCain's Democratic opponent, Barack Obama, as "The One." The video juxtaposed Obama with a scene from the movie *The Ten Commandments* in which the waters parted for Moses (played by Charlton Heston). At one point the ad stated, "He can do no wrong," and then the video showed CBS news correspondent Lara Logan asking Obama, "Do you have any doubts?" and Obama answering, "Never."

However, Obama's answer was taken out of context, as was the question that Logan asked him. The real question she asked was "Do you have any doubts about your foreign affairs experience?" The omission was designed to make it look like Obama did not have any doubts about *anything* whatsoever.

In another part of this video, Obama stated, "I have become a symbol of the possibility of America returning to our best traditions." But this too was lifted out of context. The real event transpired at a closed meeting with congressional representatives during which, referring to his speech delivered in Berlin, Obama stated that the two hundred thousand people who came to his speech came not just for him. Again, the "not just for him" part was omitted. Obama, in fact, never said he was "The One" but rather that "we are the ones we've been waiting for." Here is what Obama said:

> You see, the challenges we face will not be solved with one meeting in one night. It will not be resolved on even a Super Duper Tuesday. Change will not come if we wait for some other person or if we wait for some other time. We are the ones we've been waiting for. We are the change that we seek. We are the hope of those boys who have so little, who've been told that they cannot have what they dream, that they cannot be what they imagine. Yes, they can.

So Obama's real point was to emphasize that the people are the ones who must effect change. Yet the ad said Obama "has anointed himself ready to carry the burden of The One." Not only was this interpretation inaccurate, but Obama's point was the exact opposite—namely that the people, not he, must bear the burden. In this manner, the ad made Obama out to look arrogant with apparent delusions of grandeur.

In a society with a history of stereotyping black people as arrogant—the pejorative, racially infused word is "uppity"[9]—such a casting of Obama was unfortunate. He was the first black person in history to win the nomination of a major political party in a (soon-to-be-successful) bid for the U.S. presidency. As such, the ad was more than just deceptive. It appealed to the kind of stereotypical, prejudicial thinking that contributed to the oppression of black people in the United States in the first place.

---

9. In fact, on September 4, shortly after the ad aired, House representative Lynn Westmoreland (R-GA) actually called Obama and his wife "uppity." "Just from what little I've seen of her and Mr. Obama," he said, "they're a member of an elitist-class individual that thinks that they're uppity."

Exercise Set 22.3

Each of the following represents a different way in which something may be lifted out of its original context. For each case, explain why it commits this fallacy. What exactly has been left out of the original quote? How does this omission make it deceptive?

22.3.1
TOM CRUISE: UNBALANCED
Tom finally admits the truth!
READ MORE >>

Original context:

> How he suffered for his art as a wannabe one-eyed Nazi assassin in Valkyrie.
> The role required him to don an eye patch but as shooting continued his vision became impaired making Tommy feeling dizzy—and worse—unbalanced!
> "I was surprised," Cruise confessed to a UK glossy.
> "I lost depth perception and balance.
> "In terms of visual cinematic storytelling it was a challenge . . . especially when it was dark."
> It ain't easy being myopic, is it Tom? —*National Enquirer*[1]

22.3.2
"What occurs shortly after 8 p.m. at the Schoenfeld Theatre feels so fresh that you stop to catch your breath." —Advertisement from the producers of a 2006 Broadway revival of *A Chorus Line* quoting *New York Times* reviewer Ben Brantley.

Original context:
"What occurs shortly after 8 p.m. at the Gerald Schoenfeld Theater, where the otherwise pedestrian new revival of *A Chorus Line* opened last night, is a sort of time bending that Einstein would have trouble explaining. Light, music and a mass of bodies in motion combine to allow you to exist both in 1975, when this musical was first staged, and 2006. This is what *A Chorus Line* was when I saw it 31 years ago, and yet it feels so fresh that you stop to catch your breath. . . . Watching the show, directed by Bob Avian, is like drinking from a pitcher of draft beer: You never repeat the tang or sting of that first swig. . . . In providing us with an archivally and anatomically correct reproduction of a landmark show, its creators neglected to restore its central nervous system and, most important, its throbbing heart." —Actual review by Ben Brantley.[2]

22.3.3
"Money is the root of all evil." —Popular quotation from the Bible

Original context:
"But people who want to get rich keep toppling into temptation and are trapped by many stupid and harmful desires that plunge them into destruction and ruin. For the love of money is a root of all kinds of evil. Some people, in their eagerness to get rich, have wandered away from the faith and caused themselves a lot of pain." —What is actually stated in the Bible (I Tim. 6:10)[3]

(continued)

1. "Tom Cruise: Unbalanced," *National Enquirer,* January 7, 2009. Retrieved online on January 7, 2009, from www.nationalenquirer.com/tom_cruise_unbalanced/celebrity/66001.
2. *Orlando Sentinel,* October 18, 2006. Retrieved online on January 8, 2009, from http://blogs.orlando sentinel.com/entertainment_stage_theat/2006/10/critics_are_mis.html.
3. New Testament, International Standard Version, 1 Tim. 6:10, Biblos.com. Retrieved online on January 8, 2009, from http://isv.scripturetext.com/1_timothy/6.htm.

22.3.4

"To suppose that the eye with all its inimitable contrivances for adjusting the focus to different distances, for admitting different amounts of light, and for the correction of spherical and chromatic aberration, could have been formed by natural selection, seems, I freely confess, absurd in the highest degree."—Charles Darwin, the *Origin of Species* as quoted by Andrew Snelling[4]

Original context:

"To suppose that the eye with all its inimitable contrivances for adjusting the focus to different distances, for admitting different amounts of light, and for the correction of Spherical and chromatic aberration, could have been formed by natural selection, seems, I freely confess, absurd in the highest degree. When it was first said that the sun stood still and the world turned round, the common sense of mankind declared the doctrine false; but the old saying of Vox populi, vox Dei ["the voice of the people equals the voice of God""], as every philosopher knows, cannot be trusted in science. Reason tells me, that if numerous gradations from a simple and imperfect eye to one complex and perfect can be shown to exist, each grade being useful to its possessor, as is certain the case; if further, the eye ever varies and the variations be inherited, as is likewise certainly the case; and if such variations should be useful to any animal under changing conditions of life, then the difficulty of believing that a perfect and complex eye could be formed by natural selection, should not be considered as subversive of the theory."[5]

22.3.5

This would be the best of all possible worlds, if there were no religion in it. —John Adams quoted on Metro State Atheists (website)[6]

Original context:

"Twenty times, in the course of my late Reading, have I been upon the point of breaking out, This would be the best of all possible Worlds, if there were no Religion in it. ! ! ! But in this exclamati[on] I should have been as fanatical as Bryant or Cleverly. Without Religion this World would be Something not fit to be mentioned in polite Company, I mean Hell. So far from believing in the total and universal depravity of human Nature; I believe there is no Individual totally depraved. The most abandoned Scoundrel that ever existed, never Yet Wholly extinguished his Conscience, and while Conscience remains there is some Religion." — Letter from John Adams to Thomas Jefferson, April 19, 1817[7]

4. Charles Darwin, *The Origin of Species* (London: J. M. Dent & Sons Ltd, 1971), 167. As quoted in Andrew Snelling, ed., *The Revised Quote Book* (Brisbane, Australia: Creation Science Foundation, 1990), 18.
5. Charles Darwin, *The Origin of Species*, Encyclopedia Britannica, Great Books Series, 1952. Retrieved online on January 8, 2009, from http://toarchive.org/faqs/ce/3/part8.html.
6. John Adams, quoted on Metro State Atheists. Retrieved online on January 8, 2009, from http://metrostateatheists.wordpress.com/2008/10/26/quotes-about-religion.
7. National Humanities Center, "From the Correspondence of John Adams and Thomas Jefferson on Life, Religion, and the Young Republic." Retrieved online on January 8, 2009, from http://nationalhumanitiescenter.org/pds/livingrev/religion/text3/adamsjeffersoncor.pdf.

Exercise Set 22.4

22.4.1

Provide at least one example of the fallacy of lifting out of context. Your example(s) may be taken from newspaper articles, literature and arts reviews, websites, magazines, or other media sources. Include both the statement(s) taken out of context as well as the original source.

22.4.2
Provide at least one example of a photograph that lifts an event out of its context and is, as a result, misleading or deceptive. Explain why the photograph is deceptive. Your example might be found on the Internet or in the print media such as a magazine or newspaper.

NEWS SLANTING

News slanting is a manner of interpreting the news according to a news bias. In a general sense, a *bias* is a preference or leaning. In this sense, all news is biased insofar as it reflects the subjective perspective of the news organization. However, in the context of journalism, the term *news bias*, or *journalistic bias*, ordinarily implies unfair, discriminatory, or incompetent news reporting.[10] In this pejorative sense, a news bias can be associated with conflict of interest, as when the quality of a media company's coverage of a news story about a nuclear accident is negatively influenced by the company's financial interest in nuclear power.

Media Self-Censorship and the Playing Down of News Stories

Media bias can be reflected in the extent to which a story is covered. A media company might leave out details of a story that conflict with a vested interest, or it might fail to cover the story. The term *self-censorship* is sometimes applied by media critics to a news organization that fails to cover a seemingly newsworthy story altogether.

A news organization will rarely, if ever, admit to "censoring" a story. The standard argument is instead that choosing which stories to cover is a daunting task since there are so many potentially newsworthy stories. Thus, deciding what stories to include in the news hole is often said to be a matter of editorial discretion.

This argument, however, has lost some of its credibility as the news hole has expanded exponentially with the rise of the electronic media. In fact, most corporate media companies (including newspapers, radio, and cable and television broadcast companies) now have an Internet presence and thus more space to cover stories that do not make the conventional slots.

Moreover, the standard argument leaves out what many who have spent time in an American newsroom owned by a giant corporation can tell us: namely that decisions about which stories to cover are driven by the maximization of profit. For example, here is what Bonnie M. Anderson, a veteran of both NBC and CNN News, says about the choice of stories:

> If to achieve higher ratings also means going after the majority of viewers, who are white, by hiring white anchors and correspondents, that's considered just good business. And if easing pro-Bush politics into the newscasts appeals to more conservative

---

10. Jay Newman, "Some Reservations about Multiperspectival News," in *Philosophical Issues in Journalism*, ed. Elliot D. Cohen (New York: Oxford University Press, 1992), 205–15.

viewers, why not? The single aim was, and is, this: attracting more viewers, preferably younger and more affluent ones, to the news programs for longer periods of time.[11]

Add to these pressures the fact that the federal government has the awesome power to regulate corporate media companies out of existence or to allow them to grow larger, and we can understand how stories that may not sit well with the current administration might not see the light of day or receive the coverage they deserve.[12] Unfortunately, this does not bode well for the media's role in a democracy as a faithful government watchdog that keeps the people informed about government shenanigans.

Consider, for example, the Downing Street memo story, which was censored at first by the mainstream media and later downplayed. On May 1, 2005, the *London Times* disclosed a leaked memo containing the minutes of a July 23, 2002, meeting between British Prime Minister Tony Blair and his inner circle of advisers, which took place seven months before the U.S.-led invasion of Iraq. The memo said the following:

> Bush wanted to remove Saddam, through military action, justified by the conjunction of terrorism and WMD [weapons of mass destruction]. But the intelligence and facts were being fixed around the policy.

The memo also stated,

> It seemed clear that Bush had made up his mind to take military action, even if the timing was not yet decided. But the case was thin. Saddam was not threatening his neighbours, and his WMD capability was less than that of Libya, North Korea or Iran.

Nevertheless, said Blair, "if the political context were right, people would support regime change." And, according to the *London Times*, "a separate secret briefing for the meeting said Britain and America had to 'create' conditions to justify a war."

This was clearly a newsworthy story. In effect, these memos described a deliberate plan to take the United States to war in Iraq on false pretenses. They told a story of a government administration that was bent on lying to the American people in order to get them to support the invasion of Iraq. Given the media's role as the fourth estate, the government watchdog charged with keeping the citizens informed about government corruption, this was not a story to ignore.

Unfortunately, the mainstream media in the United States did just that. Thus, while independent media on the Internet picked up the story and ran with it, the major corporate news organizations in the United States didn't cover the story.

But as the buzz on the Internet continued to grow louder and louder, it became evident that the story could no longer be contained. So it finally bled through to the mainstream. Unfortunately, the mainstream media *played down* the story even

---

11. Bonnie M. Anderson, *News Flash: Journalism, Infotainment, and the Bottom-Line Business of Broadcast News* (San Francisco: Jossey-Bass, 2004), 10.

12. Elliot D. Cohen, *News Incorporated: Corporate Media Ownership and Its Threat to Democracy* (Amherst, N.Y.: Prometheus Books, 2005).

then. For example, in an interview on June 26, 2005, on NBC's *Meet the Press*, late veteran journalist Tim Russert interviewed then Secretary of Defense Donald Rumsfeld about the Downing Street memo. Here is the core of the exchange:

> Mr. Russert: There's been a lot of discussion of the Downing Street memo, discussion about weapons of mass destruction and not finding them, but there is one line in that Downing Street memo that the chief intelligence officer briefing Prime Minister Blair, which said this. "There was little discussion in Washington of the aftermath after military action." . . .

> Sec'y Rumsfeld: There was a great deal of post–major combat planning. . . . The commanders have an obligation in their war plans to have a postwar plan, a postwar stabilization plan, and they did.[13]

Notice that Russert focused on the question of whether the Bush administration had an exit plan for the war. He did not even ask Rumsfeld to respond to the allegation that "the intelligence and the facts were being fixed around the policy." Russert, who had been known for asking tough questions and had the secretary of defense in the hot seat, didn't probe him on this crucial issue. Instead, he focused on the question of whether the United States had an exit plan; then, he simply moved on to another issue. Given the seriousness of the charge and Russert's failure to raise it with the very government officer responsible for the formulation of general defense policy, this was clearly a case of downplaying the story.

Playing Up a Story

News organizations can also slant news stories by playing up certain aspects of a story while they downplay others. This was evident in the mainstream media's coverage of antiwar demonstrations during the Iraq War. For example, on September 1, 2008, about ten thousand anti–Iraq War protesters demonstrated near the site of the Replication National Convention in Saint Paul, Minnesota. However, it was easy to get different impressions about what happened that day depending on what media source one consulted. For example, the lead sentence of a Fox News story, "Anti-War Protest at GOP Convention Turns Violent," read as follows:

> ST. PAUL, Minn.—A protest near the site of the Republican National Convention gave way to violence Monday as demonstrators attacked members of the Connecticut delegation, smashed windows, slashed car tires and threw bottles during an anti-war march, St. Paul police said.

In contrast, the first lines of an MSNBC story, "Nearly 300 Arrested at RNC Convention Protest," read as follows:

> MINNEAPOLIS—An Associated Press photographer and a Democracy Now! TV and radio show host were among those arrested at an anti-war march on the first day of the Republican National Convention. Both were released hours later.

---

13. Meet the Press with David Gregory, transcript for June 26: Guests: Secretary of Defense Donald Rumsfeld; Bono, a lead voice for African aid as well as the rock group U2, June 26, 2005. Retrieved online on April 9, 2009, from www.msnbc.msn.com/id/8332675.

The Fox News article did not mention these arrests. Instead, it focused on the outbreaks of violence that occurred several blocks from the convention site, and it cited such details as "the violent demonstrators were mostly dressed in black and described themselves as anarchists" and "there were protesters laying on the ground, giving us the finger." These details were not included in the MSNBC article.

Burying Facts

On the other hand, immediately after its lead sentence, the MSNBC article said that most of the ten thousand estimated protesters were peaceful. The Fox News article waited twelve paragraphs to say, "Earlier in the first day of the Republican convention, nearly 10,000 veterans and protesters marched peacefully through the streets of St. Paul to the state Capitol." Such positioning of a fact at the beginning of or deep into a story is very significant. Statistically, most people tend to read the first few paragraphs of an article rather than the entire piece. Thus, *a common practice of newspapers is to bury facts that they do not wish their readers to notice. In contrast, facts that they deem important are placed near the beginning.*

Focusing on the arrest of two journalists, the MSNBC article cited an assistant AP Washington bureau chief, who said, "Covering news is a constitutionally protected activity, and covering a riot is part of that coverage," and "Photographers should not be detained for covering breaking news." The constitutional issue was not explicitly mentioned in the Fox News article. Near the end of the Fox article (five paragraphs from the bottom), it said, "Others [who looked on] were supportive. 'That's what this country is about: freedom of speech,' Janet Lowe said."

Clearly, the Fox News article attempted to paint a negative picture of the anti–Iraq War protesters by playing up the relatively few people (286 out of about 10,000) that fit its description of anarchists in black attire or who performed violent acts. In contrast, the MSNBC article attempted to play up the seriousness of the constitutional issue raised when police arrest journalists at work covering breaking news.

Exercise Set 22.5

22.5.1
Go online and search out a news story that appears to have received considerable attention from online independent media sources but relatively little coverage by big American corporate mainstream media (major broadcast and cable news companies such as NBC, MSNBC, Fox, CBS, CNN, and ABC and newspaper companies such as the *Wall Street Journal, Washington Post*, and *New York Times*). The story you find should be one that you think is important for the American people to know about. You can check to see how much mainstream media attention it received by doing a Google search of the story. Explain why you think the news story you have found should have been more thoroughly covered by the mainstream media.

22.5.2
Find a news story that plays up some aspects of the story and plays down others. Find another media source that covers the same story but plays up and down different aspects

of the story. You may look for your story online or in print media such as newspapers and news and political magazines.

22.5.3
Find at least one example of a news article (online or print) that buries important facts toward the end of the article. Explain why the facts in question are important to the story and how the burying of these facts might reflect a bias of the news organization in question.

STRAW MAN FALLACY

The salient feature of a literal straw man is that, by virtue of being made of straw, it lacks substance and can easily be blown over. The *straw man fallacy* arises when one presents another's position (argument or claim) in such a way that it can easily be blown over (defeated). One way to make a straw man out of another person's position is to leave out relevant information in an effort to weaken it.

Consider the following campaign ad put out by the Obama 2008 presidential campaign in September 2008, prior to the election:

Announcer: Three years ago John McCain campaigned for George Bush's plan to risk your Social Security in the stock market. And voted three times in favor of privatizing Social Security.

So imagine if McCain and Bush had gotten their way, and invested your future retirement benefits at Lehman Brothers? Bankrupt. AIG? Bailed out. Merrill Lynch? Sold.

John McCain—The risk is too great, trying four more years of the same.

Obama: I'm Barack Obama, and I approved this message.[14]

Here, then Democratic presidential nominee Barack Obama criticized the position of his Republican opponent, John McCain, on social security. However, these criticisms attacked a straw man.

First, Obama neglected to mention that the proposed plan that McCain endorsed was not mandatory but only voluntary. That is, this proposed plan would have forced no one to invest any future social security benefits in the stock market. Second, Obama left out the fact that, under this plan, a maximum of a third of a person's social security benefits could be invested in the stock market. Third, according to the proposal, people would not have been permitted to invest directly in the companies that were mentioned in the ad, such as Lehman Brothers, which went bankrupt. Instead, the proposal would have allowed investment only in certain broadly diversified, government-run stock funds.[15] Clearly, by leaving out these facts, Obama created a false impression of the dangers of McCain's position on privatizing social security and accordingly made arguing against it much easier than if he had revealed the truth of McCain's stance.

---

14. "More Social Security Spin: Obama-Biden Ad Misrepresents the Social Security Plan McCain Supported. Again," FactCheck.org, October 2, 2008. Retrieved online on April 9, 2009, from www.factcheck.org/elections-2008/more_social_security_spin.html.
15. "More Social Security Spin," FactCheck.org.

An appropriate antidote against someone who makes a straw man out of another's position is simply to correct the mistake. However, if the omissions are subtle enough, they may not be noticed, even by the person whose position is being distorted. Or this person may not be available to respond. When this happens in the public arena, as in a political contest, it is generally the public that loses for not having had the opportunity to obtain an accurate account of a candidate's position. Freethinkers beware!

The straw man fallacy may also take the form of exaggerating another's claim in order to weaken and defeat it. In such cases, particular statements may be changed to universal ones. For example, consider the following radio ad titled "Nightmare," put out in May 2005 by the American Family Business Institute:

> Announcer: You work hard all your life. You pay your taxes and play by the rules, and, yeah, you're proud of what you've accomplished. You'd like to leave your family farm or business to your kids. It's a legacy, something they can hold onto. It's the American dream, right? But the IRS death tax can turn that dream into a nightmare. When you die, *the IRS can bury your family in crippling tax bills.* It can cost them *everything.* What's worse, the death tax is a double tax on all you've worked to build. The death tax is wrong.[16]

However, according to FactCheck.org, in 2004, two out of five of the taxable business and farm estates valued at less than $2 million paid an average rate of only 1.6 percent, while very large estates valued at over $20 million paid just over 22 percent.[17] In other words, the tax didn't cost these families "everything" and didn't "bury your family in crippling tax bills." These claims were exaggerations put out for political purposes of repealing the death tax.

Moreover, the vast majority of estates are not even affected by the estate tax. For example, in 2002, less than 3 percent of estates were subject to the tax. However, the omission of this fact helped give the impression that the tax had a wider affect on American families than was actually the case.

Notice that exposing the fallacious character of this ad does not show that there are not good arguments for repealing the estate tax. The point is instead that the public interest is best served by an honest accounting of the facts rather than by an attempt to sway popular opinion through exaggerations and omissions of relevant facts.

Exercise Set 22.6

Each of the following quotes criticizes a specific individual or group of individuals. In your estimation, does the criticism make a straw man out of its target? Defend each of your responses. In at least some cases, you may find it helpful to familiarize yourself with the subject at hand (for example, by conducting a Google search) before responding.

---

16. "Estate Tax Malarkey: Misleading Ads Exaggerate What the Tax Costs Farmers, Small Businesses and 'Your Family,'" FactCheck.org, June 6, 2005. Retrieved online on April 9, 2009, from www.factcheck.org/taxes/estate_tax_malarkey.html.

17. "Estate Tax Malarkey," FactCheck.org.

22.6.1

"When I was in basic training, [my mother] never once wrote to me or any of that, did not attend my BCT graduation, did not attend my AIT graduation. She never once offered to come and visit me. It's always 'so, when are you coming home to visit me?' She wants me to come home so I can do things that I used to do when I was still living at home. And that's EVERYTHING. She's always complaining that she can't put up with my brothers anymore and they're stressing her out and that she has to cook and clean. Since I got pregnant, all she talks about is how she wants me and the baby home so I can help her with the household stuff while she plays with my baby. Umm, yea." —Blogger[1]

22.6.2

"Democrats view tax hikes as a 'quick fix to any and every problem, no matter how big or small,' and American taxpayers should worry about attacks on their wallets, Republican leaders are warning." —CNSNews.com[2]

22.6.3

"Republicans love war. Republicans only care about the rich. Republicans are crazy religious fanatics. Republicans are at fault for all problems in America." —*Miami Hurricane*[3]

22.6.4

"Bush was a war monger, thats all he wanted to do. He said, 'daddy? when will i get to drop bombs on unsuspecting countries.' The rest is history. . . " —Blogger[4]

22.6.5

"I'm not interested in going in there like an idiot and going, 'OK, I'm going to build ten orphanages and I'll see you guys later.' . . . I could've joined the UN and become an ambassador, visited various countries and just showed up and smiled and looked concerned. But that's not getting to the root of the problem. And neither is building orphan care centers." —Madonna regarding Angelina Jolie's activities as a U.N. ambassador and lobbyist for the world's orphaned children[5]

22.6.6

"Our opponent . . . is someone who sees America, it seems, as being so imperfect, imperfect enough, that he's palling around with terrorists who would target their own country." —Sarah Palin, 2008 Republican vice presidential candidate[6] (Palin is here referring to Democratic presidential candidate Barack Obama and his association with William Ayers, a professor of education at the University of Illinois at Chicago, who in 1969 cofounded the Weathermen, an anti–Vietnam War organization, which, through the mid-1970s, engaged in riots and bombings of federal buildings in protest of the war.)

(*continued*)

---

1. Anonymous blogger, Sex & Relationships Forum, BabyGaga.com. Retrieved online on January 9, 2009, from http://forum.baby-gaga.com/about343841.html.

2. Susan Jones, "Republicans Warn of Tax-and-Spend Democrats," CNSNews.com, August 14, 2007. Retrieved online on January 9, 2009, from http://archive.newsmax.com/archives/ic/2007/8/14/101123.shtml.

3. Jenna King, "Clearing the Record on Republicans," *Miami Hurricane*, October 12, 2008. Retrieved online on January 9, 2009, from www.themiamihurricane.com/2008/10/12/clearing-the-record-on-republicans. In this article, Jenna King attempts to defend Republicans against this popular straw man argument.

4. Blogger, CBS Sports Community, October 22, 2008. Retrieved online on January 9, 2009, from www.sportsline.com/mcc/messages/thread/11258346.

5. Tina Sims, "Madonna Shocks Angelina Jolie," National Ledger, November 14, 2006. Retrieved online on January 9, 2009, from www.nationalledger.com/cgi-bin/artman/exec/view.cgi?archive=6&num=9826.

6. Douglass K. Daniel, "AP: Palin's Ayers Attack 'Radically Tinged,'" *Huffington Post*, October 5, 2008. Retrieved online on January 10, 2009, from www.huffingtonpost.com/2008/10/05/ap-palins-ayers-attack-ra_n_132008.html.

22.6.7

"This [George W. Bush] administration can tap our phones. They can't tap our creative spirit. They can open our mail. They can't open economic opportunities. They can track our every move. They lost track of the economy while the cost of food, gasoline and electricity skyrockets. They skillfully played our post-9/11 fears and allowed the few to profit at the expense of the many. Every day we get the color orange, while the oil companies, the insurance companies, the speculators, the war contractors get the color green." —Rep. Dennis Kucinich (D-OH)[7]

22.6.8

"At the moment, I'm sad to report that many academics around the world are contributing to an atmosphere that makes peace more difficult to achieve. They are encouraging those Palestinians who see the end of Israel as their ultimate goal to persist in their ideological and terrorist campaign. By demonizing and de-legitimating Israel in the international community and on university campuses throughout the world, they send a doubly destructive message to those who must make peace on the ground. To the Palestinians, the message is don't compromise. If you hold out long enough, the next generation of leaders will buy into your efforts to de-legitimate Israel and will give you the total victory you seek. To the Israelis, the message is: Whatever you do in the name of compromise, you will continue to be attacked, demonized, divested from, boycotted and de-legitimated, so why make the compromise efforts?" —Alan Dershowitz[8]

22.6.9

"The Palestinians have nothing to offer the US. People have human rights insofar as they provide services to power. Israel provides substantial services to US power, Palestinians on the other hand provide nothing. They have no wealth, they have no power, they are mostly a nuisance. They even have a negative value because their plight stirs up antagonism in what is called the 'Arab Street,' the disdainful term for the Arab populations." —Noam Chomsky[9] (responding to a question about how the United States views Palestinians in contrast to Israelis).

22.6.10

"The Christian faith from the beginning, is sacrifice, the sacrifice of all freedom, all pride, all self-confidence of spirit; it is at the same time subjection, self-derision, and self-mutilation." —Frederick Nietzsche[10]

7. Dennis Kucinich, speech transcript for the Democratic National Convention, August 26, 2008. Retrieved online on January 10, 2009, from http://bloggingforkucinich.blogspot.com/2008/08/dennis-kucinichs-speech-transcript-for.html.

8. Alan Dershowitz, transcript of debate between Noam Chomsky and Alan Dershowitz, Kennedy School of Government, November 29, 2005. Retrieved online on January 10, 2009, from www.zmag.org/znet/viewArticle/4679.

9. Noam Chomsky interviewed by Hub Radio, "The Israel-Palestine Conflict," University of the West of England, April 23, 2008. Retrieved online on January 10, 2009, from www.chomsky.info/interviews/20080423.htm.

10. Friedrich Nietzsche, from chapter 3 of *Beyond Good and Evil*, trans. Helen Zimmern. Retrieved online on January 10, 2009, from http://infomotions.com/etexts/gutenberg/dirs/etext03/bygdv10.htm.

Appendix

Venn Diagrams

As discussed in chapter 7, Venn diagrams can be used to represent the four categorical form statements, A-, E-, I-, and O-forms. When these diagrams are used to map the two premises of a standard form categorical syllogism, they provide a means of testing the validity of the argument.

USING VENN DIAGRAMS TO TEST THE VALIDITY OF STANDARD FORM CATEGORICAL SYLLOGISMS

To construct a Venn diagram, we begin by creating three intersecting circles, each representative of one of the three terms in a standard categorical syllogism, subject (S), predicate (P), and middle term (M), respectively (see figure A.1).

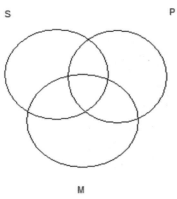

Figure A.1

Appendix

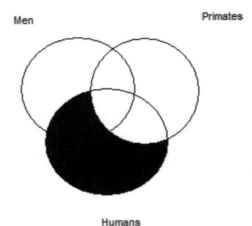

Figure A.2

Diagramming A-form Premises

For example, consider the following categorical syllogism:

All humans are primates.
All men are humans.
Therefore, all men are primates.

We first map the major premise as shown in figure A.2. Notice that the set of humans that are nonprimates is shaded out, leaving only the set of humans that are primates unshaded, thus representing the A-form statement that all humans are primates.

Second, we map the minor premise as shown in figure A.3. Notice that the set of men that are nonhumans is shaded out, leaving only the set of men who are humans unshaded, thus representing the A-form statement that all men are humans.

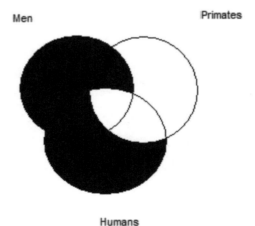

Figure A.3

Third, we look to see if the conclusion is represented by our diagram. If it is, then the syllogism is valid; if not, then it is invalid. Since the conclusion in our example states that all men are primates, only the set of men that are primates should be unshaded and the set of men that are nonprimates should be shaded out. Since this is exactly what our diagram depicts, the syllogism is indeed valid.

Diagramming E- and O-form Premises

Now consider the following categorical syllogism:

No ACLU members are NRA members.
Some liberals are not ACLU members.
Therefore, some liberals are NRA members.

We first map the major premise as shown in figure A.4. Notice that the set of ACLU members who are NRA members has been shaded out to signify the E-form statement that no ACLU members are NRA members.

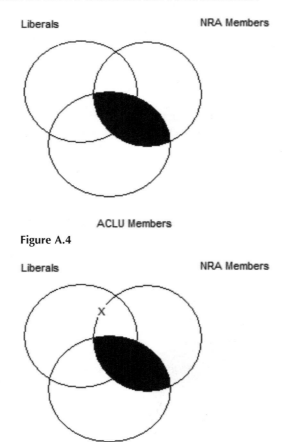

Figure A.4

Figure A.5

Second, we map the minor premise as shown in figure A.5. Notice that to map the O-form minor premise, we use an X to indicate the existence of a particular liberal. As discussed in chapter 6, this is because O-form statements are particular statements and therefore have existential import (they assert the existence of class members). Observe that the X has been placed outside ACLU members to signify the existence of a liberal that is not an ACLU member. However, observe that this X has been placed on the border between liberals and NRA members because the minor premise that some liberals are not ACLU members does not tell us anything about whether the liberals in question are, or are not, also NRA members.

Next, we look to see if the conclusion of our syllogism is diagrammed. Since the X is on the border between liberals and NRA members, our diagram does not tell us that some liberals are indeed NRA members. Therefore, this conclusion does not follow necessarily from the premises and therefore the syllogism is invalid.

Diagramming I-form Premises

Now consider this categorical syllogism:

No stereotypes are reliable generalizations.
Some media depictions are stereotypes.
Therefore, some media depictions are not reliable generalizations.

First, we map the E-form major premise as shown in figure A.6.
Second, we map the I-form minor premise as shown in figure A.7.
Since I-form statements have existential import, the I-form minor premise "Some media depictions are stereotypes" has existential import. Accordingly, an X is placed in the set of media depictions that are stereotypes to depict the existence of such an individual.

Next, we look to see if the conclusion of our syllogism is diagrammed. Since the X is in media depictions but outside reliable generalizations, the diagram

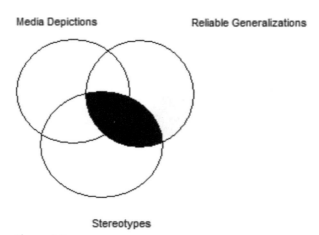

Figure A.6

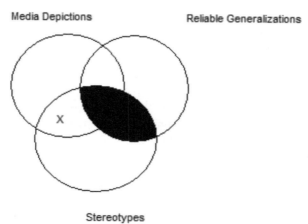

Figure A.7

does indeed tell us that some media depictions are not reliable generalizations. Therefore, the syllogism is valid.

Determining the Existential Import of Universal Premises

Now, consider the following syllogism:

All physicians are college graduates.
All pediatricians are physicians.
Therefore, some pediatricians are college graduates.

Here, we proceed in the usual way of first mapping the major premise and then the minor premise. Since both premises are A-form statements, the Venn diagram that emerges looks as shown in figure A.8.

Notice that the conclusion, an I-form statement, is not diagrammed. As such, we might be prepared to conclude that the syllogism must be invalid. However, before

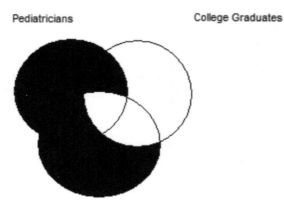

Figure A.8

writing off this syllogism, notice that the reason the conclusion is not mapped is that in diagramming the minor premise, we followed a Boolean interpretation and did not assume existential import for it.[1] But the class of physicians is clearly a class with members. Moreover, to refuse to make this assumption when we know it to be true will lead us to deny the validity of an argument that we have every good reason to accept as valid—and indeed sound.[2]

Therefore, in cases where the validity of an argument hinges on whether the minor premise has existential import, we will leave ourselves the option to decide whether or not to assume such import. *However, this option is open to us only in cases such as the present one, where there are two universal premises (A- and/or E-form statements) and a particular (I- or O-form) conclusion.*

In the present case, we can add existential import to the diagramming of the minor premise by placing an X in the unshaded region of physicians who are pediatricians, which signifies the existential-import-carrying I-form statement that some pediatricians are physicians. *In general, we can add existential import to the diagramming of a universal minor premise by diagramming its corresponding particular statement.* The corresponding particular statement of the A-form is the I-form, and the corresponding particular statement of the E-form is the O-form.[3]

When we add existential import to the minor premise in the present case, our diagram appears as shown in figure A.9. As you can see, once existential import of the minor premise is added, the conclusion is also mapped by our diagram. This is because the X we just inserted into the set of physicians who are pediatricians is now also in pediatricians who are college graduates, thus indicating that some pediatricians are college graduates.

As discussed in chapters 7 and 8, in some cases of categorical syllogisms with two universal premises and a particular conclusion, it may not be clear whether

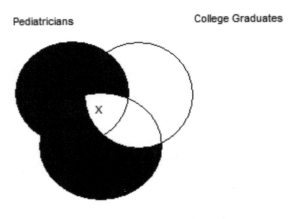

Figure A.9

---

1. See the discussion of existential import in chapter 6.

2. See the discussion of existential import in chapter 6; see also the discussion of the existential fallacy in chapter 8.

3. On the Aristotelian square of opposition, the relationship between E- and I- and A- and O-statement forms is called subalternation. See chapter 7 for a discussion of this relationship.

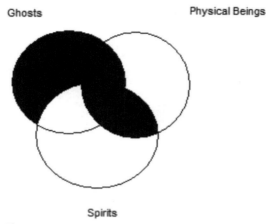

Ghosts

Physical Beings

Spirits

Figure A.10

or not existential import of the minor premise should be assumed, and the determination might sometimes be contentious. Consider, for example, the following categorical syllogism:

No spirits are physical beings.
All ghosts are spirits.
Therefore, some ghosts are not physical beings.

Mapping the major and then minor premise of this syllogism yields the Venn diagram in figure A.10.

As you can see, whether this syllogism is to be called valid depends on whether the minor premise is to be accorded existential import and therefore on whether an X is to be inserted into the area of things that are both ghosts and spirits. Since the existence of ghosts is, to say the least, contentious, you would need a rational argument to defend putting in the X. In the absence of such a rational argument, the syllogism in question would best be judged invalid.

Exercise Set A.1

For each of the following categorical syllogisms, construct a Venn diagram and use it to determine validity or invalidity:

A.1.1
All members of al-Qaeda are terrorists.
Some Iraqis are terrorists.
Therefore, some Iraqis are members of al-Qaeda.

A.1.2
No freethinkers are lockstep voters.
Some politicians are lockstep voters.
Therefore, some politicians are not freethinkers.

(*continued*)

A.1.3
All artists who use their celebrity to make political statements are affronts to the survival of democracy.
Kid Rock is not an artist who uses his celebrity to make political statements.
Therefore, Kid Rock is not an affront to the survival of democracy.

A.1.4
No veridical perceptions are imaginary beings.
All six-foot rabbits are imaginary beings.
Therefore, some six-foot rabbits are not veridical perceptions.

A.1.5
No veridical perceptions are imaginary beings.
No six-foot rabbits are veridical perceptions.
Therefore, some six-foot rabbits are imaginary beings.

A.1.6
All people who are depressed are at high risk for suicide.
Some manics are not at high risk for suicide.
Therefore, some manics are not people who are depressed.

A.1.7
All scientific theories are empirically confirmed hypotheses.
Some hypotheses are not scientific theories.
Therefore, some hypotheses are not empirically confirmed hypotheses.

A.1.8
No veridical perceptions are imaginary beings.
All six-foot rabbits are imaginary beings.
Therefore, no six-foot rabbits are veridical perceptions.

A.1.9
Some prominent members of the Obama administration are former Clinton administration members.
Hillary Clinton is a prominent member of the Obama administration.
Therefore, Hillary Clinton is a former Clinton administration member.

A.1.10
No rappers are hard rockers.
50 Cent is not a hard rocker.
Therefore, 50 Cent is a rapper.

Exercise Set A.2

Construct a Venn diagram for each of the categorical syllogisms provided in Exercise 8.3 in chapter 8. Use this diagram to determine whether the syllogism is valid or invalid.

Exercise Set A.3

For each of the arguments provided in Exercise 8.4 in chapter 8, translate it into a standard form categorical syllogism and determine its validity by means of a Venn diagram.

Index

ABC News. *See* Disney Corporation

abortion, 36, 48, 94, 151, 243, 254, 280, 355–56

Abu Ghraib, 180, 214

achievement damnation. *See* damnation, achievement

Acquired Immune Deficiency Syndrome (AIDS). *See* Human Immunodeficiency Virus (HIV)

active euthanasia. *See* euthanasia

ad hominem, argumentum. *See* personal attack

Adler, Alfred, 22

affirming the consequent, fallacy of, 38–42

agape, 267

ageism, 166

agreement, method of, 215–17; and difference, joint method of, 218–19

alcohol, drinking, 128, 210, 224, 285, 348, 360

alibi, 200

Al Jazeera, 185

al-Qaeda, 39–40, 45–46, 136–37, 166, 180, 236, 238–39, 241, 243, 354, 393

Alzheimer's disease, 223, 244

American Bar Association (ABA), code of ethics, 71–72, 362–63

American Medical Association (AMA), code of ethics of, 324

Ames, William, 49–51

ambiguity, fallacies of, 371–73

American Civil Liberties Union (ACLU), 185, 389, 390

amphiboly, 371

analogy: induction by, 177–79; insufficient, fallacy of, 179–81

Anderson, Bonnie M., 379–80

anger, 257, 258, 259, 268, 275, 289–90, 316, 365

Anselm, Saint. *See* ontological proof of God's existence

antecedent (of conditional statement). *See* conditional statement

anti-Semitism, 136, 164, 232, 280

antidotal reasoning, definition of, 266

antidote (to fallacious premise): consequent replacement, method of, 267–68; definition of, 264; finding, 264–66; guidelines for constructing, 266–67

anxiety, 6, 36, 60, 65, 259, 260–61, 263, 264–65, 268, 270, 275, 289–90, 299, 300, 301, 306, 309, 312, 316, 325. *See also* existential anxiety

approval damnation. *See* damnation, approval

Aquinas, Thomas, 18n3, 151, 244

argument, logical: definition of, 11

Aristotle: definition of truth, 280; theory of classes, 109–10; theory of virtue, 365. *See also* emotional reasoning, definition of; practical syllogism, description of; square of opposition; willpower, exercise of

Ashcroft, John, 140, 361

Ashcroft Directive. *See* Ashcroft, John